Strategic Sports Event Management

Dedicated with love to Emma, Alice, Katy and Edie,
Mum and Dad,
and to Sport and the Olympic Movement

Strategic Sports Event Management

Olympic edition

Second edition

Guy Masterman

AMSTERDAM • BOSTON • HEIDELBERG • LONDON • NEW YORK • OXFORD
PARIS • SAN DIEGO • SAN FRANCISCO • SINGAPORE • SYDNEY • TOKYO
Butterworth-Heinemann is an imprint of Elsevier

Butterworth-Heinemann is an imprint of Elsevier
Linacre House, Jordan Hill, Oxford, OX2 8DP, UK
30 Corporate Drive, Suite 400, Burlington, MA 01803, USA

First edition 2004
Second edition 2009

British Library Cataloguing in Publication Data
A catalogue record for this book is available from the British Library

Library of Congress Cataloging-in-Publication Data
A catalog record for this book is available from the Library of Congress

ISBN: 978-1-85617-523-4

For information on all Butterworth-Heinemann
publications visit our web site at www.elsevierdirect.com

Typeset by TNQ Books and Journals, Chennai, India

Printed and bound in Slovenia

09 10 11 12 13   10 9 8 7 6 5 4 3 2 1

05480536

Contents

List of Figures and Tables

Figures

Tables

List of Event Management Boxes

List of Case Studies

List of Beijing Insights

Biography

Guy Masterman is a Fellow and Head of Sport Sciences at Northumbria University and International Professor at Central University of Finance and Economics, Beijing and Shanghai University of Sport. He has been in academia since 2000 and has previously worked at New York University and the UK Centre for Events Management, Leeds Met University. He has worked in the sports and events industries for over 25 years, and since 1988 Guy has worked as an independent consultant. Early in his career he was an international racquetball player and was involved in the development of that sport in the UK and internationally. His clients have included Coca-Cola, Pepsi, Nabisco, Capital Radio Group, Chelsea FC, Leeds United FC, Team Scotland, WCT Inc. and international bodies such as the ATP Tour, the International Yacht Racing Union and the International Stoke Mandeville Wheelchair Sports Federation. He has worked extensively for charity groups such as Muscular Dystrophy, Scope and Sparks and with sports stars Seb Coe, Jody Scheckter, Steve Backley and Lennox Lewis. His event work extends across all sectors of the industry and includes Euro '96, World Games, Coca-Cola Music Festival, Pepsi Extravaganza, Nabisco Masters Doubles and the promotion of concerts for Ray Charles, Santana, BB King, James Brown and Tony Bennett. His work as Director of the UK Centre for Sport and Events Research, based at Northumbria University, focuses on strategic event planning and legacies as well as marketing communications and in particular sports sponsorship. He is in demand to speak internationally, sits on editorial boards, reviews publications and also works with a number of universities on collaborative research in these areas. He has authored three further and successful books, *Strategic Sports Event Management: An International Approach (2004), Innovative Marketing Communications: Strategies for the Events Industry (Masterman & Wood, 2006)* and *Sponsorship: A Return on Investment (2007)*.

Glossary of Terms

AELTC   All England Lawn Tennis Club, owners of the Wimbledon Tennis Championships

AFC   African Football Confederation

AFL   American Football League

After-use   The continued use of legacies after the event has ended

After-users   The organizations that manage after-use

AIBA   International Boxing Association

ANOCA   Association of National Olympic Committees of Africa

ATP   Association of Tennis Professionals, organizers of the men's tennis professional tour

AUS$ Australian dollar

BERL   Business and Economic Research Ltd

BOC   British Olympic Committee

BOCOG   Beijing Organizing Committee for the Olympic Games

BRA   British Racketball Association, NGB of British racketball

BSA   British Surfing Association, NGB for British surfing

BUSF   British Universities Sports Federation

BWSF   British Wheelchair Sports Federation, the NGB for British wheelchair sport

CAF   Confederation Africaine de Football

CAN$ Canadian dollar

COC   Chinese Olympic Committee

CONCACAF   Confederation of North, Central Americas and Caribbean Association Football

CONMEBOL   Confederation Sudamericana de Football

CRM   Customer Relationship Management, marketing technique

DM   German Deutschmark

EAC   Equivalent advertising costs, advertising evaluation technique

ECT   Estimated completion time (project management)

EOC   European Olympic Committees

E-tail   Retail operations via websites

FA   Football Association, NGB for football in England

FIA   Federation Internationale de L'Automobile, IGB for motor sport

FIBA   International Basketball Federation, the IGB for basketball

FIFA   Federation Internationale de Football Association, the IGB for football

FINA   Federation Internationale de Natation, the IGB for swimming

FISU   International University Sports Federation

FITA   International Archery Federation, the IGB for archery

49ers   San Francisco 49ers, American Football Team/Franchise

GAISF   General Association of International Sports Federations

Gantt Chart   Project management tool

GBRF   Great Britain Racqetball Federation, the NGB for British racqetball

GDP   Gross domestic product

GLA   Greater London Authority

Grand Slam   Australian Open Championships, French Open Tennis Championships, Wimbledon Championships and US Open Championships

HKSDB   Hong Kong Sports Development Board

IAAF   International Association of Athletic Federations, the IGB for athletics

IASF   International Amateur Swimming Federation, the IGB for swimming

ICC   International Cricket Council, the IGB for cricket

IGB   An international governing body of sport (same as an ISF)

IMC   Integrated Marketing Communications (marketing)

IMG   International Management Group

IPC   International Paralympic Committee

IPSF   International Paralympic Sports Federation

IOC   International Olympic Committee

IRB   International Rugby Board, the IGB for rugby union

ISAF   International Sailing Federation

ISF   An international sports federation (same as an IGB)

ISMWSF   International Stoke Mandeville Wheelchair Sports Federation, the IGB for wheelchair sport

ITF   International Tennis Federation, the IGB for tennis

IWGA   International World Games Association

KRONOS   UK based research services company

LASEC   Los Angeles Sports and Entertainment Commission

LDA   London Development Agency

LOCOG   London Organizing Committee for the Olympic Games

London 2012   London 2012 Olympic Bid Organization

MASC   Minnesota Amateur Sports Commission

MkIS   Marketing Information System, marketing support system

MUFC   Manchester United Football Club

NBA   National Basketball Association, the professional major league for basketball in the USA

NCAA   National Collegiate Athletic Association, US Colleges Sports Organization

NF   National Federation of sport (same as an NGB)

NFL   National Football League, the professional major league for american football in the USA

NGB   A national governing body of sport (same as an NF)

NHL   National Hockey League, the professional major league for ice-hockey in North America

NOC   National Olympic Committee

NSW   New South Wales, Australia

NYC2012   New York 2012 Olympic Bid Organization

OCA   Olympic Council of Asia

OCF   Oceania Football Confederation

OCOG   Organizing Committee of the Olympic Games

OGKS   Olympic Games Knowledge Service

PASO   Pan-American Sports Organization

PEST   Political, economical, sociological and technological analyses, management evaluation technique

PGA   Professional Golf Association (USA and European PGAs), organizers of professional golf tours

PIs   Performance indicators, used in evaluation of management performance

POS   Point of sale, marketing technique

PR   Public relations

PSL   Personal seat licences

SKY   BSkyB Television Company, UK

SMART   Specific, Measurable, Achievable, Relevant and Timely objectives

SOBL   Sydney Olympics 2000 Bid Ltd

SOCOG   Sydney Organizing Committee of the Olympic Games

SWOT Strengths, weaknesses, external opportunities and threats or situational analysis, management evaluation technique

TOK Transfer of Olympic Knowledge, IOC support information system

TOP The Olympic Partners, IOC and Olympic sponsorship programme

TWI Trans-World International, IMG owned television production organization

UEFA Union European Football Association

UK United Kingdom

UK Sport UK Government agency controlling elite sport development

UMass University of Massachusetts, USA

Universiade World Student Games

US$ US dollar

USA United States of America

USA Basketball NGB for US basketball

USATF USA Track and Field, the NGB of US athletics

USOC US Olympic Committee

USRA US Racquetball Association, the NGB for US racquetball

VANOC Vancouver Organizing Committee for the Olympic Games

VAT Value-added tax, UK Government taxing system

VIPs Very important persons

WBS Work breakdown structures (project management)

WCT World Championship Tennis Inc

White Elephant An obsolete structure that should be productive

WOM Word of mouth

WRC World Rally Championships

£ Great Britain pound

€ Euro

An Introduction

The Olympic Port in Barcelona: a thriving legacy for leisure, retail and hospitality from the 1992 Olympics.

THE OLYMPIC OATHS

In the name of all competitors, I promise that we shall take part in these Olympic Games, respecting and abiding by the rules which govern them, committing ourselves to a sport without doping and without drugs, in the true spirit of sportsmanship, for the glory of sport and the honour of our teams.

In the name of all the judges and officials, I promise that we shall officiate in these Olympic Games with complete impartiality, respecting and abiding by the rules which govern them in the true spirit of sportsmanship.

IOC (2003)

SETTING THE SCENE – THE IMPORTANCE OF SPORTS EVENTS

The importance of the role of sports event management is reflected in these short declarations, taken by an athlete and judge from the home nation at the opening ceremony of an Olympic Games. The oaths themselves have developed over time and are indicative of the importance of flexible management. At the ancient Olympics, athletes swore that they had trained properly and that they would abide by the rules of the Games. The importance of the oath is reflected in the fact that the trainers, brothers and fathers of athletes would also make such declarations. In more recent times, the oaths have been changed to accommodate social trends and in order to protect the integrity of an event that is seen by many to be at the pinnacle of the sports event industry. In 1920, when the first modern Olympic oath was taken, a 'spirit of chivalry' rather than sportsmanship was required and, in 2000, at the Sydney Olympics, for the first time, a commitment to participation without doping and drugs was deemed a necessary addition and a reflection of the times.

Some analysis of these oaths is useful. Abiding by the rules, for example, is important for the success of the event, but it may take more than a declaration to ensure such compliance. The development of the control of sport by governing bodies in their creation and application of rules is therefore important. Events also provide the best vehicle by which to exercise this control as they can be implemented and controlled as they happen.

We can consider the glory of sport in two ways. The first being the individual success of sporting achievement and the second, the encouragement that this achievement gives to others to then participate themselves. This is the essence of sports development and the role events play is clearly significant in putting participants, the sport, as well as the spectacle itself, into the shop window.

The linking of the glory of sport and the honour of teams (formerly country) is an important social and cultural aspect of the Olympic athlete oath. The honour at this level has been seen to have bearing on national pride and identity, manifested in large television viewing figures of key moments and providing dominant conversation topics, if only in the short term. Many host cities show even greater faith in the ability of major events to assist in the development of socio-cultural legacies by declaring them long-term event objectives.

These oaths, said in ceremony, may also indicate a longer-term perspective that implicates a wider view of the role of event management. A role that is responsible for the implementation of an event that has wide reaching and long-term impact. That is not to say that the International Olympic Committee (IOC) has any greater aim than the provision of a successful event and athlete experience. Indeed, Jacques Rogge, the current President of the IOC, declared that a successful event for spectator and athlete is their priority (Rogge, 2002). There are no IOC objectives that are concerned with the development of long-term commercial and physical legacies for Olympic host cities and yet these have developed, in recent years, as key municipal objectives with the event being seen as a catalyst for their achievement. The IOC has recognized this requirement in the development of its Transfer of Olympic Knowledge (TOK) programme and in staging its own Symposium on the Legacy of the Olympic Games (Lausanne, November 2002). It has begun to acknowledge that there is a need among host cities for a return on their investment. An investment that may entail wider and longer-term benefits than from just the staging of an Olympic event itself.

The promise of wider benefits in the form of socio-cultural and economic impact is not just an objective that is set by Olympic event organizers. Organizers of events of all scales can seek to maximize impact by using sports events more strategically. The implementation of one event can be planned so that it has a positive effect on the next. A private event organization, for example, in developing relationships with its customers at an event can increase revenue at the next. A charity can raise more funds. A municipal authority, in researching local needs, can stage an annual programme of sports events that will provide positive economic impact across its area as well as provide wider associated community activities. Sports governing bodies at all levels can utilize their events to develop future participation and audience if they facilitate opportunities at the time and incorporate appro-priate follow-up mechanisms. A strategic approach to event management is therefore of benefit across the whole industry.

Unfortunately, strategic sports event management is not widespread. There are notable and high profile examples where strategic planning has been lacking, including Sheffield, UK and Sydney, Australia. Sheffield City Council is still paying for its staging of the 1991 World Student Games and required long-term mortgage facilities to enable it to do so (Mackay, 2001).

Sydney meanwhile, 9 years after staging the 2000 Olympics, struggles to make a success of its Olympic showpiece, Stadium Australia. President Rogge of the IOC himself is reported to have referred to it as a white elephant and it remains financially challenged to date, with the stadium owners, Stadium Australia Group, recently conducting a naming rights deal with its bank ANZ in order to prevent it being financially written off (Hansard, 2001; Askew, 2006). While there are several notable exceptions that have gone on to provide positive legacies, Barcelona being one host city to have made much of its Olympics in 1992, it appears that the sports event management industry is still in its infancy in this respect.

This infancy is also reflected in a lack of research, writing and theory on the strategic management of sports events. Few books have been published in this specific area and, while there are more that are concerned with event management as a whole, they are ostensibly focused on the implementation of events as opposed to their strategic development and any long-term perspective. This book is an attempt to start bridging that gap by providing a strategic approach for sports event management that may also usefully serve across the whole event industry.

It is useful to explain one important element of the book title. Most people will have a perception of the nature, types and scales of sports events and these are discussed in Chapter 1. However, the meaning and use of the word 'strategy' does require some explanation. Consult a dictionary and the entry for strategy reveals military implications. A stratagem for example, is a plan for outwitting an enemy or gaining an advantage and strategy is the art of conducting and manoeuvring armies, planning and directing military activity. A strategic position would be a position that gives its holder an overall or long-term advantage (Oxford English Dictionary, 2006). It is hardly surprising that the word became synonymous with business.

Management theory maintains that business strategies are a means to an end (Mintzberg et al., 1998; Thompson, 2001; Johnson and Scholes, 2002) but, beyond this, there are various views and definitions, for example, on whether both goals and objectives are implemented strategically. Mintzberg et al. (1998) offer five views of strategy, as a plan, as a ploy, as a pattern, as a position and as a perspective and maintain that an eclectic view that considers all these is less confusing than trying to arrive at one single definition. Johnson and Scholes (2002), however, are clear that strategy for business is concerned with the direction and scope of an organization over the long term and for the achievement of advantage.

Further exploration of corporate strategy theory is not essential here. It is more important to identify the approach that has been adopted in this book. Strategy means different things to different people and so in order to offer an approach, an appropriate context is required. This book is essentially concerned with the implementation of events and the process required to achieve a successful outcome. The key theme that runs throughout is that this success may be measured against short-, medium- and/or long-term objectives that may or may not be achieved solely upon the execution of the event. An aim for the book is to inspire lateral, innovative and thorough planning in the management of sports events, whatever their scale, in order to achieve objectives. These objectives may involve the implementation of an event with short or long planning periods and may or may not involve aspects that the event is only a catalyst for. This may require planning that goes beyond those realms that have so far been traditionally considered a part of the business of event management.

The focus is also on the management of events and not the management of organizations. This is an important distinction. Events are ephemeral by nature and, even though they may be staged again and again, each staging is a separate and different project. The book therefore considers the management of events on two levels, the management of single events and the management of events that have a role in event programmes and series. The latter perhaps requiring a wider and longer-term strategic view.

The strategic approach in this book is therefore concerned with the direction and scope of an event in order to achieve its objectives. The approach for the book as a second edition is further to consider strategic planning of all sizes of sports events using a wide range of international examples but specifically to consider the management practice for the 2008 Olympics in Beijing.

BOOK STRUCTURE

Chapters 1 and 2 serve as an introduction to the sports event industry. The former provides some historical background on the emergence of sports events by initially focusing on ancient Greece and a path through to the modern Olympics. The various Ancient Greek Games are the providers of the genes of our current contemporary sports and sports events structure. Chapter 1 also considers the importance of events in society by analysing the types of events and the scale of the industry. Further consideration is given to the structures of events, an identification of the roles of all participants, the emergence of event management as a discipline and what the future holds for event managers. Chapter 2 considers the nature and structure of international sport by focusing on the roles of both international and national sports governing bodies. It reviews the importance of the IOC and the Olympic

Movement and the role of other events on the world stage. Lastly, it considers the various types of event owners, operators and organizers as well as the importance of volunteer groups, charities and the media.

The key focus throughout the book is an event planning process, discussed in Chapter 3. The process, intended as being appropriate for all scales of event, is iterative in nature and consists of nine stages plus a bidding stage if appropriate. This process forms a backbone for the book and, while the subsequent chapters do not follow the prescribed stages in order, the process is consistently used to identify how various planning requirements relate to each other.

Chapter 4 evaluates the successes and failures of events by generally considering what the potential impacts and legacies from sports events are. An evaluation of the strategies used and considerations for management are also discussed.

The following chapters are more directly related to the stages of the event planning process. Chapters 5 and 6 go hand in hand and are concerned first with the financial control and planning that is required prior to the decision to go ahead with an event. Secondly, in order to maximize revenue potential and even simply to get an event underwritten, the various revenue streams that are available to an event manager are evaluated.

Chapter 7 considers the management of a bid and the process undergone in strategizing to win the right to host a sports event. The process is undoubtedly political, on occasions has even been corrupt and, so, as well as looking at the actual process and what is required for a successful bid, other discussions will include scandals and tactics adopted by cities in their attempts, sometimes numerous attempts, to win. There is a particular focus on the bids for the 2012 Olympics. An inclusion for this new edition is a case that is made for 'losing bids, winning legacies', a theme that is based on research into the gaining of legacies from a losing bid. The discussion considers the seeking of a return on investment from the earliest stage of planning, to achieve objectives whether the bid for a major international sports event is successful or not.

Chapter 8, while concerned with the implementation of the event itself, does focus on what is strategically required for the longer term, including the requirements for handover and post-event evaluation.

The next three chapters have a marketing focus. The marketing planning process and how the marketing plan is implemented are covered in Chapter 9. The emphasis here is on the importance of competitive advantage and how it can be achieved. As customer expectation grows, the event manager has to provide an event that not only competes with other events, but also with other activities for the same disposable income and even last year's event. The critical importance of 'the show' and how sports events are entertainment is emphasized.

There is an approach for innovative event communications in Chapter 10. This is in two sections, with the first making the case for an integrated marketing communications approach. The second provides a 'toolbox' and discusses the use and merits of the various communications tools on offer to an event manager.

The development of successful sponsorship programmes is considered in Chapter 11. The sponsorship recruitment process is reviewed in detail covering the essential research required and the provision of bespoke proposals. Sponsorship is a mutually beneficial process and, for the event to recruit a sponsor, it must first learn about what the sponsor wants. Ideally, it will recruit a sponsor that will support and exploit its purchase of the sponsorship rights.

The final chapter is focused on research and from two perspectives. The first considers the importance of conducting research throughout the event planning process and how that contributes to the strategic development of events. The second is concerned with the use of research post the event and, in particular, on the importance of evaluating events against their objectives. A strategic approach to event evaluation undertakes research and then evaluation immediately after the event but, if there are longer-term objectives that involve legacies, then these too require evaluation.

In appropriate places there are case studies covering a whole range of different scales and types of sports and events in order to exemplify key points. In addition, there are examples of all types of sports event from all around the world that are used throughout to show both similarities and differences in the business of sports event management. For example, there are a number of references used from three case studies where primary research has been conducted, Manchester and Sheffield in the UK and Sydney in Australia. To support further key points, there is also the use of 'event management boxes', where specific practices are further explained. 'Beijing insights', focus on the 2008 Beijing Olympics and are a new addition for this edition that cover the whole of the sports event planning process implemented during one Olympiad.

To aid both student, professor and industry practitioner there are questions and references at the end of each chapter.

Finally, here is one humorous introductory note that is worthy of consideration and perhaps not as far-fetched as it first sounds. While the sports calendar is undoubtedly crowded, new sports events continue to emerge and grow. In order to be competitive therefore, a sports event manager has to be aware of an ever-increasing market and deliver an innovative and wonderful product. For this, the manager has to know what the future will bring.

In February 1971, Captain Alan Shepard of Apollo 14, drove two golf balls on the moon with his Spalding 6-iron (Fotheringham, 2003).

The overall aim for this book is to throw a little light on the fantastic world of sports event management and hopefully do three things: enthuse future sports event managers, give them some insight into the importance of planning and also the importance of going about that planning strategically.

REFERENCES

Askew, K. (2006). Debt sinks Stadium Australia: ANZ to take control for $10m. *The Sydney Morning Herald*, 16 November, 2006. www.smh.com.au (accessed 22 January 2008).

Fotheringham, W. (2003). *Fotheringham's Sporting Trivia*. London, Sanctuary.

Hansard (2001). House of Commons Hansard Debates. 11 December 2001. United Kingdom Parliament. www.parliament.the-stationery-office.co.uk/pa/cm200102/cmhansrd/vo011211 (accessed 6 January 2004).

IOC (2003). www.olympic.org/uk/games/past/index_uk (accessed 7 January 2003).

Johnson, G. and Scholes, K. (2002). *Exploring Corporate Strategy*, 6th edn. Harlow, FT Prentice Hall.

Mackay, D. (2001). Sheffield calls off bid. *The Guardian*, 28 November, Manchester, The Guardian Media Group.

Mintzberg, H., Quinn, J. and Ghoshal, S. (1998). *The Strategy Process*, revised european edn. Hemel Hempstead, Prentice Hall.

Oxford English Dictionary (2006), 11th edition revised. Oxford, Oxford University Press.

Rogge, J. (2002). *Opening address at the IOC Annual Symposium: Legacy, Olympic Museum*, November 2002. Lausanne IOC.

Thompson, J. (2001). *Understanding Corporate Strategy*. London, Thomson Learning.

CHAPTER 1

The Sports Event Industry

The Stadium, Ancient Olympia, Greece.

CONTENTS

LEARNING OBJECTIVES

After studying this chapter, you should be able to:

- understand the origins of sports events and the sports event industry
- determine the international importance of sports events
- identify the importance of scale in planning and managing sports events

1

■ identify the different structures and formats of sports events

■ identify the range of roles of the personnel at sports events

INTRODUCTION

Putting today's sophisticated sports event industry into historical perspective is important if an understanding of how modern day sports events are governed and structured is to be achieved. The importance of organized sport in early Greek, Chinese and Egyptian cultures, for example, has ultimately led to what exists today, an industry that consists of a multi-levelled range of events, varying in scale from the locally to the globally significant. This chapter briefly considers a historical perspective and moves on to dissect the industry into various components by considering the importance of the industry at large, not simply from an economic viewpoint, but also its social, political and technological impact. Then the different scales of event, event ownership and governance and event formats, including competition structures, are discussed. It is people that are at the heart of all industries and so, finally, the role of the event manager is considered.

HISTORICAL PERSPECTIVE

The study of the history of sport is a considerable academic area and the question of a chronological order for the development of sport is a fascinating focus for these studies. When and how sports events were first and then subsequently organized throughout history is important for an understanding of how current events emerged. However, this is not a sports history book. What is required here is an awareness of what are considered to be the origins of organized sport.

It perhaps comes as no surprise that there is some debate regarding these origins. The credit lies somewhere between Greek, Chinese and Egyptian historical accounts and, indeed, it is only in the last 20 years or so that research from beyond the Mediterranean has come to light. Chinese scholars have added to the wealth of western knowledge with the publication of numbers of studies, in English, that at least raise questions about the chronology of the origins of sports (Peiser, 1996).

Prehistoric cave art unearthed in France, Africa and Australia and the application of carbon dating show that ritual archery was in evidence up to 30 000 years ago. The art points to leisure pursuit at the very least as opposed the more basic function of staying alive. While this is not sport, they are still important foundations.

There are also archaeological finds that have led to the dating of sports. The 1994 Winter Olympics in Lillehammer, Norway commercially utilized the images of 4000-year-old rock carvings of sports people in action. There are the somewhat younger 2000-year-old drawings on pharaonic monuments in Egypt that depict competitive action such as the tug-of-war, swimming, boxing and others that have led to the claims that the Egyptians laid down rules for games, had player uniforms and that there were awards for winners. In literature, Homer's Iliad refers to an athletic competition as being part of a funeral event (Graham et al., 2001). Further afield, there is evidence of lacrosse in North America and, in ancient Mayan and Aztec civilizations, signs of ritualized ball games.

Of course, more widely acknowledged history refers to the origins of what are now the Olympic Games but less commonly known is that the ancient games of Olympia in Greece were also a part of a wider festival. From humble beginnings, the games at Olympia may have existed as early as the 10th or 9th century BC where they were a part of a religious festival in honour of Zeus, the father of mythological Greek Gods. Olympia, in the Peloponnesos region of Greece, was a rural sanctuary and the original festival was attended by those who only spoke the same language and shared the same religious beliefs (University of Pennsylvania, 2003). As the games became more widely known, they attracted athletes from farther afield and, from 776BC, the date from which historical records are more clear, the games were held in Olympia every 4 years for possibly 10 centuries. Sports were added each year and, in the 5th century BC and at its height, the festival consisted of a 5-day pro- gramme with athletic events including three races on foot (the stadion, the diaulos and the dolichos) and the pentathlon, which incorporated the five sports of discus, javelin, long jump, wrestling and a foot race (Toohey and Veal, 2000).

The games at Olympia were not the only sporting festival of the time. They were one of four that are now referred to as the Panhellenic Games. The others were the Pythian Games in Delphi (every 4 years and 3 years after the games at Olympia in celebration of the God Apollo), the Isthmian Games in Corinth (every 2 years in celebration of the God Poseiden) and the Nemean Games in Nemea (every 2 years and in the same year as the Isthmian Games in celebration of the God Zeus) (Toohey and Veal, 2000). Even by todays standards, the attendance was high, with the games at Olympia drawing what is believed to be crowds of up to 40 000 at their peak.

The ancient Olympic Games faded and finally came to a halt in 393AD when the Christian Roman Emperor, Theodosius I, abolished them because of their links to Zeus. They were rejuvenated as the modern games in 1896. The Frenchman Baron Pierre de Coubertin was responsible, having first proposed the idea in 1894 with the intention of reviving the games in 1900 in Paris. Instead, it was decided that the first modern Olympics should be returned to Greece and were staged in Athens in 1896. The 4-year cycle was re-adopted but, significantly, for a different location each time and later, in 1924, a Winter games was introduced. More recently, in 1994, the Winter Olympics cycle was altered so that every other year would be an Olympic year (Table 1.1).

Much of the time between the end of the ancient Olympics and early medieval times there is little evidence of sport, certainly in western Europe, with many commentators referring to it as a dark period. However, throughout the medieval period, there are traces of modern sport in the local and rural games that were played and with many references to violence. A lack of rules was certainly prevalent. Hurling, for example, was very crude and violent in comparison with today but it is clear that the game had its origins at that time.

From the 1700s, rules began to be introduced and, in particular, to prizefighting, the London Prize Ring rules coming in 1743. It was from this time that the aristocracy started to be more influential and with a direction that took them away from the rough and tumble of the rural countryside. Organized horse racing developed at this time, for example. Public schools also played their part with the introduction of sports, particularly football games that were deliberately less violent.

A key time in Europe though came with the Industrial Revolution with more people moving into the cities where there was more influence from the middle and upper classes on the development of sport. The rules that were being developed, in schools in particular, began to be rolled out across society. Governing bodies for sport began to emerge in the UK, in particular, the Football Association for example being founded in 1863, although it was in the USA where baseball was one of the earliest sports to formalize and codify its rules in the 1840s. Cricket had long been an organized game in the USA but the popularity and codification of baseball helped push that earlier sport into relative obscurity.

We now have a number of multi-sport events in addition to the Summer and Winter Olympics and, while they are not of the same scale, they are nevertheless of importance to societies. These would include, among others, the Commonwealth Games that purports to develop trade links between countries of the Commonwealth, the World Wheelchair Games that helps to develop sport for the disabled bodied, and the Islands Games that create links between many small island communities around the world.

Table 1.1	The Modern Olympic Games	
Year	**Summer**	**Winter**
1896	Athens	
1900	Paris	
1904	St Louis	
1908	London	
1912	Stockholm	
No games were organized during World War I		
1920	Antwerp	
1924	Paris	Chamonix
1928	Amsterdam	St Moritz
1932	Los Angeles	Lake Placid
1936	Berlin	Garmisch-Partenkirchen
No games were organized during World War II		
1948	London	St Moritz
1952	Helsinki	Oslo
1956	Melbourne	Cortina d'Ampezzo
1960	Rome	Squaw Valley
1964	Tokyo	Innsbruck
1968	Mexico City	Grenoble
1972	Munich	Sapporo
1976	Montreal	Innsbruck
1980	Moscow	Lake Placid
1984	Los Angeles	Sarajevo
1988	Seoul	Calgary
1992	Barcelona	Albertville
1994		Lillehammer
1996	Atlanta	
1998		Nagano
2000	Sydney	
2002		Salt Lake City
2004	Athens	
2006		Torino
2008	Beijing	
2010		Vancouver
2012	London	
2014		Sochi

Source: IOC (2008)

A key point in recent history has been the gradual change in definition of amateur status and the emergence of professionalism across sports that not too long ago were sacrosanct and commercially untouchable. For example, the emergence of professional tennis in the 1960s and the eventual acceptance of the grand slam 'Opens' for professional players. Earlier in the century there were illegal payments to UK footballers and, as a result, clubs like Leeds City Football Club were disbanded. In the USA in the1880s, the major controversy in college sports was the use of professional coaches and the use of 'tramp' players (those who would regularly switch teams sometimes for inducements).

IMPORTANCE OF SPORTS EVENTS

How important are sports events? History reveals that they have played a significant role in the development of society and that key individuals have managed, sometimes against all odds, to start from small beginnings a wide reaching sports event industry. Consider these wide ranging examples below.

The eventual transformation of illegal bareknuckle prize fights into the Marquis of Queensberry 1867 rules for boxing is an example of the development of a sport over a very long period. Other and varied examples include the development of a sport intended as a recreational indoor game at a New England School for Christian Workers by James Naismith in 1891. He developed the original 13 rules of basketball, a game that is now played in events all over the world by over 300 million people (Basketball Hall of Fame, 2003).

On Christmas Day in 1914 it is reported that World War I enemies temporarily ceased warfare and contested an inter-trench football match and, although reports are varied, the idea at least has affected many and is legend now (Bancroft-Hinchley, 2000).

Shortly after World War II in 1948, Ludwig Guttmann organized a competition for war veterans with spinal cord injuries in Stoke Mandeville in the UK. Four years later the Paralympics was founded, the first games taking place in Rome in 1960 (Paralympic Games, 2003).

Tom Waddell is credited with having conceived the idea of the Gay Games, originally intended as the Gay Olympic Games, but as an event that would have no minimum ability as criteria for participation. The first event was held in 1982 in San Francisco and Gay Games VIII will be staged in Cologne in 2010.

More recently, in 2003, football became the number one sport for women in the UK, a game that has traditionally been developed and played by men and England hosted the 2005 Union European Football Association (UEFA) European Women's Championship. In 1999, the US team won the Federation International de Football Association (FIFA) Women's World Cup in front of a crowd of 90 125 in the Rose Bowl, Pasadena (Blum, 2003).

These varied examples go some way to explain and explore the importance of sports events and their contribution to society but, of course, the significance of each is an individual perception and, while there is no research to show that there is undivided acceptance of say Gay sports events, their existence is at least a reflection of the flexibility of society. The creation of these events has clearly helped trailblaze for issues that were of wider significance to society than just the staging of a sport event.

The breadth of the sports event industry is so great that it is difficult to establish the extent and scope of markets. It is made more difficult by having to decide which sectors should be included. Consider two different perspectives. Economically, there is venue revenue, the monies spent on the leveraging of sports sponsorship as well as event revenues themselves and, from a sports development perspective, there is the vast range of participation numbers, from school sports days to major international events. Sports participation figures are available for certain sports and they can also be supplemented by percentage year-on-year growth. Unfortunately, the availability of data is sparse on anything more than a national scale and beyond only a selected number of countries. However, the data are useful when available. Using US soccer as an example again, it is reported that in that country 9 million women play the game and it ranks number 2 in FIFA's 'big count' research with the most male and female registered players (FIFA.com, 2008).

Keeping politics out of sport is a recurring issue. On the one hand, there is the argument that sport should be considered above all politics and governmental and party politics. This is a debateable area of course and, when it comes to certain events, it may simply not be possible. All scales of events are influenced politically in many ways as there is no getting away from the requirement to conform to numerous sets of regulations such as the likes of those for health and safety, employment, fiscal reporting and licensing. On the other hand, political intervention is quite different and there are all levels of politician that see fit to play a role in the management of sports events and/ or use such for political ends. Prime ministers have been seen to increase their opinion poll results and political messages have been made all the more vehemently by individuals and minority groups as a result of associating themselves with major events (see Chapter 4).

The role of technology in sport has been intrinsically involved in the development of sports events. Customer expectations and the demands of the media again have led to all kinds of innovation and its use in the advancement of the presentation and control of sports events. Examples include tennis where wooden to metal to carbon fibre racket development has led to the enhancement of player performance. Footballs for the FIFA 2002

World Cup were lighter in an attempt to make the game more entertaining, although the expected shooting and goals from long range did not appear to materialize. The development of a reflective ball in the 1980s was intended to lead to an increased and much needed television coverage of the sport of squash as was the use of one-way see-through glass. Technology worked against South African double-amputee sprinter Oscar Pistorius in 2008 when his state-of-the-art carbon fibre prosthetics were deemed to be technical aids and an illegal advantage by the International Association of Athletics Federations (Robinson, 2008).

Call centre services have made ticket selling a less frustrating customer activity and giant plasma screens have made the action replay possible at an event. Digital timing has clearly enhanced athletes' performance indicators and the introduction of Cyclops and then Hawk-Eye (equipment for judging line calls) has made a big difference to line calling in tennis and wicket taking in cricket. This simulation software has helped to educate viewers on the finer technicalities of cricket and improved the spectator and television viewer entertainment in tennis. The challenges that can now be made by tennis players so that the software can be run to see if a ball was 'in or out' has very quickly become a part of the game. Technological development of broadcast equipment has also improved the televised viewing of events and is also utlized to improve viewing figures. Another good example is the software that is now in widespread use by the agencies that analyse football matches for their client clubs. ProZone works for many of the English Premier League clubs and produces comprehensive reports on match and player statistics 24 hours after the game.

One can see how much the development of technology has also added to the communication potential of events by increasing the opportunities for an event to increase spectator and viewer numbers and, at the same time, increase revenue with various types of sponsorship and advertising vehicles. The FIFA 2002 World Cup 'fevernova' footballs that were provided by Adidas and the digital timing and scoring services, supplied by various organizations such as Siemens, received their own on-air television exposure. Adidas actually do this very well and, at each FIFA World Cup, they introduce new footballs that are reported as being 'technically' superior, the latest being the +Teamgeist ball at the 2006 FIFA World Cup in Germany which was claimed by the manufacturer to be 'more round' due to its fewer seams and revolutionary panels (soccerballworld.com, 2008). Plasma screens not only attract the eye towards replays, they also show advertisements. Lastly, though probably not finally, the Internet has clearly had an effect by becoming a major vehicle for marketing communications, not just for tickets, but for event webcasting and merchandise sales.

The development of sport itself relies on the unique showcase that events supply. The more people that watch a sports event the more likely it is that sports participation figures will increase and participation-led events are vehicles for newcomers as well as more experienced performers. However, this is not necessarily sustained development. In the UK, for example, the public tennis courts appear to fill up during Wimbledon fortnight but then return to lesser use afterwards. The task of governing bodies is therefore not just to make use of events as showcases and as opportunities to see and try, but also to ensure there are mechanisms that convert these experiences into long-term participation.

SCALE OF THE INDUSTRY

The industry can be dissected into various conceptual dimensions in order to ascertain the scale involved. Sports events are organized throughout the world for able and disabled bodied men and/or women of all ages. There are single and multi-sport formats, some of which are universally available and others that are specific to only one region of one country. In a time dimension, there are various competition formats from one-day tournaments to year-round championships. In a socio-economic dimension, there are amateur and professional events and those that are spectator or participant led. There is also the dimension of ability and attainment, at the heart of competition, with grassroots sports events for those who are new to the sport and elite events that are organized for skilled performers.

Some events can be classed as being either spectator or participant led. This is essentially a commercial classification in that the main revenue is earned via one and/or the other. For example, a 32-player draw badminton tournament may be watched by thousands of spectators if it is a national competition such as the British Open. However, if it is a club competition, it is unlikely that many more than friends, family and other players will watch. Revenue for the former would probably be predominantly made up of spectator ticket sales, whereas the latter may involve only player entry fees. For multi-sports events such as the Commonwealth Games, Olympic Games and Pan-American Games, however, there is a case for classifying them as both spectator and participant led, such is the extent of the revenue and numbers of both spectators and participants.

Event organizers and owners determine who participates in their event and a diverse range of sectors is involved. Educational institutions are possibly the first to introduce most sports at the earliest ages and schools, colleges, universities are all involved with events at intra- and inter-competition levels. Television, as an informer, also plays an ever-increasing role. Events are staged at schools, colleges and universities and at district, county, state, regional, national and international levels. Similarly, there are sports clubs for all ages, some of which have their beginnings entrenched in religiously based institutions such as church groups. Some older clubs were founded for amateur sport but evolved into professional organizations. For example, the founding member teams of the English Football League started out from such beginnings. One founding club was St Domingo FC, began in 1878 for the people of the Parish of St Domingo's Church in Liverpool in the UK so that their cricketers could play a sport in the winter. The club changed its name to Everton FC a year later. Aston Villa FC had similar beginnings and was founded in 1874 by the cricketers in the Parish of Villa Cross Wesleyan Chapel in Aston, Birmingham.

Many sports events are a part of a wider entertainment delivery. Larger events that cover a range of leisure and recreational activities may have sports as one element but with arts, music and other socially integrating elements alongside. Multi-sported events such as the Olympics and Commonwealth Games have sports competitions as their central focus but incorporate programmes of events that often extend well before and after these take place. The Spirit of Friendship Festival began in Manchester in early 2002 and several months before the Commonwealth Games. It incorporated arts, music and educationally based activities for all age ranges of local residents as well as tourists. Manchester's 2002 torch relay, modelled on Sydney's 2000 Olympic event, took 3 months to tour Commonwealth countries and the UK and was the catalyst for municipal events in many towns and cities.

Not all sports related events have sports activity and competition at their heart. There are also sports related exhibitions and conferences, sports product launches, sports personality appearances at corporate events and, while there is no sports activity at the BBC's Sports Personality of the Year Award ceremony, there is certainly competition for the coveted prize.

While this text is predominantly concerned with those events that consist of sports competition, it is important to place this industry into the more generic sports industry. The sports industry consists of three elements: consumers of sport, sports products and suppliers of sports related products (Shank, 2002).

Consumers

Among other sports products, there is the consumption of sports events themselves. In the broadest sense of the word, consumers can be spectators of two basic kinds, corporate and individual. Corporate consumers at sports events can be sponsors, corporate hospitality purchasers and guests. Individual spectators may be ticket buying, complimentary guests or free entrants. Sports event consumers can also be participants in the form of teams or individual competitors as well as trainers, medical staff and even agents. Officials such as referees, umpires and judges are also included here because they too take part and consume the event. An event consumes too as it is supplied with necessary resources.

Products

These products consist of sports goods and equipment. There is also sports information and data including results and media fed broadcast, live or by delay. There are also training services and facilities that are provided to those that require them. Funding, grants and commercial input can also be described as products from an events perspective. An event itself is also a product or an offering.

Suppliers

The suppliers of such products are therefore not just limited to the manufacturers of sporting goods and equipment. They also include sponsors and other organizations with the supply of equipment and services as well as funds. The media are the suppliers of information and broadcasts to both individual consumers and are of course brought in as event partners. Agents can also be suppliers of elite performers as well as the facilitators of broadcast deals for events.

One concept prevails across all sports events. They are all entertainment. This is true whether the event has spectators or not because participants take part for their own entertainment, even if they sometimes make it look like hard work. Of course, there are poor experiences for both spectators and those taking part and the aftermath may well be one of negative reflection, however, sports events are a significant part of the entertainment industry. Whatever the scale there is a show to be put on.

Establishing the three elements of the wider sports industry above provides an understanding of the relationships that are important for the event. What should be clear is that the sports event industry and its entertainment product is no different from any other industry and the focus for those that provide events has to be on the needs of the consumer.

There has been mention of large- and small-scale events and, in identifying so many different kinds of events, it becomes clear that terminology may be an issue. For example, what is a mega-event and how much lesser is a minor event than a major event and in what ways?

These differences in the definitions and terms occur in event planning literature. For example, an event is temporary, can be planned or not, has a fixed length and, most importantly, is unique (Getz, 1997). The field of event management is concerned with those events that are planned and, to mark the differences, some refer to these events as special events (Getz, 1997; Allen et al., 2002). At this point, the terminology differs. There are hallmark, mega-, major and minor events referred to by various authors. Goldblatt (1997) and Hall (1992) refer to any Olympic Games as a hallmark event, whereas Getz (1997) and Allen et al (2002) bill them as mega-events and describe hallmark events as those that recur in a particular place where the city and the event become inseparable, take for instance Wimbledon, the tennis championships. Getz (1997) identifies mega-events by way of size and significance and as those that have a high yield of tourism, media coverage, prestige and economic impact for the host.

Jago and Shaw (1998) offer a useful model that appears to encapsulate all these terms in a ranked structure that indicates scale and size, along with an explanation of the relationship between the various types of event. They describe a relationship between major, hallmark and mega-events. Their model begins with events that are either ordinary (unplanned) or special (planned). Secondly, special events are minor or major. Thirdly, major events are either hallmark events that are infrequent and belong to a particular place, or mega-events that are one-off and change location (Figure 1.1). They define a major event as a special event that is high in status or prestige, one that attracts a large crowd and wide media attention, has a tradition and incorporates festivals and other types of events, are expensive to stage, attract funds to the host region, lead to demand for associated services and leave behind legacies.

In accordance with this definition, major events can be one-time or recurring events, one or several days in nature, and size and scale can differ enormously. Thus the sorts of major international sports events referred to in this book vary greatly in scale and profile. On the one hand, there are the Winter and Summer Olympics, Asian Games, FIFA World Cup, UEFA European Championship, Super Bowl, Rugby Union World Cup and many sports international championships such as those for athletics, swimming, judo, cycling and so on, which are all one-time staged as far as the hosts are concerned and are often bid for. On the other hand, there are recurring events such as the four Grand Slams in tennis, the Football Association (FA) Cup Final, US and European Golf tour events and Formula One motor racing Grand Prix.

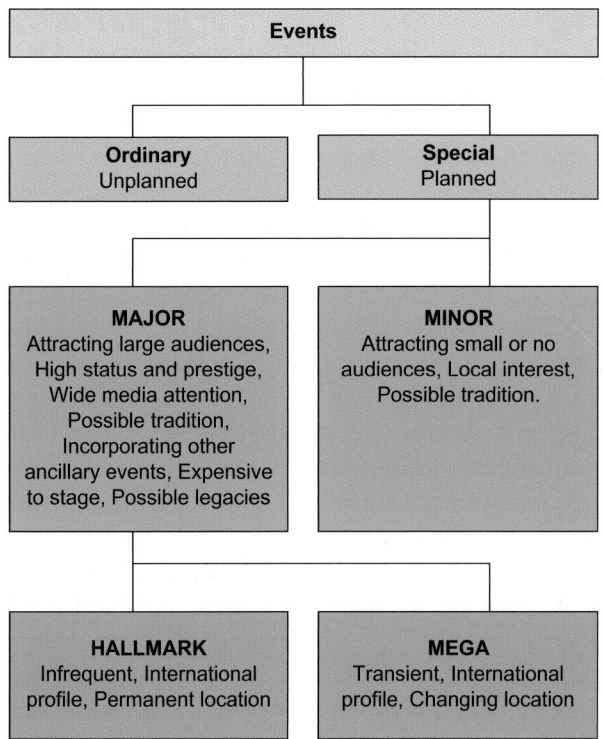

FIGURE 1.1 *A definition for events (adapted from Jago and Shaw, 1998).*

There would be no advantage gained here in reviewing the literature further. The purpose in doing so at all is to show that there are no standards in the use of terminology. It might be argued that a standard use of definition and terminology across the event industry might be beneficial for those writing about it and it could serve that purpose here. However, most event attendees, whatever type of consumer they might be, will not need to know if the event is mega or hallmark, or major or minor, they will be able to determine the scale themselves. The same may be said of event managers.

STRUCTURES

Each and every year there are many sports events staged all around the world and the structures and formats of these events are determined by a number of different kinds of owners. These owners fall into one or more of several categories, local government and authorities, sports governing bodies and competition organizations, corporate organizations, volunteer and charitable organizations and educational institutions and organizations. These are discussed in greater detail in Chapter 2. In many instances, particularly when the impact of the event is wider spread, there are collaborations between two or more of these owners and organizers in the control, development and implementation of their event. These event-managing bodies determine the kinds of competition and entertainment that goes on show.

Whether it is the local church, scout group, regional sports body or a host city, the same basic competition formats are available. These formats have been developed over time and as a result of the influence of key drivers, such as increasing consumer expectations and, more recently, for some events, televized expectations. For example, straightforward knockout draws have been made more sophisticated with seeding in order to keep the better players in the event longer and the better matches until later in the event. These have been further developed with the introduction of earlier staged mini-leagues or round-robin formats where more matches can be seen by partisan fans. The spectacle of knock-out can then still be enjoyed but between those competitors that were able to sustain their efforts, in other words protecting the interests of the supposed better performers. This can mean more ticket revenue as well as improved media rights take up for larger events. There is nothing wrong with this. It is good commercial sense and remains consumer focused.

Competition formats are universal. They are applicable in any scale of event. Knockout tournaments, long- or short-term league championships, round robins, challenge tables, pre-qualification and group stages are formats that can be used by all event managers, although some are more common at certain sizes of event. The basic principles behind each format are explained, using examples, in Case study 1.1.

Case Study 1.1

Event Competition Formats

Knockout Tournament

Entries are received from interested participants (teams or individuals) by a certain time (entry deadline). The number of entrants may be limited to a certain number too (limited draw) and the eventual number of entrants determines the shape of the draw. The draw consists of the random selection of each entrant against an opponent whereby the match can be played by or at a certain time or date that can be prescribed or self-arranged. The aim of the draw is to end up with an even number of matches/fixtures (rounds) so that quarter finals, semi-finals and a final can result. This provides a winner. For example, an entry level of

128 participants will result in there being four quarter finals, two semi-finals and one final (127 matches in all). It is of course possible to have any number of entrants and still devise a draw that results in the same way.

An example of the results of the final rounds of the 2007 US Tennis Open Men's Singles event that began as a 128-man draw is given in the following adapted results sheet.

US Tennis Open 2007, Men's Singles

Quarter Final	Semi-Final	Final
R. Federer (1)		
V	R. Federer	
A. Roddick (5)		
	V	R. Federer
N. Davydenko (4)		
V	N. Davydenko	
T. Haas (10)		
		V R. Federer
		(Winner)
C. Moya (17)		
V	N. Djokovic	
N. Djokovic (3)		
	V	N. Djokovic
J. Chela (20)		
V	D. Ferrer	
D. Ferrer (15)		

The numbers in brackets behind the names in the first column (quarter-final round/last 16) are the seedings that were given to those players. Seedings are a ranking starting with the favourite at number one. They are decided by tournament directors or committees and are used to keep the better players apart until their respective seedings bring them together. A seeding process that has been 100% successful would have the top eight seeds winning through to the quarter finals, with the top four seeds going through to the semi-finals and the top two seeds playing each other in the final. In this particular example, it can be seen that the seedings were quite successful with no non-seeded players reaching the quarters and the number 1 seed playing the number 3 in the final with the number 1, the irrepressible Roger Federer, winning.

Completed tournaments of this sort produce a regular update of results and make it available to competitors and spectators as well as the media. After the event, the result sheet would feature every match score (US Open, 2008).

Knockout Stalemate Solutions

A number of elements have been introduced to knockout competition formats in order to make them more attractive and efficient. Those matches that end in draws or stalemates have previously required a replay, sometimes on neutral territory at a later date. Extra time at the end of normal time has long been used to find a winner but, of more recent use, have been shoot-outs or penalty competitions, silver goals and golden goals systems (first goal wins scenarios). Tie-breaks in racket-related sports have also been introduced in order to keep the duration of matches manageable, not just for participants and spectators but also for event managers. Tie-breaks in tennis, when they are in use, are played when a set is tied at 6 games all and the winner is the first to reach at least 7 points with 2 clear points. At the 2007 US Open, Federer beat Djokovic in three sets with the first two sets going to tie-breaks. The final match score was recorded as 7–6 (4), 7–6 (2), 6–4 which shows that Federer won those tie-breaks 7–4 and 7–2 respectively.

Leagues

Leagues are generally used over longer competition periods and involve everyone or every team playing each other at least once. Each participant is then automatically placed in rank in the league according to points won for winning or drawing matches. Most leagues also accumulate the points and then the goals (for and against), tries, runs, etc. for each participant/team, to also determine ranking when points are equal.

Round Robin

Round-robin competitions are where everyone plays each other. They are particularly appropriate for limited entry day-long events. They are used productively in combinations, see below.

Continued

Challenge Tables

These are more appropriately used when the competition is long-term or flexible and for individually played sports such as tennis, racquetball, squash and badminton. Entrants are placed on a ladder or league whereby they are initially ranked in order, probably by a seeding process. Challenge rules are then agreed whereby a participant on the ladder can challenge someone above them (for example, up to two places). A match is self-arranged and played. If a challenger wins they move into the other persons place and everyone else below moves down one place. If the other person wins, the positions remain unaltered. At a declared time/date all challenges are ceased and a ladder winner and all other final positions are determined.

Group Stages

These consist of mini leagues usually with small numbers of participants whereby round-robin matches are played over a given time and then the group winners and or runners-up go through to further competition. This can involve the use of further mini-leagues, such as for the UEFA Champions League where there are two group stages then followed by a knockout competition format.

Tours

Tours consist of a series of events and can result in end of tour champions, possibly via a play-off event. Usually the same players, probably with some kind of tour registration, play each event. The idea may well have originated out of the same athletes visiting ancient games and now we have the likes of the Professional Golf Association (PGA) Tour and the Association of Tennis Professionals (ATP) Tour. The latter takes its top eight players over the year round tour and stages an end of tour championship play-off that uses a combination of competition formats; two groups of four players in a round robin with the top two in each group going through to knockout semi-finals and then a final.

Pre-Qualification Stages

These consist of competitions of any format and they are staged prior to the main competition in order to provide participants for the main event. Some pre-qualifying events only provide limited numbers of places in the main competition where others can be the sole providers of entrants for the main event albeit with a prescribed number of places available. An example of the latter would be the qualifying rounds of the FIFA World Cup where there are international group zones and the fixtures take over a year to complete. Group winners and some runners-up, qualify for the finals.

Stroke Play

Used widely in golf where, unlike in most other sports, the players are hitting their own ball and trying to keep as low a score as possible by getting around the course in as few strokes as possible. The person with the lowest stroke count overall is the winner. Competitions can be organized whereby participants play in groups, usually of two or four, and each group starts their round (usually an 18 hole course) at a certain time (tee-off). Any number of participants can take part and, because it is your own number of strokes at stake, there is no real handicap in who your partner is in your group. When all rounds have concluded the participants are ranked according to their strokes played and prizes can be awarded. Golf is unique in this way but there are other games where you play your own ball. For example, croquet, ten-pin bowling and crown green bowling where there is the added interest of the opportunity to hit and affect your opponent's shots.

Combination Formats

As can be seen in some of the above examples, there are a number of events that combine competition formats in order to be more efficient, conclude within certain time limitations and as a result provide more exciting and entertaining spectacles for those who watch and play.

The sports and their competition formats for the Beijing 2008 Olympics are considered Beijing Insight 1.1 and, in particular, focus on the complexities that face the event manager in the scheduling for the sport of cycling and its road, mountain, BMX and track cycling disciplines.

Beijing Insight 1.1
2008 Olympics: Olympic Sports and Competitions
The 2008 Olympics in Beijing consisted of the following 28 sports and their disciplines:

Archery

Athletics

Aquatics – swimming, synchronised swimming, diving and water polo

Badminton

Baseball

Basketball

Boxing

Canoe/kayak – flatwater and slalom

Cycling – road, mountain biking, BMX and track

Equestrian – jumping, dressage and eventing

Fencing

Football

Gymnastics – artistic, trampoline and rythmic

Handball

Hockey

Judo

Modern pentathlon

Rowing

Sailing

Shooting

Softball

Table tennis

Taekwondo

Tennis

Triathlon

Volleyball and beach volleyball

Weightlifting

Wrestling – Greco Roman and freestyle

Across these sports there were 165 mens events, 127 womens events and 10 mixed – a total of 302 competitions.

Many of these sports, each governed by an International Federation, consist of a number of competition areas. In Beijing, the task was to stage 302 competitions in

Continued

Beijing Insight 1.1—cont'd

an overall event timeline that lasted 16 days, 9–24 August. Here, as an example of the complexity of this task, is the sport of cycling and details of the competitions for its four very different disciplines of road, mountain biking, BMX and track cycling.

Sport: Cycling

International federation: International Cycling Federation (UCI)

Discipline: Road Cycling

Location: Beijing, urban road course
  Dates: 9 (11.00–17.30), 10 (14.00–17.30) and 13 (11.30–17.30) August, 2008

Competitions

Individual Road Race   Men

Mass start for 143 riders to a 239 kilometre course
  Gold: Samuel Sanchez, Spain

Individual Time Trial   Men

A race for 39 riders against the clock over 46.8 kilometres with riders starting at 90 second intervals
  Gold: Fabian Cancellara, Switzerland

Individual Road Race   Women

Mass start for 66 riders to a 120 kilometre course
  Gold: Nicole Cooke, Great Britain

Individual Time Trial   Women

A race for 25 riders against the clock over 31.2 kilometres with riders starting at 90 second intervals
  Gold: Kristin Armstrong, USA

Discipline: Mountain Bike

Location: Laoshan Mountain Biking Course, hilly natural terrain
  Dates: 22 (15.00–17.00) and 23 (15.00–17.30) August, 2008

Competitions

Cross Country   Men

A race for 30 riders over a 40 to 50 kilometre course, the exact distance of which is determined the day before the competition once weather and terrain have been considered. The aim is an optimum finishing time of 2 hours and 15 minutes for the winner after 6 to 7 laps of the course.

Gold: Julien Absalon, France

Cross Country   Women

A race for 30 riders over a 30 to 40 kilometre course, the exact distance of which is determined the day before the competition once weather and terrain have been considered. The aim is an optimum finishing time of 2 hours for the winner after 5 to 6 laps of the course.

Gold: Sabine Spitz, Germany

Discipline: BMX

Location: Laoshan Bicycle Moto Cross (BMX) Venue

Dates: 20 (09.00–11.40) and 21 (09.00–11.40) August, 2008

Competitions

Individual   Men

The same format is implemented for both competitions. Eight riders compete in each heat (qualifying rounds, quarter-finals, semi-finals and finals) with the top four riders qualifying for the next round. The races are held on circuits of approximately 350 metres that include jumps, banks and obstacles.

Gold: Maris Strombergs, Latvia

Individual   Women

As above

Gold: Anne-Caroline Chausson, France

Discipline: Track Cycling

Location: Laoshan Velodrome

Dates: 15–19 (10.00–11.45, 16.30–19.50) August, 2008

Competitions

The full programme consists of 10 competitions based on the 42 degree banked indoor oval track:

Individual Pursuit   Men

Gold: Bradley Wiggins, Great Britain (set Olympic record of 4:15.031 in qualifying)

Individual Sprint   Men

Gold: Chris Hoy, Great Britain (set Olympic record of 9.815 in qualifying)

Continued

Beijing Insight 1.1—cont'd

Keirin Men

This is a 2000 metres race with finals for 12 riders. In a paced mass start all riders follow a motor derny for 1400 metres and when the derny pulls off the track they sprint for the finish.

Gold: Chris Hoy, Great Britain

Team Pursuit (4000 m) Men

Teams of four riders

Gold: Great Britain (Ed Clancy, Paul Manning, Geraint Thomas, Bradley Wiggins set new Olympic and world records twice, 3:53.314)

Points Race Men

23 riders in 16 sprints to amass points

Gold: Joan Cloneras, Spain

Olympic Sprint Men

This is a team competition with teams of three. Two teams compete by starting at opposite ends of the track and the aim is to catch the opposing team or finish 3 laps of the track first. Each rider must lead his team for one lap. The time for the third finishing rider in each team is the recorded time for the team.

Gold: Great Britain

(Chris Hoy, Jason Kenny, Jamie Staff)

Madison Men

This is a team competition with teams of two riders, only one of whom is on the track at any one time. Riding for a number of laps, each rider gains points for intermediate and finishing sprints. As a rider leaves the track he holds on to his team mate and propels him via a hand sling on to the track for his turn.

Gold: Argentina (Juan Curuchet, Walter Perez)

Individual Pursuit Women

Gold: Rebecca Romero, Great Britain

Points Race Women

Gold: Marianne Vos, Netherlands

Sprint Women

Gold: Victoria Pendleton, Great Britain (set Olympic record of 10.963 in qualifying)

Volunteers ready to line the street side await the start of the Individual Road Race for Women.

The Individual Road Race for Women underway from a park in Yongdingmen in south Beijing. The 102.6 km route took the cyclists through central Beijing into the Badaling Great Wall area north of the city.

Source: Beijing 2008 (2008)

PARTICIPANTS

The participants of a sports event are often perceived as being only the sportsmen and women who take part in the competition. Of equal importance, however, are a number of other 'players' as intimated above in the list of sports industry consumers. The stakeholders listed below can be considered to be participants as the event may well be worse off without them.

Competitors

The men and women who compete against each other, either as individuals or in teams of two or more and either for their own gratification and achievement or for some representative body such as a school, club, district, county, state, region, league, conference or nation. Competitors can take part in an event by paying an entry fee and may also buy tickets for themselves and their families. They can also spend money at the event in a variety of ways. At larger events, of course, there are those participants that are needed by the event to help it sell itself and so prize money structures and appearance fees play a part. To go out of the competition in the first round at Wimbledon earned 64 male and female tennis players £10 000 each in 2007 (Wimbledon, 2008).

Officials

Sometimes professional but often volunteers, the officials at sports events include scorers and recorders as well as the referees, umpires and judges that are required for arbitrary decisions and keeping score. The call for volunteer parental assistance here is often the difference between being able to stage the event or not. While officials are an intrinsic part of the management of the event, they are also stakeholders in that they watch the event when they are not officiating and often spend their own money at the event on event services and products.

The entourage

This is a collective description for the men and women who accompany the competitors, sometimes through necessity and sometimes as a result of indulgence. Whatever the reason, the event manager has to be aware that the trainer or coach, the wife and children, the doctor or physiotherapist may need tickets, car parking, accommodation and somewhere to provide whatever service they provide. There are also official governing body executives and council members, team managers and agents to consider too. At larger events, they require event expenditure but they may also spend their own money.

Suppliers

Suppliers include all the providers of equipment and services that are required by the event. They may be front line services where there is direct contact with other stakeholders and they, of course, may be key stakeholders themselves. Security services, sponsors, sports equipment manufacturers and caterers all come into this category.

Event management

Event managers, whether they be owner/operators or not, make the event the show it needs to be. As owners they are shareholders and whether they are employed or contracted they are stakeholders.

Staffing

In addition to management, there are also paid casual employees or volunteers who staff the event in all kinds of roles. These include stewarding, table waiting, kiosk attendance, ticket selling and being a part of the ball-boy/girl team. They are both spectators and money spenders at the event in many cases.

Spectators

Spectators are all those who watch the event whether they buy a ticket or not and, as such, they are very much a part of the event. The interactions between a peanut seller and a seat holder at a major league baseball game can provide much needed entertainment between innings. The interaction between fans and the response of audience to action are also a fundamental part of the event. Empty stadiums do not attract strong media interest nor do they impress those who attend. Event managers have just as much a job to do with the empty seats as they do the full ones in this respect. If people on seats are important, then contingency plans to fill them at the last minute are a key management responsibility and contingency.

Media

The provision for the representatives of the media at events is becoming increasingly sophisticated. Elaborate media centres with state of the art technology and dedicated communications and liaison executives are now common at many events. In this respect, they are stakeholders. The media are also an important vehicle for the delivery of information to others before, during and after the event.

Cheering from Beijing workers, provided via a strategy for creating atmosphere at the 2008 Beijing Olympics, happily and noisily performed by recruited volunteers.

Very important people

The very important people (VIPs) who attend an event often do not have to pay anything for anything but they are, nevertheless, key consumers. They can be sponsors, government officials or other stakeholders whose opinions are important for the future of the event. They can also be important additions to the event programme in that they can present trophies at awards ceremonies or simply add presence to the spectacle of the event. Why else would we want to classify our celebrity lists from A to C?

THE DISCIPLINE OF EVENT MANAGEMENT

Clearly, event managers and the skill of event management have been around for a long time, but it is only in the last decade that both literature and qualifications in the field have emerged to any great extent.

Much of the literature that has been written on the practice of event management is first of all related to the industry as a whole. It is a practical approach that has been adopted by most, with an emphasis on planning and operation. Authors such as Allen, O'Toole, McDonnell and Harris in Australia, Catherwood, Van Kirk, Getz and Goldblatt in North America and Hall from New Zealand, have contributed much to the development of the discipline and the emergence of event management courses in higher education in the USA, Australia and the UK in particular.

There are few dedicated sports event management English texts though the subject does receive coverage to some extent in sport management and sport marketing related literature.

In the early 1990s, event management certification emerged in the USA, principally at George Washington University. Not too much later, in 1996, Leeds Metropolitan University in the UK launched the first BA Honours degree in event management with a Higher National Diploma in 2000 followed by a Masters degree in 2002. To date, there are 75 institutions offering higher education qualifications in event management in the UK, thus demonstrating significant development in just 12 years. The emergence of sports event management as an integral part of this provision has been a natural development and the launching of sports event management undergraduate and postgraduate degrees is beginning to take place. In the USA, sports event management has for some time been a part of the delivery of wider sports management programmes.

There are numbers of event industry related associations. This provides a point of contention. There is a distinct lack of cooperation between these bodies and the formation of more universal representation. There are those that advocate that this is a necessity and yet the simple consideration of the extent of the industry, its broad inclusion of arts, music, conference, exhibition, festivals and sports sectors is perhaps evidence enough that single body representation is barely a practical opportunity. Those that organize sports events are inextricably linked if not articled with national and international governing, organizing and owning bodies and are, therefore, well served with information and support by such. The International Olympic Committee (IOC) itself is also involved in the endorsement of educational programmes. Along with the European Olympic Committees, it supports the delivery of a postgraduate degree in sports administration that is based at different sites across Europe. In the sports sector of event management at least the bodies that exist serve well.

EVENT MANAGERS

There have clearly been sports event managers long before any formal qualifications were available. This begs the question, is there a need for formal qualification in an area that has been well served by expertise from all kinds of other disciplines? Great event managers have emerged from backgrounds in law, marketing, human resources and accounting and, indeed, out of non-certificated routes into management. The reason for their success is that event management encompasses all of these disciplines and an event requires a multitude of management and business skills. Event management qualifications from higher education institutions are not able to offer these disciplines in as much singular depth, but they do allow for a multi-skilled and equipped graduate that can only be of benefit to the industry. The recent development of so many new programmes is a result of industry asking for more qualification in this area.

THE FUTURE

What of the future? There are perhaps several areas of concern for the future of sports events. One is the development of some sports at the expense of others. In the UK, the top 10 sports received 90% of all the money spent on sponsorship and, of those, the top two sports, motor sport and football, received the majority of the increase in spend (Mintel, 2000). The concern is the increasing influence borne by television revenue, the related attraction of sponsorship to events and, as a result, a polarization effect. This polarization continues and, while the spend on football in particular is increasing and as a proportion of marketing communications spend, it is the sports at the top that are receiving increased benefit. While the successful get more so, is this at the expense of minor sports that may well be regressing? Significantly, events may disappear as a result of lesser demand from television and thus much needed sponsorship funding. The irony of this is that there will then be fewer events to help develop those sports.

The increasing influence of the media on sport goes still further. It is now a common occurrence for televised games across many sports to be scheduled according to the timings of commercial breaks and for peak audiences. This has meant that the traditional Saturday fixtures for many sports have now become Sundays and Mondays and at all kinds of start times. A Sunday 4.05 p.m. kick-off time for a Sky televised football match in the UK allows for two pre-game advertising slots within 5 minutes. In addition, those sports with natural time-outs can get more coverage because they allow for more commercial breaks. This does go someway to explain the growth of the major league sports in the USA compared with soccer, the latter requiring a straight 45 minutes minimum of uninterupted broadcast.

There are other examples of where the drive for success and commercial gain is having an effect on the integrity of sport. The opportunity for drug abuse and performance enhancement has increased and sport has had to move with that to control it. Sports marketing techniques are so well advanced that there are now sophisticated controls developed to protect against ambush marketing. All these developments are indicative of the external commercial forces that are at play and of the extent of the skills that are now required in order to put on the event successfully. The event manager's remit and scope of duty has grown significantly in the last decade.

These concerns for the future are indicative of the importance that is placed on sport. The popularity of sports events in society has led to increased commercial interest and greater competition on and off the field that have in turn led to the need for increased controls to keep sport within the limits of social standards and values.

SUMMARY

The origins of modern sports events can be clearly seen in the models that were created in ancient cultures. From the likes of the ancient Greek Games have emerged sports events that have played significant roles in the development of society. The industry now is important on a global scale, economically, socially, politically and technologically.

In determining the scale of the sports events industry, this chapter has considered various conceptual dimensions, the structures of competition and the stakeholders involved. These stakeholders include the organizers, competitors, suppliers and spectators of events that can range from local to international in profile. The identification of the various roles that stakeholders play is important in understanding the relationships that event managers have with each stakeholder group. The management of events is clearly historically important, however, the academic discipline of event management, both in terms of certificated education and writing, is more recent. As it develops, these relationships and the issues that arise out of them, will become the focus for further understanding and, thus, better performance within the industry.

QUESTIONS

1. Sports events are an important social phenomenon. Critically discuss this statement.

2. Sport has been criticized for its negative impact on society, football hooliganism, the bad influence of role models, corruption and drug abuse being cases that occur on a regular basis. Select an issue and critically assess if this is society's or sport's problem to solve.

3. Analyse how scale is important in the planning of sports events by using examples of events from your own research.

4. Explain how the basic sports competition formats have developed into the sophisticated events that exist today and identify the driving forces that have led to them.

5. Identify the relationships between, and the roles played by, the various participants of a sports event of your choice.

6. What are the main future concerns for sports event managers? Select one event and comment on the decisions its managers will need to make.

REFERENCES

Allen, J., O'Toole, W., McDonnell, I. and Harris, R. (2002). *Festival and Special Event Management*, 2nd edn. Queensland, John Wiley & Sons, Chapter 1.

Bancroft-Hinchley, T. (2000). *Football Match between First World War Enemies on Christmas Day 1914 really took place*. www.english.pravda.ru/sport/2001/01/01/1795 (accessed 22 May 2003).

Basketball Hall of Fame (2003). www.hoophall.com/halloffamers/Naismith (accessed 22 May 2003).

Beijing 2008(2008). www.beijing2008.cn/cptvenues/sports (accessed 1 February, 2008).

Blum, R. (2003). *US: Sweden Place Women's World Cup Bids. Miami Herald*. www.miami.com/mld/miamiherald/sports/5896707 (accessed 22 May 2003).

FIFA.com. (2008). Big count. www.fifa.com/worldfootball/bigcount (accessed 29 January, 2008).

Getz, D. (1997). *Event Management and Tourism*. New York, Cognizant, Chapter 1.

Goldblatt, J. (1997). *Special Events: Best Practices in Modern Event Management*. New York, John Wiley & Sons, Chapter 2.

Graham, S., Neirotti, L. and Goldblatt, J. (2001). *The Ultimate Guide to Sports Marketing*. New York, McGraw-Hill, Chapter 1.

Hall, C. M. (1992). *Hallmark Tourist Events – Impacts, Management and Planning. London*, Bellhaven Press, Chapter 1.

IOC (2008). www.olympic.org/uk/games (accessed 19 January 2009).

Jago, L. and Shaw, R. (1998). Special events: a conceptual and differential framework. *Festival Management and Event Tourism*, **5**(1/2), 21–32.

Mintel (2000). *Sponsorship 2000*. Sports Sponsorship: Market Overview. 5 July.

Paralympic Games (2003). *Paralympic Games*. www.paralympic.org/games/01 (accessed 22 May 2003).

Peiser, B. (1996). *Western Theories about the Origins of Sport in Ancient China*. www.umist.ac.uk/sport/peiser2 (accessed 7 May 2003).

Robinson, J. (2008). Amputee ineligible for Olympic events. New York Times. 14 January, 2008. www.nytimes.com/2008 (accessed 29 January, 2008).

Shank, M. (2002). *Sports Marketing: A Strategic Perspective*, 2nd edn. Upper Saddle River, Prentice Hall, Chapter 1.

Soccerballworld.com. (2008). Teamgeist World Cup 2006. www.soccerballworld.com (accessed 29 January, 2008).

Toohey, K. and Veal, A. (2000). *The Olympic Games: A Social Science Perspective*. Oxford, CABI, Chapters 2 and 3.

University of Pennsylvania (2003). www.upenn.edu/museum/Olympics/olympicorigins (accessed 7 May 2003).

US Open (2008). *2007 US Open Draws*. www.usopen.org (accessed 1 February 2008).

Wimbledon (2008). 2007 Wimbledon prize money. www. wimbledon.org (accessed 29 January 2008).

CHAPTER 2

Event Organizations

The Mutua Madrilena Masters Madrid, Recinto Ferial de la Casade de Campo, Madrid (courtesy of the Mutua Madrilena Masters).

CONTENTS

LEARNING OBJECTIVES

After studying this chapter, you should be able to:

- understand the structure of international sport
- identify the role played by sports governing bodies in the governance of sport on a local to a worldwide level
- identify the various types of sports event owners and organizers and the roles they play

31

INTRODUCTION

Who do event managers work for if they want to organize sports events and for those that have the ambition, who are the best and the most deserved of emulation in the industry? This chapter considers the bodies and organizations that play key roles in the sports event industry. First, it is important to describe the structure of international sport and the mechanisms that are used to govern and control sport. This governance is ostensibly universal and thus applies to all owners and organizers of sports events whether they are national governments or local authorities, professional sports franchises or amateur sports clubs. Secondly, the various types of event owners and organizers and the key relationships that exist between them will be discussed.

INTERNATIONAL SPORT

International and national governing bodies

While there is a plethora of bodies that represent the interests of sports, the basic structure of international sport and its governance is not difficult to understand. The accepted and guiding principle, though not universal across all sports, is that there is one recognized international governing body (IGB). Even where this is not the case, it is generally accepted that it is the optimum aspiration. This one body is responsible for the development and control of that sport including its rules of competition. This control is exercised and maintained via membership whereby all those who wish to play a sport, particularly at events, are governed by the rules and conditions of that body. For example, the rules for archery, basketball and cricket are governed by three organizations: the International Archery Federation (FITA), the International Basketball Federation (FIBA) and the International Cricket Council (ICC), respectively. These bodies govern their sports at all levels and, therefore, control the rules whether played by children or adults, by amateurs or professionals, or at school or world championships.

When new sports develop, sometimes a number of organizing bodies may emerge but, generally, and ultimately, one body becomes the recognized authority. The most widely developed sports on a global basis are those with long established IGBs. For example, those of athletics, boxing, football and swimming are the International Association of Athletic Federations (IAAF), International Boxing Association (AIBA), Federation Internationale de Football Association (FIFA) and International Amateur Swimming Federation (IASF). Collectively, these governing bodies are referred to as IGBs in the

USA and UK or International Federations (IFs) by the Olympic Movement and most are members themselves of the General Association of International Sports Federations (GAISF), a forum that allows for discussion on common issues and policy. They can also be a part of the Olympic Movement either as an Olympic participating or Olympic recognized sport.

The more widespread the sport, the more levels there are in the organizational structure that is then developed by the IGB in order to maintain governance. Control is maintained essentially in two ways. First, only one national governing body or national federation (NGB or NF) can be recognized in each country and secondly, that national body governs its territory according to the international rules and regulations set by the respective IGB. In between the international and national forums there may also be international regional bodies, generally called confederations. For example, the Football Association of England (the FA) is a member of Union European Football Association (UEFA) that ultimately sits under the governance of FIFA. UEFA operates within a territory (Europe) and alongside similar confederations that operate within Africa, Asia, North and Central America and the Caribbean, Oceania and South America. The international structure of football and how it relates to local member clubs and players in England is illustrated in Case study 2.1. Similar structures and relationships between bodies apply for each NGB of football.

There are other relationships that are peculiar to each IGB/NGB and are concerned with the organization of competitions and events and this is where the structure may be more sophisticated. In some cases, the organizations that emerge as event and competition organizers are perceived as being just as powerful as the governing bodies. For example, the Football League and the Premier League in England are responsible for various professional football competitions and events but play to the rules of the game as prescribed by FIFA and as controlled at national level by the FA. The Association of Tennis Professionals (ATP) runs the worldwide tour (ATP Tour) of men's tennis tournaments but to the rules of tennis as laid down by the International Tennis Federation (ITF). As powerful as the National Basketball Association (NBA) is in the USA, the matches are played to rules that derive out of FIBA and its nationally affiliated body, USA Basketball.

In addition, IGBs and NGBs own and/or organize their own events and competitions. To illustrate the point and use the same sports, UEFA has its Champions League (for club teams) and European Championships (for national teams), the ITF has the Davis Cup and FIBA has World Championships for national men's and women's teams at senior, youth and junior levels as well as for wheelchair teams.

For some sports, the international body appears to be less powerful than say a prominent national body. This tends to represent a relatively early

Case Study 2.1

International Sports Structures: Football

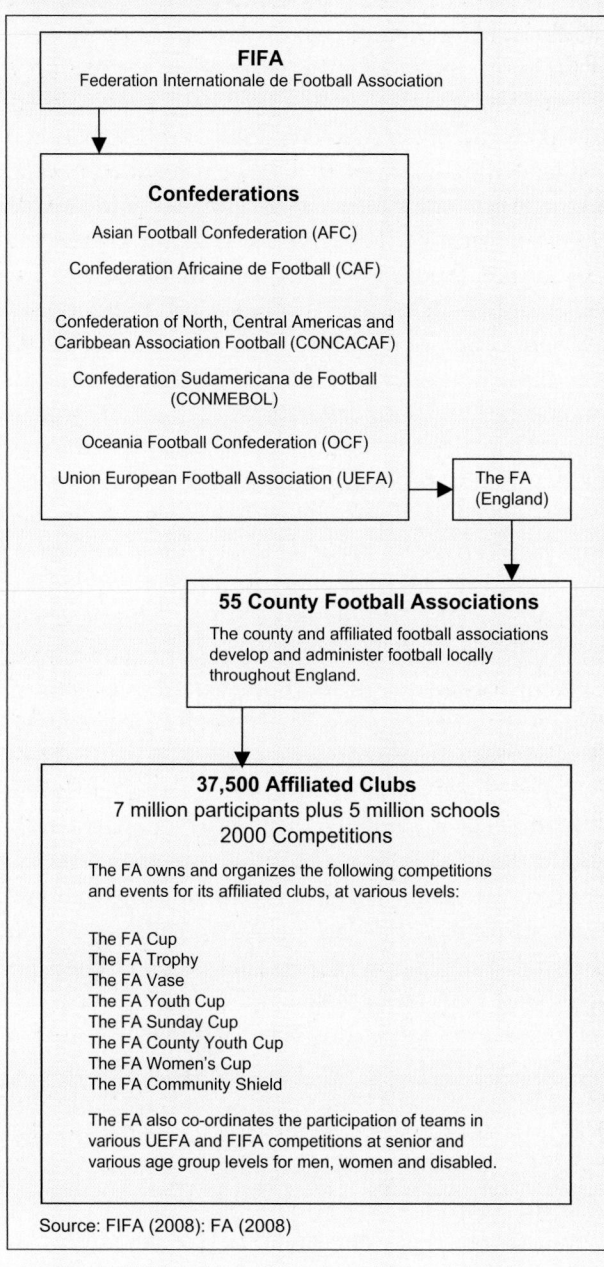

FIFA
Federation Internationale de Football Association

Confederations

Asian Football Confederation (AFC)

Confederation Africaine de Football (CAF)

Confederation of North, Central Americas and
Caribbean Association Football (CONCACAF)

Confederation Sudamericana de Football
(CONMEBOL)

Oceania Football Confederation (OCF)

Union European Football Association (UEFA)

The FA
(England)

55 County Football Associations

The county and affiliated football associations
develop and administer football locally
throughout England.

37,500 Affiliated Clubs
7 million participants plus 5 million schools
2000 Competitions

The FA owns and organizes the following competitions
and events for its affiliated clubs, at various levels:

The FA Cup
The FA Trophy
The FA Vase
The FA Youth Cup
The FA Sunday Cup
The FA County Youth Cup
The FA Women's Cup
The FA Community Shield

The FA also co-ordinates the participation of teams in
various UEFA and FIFA competitions at senior and
various age group levels for men, women and disabled.

Source: FIFA (2008): FA (2008)

stage in the life-cycle of that body and its influence on an international basis. The game of racquetball has been a significant sport within the USA since the 1960s and has had a strong NGB in the US Racquetball Association (USRA) since 1968. In the 1970s and 1980s, there was also a very strong professional circuit for individual players in the USA. The International Racquetball Federation (IRF) was formed in the late 1970s and remains a relatively smaller body with an executive member of USRA serving as its secretary. Another sign of early growth is the existence of more than one body purporting to be the NGB and racquetball again provides a good example. The growth of racquetball and the emergence of the sport's NGBs and IGBs are described in Case study 2.2. Similarly, the International Stoke Mandeville Wheelchair Sports Federation (ISMWSF), the IGB for wheelchair sport operates a two-person office and is based at the Guttmann Sports Centre along with the much larger NGB, the British Wheelchair Sports Foundation (BWSF).

Case Study 2.2

International and National Governing Bodies: The Growth of Racquetball

IRF

The International Racquetball Federation (IRF), previously called the International Amateur Racquetball Federation (IARF), held its first World Championships and Congress in 1981 in Santa Clara, USA where only six national teams took part. Since the second championships in Sacramento, USA in 1984, the event has been held every 2 years and, in 2002, featured 40 teams from six continents. The sport has been a medal sport for national and individual men's and women's entries at the World Games since they began in 1981 and, since 1995, at the Pan-American Games. The sport is now recognized by the IOC and is played in over 90 countries by over 14 million players. This is a Federation that does have Olympic aspirations.

USRA

The United States Racquetball Association (USRA) was founded some time before the IRF, in 1968, and has been at the forefront of the development of the sport including in the founding of the IRF. It has 25 000 members and there are nearly 7 million players in the USA.

BRA vs GBRF

In Great Britain in the early 1980s, two racket manufacturers (Slazenger and Dunlop) and key sports/squash club managers discussed and founded the British Racketball Association (BRA). Their aim was to promote the sport in British squash clubs and on squash courts. The racquetball court is fundamentally different from the squash court in that there is no front tin, it is longer and racquetball shots can be played off the ceiling. There were commercial reasons for forming the body and these were to sell the game to an off-peak hours target audience. It consequently grew and still thrives today. In 1982, a number of British style racketball players were selected to represent Great Britain at the European Racquetball Championships in Holland. Having sampled the international game they returned and a new governing body was founded, the Great Britain Racquetball Federation (GBRF) for the promotion and development of that sport and it remains a member body of the IRF as the NGB for racquetball in Great Britain.

Source: USRA (2008)

The importance of an IGB is not so much about its size but the role it can play in the development of its sport and the control of the development of a sport that is standardized. According to Thoma and Chalip (1996), the objectives for a typical IGB, or IF, include the development of competition between NFs under common rules. For example, USA Basketball is responsible for the selection, training and fielding of US teams in FIBA competition and some national competitions (USA Basketball, 2008). This highlights the importance that is placed on events. On the one hand, they are used to develop individual and team performance. On the other, they are used to put the sport on show in order to encourage participation generally in that sport. Thereby they also become the mechanism by which governing bodies exert their control. The way in which even a local event is played to the same rules as an International Championship is down to the governance that is disseminated down through the structure of that sport.

The Olympic Movement

An understanding of Olympic sport and structure is key to an understanding of international sports governance generally. As indicated in the previous chapter, the Olympic Games have played a significant historical part in the development of sport and sports events. Olympic sport has also served as a model for many sports in how they have structured themselves at all levels.

The IOC retains the rights to Olympic properties such as the five rings symbol and awards a host city the rights to use such in their organization of a Games. The Lausanne (Switzerland) based organization is not associated with any one country or government, is non-profit making and is governed by individual members who are elected by the organization itself. The funding it requires to exist is self-generated via its own marketing programme. An IOC member is a representative of the IOC in their respective country not a representative of that country. The ideals of Olympism are surrounded by debate but the IOC does maintain that it is concerned only with the development of the Olympic Movement.

The Olympic Movement is defined as consisting of the IOC itself, recognized IFs, NGBs and all those who belong to them including of course sportsmen and women. The Movement also consists of National Olympic Committees (NOCs) and Organizing Committees of the Olympic Games (OCOGs).

Each NOC is responsible for the development of the Movement within their country and this includes the encouragement of elite sports performance in that country and the leading of the national teams to Olympic Games. The NGBs that are Olympic recognized sports are affiliated to their own NOC and together they determine the teams that represent their country at Olympic Games. NOCs also have the right to determine which city from their country may bid to host an Olympic Games.

Following a successful bid, an OCOG is formed by the NOC and the host city concerned. The IOC members in that country, the President and Secretary General of the NOC, at least one host city representative plus municipal authority and other suitable members are sought to form what is the controlling body for the organization of a Games. (See Beijing Insight 2.1 for details on the relationship between the IOC, IFs, NOCs and the Organizing Committee for the Olympic Games in Beijing (BOCOG).)

Beijing Insight 2.1
The IOC and Beijing 2008 Olympics and Other Key Relationships

Olympic Movement
The Olympic Movement encompasses organizations, athletes and others who comply to be guided by the Olympic Charter.

The International Olympic Committee (IOC) is the ultimate authority of the Movement and has a role to promote 'top-level' sport for all members of the Movement including the regular and successful celebration of the Olympic Games.

IOC
The IOC comprises a maximum of 115 co-opted committee members and meets at least once per year. It elects a president for a term of eight years and may renew that election for a further four years in addition to a new Executive Board every four years.

The IOC retains all rights to the Olympic Games in all its aspects (marketing, broadcasting etc.) and exists purely on the income received from the sale or licence of those rights.

In 1998, following allegations against the Bid Committee for the 2002 Winter Olympics, Salt Lake City, a review of the IOC and the Olympic Games was conducted by the Commission with a number of key outcomes. These included:

- IOC committee membership lasts eight years and is renewable by election
- 15 members come from International Federations (IFs)
- 15 members come from National Olympic Committees (NOCs)
- 70 individual members
- Members maximum age: 70 years
- A new Ethics Committee and the World Anti-Doping Authority were created
- The transparency of the work of the IOC is promoted via the publication of financial reports and via the opening of IOC Sessions to the media

Continued

Beijing Insight 2.1—cont'd

The Executive Board consists of the President, currently Jacques Rogge from Belgium, four Vice-Presidents and 10 other members (currently from China, Greece, Germany, two from Italy, Japan, Mexico, Norway, Puerto Rico, Singapore, South Africa, Sweden, Switzerland, Ukraine) and its role is to manage the affairs of the IOC. This includes the management of its finances, administration, the process by which the Olympic Games are awarded to host cities and their compliance with the Olympic Charter.

IOC Sessions appoint committee members to Commissions to oversee areas of work. Currently, there are Commissions for Athletes, Collectors, Coordination Committee, Culture and Education, Ethics, Finance, International Relations, Juridical, Marketing, Medical, Nominations, Olympic Congress 2009, Philately, Olympic Programme, Solidarity, Press, Radio and Television, Sport and Environment, Sport and Law, Sport for All, Television Rights and New Media, Women and Sport.

The Executive Board appoints lead administrators including a Director General, currently Urs Lacotte, and the Directors for the Olympic Games (Gilbert Felli), International Cooperation and Development, Finance and Administration, Sports, NOC Relations, Technology, Communications, Information Management, Television and Marketing Services, Legal Affairs, Medical and Scientific, Olympic Museum, Olympic Solidarity.

The main areas of administration include:

- The implementation of Session, Executive Board and President decisions

- Implementation of Commission derived decisions

- Liaison with IFs, NOCs and Organizing Committees for the Olympic Games (OCOGs)

- Coordination of the preparation for all Olympic Games including the new Olympic Youth Games

- Advice to Olympic and candidate cities

- Liaison with governmental and non-government organizations responsible for sport, education and culture.

IOC Olympic Role

A role of the IOC is to establish the candidature and election process and then the selection of host cities of the Olympics. The selection is the perogative of the IOC Session, the general assembly of the IOC members. The final selection event takes place in a country that has no current candidate city for the Games in question.

Rule 34, Chapter Five of the Olympic Charter outlines the governance of the selection of an Olympic host city (see Chapter 7 for further details).

The Olympic Games are competitions for athletes in individual or team events and are not between countries – they are athletes that have been designated by their respective NOCs and accepted by the IOC to compete in a given sport. They compete under the technical direction and rules of the respective IFs of that sport.

Governing Bodies of Sport (International and National)

The IFs of Olympic participating sports are international organizations that are recognized by the IOC as administering one or more sports on a global basis. National Governing Bodies (NGBs) are recognized by IFs as administering those sports in one country.

The mission of an IF for an Olympic sport, an International Olympic Federation, is to manage the everyday running of that sport(s) on an international basis as well as the supervision of the development of athletes at all levels of participation. It will conduct this through its relationships with its constituent NGBs. In addition, it also has the responsibility of the practical organization of the events in their respective sport(s) at Olympic Games. IFs may formulate proposals for the IOCs consideration and these may include reference to the Olympic Movement and Charter and opinion concerning the candidatures of cities for Olympic Games.

In order to expediate common areas of concern, the International Olympic Federations belong to various associations, Association of Summer Olympic International Federations (ASOIF), Association of International Olympic Winter Sports Federations (AIOWF), Association of IOC Recognized International Sports Federations (ARISF) and General Association of International Sports Federations (GAISF).

NOCs

National Olympic Committees (NOCs) maintain and develop the Olympic Movement in their respective countries (independent territories, commonwealths, protectorates or geographical areas are also recognized). There are 205 NOCs on the five continents and they meet at least every two years by way of the Association of National Olympic Committees (ANOC). ANOC consists of five continental constituent bodies, African NOCs (ANOC), American NOCs (PASO), Asian NOCs (OCA), European NOCs (EOC) and Oceanic NOCs (ONOC). These bodies stage their own sports events as described in this chapter.

The further role of an NOC is to facilitate the participation of athletes from their countries at Olympic and other Association Games – only an NOC is able to select and send a team to an Olympic Games. NOCs and NGBs relate to each other in this process.

NOCs also supervise the selection of one city from any cities from their respective countries that wish to bid to host the Olympic Games. It is the respective NOC that names that selected city to the IOC as a candidate to host a Games (see Chapter 7 for further details on the candidature process).

Organizing Committees

Once a candidate city has been selected following the two phases of the IOC selection process to host the Olympic Games, the IOC entrusts the organization of that Games to the respective NOC and host city. The NOC then appoints an Organizing Committee of the Olympic Games (OCOG) to manage that Games and report directly to the IOC on that task. The IOC directs that OCOG in its task.

Continued

Beijing Insight 2.1—cont'd

The OCOG must comply with the Olympic Charter and the contract that is drawn up for it with the IOC and the NOC. There is a period of approximately 7 years of planning and implementation by the OCOG in respect of this task after its subsequent formation following the city's selection at the appropriate IOC Session.

Beijing Organizing Committee of the Olympic Games

The Organizing Committee of the Olympic Games in Beijing (BOCOG) was charged and contracted with the organization of the Games for the XXIX Olympiad, the 2008 Games. This included ensuring that the sports competitions were staged according to the rules of the respective IFs, that no political demonstration took place on Olympic sites and the supply of structures and sites to enable the Games to operate, including if required, new venues. It also included the provision of athlete accommodation and services, transportation systems to sites and beyond, media services that ensured best possible information on the Games, a cultural programme and a final evaluation report.

BOCOG consisted of a President, Qi Liu (Mayor of Beijing), a Vice-President, three Executive Presidents and eight Executive Vice-Presidents. One Executive Vice-President was appointed Secretary General, Wei Wang. BOCOG was formed in December 2001, 5 months after the games was awarded to the city from which time these directors oversaw the work of up to 4000 staff in 30 departments for both the 2008 Olympic Games, including co-host cities Qingdao (sailing), Hong Kong (Equestrian), Tianjin, Shanghai, Shenyang and Qinhuangdao (football) and the Paralympic Games.

A General Office, responsible for liaison with various Government departments and the co-host cities, oversaw the work of an initial 25 departments focused on the following areas:

Project management – overall planning

International relations – liaison with the IOC, NOCs etc

Sports – organization of all competitions

Media and communications – media relations and information services

Construction and environment – supervision/construction of the venues

Marketing – fund raising activities of sponsorship and licensing

Technology – technical services for results and telecoms

Legal affairs – contracts and legal protection of intellectual rights

Games services – housing, transport, registration and spectator services

Audit and supervision – supervision of BOCOG funds and staff performance

Human resources – recruitment, training and management of staff

Finance – compilation and management of the budget

Cultural services – Olympic Youth Festival and other cultural events

Security – event security and public order

Media operations – main press centre and venue press centres operations

Venue management – coordination and promotion of the venues

Logistics – materials and services for the Games

Paralympic Games – preparatory work and liaison with IPC and IPSFs

Transport – for the Olympic family and Games generally

Olympic torch relay centre – coordination and promotion of the event

Accreditation – spectator, athlete, official, staff and dignatory

Opening and closing ceremonies

Olympic villages – villages operations

Volunteers – recruitment/training of all volunteers and volunteer management

Ticketing centre – ticket programmes and sale

Source: IOC (2008a; 2008b; 2008c); Beijing 2008 (2008)

The BOCOG offices in the Haiden district of Beijing, near to the Olympic Green.

The BOCOG offices reception area contained a large welcome desk, various media and meeting areas plus a merchandise retail space.

In addition, the Movement also consists of regional organizations. These are the Pan American Sports Organization (PASO), Association of National Olympic Committees of Africa (ANOCA), Olympic Council of Asia (OCA), European Olympic Committees (EOC) and Oceania National Olympic Committees (ONOC). PASO, like the other bodies, is responsible for the development of the Movement, but is also responsible for other events, in this case the Pan American Games. OCA is responsible for the Asian Games. Both these multi-sports events feature Olympic recognized sports. This general structure provides a model for many IGBs, particularly those that represent Olympic sports. One example is FIFA, as seen in Case study 2.1.

There are currently seven Winter Olympic sports and 28 Summer Olympic sports involving 34 different IFs/IGBs and up to 400 events in the whole Winter/Summer programme (IOC, 2008a). In addition, the IOC recognizes other sports and has on occasion staged them as demonstration events at Olympic Games (but with no medal awards). Non-participating but recognized sports include climbing, bridge, golf, roller-skating and surfing (see Table 2.1 for a full list of Olympic sports and recognized sports). In order to retain that sought after IOC recognition, the IFs concerned are charged with administering their sports according to the Olympic Charter. This conformity includes for example, the application of the Olympic Movement Anti-Doping Code.

CHAPTER 3

The Sports Event Planning Process

The new National Stadium, popularly named the 'Bird's Nest', still in construction in December 2007 and already impacting on the Beijing skyline (see Chapter 4 for a view of the finished stadium).

CONTENTS

LEARNING OBJECTIVES

After studying this chapter, you should be able to:

■ understand the importance of following a planning process for the organization of sports events

■ recognize the need for the process to consider short- to long-term objectives

■ recognize the need for a staged and iterative process that allows continuous alignment with objectives

INTRODUCTION

The importance of sports events in terms of their impacts and benefits, particularly major international events, is well documented and also well covered in the media. In the main, it is the economic benefits that receive the most attention, due mainly to the fact that they are more easily quantified (UK Sport, 1999; Jones, 2001). However, it is the other less quantifiable benefits, those that involve regeneration, physical legacies, cultural, social, environment, tourism and sports development, which may be of more significant value over the long term.

In 2001, a lack of planning led to the loss of the 2005 World Athletic Championships for the UK. The government promised a London venue in its bid with Picketts Lock intended as a long-term legacy for the sport. Upon discovering the costs would be too high, the government tried to offer an alternative location away from London. This resulted in the International Amateur Athletics Federation (IAAF) deciding to put the event out to bid again. While it is commendable that an uneconomic project was aborted, a potentially beneficial event and its stadium legacy might have been better planned for. Alan Pascoe, who ran Fast Track, the organization responsible for UK Athletics' commercial activities, estimated at the time that the loss for athletics was £15–20 million but recognized that it was not just about the financial loss. The world championships could have helped the development of the sport as well the creation of the legacy of a national stadium for future athletics events (Hubbard, 2002).

Much of the theory that underpins the teaching of event management in higher education is centred on how important the event planning process is for organizers of events. An evaluation of the theories of Allen et al (2002), Bowdin et al. (2006), Getz (1997), Shone and Parry (2004), Torkildsen (1999) and Watt (1998) shows that they propose that event planning is a staged process. Westerbeek et al (2006) provide an event 'life-cycle' approach that encompasses basic stages of pre-, event and post-event stages. Others such as Catherwood and Van Kirk (1992), Goldblatt (1997) and Graham et al (1995) propose a less formal approach to event planning.

These theories and models generally accept that event organizations should strategically plan for the long term including there being a responsibility for the ongoing and long-term management of the financial and physical legacies of major events. Getz (1997, 2007) maintains that long-term gains and losses should be assessed at the feasibility stage of the planning process. Allen et al (2002) and Bowdin et al (2006) follow a similar approach. Westerbeek et al (2006) have much detail on the importance of feasibility testing and a comprehensive process for going about that. Hall (1997) stresses the importance of long-term planning with the acceptance that it is the long-term legacies of an event that have the most consequence. Several of the theories also consider wind-up or shutdown (Catherwood and Van Kirk, 1992; Getz, 1997; Allen et al, 2002; Shone and Parry, 2004). Shone and Parry (2004) recognize that some thought should be given to intended legacies in the formation of objectives at the beginning of the planning process.

The theory that is generally on offer in the literature appears to cater for the short-term benefits that events can bring rather than the long-term value that major international events can be strategically planned for. What the planning models tend not to cover is where the development of strategies for successful long-term legacies should sit in the process. In particular, there is a need for the inclusion of specific long-term strategies when planning major international sports events and strategies that will extend beyond the end of the event itself. Since the first edition of this book, only a small number of sports events management related texts have been published, but at least the importance of strategically planning for long-term benefits is gathering momentum. Pruess (2004), for example, recognizes that major international sports events, and Olympics in particular, can act as catalysts for fast–track urban development and that they can therefore be viewed as opportunities for more than just the staging of an event. He maintains that to do this successfully, however, it is first necessary to compare any existing long-term development plans with any Olympic plans for structural development and second, to do that prior to submitting any bid. In addition, this text acknowledges the importance of planning the post-Olympic utilization. Westerbeek et al (2006) acknowledge the importance of the potential role sports events can have in their strategic involvement in long-term regeneration but focus on the short-term planning process for staging sports events and the management of facilities rather than the 'where and how' this is planned.

Generally, then, a more comprehensive process is required, one that can encompass the specific needs of sports event planning, can accommodate sports events of all scales and intentions, accommodate those events that require bidding processes and includes stages where benefits in the longer as well as the shorter term can be planned for.

THE EVENT PLANNING PROCESS

It is essential that any potential long-term benefits intended as attributable to the event be comprehensively covered by strategies that ensure that long-term success. There are a number of key factors required in order to do this. First, the inclusion of a cost–benefit forecast at the feasibility stage of the event planning process would enable organizers not only to forecast the extent of the benefits of their events and budget accordingly, but through that forecast gain support for the event at an early and appropriate stage.

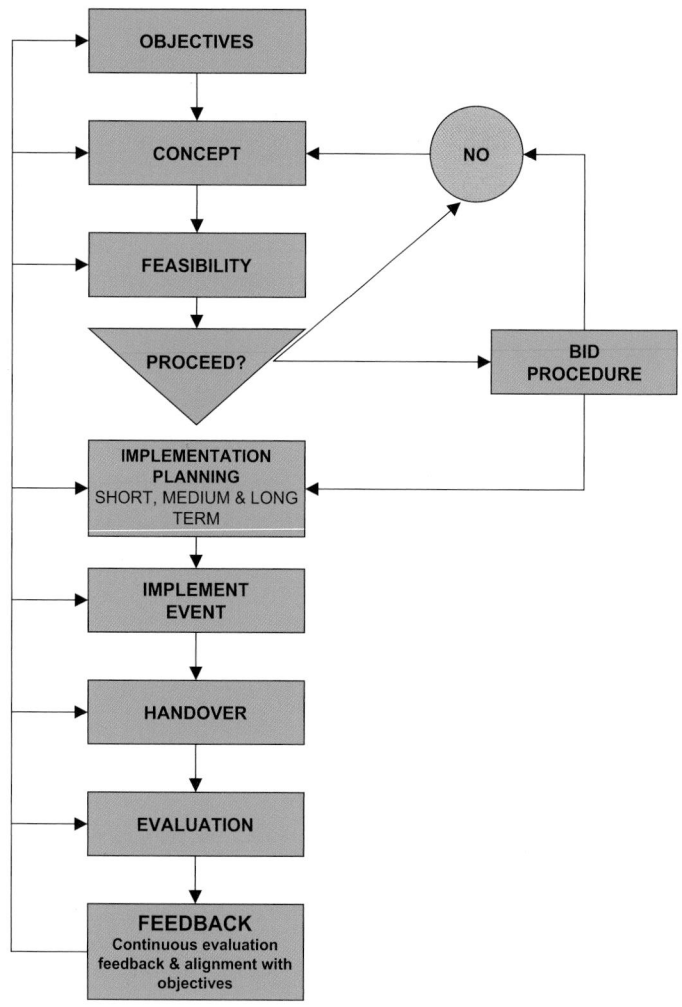

FIGURE 3.1 *The event planning process (source: Masterman, 2003a, 2003b, 2004).*

Secondly, implementation strategies for the use of any new facilities and/or regeneration projects need to be built-in to ensure their long-term futures.

Thirdly, assessing the impact of such an event requires not only an evaluation of short- and medium-term economic and cultural benefits. It also requires a long-term evaluation, possibly even 10 years on or more, of the sustainability and durability, in other words, the success of the regeneration and the legacies that were created as a result of staging the event.

Fourthly, in order for objectives to be met there is a case for the inclusion of mechanisms in the process that will allow continuous alignment with short-, medium- and long-term plans.

The remainder of this chapter is devoted to explaining the sports event management process, a process that encompasses both short-term requirements for the implementation of the event and the long-term objectives that become the legacies of the event (Masterman, 2003a, 2003b, 2004). The model is intended to address the planning process that is required for all scales of event and, while this book is concerned with the management of sports events, it is suggested that this process is universally applicable across the events industry (see Figure 3.1 and Event management 3.1).

EVENT MANAGEMENT 3.1

The Event Planning Process – stage by stage

Objectives

Determine why the event is to be held, what it is to achieve, who is to benefit, and how they are going to benefit; are there political, social, cultural, environmental, sports and/ or economic benefits and over what time span?

Any briefs or bidding processes should be considered as early as this stage.

Concept

Determine what the event is and what it looks like? Design the outline by completing a situational analysis and a competitor analysis (particularly if there is a bid involved).

Consider scales of event and operation, timings, locations and venues, facilities required and available, target markets etc.

Identify strategic partners: local and national government, national and international governing bodies, event owners and promoters, charities, sponsors, participants and after-users.

Identify all internal and external decision-makers.

Identify the stakeholders and organizers: determine if there is to be limited company status, the after-use and after-users for any facilities and infrastructure, and the publics that are affected.

Ensure the design is in alignment with the objectives – short to long term.

Feasibility

At the feasibility stage the event design is tested:

- Identify who is responsible for the delivery of the short- and long-term objectives

- Identify resources required: HR, facilities, equipment, marketing, services etc

- Consider the coordination of any bidding process, the event's implementation and the handover of legacies and returned facilities/ venues/equipment

Continued

- Specifically consider long-term usage of facilities and their future management
- Determine the nature and timing of partnerships to be involved including those required at this stage of the process, i.e. bidding finance if applicable, any finance required to underwrite the event, any handover agreements or operational strategies required for the long-term usage of the facilities used for the event
- Identity any partners not previously identified: particularly those that can provide financial support
- Budget according to these requirements
- Perform a costs versus benefits analysis for the event and also for any long-term objectives
- Determine the critical path required – short and long term
- Ensure alignment with short- and long-term objectives

Proceed?

All of the identified decision-makers are involved in deciding if the event is feasible and will achieve the objectives …

If the answer is NO then evaluate and feedback to the concept stage to re-shape and begin the process again and/or ABORT the project…

If the decision is to PROCEED:

- … and if there is a *Bid Procedure* ….prepare, market, and present the bid
- … if the bid is not won abort the project but evaluate the process and feedback for future use and continue planning for the achievement of any objectives that are intended despite a failed bid
- … if the bid is won or there is no bid procedure then move on to the next KEY stage….

Implementation Planning

It is at this stage where often only the short-term requirements of the event are considered.

Determine all the operational strategies: financial, HR, partnerships, suppliers, services, facilities, equipment,

sales and marketing – include in those: the requirements for after-use, after-users input and what the handover arrangements will be, including how the evaluation over the long term will be completed.

Develop the critical path and the performance indicators so that they incorporate all the fine detail required to execute the event in the short term and for the achievement of the benefits in the long term.

Alignment with the short- and long-term objectives can then be made.

Implement Event

The implementation plans are then executed and the event staged. However, having completed this implementation, there are still key stages of the event planning process remaining.

Handover

The handover of facilities or even equipment is key for all scales of event. The planning for this has already been conducted in previous stages and now managers implement the handover of facilities to the identified or contracted organizations for their continued operation and/or development.

In addition, there is the handover of the responsibility for the evaluation of the legacies such as facilities over the long-term – to determine the level of success according to the long term objectives.

Evaluation

Post-event evaluation is performed against original objectives, short and long term:

- Short term evaluation: of the costs, benefits, impacts of the event itself are performed immediately after the event
- Medium- and long-term evaluation: of the costs, benefits and impacts after a predetermined time and in particular of the legacies to see if they are achieving the objectives set for them

Continuous evaluation: by using performance indicators (budget targets, deadlines for contracts to be achieved etc) in evaluation at all stages of the process, continuous alignment with the objectives is achieved.

Feedback

The evaluation is not complete without feedback:

    The process is iterative by conducting evaluation at all stages thus ensuring feedback is continuous throughout the lifecycle of the event.

Post-event feedback following the short- and/or long-term evaluation includes recommendations that feed into the process for the next event whenever or whatever it is.

Source: Masterman (2003a, 2003b, 2004)

STAGED PROCESS

The event planning process model consists of up to 10 different stages.

There is justification for a staged process where progression through the planning process is made step by step. Manchester, for example, decided on urban regeneration objectives before it decided to bid for both the 2000 Olympics and the 2002 Commonwealth Games (Department of Environment, 1993; Bernstein, 2002). It then looked at the feasibility of the latter being able successfully to deliver the objectives over the long term. On deciding to proceed, the city then went to bid for the event. There was then the development of strategies prior to the event, so that the event would deliver over the long term: for example, the building of the venues and the ensuring of their after-use prior to construction. The policy to build only permanent facilities when after-use and users were secure demonstrates that the city was not only planning for the long term at a pre-event stage but it was also not prepared to progress to the next stage in its planning until these requirements had been met (Bernstein, 2002).

Sydney also decided on its long-term objectives first and then developed the concept for the 2000 Olympic Games (Adby, 2002). Feasibility was next assessed, albeit not to the same level as in Manchester, prior to submitting a bid. Sydney did not have, for example, secure after-use for its new facilities in place prior to the construction of the building.

A handover stage followed the implementation of each event and then similarly evaluation and feedback followed as the final stage.

A review of literature pertaining to the event planning process also supports a staged model (Getz, 1997; Hall, 1997; Watt, 1998; Smith and Stewart, 1999; Torkildsen, 1999; Allen et al., 2002; Shone and Parry, 2004; Bowdin et al., 2006) with the remainder of the literature demonstrating no arguments against such (Catherwood and Van Kirk, 1992; Graham et al., 1995; American Sport Education Programme, 1996; Goldblatt, 1997; Cashman and Hughes, 1999). The main advantage of a staged process being that it is an efficient way of not advancing too quickly and finding out that effort and budgets have been committed unnecessarily.

There is also justification for each stage to be completed prior to progression to the next in order to maintain efficiency in both time and finance. This is also advocated by Allen et al (2002), Bowdin et al (2006), Getz (1997) and Shone and Parry (2004).

A description of each stage in the process now follows with the 2000 Olympics in Sydney, the 2002 Commonwealth Games in Manchester and the 1991 World Student Games in Sheffield used to exemplify key points.

Objectives

It is important to identify why the event is to be staged prior to deciding what the event will be or what it looks like and so objectives are the first stage in the process. The objectives determine the nature and scale of the event. For example, major international sports event host cities may well have regeneration objectives such as the redevelopment of derelict lands for new facilities, housing and business opportunities. The event in effect becomes the catalyst for the achievement of such objectives. Therefore, for this scale of event it is important to consider how event objectives might fit into wider urban plans. For all scales of event, of international or local importance, the objectives are concerned with what the event itself is to achieve. These could be for monetary profit, to develop participation in sport, create employment or to engage communities in social and cultural activities. Whatever the objectives are, they are what the event will be evaluated against in order to determine whether it has been a success or not.

The use of objectives is not necessarily widespread in the industry. Emery (2001), for example, researched 400 major sports event organizers and found that while 64% of the respondents maintained that they used aims and objectives, they were generally a single general aim and/or lacked detail. There may be a number of reasons for this. One may be management complacency, but it may also be due to a perception that setting objectives is too difficult a task due to the diverse nature of the various stakeholders involved. Setting objectives for a long planning process may also be seen to be too inflexible an approach when so much can change in the meantime. Also, because objectives are used as the eventual benchmark for an event, there may also be a reluctance to use them politically. After all, not many people want to be seen to fail.

The argument in favour of the use of event objectives is that they provide the direction for planning and execution. Event management texts agree that the use of objectives is necessary for the production of a successful event (Graham et al, 1995; Hall, 1997; Getz, 1997; Goldblatt, 1997; Watt, 1998; Smith and Stewart, 1999; Torkildsen, 1999; Allen et al, 2002; Shone and Parry, 2004; Bowdin et al, 2006). However, not all agree that they should be ahead of the development of the event concept in the planning process. Some describe a process that begins with a concept and include an intention to bid for an event where appropriate (Getz, 1997; Allen et al, 2002), or an idea and a proposal (Watt, 1998; Torkildsen, 1999). Getz (1997) and Watt (1998) propose that scanning the internal and external environments is necessary prior to setting the vision and goals for the event. Shone and Parry (2004) at least wrap all of these elements into one initial stage that includes the setting of objectives and Allen et al (2002) and Bowdin et al (2006) agree that objectives are required before any situational analysis. The process featured in Figure 3.1 and Event management 3.1 recognizes the necessity for objectives to be the first stage in the planning process by demonstrating that the concept is the vehicle that is designed to achieve the objectives and can only be designed once objectives have been set.

Much is made of objectives being SMART, where they are specific, measurable, achievable, realistic and timely. For them to be achievable and realistic for sports events, the next stage in the process, feasibility, is key. That they are specific, are to be achieved in a certain timeframe and have performance indicators that can be measured, aids the penultimate stage of the process, evaluation.

In order that objectives can be determined, it is necessary for all stakeholders to be identified and their requirements considered in this first stage so that they can be incorporated into the planning of the event. This includes considering potential partners and linked strategies. The basic questions that should be asked at this stage include, why is the event to be held, what is to be achieved, who is to benefit and how? While it is not necessary to categorize sports event objectives in order to determine them, in analysis, they may well be political, social, cultural, environmental or economic in nature. Such a categorization may well assist in determining who the people and/or organizations are that have an influence on the staging of the event, in other words its stakeholders.

Stakeholders

- *Customers*: seat and corporate ticket buyers, sports players or competition participants, advertisers, corporate package buyers such as those for franchized space, sponsors, merchandise buyers.

- *Suppliers*: the organizations that are used to supply equipment, services or goods in connection with the event, for example, tournament equipment, legal advice, food and beverages, transportation and emergency services.

- *Partners*: many sports events are not possible without the sanction of the relevant regional, national and international governing body and these bodies also run their own sports. Other partners may well be local, regional or national government or their agencies. Separate event management organizations may well combine forces to execute an event. Sponsors are often referred to as partners both in their title rights and because of the longevity and/or closeness of the relationship, as too are those media organizations that purchase event rights.

- *Investors*: some of the above partners may also be investors in that they have a vested interest as a result of providing funding either monetarily or via services/goods in-kind. This interest may result in a monetary return on investment but not always. Municipal or agency investment may require non-financial returns such as sports, cultural or social development.

- *Staff*: permanent staff, short-term event hired personnel, those that are sub-contracted and volunteers can fall into this category.

- *External influencers*: these include the event publics that are important for the success of the event and therefore influence any decision-making even if they are not directly connected to the event in any of the above terms. For example, the local community in which the event is delivered, pressure groups, local and national governments from legislative, economic, health and safety, cultural and social perspectives, individual politicians and the media.

At this stage, it is also important to consider any briefs that have been received for the event. Competition to win the right to stage an event, for example, is increasingly in use by event owners. In the corporate world, pitching against others in order to run a sports event on behalf of event owners is growing. A sports management agency will need to discuss, negotiate and fulfil the latter's stipulated conditions and targets. Even if there is no competition there is likely to be such a brief. In the same light, bidding is also being increasingly used by event owners where host cities compete for the right to stage major events. Again, various stipulated conditions or criteria will have to be met by any bid in order to be successful.

It is important that the planning process has built-in alignment mechanisms that ensure that objectives are evaluated throughout all stages of the planning process. Sydney was able to change its 2000 Olympic masterplan on three occasions (Sydney 2000, 2001; Adby, 2002) and Manchester conducted independent reviews of its performance at various stages of the planning process undertaken for the 2002 Commonwealth Games. Alignment can be achieved with the identification of performance indicators and targets. For example, in setting objectives that include the long-term success of facilities and a resultant economic gain from the staging of an event, the planning process automatically gains performance benchmarks. For all scales of sports event, the setting of deadlines for the achievement of certain levels of income, prescribed levels of media coverage or the signing of appropriate contracts ensures that the process gains its own integrated indicators. Incorporating mechanisms and operational systems throughout the implementation planning stage and thus allowing for further thinking on how a project can be improved, will also ensure that, ultimately, the event achieves what it is supposed to achieve.

Concept

Having determined the objectives the concept for the event can be designed.

The previous stage identified all the stakeholders that could or should be involved. Now the decision-makers need to be identified. In designing facilities that were to be used after the 2002 Commonwealth Games, Manchester found it critical to involve the after-users so that they could contract them at an early stage and, in some cases, receive funding in order to proceed. Indeed, without an identified and signed after-user, any new facility would have been of only temporary build (Bernstein, 2002). Sydney was also able to involve relevant municipal agencies at the concept stage with the design of its facilities and Sydney Olympic Park incorporated as part of the strategy for the development of Homebush Bay.

The key questions asked at this stage of the process are what is the event and what does it look like? A situational analysis, including an evaluation of competition, is required in order that the concept can be fully developed to achieve the objectives. There are contrasting examples provided by the 2000 Olympics and the 2002 Commonwealth Games. Manchester planned early to consider its choice of new facilities from a long-term business perspective. It researched the need for a stadium that could house athletics and field team sports for the Commonwealth Games and the long-term contracted use by Manchester City Football Club (FC) and itself in bringing other major events to the city. Sydney, on the other hand, failed to recognize the events expertise and established facilities that were already in place in Melbourne and the high level of competition they would bring.

Consideration of the scale of the event, how it will operate, the timing involved, locations and venues, the facilities and equipment required and already available are all key issues at this stage. The identification of potential strategic partners, possibly local or national government, sports governing bodies, event owners and promoters and charities are also early considerations in forming the concept.

Consideration should also be given at this stage to the show. Sports events are entertainment and can be expensive to stage. It may be tempting to keep the event at its bare bones and not add interval entertainers, extra floral decoration, ceremonies with pomp and style and it will always be a cost versus benefits decision, but this needs to be viewed with a long-term perspective. For those events that want to view their customers in terms of life asset value and from a relationship management perspective, there is a need to evaluate the event experience and how it will attract them next time. The National Basketball Association (NBA) spends US$1 million on research to help its teams find out what its fans want and, in particular, what will make season ticket holders renew year after year. In the top 10 reasons for renewing seat tickets, fans indicated that they viewed in-game entertainment and gifts as the seventh and eighth highest motivations, respectively. A clean arena was placed sixth, and the attitude and behaviour of neighbouring fans in your seat area was placed fourth (Cann, 2003). It can be argued that if it is customer orientated, in other words if the customer values it, then it is a part of the show and such items become important budget considerations. 'How much extra cleaning' and 'how many more floral bouquets' is clearly a subjective managerial decision but the NBA shows that such decisions can be aided by customer research at this stage of the planning process. Setting a budget for these elements is the solution so that as the planning develops and certainly after the decision has been made to go ahead, there is a cost centre to use and the flexibility to respond to changes in requirements nearer to the implementation of the event.

One of the key findings in the NBA research was the dependence of fans on their neighbours in the stands. It showed that one of the most influential aspects on an event experience is the person who sits next to you. You and they are part of the show. Individual experiences on this level would appear to be beyond the control of the event manager but, in at least making sure the seat is occupied, the atmosphere for spectators and participants can only be enhanced. Making sure that each and all are entertained becomes a key aspect of the delivery of the event. At the 2002 Commonwealth Games for the 7 a'side rugby matches, fans for each of the participating national teams were sat side by side. They sang together and entertained themselves with humorous banter. The organizers had done their homework and their knowledge of rugby fans was sufficient to ensure that, not only was it safe for fans to sit together, it was actually preferable for the most conducive atmosphere. A host announcer, music and screen video footage was used to ensure that this was encouraged.

There are two further decision areas that should be highlighted for this stage. The first is that of after-use. Whatever the scale of the event, there is use of the facilities, equipment and venues after the event has concluded, unless it is temporary. Even then, a temporary structure may be used or moved on for use elsewhere. For example, London 2012 plans to do this with a number of training facilities. For major events, this may include handing over newly built sports stadiums and, for locally important events, it may be the handing back of the venue to the owners for everyday use. Either way there is a need to consider how this handover will be achieved at this early stage of the planning process.

The second concerns target markets. If it has not already been done as part of the previous stage, it is important to identify who the target customers for the event will be. This will include targets of participants or sports competitors as well targets for sponsorship, advertising and ticket sales. For instance, the sportsmen and women who take part in the event may or may not bring in revenue in participation or entry fees but they are, nevertheless, clearly critical. There is no concept without them. It is important that they are identified as a realistically achievable target and this is often decided in tandem with all the other considerations above. Are the two exhibition tennis players available on the right date, how many ticket buying fans will be able to be seated, what ticket sales price strategy will be appropriate for the audience demographics? The answers to these questions can help determine what the event is.

While the next stage of the planning process is concerned with deciding if and how the concept can run, as long as there is enough flexibility, the concept can be revisited until feasibility is ensured.

Having determined the objectives at the outset, all of the subsequent stages of the planning process require the implementation of a system of constant alignment with those objectives. While it is not simple to achieve, in theory, if alignment with all the objectives at every stage of the event planning process is achieved, then the event has to be a success. More practically, best event management practice is where managers are aware of the objectives throughout the planning and execution of the event and identify when and where re-alignment is necessary.

Feasibility

Feasibility is a key stage that is recognized by the majority of event theory (Getz, 1997; Watt, 1998; Smith and Stewart, 1999; Torkildsen, 1999; Allen et al., 2002). Having determined the concept for an event and what it is to achieve, it needs to be tested to see if it will work. This does not entail a dress rehearsal but, for major events, it may involve the delivery of one or more events that are used as learning curves. In Manchester, prior to the 2002 Commonwealth Games, the city ran a series of events that were significant in their own right but were still used to test various event management aspects not least the performance of new venues. One such example was the delivery of national swimming championships in the newly built aquatics centre. In a 2-year period, 2000–2002, the city delivered major championship events in sports such as squash, table tennis and cycling, and used them as part of their learning process for the management of the 2002 Commonwealth Games. This is now common practice in Olympic host cities.

Whatever the scale of event, the feasibility stage needs to include a cost–benefit evaluation in order that the budget can be set. This will enable organizers to forecast the extent of the benefits. Through that forecast they can gain important stakeholder's support for the event and by determining costs versus benefits prior to any proceed decisions, organizers can also ensure that unnecessary costs can be kept to a minimum. This may involve the identification of long-term after-use and users or the need for handover of legacies at the end of the event that come with an advantageous financial position. In order to conduct the cost side of this exercise, a number of considerations are required:

- identify who is responsible for the delivery of the objectives (short- or long-term) and the timings involved

- identify the resources required and sources where possible, including financial, personnel, facilities, equipment, marketing, services, etc. and the timings for payment involved

- any bidding process criteria and finance required and the capacity to write that off or benefit from a losing bid

- event implementation, execution and evaluation requirements and timings

- legacies handover and any requirements of long-term after-use of facilities.

These considerations lead to the forming of an event budget and therefore provide a view on the cost at which the event benefits will be achieved. The budget goes on to act as a performance indicator and means by which alignment with the objectives can be continually assessed.

Getz (1997) agrees that long-term gains and losses should be assessed at this stage but maintains that it should also concern an assessment of social, cultural and environmental factors. He sees feasibility as a comprehensive evaluation that also includes 'fit', whereby matters of track records in events, the interests of the community, the availability of personnel and local politics and ideology are all considered.

At this stage, it may be difficult to give any due credence to non-economic-related criteria simply due to the fact that these issues tend to dominate. Most stakeholders are interested first in the economics of whether the event will pay its way. Jones (2001) goes one stage further and suggests that even a balanced economic analysis of whether to host an event may get overshadowed by the political objectives of event organizers, and local and national politicians. Hall (2001) supports this and discusses the lack of feasibility assessment in what he terms 'fast-track planning.' This is where government reaction to short timeframes in hosting events results in the pushing through of proposals without due economic, social or environmental evaluation procedures. Clearly, unbiased feasibility assessment would appear to be critical in aiding the decision of whether to go ahead or not.

Next, it is important to determine a critical path whatever the scale of event. This should include the short- and long-term implementation of the event and any handovers and management of after-use and legacies, physical or non-physical. The importance of this at this stage is to ensure that the timings that are considered necessary are mapped out to see that they can indeed deliver. This is covered in greater detail in Chapter 8.

The benefits an event can achieve should be inherent within the objectives and, if these objectives are specific and measurable, they can be compared with the costs and therefore determine if the event is of value.

In many cases, cost–benefit exercises involve subjective views and forecasts. The greater the scale of event perhaps the greater the need is for a more objective view due to the increased need for accountability. Independent evaluations can entail further expense. For example, the Arup Report produced in May 2002 (Arup, 2002), commissioned jointly by the Greater London Authority, the UK Government and the British Olympic Committee (BOC), reported on the feasibility of London staging the 2012 Olympic Games. It included a forecast of costs and an estimation of the extent of possible benefits. Whatever the scale of the exercise and whether or not it is an internal or external audit, the expense does need to be included in the costs for the event. Interestingly, both Manchester, for 2000, and London, for 2012, went ahead with their Olympic bids without knowledge of the full costs and implications. Both bids acknowledged that value added tax (VAT) 'may or may not' be applicable on event income. London remains in this position to date.

The essential focus of the feasibility stage is to determine if the event can deliver the objectives. Only through continuous alignment of the planning process with the objectives can this be assured.

Proceed?

The decision whether to proceed or not is dependent upon the objectives being feasible and this requires the involvement of all decision-makers. Both Allen et al (2002) and Getz (1997) include this as a stage in the planning process models.

The reason why it is necessary to separate this stage from the previous one is that, when the event is deemed unfeasible, there may well be a case to revisit the concept stage using feedback from the cost–benefit exercise to reshape the event. Additionally, there is also the decision to abort the event completely.

If the event is feasible then the decision to proceed can be made.

Bidding

If there is a bid procedure then the bid needs to be prepared, marketed and presented and, clearly, there are costs involved (Getz, 1997; Allen et al., 2002). The decision to progress from feasibility to the one of proceed must be informed by the identified sunk costs that have been incurred in not winning the bid. If these are not acceptable then the decision not to proceed should also include relevant feedback for future decisions. Manchester was able to feed its experience of its failed 1996 and 2000 Olympics bids into the process by which it won the bid to host the 2002 Commonwealth Games. This too is a common occurrence in Olympic host cities. Athens lost out for 1996 before winning its 2004 bid. Beijing also lost out for 2000 prior to winning for 2008 and, while there is little evidence to support the notion, there are those observers that maintain that a city has to experience a failed bid before it can win. Interestingly, in recent years, several cities have lost out more than once but have kept on bidding without yet winning, Paris (1992, 2008, 2012), Belgrade (1992, 1996), Toronto (1996, 2008) and Istanbul (2000, 2008).

It may also be the case that the bid itself can deliver a number of objectives and that a successful bid concerns a further set of objectives. This makes the bid both a means to an end and a worthwhile project in its own right. Torino, for instance, in its bid for the 2006 Winter Olympics, arguably formulated a bid that would achieve a set of objectives, win or lose and New York City clearly set objectives to gain physical legacies whether it won its 2012 bid or not. As concern grows over the increasing costs of bidding and the threat of fewer bidding cities increases, the premise that all bidding cities need to plan for legacies is a topical question and one that is discussed further in Chapter 7.

Implementation planning

The next stage, bid process or not, is the planning for the implementation of the event concept. This involves the determination of strategies that can achieve the objectives. It is at this stage where often only the short-term requirements of the event are considered in depth.

For the delivery of the event itself, there are operational strategies. These entail the considerations for the delivery of the event, such as the requirements for finance, human resources (HR), partnerships, services and suppliers, venues, facilities, equipment and marketing.

If the event has no long-term objectives, it is implemented via relatively short-term strategies. However, if there are long-term objectives, it is important that long-term strategies are implemented at this stage. Sydney intended that its 2000 Olympics facilities would be of long-term use for the cultural and sporting development of its residents and of national tourism importance. While it had long-term benefits in its sights, its strategies for Stadium Australia failed and the stadium remains a 'finacial challenge'. Sheffield saw the importance of an events strategy over the long term as a legacy of its investment in the facilities it built for the 1991 World Student Games. The objectives were to regenerate an urban area that had been stricken with unemployment. The Sheffield Event Unit, a city authority department, was set up accordingly to attract new events to make use of the new facilities and has been successful in that with over 500 events staged to date (Coyle, 2002). The cost of building the facilities, however, is still a financial millstone around the city's neck and it will continue to pay off its debt until 2025 (Wallace, 2001). Montreal has also experienced similar conditions and has only recently, at the end of 2007, reached financial stability on its 1976 investment in the Olympics. On the other hand, it would appear that Manchester was only going to build its new 2002 Commonwealth Games facilities if they could be a catalyst for regeneration, with jobs, tourism, sports and cultural development the intended impact over the long-term (Bernstein, 2002). In order to achieve this, it implemented a strategy that entailed the commencement of building only when the long-term after-users for the facilities were in place. The identification of Manchester City FC as the user of a new stadium for example was made as early as 1993 in the city's 2000 Olympic bid (Department of Environment, 1993). In failing with that bid, the strategy was still brought to fruition with the subsequent bid for the 2002 Commonwealth Games.

The strategies that are required to deliver the event and its short- and long-term objectives need to be tied into the further development of the critical path. This stage of implementation planning is closest to the delivery of the event itself and, whatever the length of period, it is necessary to add all the fine detail that is required in order to deliver a successful event. Day-to-day itemization is needed in this lead-up time and so the staffing, catering, equipment requirements, for example, are mapped out to deadlines and costs, as are the receipts of ticket, hospitality, entrant fees and sponsorship revenue to deadlines and income. At the same time, as is noted above, the negotiations with new after-users concerning handover or previous users/ owners concering handback need to take place.

The alignment of these strategies with the event objectives is again a key element and the re-addressing of the budget requirements and the assessment of performance indicators throughout this stage of the process can help to assure this.

Implement event

The successful delivery of the event involves the implementation of the strategies that ensure that the short-term objectives of the event are met. The success of these short-term objectives is also of critical importance for the success of any long-term benefits. The attraction of future events to a new stadium will be influenced by how successful the event was and the long-term objectives of sport development may well be dependent upon how successful the spectacle was for example.

Handover

This stage involves the shutdown of the event and, as highlighted earlier, this needs to be considered at the concept and feasibility stages. While several authors consider this an important stage in the planning process (Getz, 1997; Allen et al, 2002; Shone and Parry, 2004), they do not highlight the nature of the planning that is required for the handover of legacies that are to be managed in the long-term. If there are facilities to be handed back to owners, or new venues to be divested or handed over to after-users, the strategies that ensure this is to be achieved are dealt with early in the process. In Manchester's case, no construction of new facilities was undertaken until the after-users were in place and so handover actually involved strategies that had been implemented at the concept stage. In contrast, Sydney's after-use strategies for Stadium Australia were considered after the bid had been won and then, when these strategies failed, the venue was left with financial issues. Earlier consideration of the competition and a more effective cost–benefit analysis may have led to more success in this case.

Shutdown involves clearing out and clearing up and a strategy has to be in place so that this is a seamless activity. This is therefore a stage of the process that when reached, has already been diligently prepared at the implementation planning stage. Equally important for event managers at this stage is the need to prepare for and execute the handover of the facilities and equipment used. This could involve a hand-back to owners of a building that was overlaid for the event or a handover of a new legacy to new operators.

There is one further aspect that may require handover too. If there are long-term objectives, the handover of the responsibility for the evaluation of the legacies and facilities over the long-term is also necessary if the event managers/owners are not going to perform it themselves. Sydney Olympic Park was a resulting legacy of the 2000 Olympics and entailed the handing over of facilities to a new organization in 2002 and their strategy for the Park's future management and development involves evaluation after 15 years of operation (Adby, 2002). Manchester too promised long-term (10 years) evaluation (Bernstein, 2002).

Evaluation

The role and place of evaluation in the process is generally agreed in the literature. In one form or another, theories and planning models identify that evaluation of the event, and then feedback to aid future practice, is a key component. There is agreement in that evaluation is performed after the event but, unfortunately, there is little consideration for longer-term evaluations. Getz (1997) does make the point about event objectives being measurable targets with various timeframes but, for major sports events, there is a need for specific planning for longer-term measures. Assessing the impact of an event may require both short- and long-term evaluation. In the longer-term, it is the sustainability and durability, in other words, the success, of the regeneration and the legacies that were created as a result of staging the event that are to be measured. In Manchester, there was the intention of regular evaluation against objectives and, with a 60-year contract in-place for the use of its stadium, it also had its performance indicators already in place. The Sheffield Event Unit evaluates its events prior to agreeing to host them and also assesses how each event will impact on its overall event strategy. It regularly reports the accumulative impact since the 1991 World Student Games for example.

It is therefore evaluation at the end of the process, rather than at the end of the event itself, that is required. However, evaluation is not just necessary at the end of the process. If continuous alignment with the objectives is to be achieved, than evaluation is required throughout the process. This is important no matter what the scale of the event but it is critical for the planning process for major international sports events. The planning for such events extends over a number of years and it is necessary to adapt to new business, social, cultural and political expectations and conditions. Continuous reassessment of how the objectives are going to be met is therefore required and, consequently, evaluation has a role throughout the process at all stages as well as over various timeframes after the event.

Whatever the scale of the event, performance indicators, such as budget targets or deadlines for completion of contracts, can be used continually to evaluate whether alignment with objectives is being achieved. Sydney and Manchester both had sets of targets as part of their objectives and were able to measure against those. For example, by how much their employment, economies and tourism were performing against target. Evaluation methods include the use of economic impact analysis, employment statistics and tourism data but may also include the use of participation data in order to measure sports development. Similarly, data regarding the continued participation in community activities following an event may be used to assess cultural impact in the long-term. Sheffield set no such targets and consequently cannot assess how successful or not it has been against its original objectives for the 1991 World Student Games. Evaluation requires specific and measurable objectives. These need to be set as part of the first stage of the process, in order that success can in fact be evaluated at whatever point, during or at the end of the planning process. There is more on evaluation in Chapter 12.

Feedback

Evaluation is only of use if the results are fed back into the decision-making process. At whatever stage the evaluation is being implemented, it is critical that future plans incorporate why and how previous strategies worked and failed and so feedback is necessary. This is equally true of short- and long-term evaluation periods, as the next event should always benefit from the feedback from a previous event.

Feedback after a 20-year evaluation period for the legacies of a major event would clearly be too late for any follow-up events that occur earlier, but that is where regular evaluation and alignment throughout the process is appropriate.

Thus evaluation is conducted at all stages and therefore feedback is also continuous throughout the process.

A formal overall evaluation report is required at the end of the process. This enables the managers of the next event to refer easily to how the new event should be delivered. A small-scale event for example, may be an annual occurrence, but memories for detail fade. However, the use of such reporting is uncommon in the events industry and the sports sector is no better even at the highest levels. It was only in 2002, for example, that the International Olympic Committee (IOC) finally incorporated a feedback system for Olympic hosts with its Transfer of Olympic Knowledge (TOK), whereby current hosts can access evaluation reports from previous games (Felli, 2002).

Certain aspects of the planning process Beijing underwent between 2001 and 2008 are considered in Beijing Insight 3.1.

Beijing Insight 3.1

Beijing 2008 Olympics Planning Process: One World One Dream

Sydney was declared host for the 2000 Games in 1993. As a result of coming second in that process, Beijing declared its interests and began its preparation for a bid for the 2008 Olympic Games.

Work began on the bid and its book in earnest in 1998 under the general auspices of a mission of *'One World One Dream'*.

This mission and core statements fed the setting of the following objectives:

General goal: 'To host high-level Olympic Games and high-level Olympics with distinguishing features, to realize the strategic concepts of "New Beijing, Great Olympics" and to leave a unique legacy for China and world sports.'

Distinguishing features: A high-level provision of:

- Sporting venues, facilities and competition organization
- Opening ceremonies and cultural events
- Media services and favourable press commentary
- Security work
- Volunteers and services
- Transportation and logistics
- Civility and friendliness
- Performances by athletes from around the world

Continued

Beijing Insight 3.1—cont'd

While the basic concept of an Olympic Games is already prescribed by the IOC and ensured by their criteria, each Games is unique due to an overlying focus. Beijing adopted three main concepts for a 'core and soul' for their Games:

'Green Olympics, High-tech Olympics and People's Olympics'

Green Olympics

With protection of the environment a fundamental, Beijing specifically wanted to produce environmentally friendly structures and venues, urban and rural afforestation, promote environmental awareness for green consumption and engagement in improvement activities – for a better ecology and city to live in.

High-Tech Olympics

The Games were designed to utilize the latest domestic and international technology, enable the upgrading of scientific innovation capability, implement high-tech innovation in industry and showcase high-tech achievements and innovation.

People's Olympics

The spreading of the modern Olympic ideas in combination with Chinese culture was a key requisite so that Beijing's historical and cultural heritage and its residents' positive outlook could be highlighted. The Games were seen as an opportunity to exchange and deepen understanding between China and the rest of the world. As the Games are an athlete-centred event, the wider opportunity to foster a people-centred philosophy via quality service that met all expectations was adopted.

A New Beijing

Another overlying focus for the concept was 'a new Beijing'. While this was a municipal objective, it was the Games that was to act as the catalyst.

This was a large undertaking and following a strategy to 'Rejuvenate Beijing' some of the ancient and cultural buildings to receive treatment included the major tourist attractions of the Summer Palace, Ming Tombs, Temple of Haven, parts of the Forbidden City and 20 sections of the Great Wall. In addition, the city focused on a central axis, a spine of buildings running through the city, whereby a number of parks, temples, palaces, bridges and pagodas underwent refurbishment.

Personnel

Key aspects of interest at this stage are also their selection of members of BOCOG. As well as national party members and Beijing city municipal committee members, there were also prominent industrialists and bankers appointed in order to maximize the achievement of objectives.

Budget

The budgets were finalized on 14 December 2000 prior to submitting the bid in early 2001. The BOCOG Games budget consisted of total income targeted at $1.62US billion and expenditure at $1.43US billion; $190US billion of this expenditure was long-term capital investment in facilities, with the remainder, $1.24US billion allocated for Games operations.

City, regional and state spending plus private investment on construction was seperately budgeted at a total of $14.25US billion and this included environmental protection, roads, railways, airport expenditure. Of this, $1.86US billion was on sports venues and the Olympic Village.

Short-Term Planning

Some of the upgrading to existing facilites was implemented early to enable a number of events to be staged. These events served as test-runs and were used to evaluate strengths and weaknesses for Games operations, for example, the International Taekwondo Invitation Tournament. In addition, the new Aquatics Centre was completed and opened to enable a number of swimming events to be staged in the final few months run-up to the Games, including the 16th FINA Diving World Cup, the Swimming China Open and the Water Polo China Open.

The Olympic Cultural Festival programme was started early in order to keep momentum and public interest active throughout the planning process. The programme consisted of five festivals in all and began in 2005. The goal was to engage the local population in mass sports, discussion forums and cultural performances and promote unique characteristics of Chinese and Beijing culture internationally.

Similarly, the Beijing Olympic Educational programme began in 2006 with projects such as the Heart-to-Heart Partnership which engaged 200 primary and secondary schools in the city with 205 NOCs. Contacts between the partners were sustained through to the Games themselves and culminated with meetings both at the schools and the Olympic Village during the Games.

Long-Term Planning

The sports building strategy was to build new where required but upgrade where possible. On the whole, the BOCOG budget was used to fund upgrading and the municipal budget focused on new build. The municipal budget, for example, funded 19 new facilities including the new National Stadium and the Aquatics Centre, fondly called the 'Bird's Nest' and 'Water Cube' respectively, plus the new Indoor Stadium. The BOCOG budget did contribute towards one new build, the Olympic Village, but otherwise provided funding for the upgrading of 21 existing facilities, 3 with additional municipal funding.

After-use and contracted post-games ownership for all 37 sports venues were identified in the bid document. Predominantly, venues are municipally owned although one venue was returned to a University (see Beijing Insight 4.2).

Continued

Beijing Insight 3.1—cont'd

Beijing's new Aquatics Centre, nicknamed the 'Water Cube' nearing completion in late 2007 standing alongside its fellow icon the 'Bird's Nest'.

Source: Beijing 2008 (2008)

SUMMARY

The event planning process model provided in this chapter highlights the need strategically to address the long-term legacy needs in the planning of major international sports events. A review of the pertinent literature since the first edition of this book shows little development in this area despite the currency of the issue.

A staged process is important so that clear progression can be made without unnecessary action being taken too early. Attempting to complete each stage prior to progressing to the next is good management practice though it is only common sense to realize that the boundaries between each stage can be less than clear at times. Consistent alignment with the objectives of the event is important and this is made more effective via evaluations of such at each stage. Thus the process is iterative in nature allowing adjustments to be made where necessary as a result of evaluation feedback. Objectives that are specific, measurable, achievable, relevant and timely (SMART) have built-in performance indicators and will make this continuous monitoring easier.

The setting of objectives prior to any concept development allows the whole planning process to be driven towards the event's intended goals and, in many cases, these two stages can be delivered at minimal expense. Testing the feasibility of the event next is critical thus ensuring that any expenditure of time or money is not going to be superfluous. The assessment of costs versus benefits here will determine whether it is worth pursuing the objectives and a particular concept at all.

The next stage of strategy implementation is where there are cases of neglect. If there are long-term objectives and legacies requiring post-event development, management and after-use, then the strategies that will ensure this need to be inherent at this stage. Much of the literature does not consider this relationship and, in industry, there remain concerns when such high profile cities do not undertake such planning.

Despite this being an iterative process, there is still a clear need for an evaluation of the event after it has been executed. However, it is important to understand that an event is only a success if it has achieved its objectives and post-event evaluation against such can reveal to what degree this has been the case. Therefore, the timely nature of the objectives is a key factor in determining when this evaluation is performed. The success of achieving sales and expenditure targets is a short-term task, but the success of the after-use of a new arena may require evaluation over a much longer period. Whenever evaluation is completed, it is its use of feedback for future performance that is important.

QUESTIONS

1. Consider the implications of not setting objectives and designing an appropriate event concept? Support your analysis with your own researched examples.

2. The success of an event can be identified at any point during the event planning process. Identify how this can be effectively achieved by applying appropriate management techniques. Relate your answer to specific event examples.

3. Evaluate the arguments for and against the use of short- and long-term objectives for events.

4. Attempt to review an Olympic bid book. Identify any SMART objectives in evidence.

5. Using the same bid book, analyse whether after-use and after-users have been strategically planned. Visiting Lausanne and the Olympic Studies Centre if you get the opportunity will make this an enjoyable task, but bid books are also available on-line.

6. Long planning periods require flexible management. What issues if any do you see being important considerations for the success of long-term planning?

7. Analyse the role of evaluation and feedback in the planning process, both as an iterative and final stage tool. Discuss the issues with the evaluation of long-term objectives?

REFERENCES

Adby, R. (2002). Email Questionnaire: Director General, Olympic Co-Ordination Authority 2000 Olympics. 9 July.

Allen. J., O'Toole, W., McDonnell, I. and Harris, R. (2002). *Festival and Special Event Management,* 2nd edn. Queensland, John Wiley & Sons, Chapters 2, 5 and 13.

American Sport Education Programme (1996). *Event Management for Sport Directors*. Champaign, Human Kinetics.

Arup (2002). *London Olympics 2012 Costs and Benefits: Summary*. In association with Insignia Richard Ellis, 21 May. www.olympics.org.uk/library/boa (accessed 11 November 2002).

Beijing 2008 (2008). www.beijing2008.cn (accessed 11 February, 2008).

Bernstein, H. (2002). Interview: Chief Executive, Manchester City Council at Chief Executive's Office, Manchester City Council, Town Hall, Manchester. 3 p.m., 28 June.

Bowdin, G., Allen, J., O'Toole, W., Harris, R. and McDonnell, I. (2006). *Events Management*, 2nd edn. Oxford, Butterworth Heinmann.

Cashman, R. and Hughes, A. (eds) (1999). *Staging the Olympics: The Event and Its Impact*. Sydney, University of New South Wales, Chapter 16.

Catherwood, D. and Van Kirk, R. (1992). *The Complete Guide to Special Event Management: Business Insights,* Financial Strategies from Ernst & Young, Advisors to the Olympics, the Emmy Awards and the PGA Tour. New York, John Wiley & Sons, Chapters 1 and 11.

Cann, J. (2003). NBA Research Overview. Presentation by NBA Senior Manager for Market Research and Analysis, NBA Store, New York, 2 December.

Coyle, W. (2002). Interview: Manager, Events Unit, Sheffield City Council at Events Unit. Sheffield City Council, Sheffield, 12 noon, 19 July.

Department of Environment (1993). The Stadium Legacy. In *The British Olympic Bid: Manchester 2000*, Section 12, Vol. 2. Manchester, Department of Environment.

Emery, P. (2001). Bidding to host a major sports event: strategic investment or complete lottery. In Gratton, C. and Henry, P. (eds), *Sport in the City: The Role of Sport in Economic and Social Regeneration*. London, Routledge, Chapter 7.

Felli, G. (2002). Transfer of Knowledge (TOK): A games management tool. A paper delivered at the IOC-UIA Conference: Architecture and International Sporting Events, Olympic Museum. Lausanne, IOC. June.

Getz, D. (1997). *Event Management and Tourism*. New York, Cognizant, Chapters 3 and 4.

Getz, D. (2007). *Event Studies: Theory, Research and Policy for Planned Events*. Oxford, Butterworth-Heinemann.

Goldblatt, J. (1997). *Special Events: Best Practices in Modern Event Management*. New York, John Wiley & Sons, Chapter 2.

Graham, S., Neirotti, L. and Goldblatt, J. (1995). *The Ultimate Guide to Sport Event Management and Marketing*. Chicago, Irwin, Chapter 13.

Hall, C. M. (1997). *Hallmark Tourist Events – Impacts, Management and Planning*. London, Bellhaven Press, Chapters 3–7.

Hall, C. M. (2001). Imaging, tourism and sports event fever. In Gratton, C. and Henry, I. (eds), *Sport in the city: The Role of Sport in Economic and Social Regeneration*. London, Routledge, Chapter 11.

Hubbard, A. (2002). The Interview: Alan Pascoe: A sport stabbed in the back, a nation and its youngsters badly let down. In *The Independent on Sunday*. London, The Independent, 6 January.

Jones, C. (2001). Mega-events and host region impacts: determining the true worth of the 1999 Rugby World Cup. *International Journal of Tourism Research*, **3**, 241–251. London, John Wiley & Sons.

Masterman, G. (2003) The event planning process. In Moragas, M., de Kennett, C. and Puig, N. (eds), *The Legacy of the Olympic Games 1984–2000*, Lausanne, IOC.

Masterman, G. (2003). Major international sports events: planning for long-term benefits. In Ibbetson, A., Watson, B. and Ferguson, M. (eds), *Sport, Leisure and Social Inclusion*. Eastbourne, LSA.

Masterman, G. (2004). Sports events. a new planning process: In McMahon-Beattie, U. and Yeoman, I. (eds), *Sport and Leisure: A Services Operations Approach*. London, Thomson Learning/Continuum, Chapter 13.

Preuss, H. (2004). *The Economics of Staging Olympics: A Comparison of the Games 1972–2008*. Cheltenham, UK., Edward Elgar.

Shone, A. and Parry, B. (2004). *Successful Event Management: A Practical Handbook*, 2nd edn. London, Continuum, Chapters 6 and 12.

Smith, A. and Stewart, B. (1999). *Sports Management: A Guide to Professional Practice*. Sydney, Allen & Unwin, pp. 249–261.

Sydney 2000 (2001). www.gamesinfo.com.au/Home/Sydney2000OlympicGames Report (accessed 4 July 2002).

Torkildsen, G. (1999). *Leisure and Recreation Management*, 4th edn. London, E & F N Spon, Chapter 15.

UK Sport (1999). *Major Events: A Blueprint for Success*. London, UK Sport.

Wallace, S. (2001). Behind the headlines. *The Telegraph*. London, Telegraph, 15 June.

Watt, D. (1998). *Event Management in Leisure and Tourism*. Harlow, Addison Wesley Longman, Chapter 1.

Westerbeek, H., Smith, A., Turner, P., Emery, P., Green, C. and van Leeuwen, L. (2006). *Managing Sport Facilities and Major Events*. London, Routledge.

Impacts and Legacies

The Olympic Park site for London's 2012 Olympics undergoing early preparation in May 2006.

LEARNING OBJECTIVES

After studying this chapter, you should be able to:

- understand the importance of sports events as catalysts for the achievement of short-term benefits and long-term legacies
- identify the various forms of impact that can be gained from sports events

83

- demonstrate how the positive impacts of sports events can be maximized

- demonstrate how the negative impacts of sports events can be minimized

INTRODUCTION

The impacts of sports events on their immediate and wider environments can be both negative and positive and the key to minimizing negative impacts and achieving potential positive impacts is in the effective planning of the event. Impacts can have effect over the long term as well as during and immediately after the event and so the planning needs to reflect an understanding of the different strategies that are therefore required. Even in some of the highest profile sports events this has not always been the case as will be revealed in this chapter.

Long-term impacts as a result of staging events are referred to as the event's legacies and, as discussed in the previous chapter, there is a necessity to include long-term strategies in the planning of events at appropriate early stages in order to achieve successful legacies. The long term is the point at which the physical and non-physical legacies begin, generally referred to as after-use. The medium term is concerned with the impacts that occur post-event after the original event has closed down. The short-term impacts are those that take place during the event and may also refer to those impacts that occur prior to and immediately after the event. Generally speaking, there is no defined timeline used to identify when short-, medium- or long-term impact periods begin or end other than those that might be specified by an event itself. The difference in the nature of shorter- and longer-term impacts is that, more often than not, the latter, the legacies, are not managed or developed by the original event organizers. At some stage after the event, a handover of some kind has been implemented and the expectation of success over that term is passed to new users. It would only be good managerial practice, therefore, for these after-users to want to be involved in those parts of the planning process that bear influence on those legacies.

Spilling (2000) lists the main potential long-term impacts of events as falling into four categories: enhanced international awareness, increased economic activity, enhanced facilities and infrastructure, and increased social and cultural opportunities. While the political impacts of events are acknowledged by Spilling, the research he has conducted is focused on what are termed, the long-term 'industrial' impacts. Getz (1997) makes distinctions between various economic impacts including those of tourism whereby the event acts as a marketing mechanism for the host city as a destination. UK Sport (1999) identifies three main impacts: winning performances and the social effect that has (the development of sports) and economic benefits. Allen et al (2002) split the impacts into four spheres: social and cultural, physical and environmental, political, and tourism and economic. Therefore, there is general agreement on what the main impacts are, with the only difference being the way they are grouped or categorized.

What is intended in this chapter is an overview of the potential benefits that are attributed to both larger and smaller sports events. Examples are used to identify where events have been used as catalysts for the achievement of short-term benefits and longer-term legacies. In addition, the chapter considers the negative impacts that can occur as well as the strategies that can be undertaken as part of the event planning process to ensure that they do not.

LAND REGENERATION

There is some agreement among other authors on the capacity for major international sports events to produce physical legacies in the form of built facilities that can ultimately bring economic benefit (Getz, 1997; Allen et al, 2002; Bowdin et al, 2006). However, the decision to bid to stage a major international sports event will depend on more than just potential budgeted economic benefits. The wider benefits that can be gained by incorporating regeneration projects and new facility provision can lead to critically important local community support as well as political and financial assistance to ensure the bid goes ahead (Hall, 1997; Preuss, 2004). An event that necessitates the development and utilization of land that would otherwise not be used, can then leave physical legacies for future social, cultural and economic benefit and, for some, these can help the initial event staging costs. Indeed, without such support the bid may not even get off the ground.

Cities that have made bids for the right to stage major sports events in recent years have included plans to build new facilities. In many cases, these plans have had to look to the regeneration of land and buildings due to the scarcity and cost of utilizing prime inner-city development sites. In the cases of Sydney and Manchester, this necessitated the development of land beyond inner-city boundaries; the Homebush Bay area in Sydney Harbour for the 2000 Olympics, and Sports City, on the east side of Manchester, for the 2002 Commonwealth Games. This not only allowed for the development of disused and derelict land but also the opportunity to create a central site and focus for each event. The municipal justification in each case being that the regenerated land would have remained derelict if it were not for the opportunities given by the requirement to have new state-of-the-art sports facilities for these events. Further examples include the 1996 Atlanta Olympics which revitalized downtown areas with the creation of Centennial Park, a new stadium, college sports facilities and residential housing (Roche, 2000). In Melbourne, the revitalization of its Docklands area featured in Olympics and Commonwealth Games bids at various stages throughout the 1990s (Hall, 1997, 2001). Also in Australia, there was the development of Fremantle for the 1987 America's Cup.

There were clear regeneration objectives set by Manchester that were a part of, first of all their 2000 Olympics bid and, subsequently, their 2002 Commonwealth Games planning. The objectives were concerned with the regeneration of an inner-city area for the development of jobs and economic growth. The city concluded that these objectives would be best delivered via a sports-led strategy that included the building of major new facilities. In what it entitles its 'Sustainable Strategy,' Manchester 2002 Ltd (1999) declared that the new sporting facilities for the 2002 Commonwealth Games were to provide an important legacy for future improved health, jobs and the regeneration of derelict urban land.

FACILITIES AND SERVICES

Buildings that are newly erected and redeveloped to house major sports events are generally seen as long-term legacies and the appropriate city authorities have to look to justify their investment by looking to their usage beyond the end of the event. They can look for two types of usage: sports, leisure and recreational use by the local community and/or the further staging of more events. Roche (2000) recognized that the 1992 Barcelona Olympics were a part of a wider long-term city strategy for modernization. The strategy, 'Barcelona 2000' was implemented in the mid-1980s and included new sports stadiums, an Olympic Village on the waterfront (see the photograph in the Introduction at the beginning of this book), a new airport and communication towers. Two distinct organizations were created to manage the legacies. One was to attract and run major events and the other was for the development of public sports participation. Roche (2000) maintains that this strategy assisted in ensuring after-use by the general public and the development of public and private sector initiatives to manage the facilities in the long-term was achieved.

The redevelopment of the Faleron Bay is another example. This area in Athens had been a municipal regeneration objective since the early 1960s and formed the basis of the Athens proposals for their candidature for the 1996 and 2004 Summer Olympic Games. Having been awarded the 2004 Games, the city used the event as a catalyst to provide a number of new facilities that were desired long before they intended on bidding for either games. These include a water plaza and esplanade, nautical sports complex and the post-games transformation of the beach volleyball arena into an open-air amphitheatre (Marcopoulou and Christopoulos, 2002). Unfortunately, many of the facilities now lie unused as a consequence of not planning either after-use or required after-users.

In contrast, Melbourne provides an example of the sustainability of legacies. The Melbourne Sports Precinct was originally built for the 1956 Olympics, as discussed in Chapter 2, and now provides a home for a host of important national and international events such as the Australian Open Tennis Championships. This represents nearly 50 years of after-use.

More recently, the preparations Germany made for the staging of the FIFA World Cup in 2006 were focused on getting the country 'fit for football' (Dawson, 2004). The development of stadiums for the event included a refurbishment as well as new build strategy with seven stadiums refurbished and five newly built. The country felt that its stadiums were lagging behind that of the major football powers in Europe and, so, when it bid for the event and beat off competition from England, it promised 12 new facilities that would provide 12 established German football clubs with new and improved facilities for the long-term. Thus, the after-use and users were already determined.

The importance of planning after-use has already been highlighted, but the after-users themselves should also play a key part in the planning process. Those that will be using a facility in the long-term are going to be interested in how it is designed and there is, therefore, an argument that they should be involved at the stages of the event planning process when this input is the most useful. Meinel (2001) maintains that, in practice, after-users are involved mainly after the facility has been designed. He maintains that 50–80% of subsequent operating costs are determined at the planning stage of a facility and argues that, for a facility to be a long-term success, there should be consideration of the needs of both the after-use and the users at the time of its design.

An analysis of New York's bid for the 2012 Olympic Games provides an example of a city that had planned to benefit from its bid, win or lose. The IOC requires Olympic bids to detail specifically how a host city will provide legacies and so New York provided details on how they would be providing social, cultural, economic and sports legacies. Their plans for the infrastructure and physical building of facilities for long-term use at the time of their bids (November 2004) though was quite different. As indicated earlier, the IOC does not require that a host city build new facilities and therefore does not require that there be physical legacies of any sort. It does, however, look to protect against the prospect of 'white elephants' and therefore does require that if new facilities are to be built, there are long-term after-use plans in place (Olympic Review, 2005a). A bidding city can therefore be judged on the planning details it provides in a bid book.

Despite the confusion over whether its preferred new main Olympic stadium would be on the west side of the city (Manhattan) or not, every single one of its planned permanent sports venues at the time of the bid not only had its after-use decided, but also had its after-use management and operators nominated and therefore in place (Gonzalez, 2004). There was a firm statement by the city that 'every proposed Olympic venue has a detailed post-use plan' and the bid itself stated that a New York Olympic Legacy Foundation would be set up to help maintain facilities in the long-term (NYC2012, 2004, 2005). Perhaps more importantly though, every single one of its planned new sports facilities, apart from a bridge that was a part of the rowing lakes development, was to be built whether the city won the bid or not (Gonzalez, 2004). Indeed, the city at the time of its bid had already started investing in new facilities 'to meet a growing revival of Olympic sports in the city'. An outdoor athletics complex, a pool and an 18 000-seat multi-sport arena, all part of the 2012 bid provision, were already underway in 2004 (NYC2012, 2004). The city, while clearly intent on winning the right to stage the 2012 Olympics, was, however, not prepared to waste the opportunity of using an Olympic bid as a catalyst to drive the city plan forward. New York was already committed to expanding its central business districts by developing underutilized areas in Midtown Manhattan and Downtown Brooklyn and new sports facilities were seen as 'anchors for these revitalized neighborhoods' that would spur 'the construction of office space, housing units, and new and enhanced parkland' (NYC2012, 2004). Figure 4.1 shows an excerpt from the city's Olympic Legacy Plan (2005) and clearly states the after-use, names the after-users and shows that these plans were also financially secured in the main with declared sources for after-games financing. Figure 4.2 provides similar detail for Beijing's long-term approach for its 2008 Olympic facilities. All 37 sports facilities had assigned post-games usage and contracted post-games proprietors in place at the time of its bid, details of which were provided in a 'Guarantee of use' section in Volume 2, Theme 7 of its bid book (Beijing 2008, 2008).

A question arises here. At what point in the event planning process should a host city of a major international sports event devise and then implement a strategy that will achieve a successful legacy. Torino planned the building of

Venue	Games Use	Post-Games Use	Venue Owner	Post-Games Funding
369th Regiment Olympic Arena	Boxing	Multi-sport arena	NY State Dept of Military	NY State Dept of Military
Bronx Velodrome	Badminton Cycling	Multi-sport arena	NY City Dept of Small Business Services	NY City Dept of Small Business Services
Brooklyn Olympic Arena	Gymnastics	Multi-Sport arena	Brooklyn Arena LLC	Brooklyn Arena LLC
Gateway Park Olympic Marina	Sailing	Permanent Marina	National Parks Service	National Parks Service
Greenbelt Equestrian Center	Equestrian	Permanent Equestrian Center	NYC Dept of Parks & Rec	NYC Dept of Parks & Rec Legacy Foundation
Olympic Aquatic Center, Williamsburg	Aquatics Water Polo	City Park with swimming	NYC Dept of Parks & Rec	NYC Dept of Parks & Rec Legacy Foundation
Olympic Water Polo Center, Flushing	Aquatics Water Polo	Permanent Pool	NYC Dept of Parks & Rec	NYC Dept of Parks & Rec Legacy Foundation
Olympic Archery Field, Flushing	Archery	City Park and Rec Field	NYC Dept of Parks & Rec	NYC Dept of Parks & Rec Legacy Foundation
Olympic Regatta Center, Flushing	Rowing Canoe/Kayak	Permanent Rowing/Kayak Lake	NYC Dept of Parks & Rec	NYC Dept of Parks & Rec Legacy Foundation
Olympic Shooting Center, Pelham Bay Park	Shooting	NYPD Shooting Range	NYPD	NYPD Legacy Foundation
Olympic Stadium, Manhattan?	Athletics Football	Multi-Sport Stadia	Jets Development LLC (NY Jets)	Jets Development LLC (NY Jets)
Olympic Whitewater Center, Flushing	Canoe/Kayak	Permanent Canoe Center	NYC Dept of Parks & Rec	NYC Dept of Parks & Rec Legacy Foundation
Staten Island Olympic Cycling Center	Cycling BMX Mountain Biking	City Park and BMX/Mountain courses	NYC Dept of Parks & Rec	NYC Dept of Parks & Rec Legacy Foundation
Icahn Stadium	Olympic training site (various)	Multi-Sport Center	NYC Dept of Parks & Rec	NYC Dept of Parks & Rec Legacy Foundation
Randall's Island Competition Site	Olympic training site (various)	Multi-Sport Center	NYC Dept of Parks & Rec	NYC Dept of Parks & Rec Legacy Foundation

FIGURE 4.1 *NYC2012 legacy plan – venue after-use and users.*

Venue	Games Use	Post-Games Use	Venue Owner
National Stadium	Athletics	Multi sports purpose	Beijing Municipal Government
National Indoor Stadium	Gymnastics	Multi sports purpose	Beijing Municipal Government
National Swimming Centre	Swimming	Swimming events	Beijing Municipal Government
CIEC Hall A	Table Tennis Trampoline	Multi sports purpose	Beijing Municipal Government
CEIC Hall B	Shooting Fencing	Multi sports purpose	Beijing Municipal Government
CEIC Hall C	Wrestling Rhythmic Gymnastics	Multi sports purpose	Beijing Municipal Government
CEIC Hall D	Badminton	Multi sports purpose	Beijing Municipal Government
Archery Ground	Archery	Multi sports purpose	Beijing Municipal Government
National Tennis Centre	Tennis	Tennis events	State Sport General Administration
National Hockey Stadium	Hockey	Multi sports purpose	State Sport General Administration
Olympic Sports Centre Stadium	Football Modern Pentathlon	Sports events	State Sport General Administration
Olympic Sports Centre Gymnasium	Handball	Multi sports purpose	State Sport General Administration
Olympic Sports Centre Softball Field	Baseball	Multi sports purpose	State Sport General Administration
Ying Tung Natatorium	Water Polo	Public sports provision	State Sport General Administration
Beijing Shooting Range	Shooting	Public sports provision	State Sport General Administration
Beijing Shooting Hall	Shooting	Public sports provision	State Sport General Administration
Laoshan Velodrome	Track Cycling	Cycling events	State Sport General Administration
Laoshan Mountain Bike Course	Mountain Bike	Public sports provision	State Sport General Administration
Road Cycling Course	Road Cycling	Returned to public use	Beijing Municipal Government
Wukesong Indoor Stadium	Basketball	District public recreational use	Haidian District Government

FIGURE 4.2 *Beijing 2008 – venue after-use and users. Adapted from the Beijing 2008 Bid Book (Beijing 2008, 2008).*

Wukesong Baseball Field	Baseball	District public recreational use	Haidian District Government
Fengtai Baseball Field	Baseball	District public recreational use	Fengtai District Government
Forbidden City Triathlon Venue	Triathlon	Returned to public use	Beijing Municipal Government
Shunyi Olympic Aquatic Park	Canoe/Kayak	Events/Public use	Shunyi District Government
Beijing Country Equestrian Park	Equestrian	Events/Public use	Shunyi District Government
Shoutiyuan Sports Hall	Taekwondo Judo	Education use	Beijing Municipal Education Commission
Beihang Gymnasium	Weightlifting	Returned for University use	Beijing University of Aeronautics and Astronautics
Beitida Sports Hall	Volleyball	Multi sports purpose	State Sport General Administration
Capital Indoor Stadium	Volleyball	Events	State Sport General Administration
Workers Stadium	Football	Events/Football	Beijing Federation of Trade Unions
Workers Indoor Arena	Boxing	Events	Beijing Federation of Trade Unions
Tiananmen Beach Volleyball Ground	Beach Volleyball	Returned for public use	Beijing Municipal Government Venue later changed
Qingdao International Marina	Sailing	Marina and international sailing events	Qingdao Municipal Government
Tianjin Stadium	Football	Events/Football	Tianjin Municipal Government
Qinhuangdao Stadium	Football	Events/Football	Qinhuangdao Municipal Government
Shenyang Wulihe Stadium	Football	Events/Football	Shenyang Municipal Government
Shanghai Stadium	Football	Events/Football	Shanghai Municipal Government

FIGURE 4.2   *Continued.*

several new facilities for the 2006 Winter Olympics and determined their after-use some two years prior to their Games. However, the design and therefore the after-use of their ice sports stadiums for example, were not considered until after the city had been awarded the games. The International Olympic Committee (IOC) had to advise them, a year after the awarding of the games in 2001, to consider leaving a legacy for ice sports in the city (Felli, 2002).

There are numerous further examples of cities that did not plan for the long term adequately. The Millennium Stadium in Cardiff, built to stage the 1999 Rugby World Cup, was designed ultimately to house different events and not just sports. The proposed location for the venue was very accessible to central Cardiff and there was a good case that argued for the need for a national venue. Arguably, the stadium is now a successful business, however, according to Cardiff City Council (2000), the urgency of the task in building the stadium meant that there was little time to consider future usage at the planning stage and that bookings were acquired after the event via post-event marketing. Similarly, the planning of the Stade de France for the 1998 Federation Internationale de Football Association (FIFA) World Cup consisted of a complicated process in order to justify the build in Paris where there were already many other stadiums. At one point, this included the moving in of a top-flight football club as one of several solutions to a long-term after-use problem. There was even thought given to creating a brand new football club for that purpose when there was no agreement on which existing club should go in (Dauncey and Hare, 1999). The thoughts as to future usage in both these cases were retrospective to the already done deals to build and, unfortunately, this is a somewhat common approach.

London's 2012 bid highlighted an ambiguous approach for its planning of the after-use of the venues it would build. In what it calls a 'thorough plan', the bid refers to a Legacy Masterplan and claims that all Olympic venues would have an agreed owner and after-use going forward (London 2102, 2004). However, the bid book, in detailing how venue assets would be disposed of after the Games, failed to identify many of the destinations of facilities that were to be relocated and, perhaps more importantly, left many of the after-users of retained venues unidentified. For example, its planned Olympic Park consisted of five main components: a stadium (to be reconfigured to a capacity of 25 000 seats); an aquatics centre (to be reconfigured to a capacity of 3500 seats); a velopark (cycling velodrome, BMX, track etc), four indoor arenas (one permanent, two to be relocated and one temporary) and a hockey centre. Two of the arenas were to have been deconstructed and relocated to another region of the UK, but the receiving regional authorities that would then become responsible for them remained unidentified. The new Greenwich arena, an indoor shooting hall and temporary swimming training pools were also to be relocated to unidentified regional local authorities.

Only the aquatics centre and the velopark had an identified post-Games operator in place at the time of the bid, the Lee Valley Regional Park Authority. For the stadium, a facility that was to remain in-situ, the bid simply stated that the facilities would be operated by an 'as yet to be identified not-for-profit company through a contract with a specialist commercial operator'. It was the same case for the hockey centre. It is clear that London submitted its bid with the intent on staging an Olympic Games and yet it had not strategically planned its disposal of assets to a point where it could be financially confident. It had also committed to a Games and yet it had no firm plans on how many of its new venues would become physical legacies and avoid being 'white elephants', despite its declared intent on avoiding the very same and of course the IOCs requirement for such. The confidence the city no doubt had in fulfilling these voids over time might be likened to the approach Sydney had at a similar stage of its planning for the 2000 Olympic Games and Stadium Australia in particular. Unfortunately, Sydney failed to follow through and, to date, London's new Olympic Stadium does not have a contracted after-user.

The attraction for many cities is the speed with which regeneration can be effected via the use of a major international sports event as a catalyst. On frequent occasions, Olympic planning, for example, has overridden rigid political procedures in order to fast-track developments (Preuss, 2004). Unfortunately, 'fast-track' planning, for faster reaction to short timeframes in hosting events, can result in the pushing through of proposals that do not receive appropriate economic, social or environmental evaluation (Hall, 2001).

An important factor to consider is the danger of obsolescence in planning early, for example, where even the most advanced facility designs may not be socially or legally acceptable in 10 years time because of new standards in health and safety or for the environment. Sports too may become less popular over time. This is something Japanese architect Isozaki (2001) suggests is a concern to some sports architects and that they therefore consider sustainable design for sports facilities as an insurmountable problem. However, far from advocating that long-term planning is not necessary, he suggests that the answer lies in adaptability of design, where good design will allow for change of use over time. Such design would necessitate the early planning of after-use and identification of after-users. It would also require the inclusion of architects very early in the planning process.

Negative impact mainly comes in the form of superfluous physical structures. The term often used is 'white elephant' and host cities and supporting governments are keen to avoid such obsolescence and drains on further funding. The Olympic Stadium built for the Montreal Olympics in 1976 is a famous example and has often been referred to as a white elephant. The cost of the building of the stadium left the city with enormous debt. The stadium was unfinished at the time of the Olympics and cost overruns and engineering problems meant that it was not completed until 1987. In order to pay off the debt, the government used national lotteries, taxes on tobacco products and property to diffuse the cost onto Quebec citizens. It eventually achieved final payment only in late 2007.

In addition to new facilities and venues, there is also the need to plan for the infrastructure that is required to serve these facilities. In building facilities in disused and outer-city areas, there arises the need to provide adequate transportation if only for the event itself. Depending on the size of the event, of course, there may be a need to enhance existing inner-city provision too. High on the list of any scrutiny of Olympic bids are the provisions made for people flow (IOC, 2002). For example, intended for Athens 2004 were, 120 kilometres of new roads, an expanded metro system, a new traffic management centre and a new international airport (Athens 2004, 2002a). The planning for the provision of transportation infrastructure clearly goes hand-in-hand with the plans for facilities.

The link between the new facilities that are built for major international sports events and the other physical legacies in the form of the infrastructure that are put in to support them is an important one that deserves greater focus in literature. In Tokyo (1964 Olympics), it took 22 new highways and two underground lines, in Sapporo (1972), extensions were required for two airports together with improvements to 41 roads and, in Seoul (1988), three new underground lines were required. At Greenoble (1968), 20% of the total investment in its Games was on road infrastructure. In each of these cases, the transport developments were implemented in order first to accommodate the short-term needs of the event and then for the long-term needs of the city generally.

If facilities are going to be a legacy of any success at all then the planning for the provision of transportation infrastructure goes hand-in-hand with those for facilities. Clearly, this requires further investment, AU$80m in Sydney's case (Holloway, 2001) and its future use becomes reliant upon the long-term success of the facility it serves. Hence, the importance of integrating the long-term strategic plans for both a new facility and the infrastructure that supports it. Germany invested EU3.7billion on its national motorway system throughout 2005 as part of its fast-tracked provision of transport infrastructure to accommodate the three million people that travelled to the 2006 FIFA World Cup in that country (Stadia, 2005).

In contrast, events do not in general provide great stimulus for legacies in the form of accommodation, hotels and room increases etc. There are fewer examples in this industry of new build, refurbishment and even renovation and this is because the increases in event tourism are not proven as sustainable tourist numbers are usually short-lived (Hughes, 1993; Essex and Chalkley, 2003). Consequently, investment in hotels becomes a rarity. For the 2004 Olympics, Athens used cruise ships to accommodate its extra numbers rather than attempt to encourage private investment in new hotel development that would not be required in the long-term. For the most part, Olympics participants are housed in Olympic Villages. These can be refurbished for the event, even temporarily provided out of existing facilities for the event and then returned to former use. Prior to the 1960 winter Olympics, for example, existing accommodation was generally utilized because a newly constructed village would not have been viable in the long-term due to the low local housing requirement in Squaw Valley. While there are exceptions (Helsinki in 1952), even recent winter Games villages have been provided on a temporary basis; Albertville in 1992 and Lillehammer in 1994 (Chappelet, 1997). However, for summer Games, villages can normally be more easily justified and therefore newly built with firm after-usage already in place. In most cases, this kind of legacy is in the form of residential housing that the city has identified as a priority. This was the case in Sydney (2000) and is also what is intended for the London 2012 village.

An important consideration is that if infrastructure, as well as the facilities they serve, becomes underused then the knock on effect can be that they too become white elephants.

Another important and related legacy here is the event management expertise that is gained in staging an event. If the facilities are intended to stage further events, then such management expertise not only serves as an attractive asset in future event bids but also gives the city itself an internal understanding of what it is capable of. This will, of course, enable it to improve its performance. The dedicated municipal department in Sheffield, for example, was set up in the city in 1990 to make full use of the facilities built for the 1991 World Student Games and remains in force today.

The development of local facilities is important too, despite their less significant profile. The raising of funding via one or more sports events can and has resulted in the provision of facilities in many community-led sports and leisure provision, including new courts, clubhouses, pitches and the like. Case study 4.1 considers physical legacies in the surfing sector.

Case Study 4.1

Physical Legacies: Surfing Sector

Fistral Beach, UK

Fistral beach is one of the beaches in Newquay, a tourist town in the county of Cornwall in England. In 2002, the facilities were only basic with only two cafes, kiosks and lavatories, but the beach had already become a major surf attraction due to its superior wave conditions.

Continued

The local municipal authority, Restormel Council, decided to upgrade these facilities via a surfing industry focused strategy that would work as a catalyst generally for regeneration projects. In an attempt to capitalize on the buoyant impact of the surfing industry, it sought to invest in legacies in the form of new facilities as a focus for future beach visitors including event tourists and the staging of international events. It was hoped that that would lead to increased economic impact as well as jobs, business investment and sports development.

Britanic Industries won the tender as the preferred developer of these facilities and invested the bulk of the money required but investment partners also included Restormel and Cornwall County councils. A grant was also awarded in the form of European 'objective one' funding. The investment provided a £1.8m international surf centre with retail, restaurant and changing facilities.

The surf industry has, as a result, become increasingly important to Cornwall's economy and is estimated to be worth £40m per year. Year round, Newquay attracts 2m visitors and most visit the mile long beach.

Regular events include The Rip Curl Boardmasters festival, the annual British leg of a world tour and a nine-day event featuring professional surfers that attracts an estimated 100 000 visitors to the town of Newquay each year. The centre, built in 2002, now houses the British Surfing Association, Newquay Life-saving Club, lifeguards, creche and event competition and training quarters.

More recently, the town has won the Surf Life Saving Great Britain's (SLSGB) bid to host the Rescue 2010 World Lifesaving Championships, a bid that was developed along with the Royal National Lifeboat Institution (RNLI) in a wider strategy to develop life-guarding. The event will attract 6000 competitors and officials from 55 nations and will incorporate 120 events in and out of the water. The opening ceremony will be staged at the Eden Project in nearby St Austell in order to widen the impact. All told, this one event will attract 40 000 spectators and, with that, an economic gain for the region.

This one example demonstrates the success of sports led regeneration strategies at a regional level for economic, social and sports impacts and legacies as well as national lifesaving development.

Source: Benjamin (2002); www.surfnewquay.co.uk (2008)

While London did not diligently plan a new park prior to its bid for the 2012 Olympic Games, it has at least developed a plan for the further development of the Olympic site after the Games. Similar to Sydney, it will turn its site into an urban park, incorporating the new sports facilities but adding much more. Case study 4.2 provides the details.

Case Study 4.2

Physical Legacies: London Olympic Park

Olympic Park

London plans a social and health legacy out of its Olympic site. Costing a projected £200 million, a new 270 acre park will be created to give East London a recreation and leisure focal point. If it is achieved, it will be the largest urban space to be created in the UK since the early 1800s.

The expanse of asphalt that will be laid to accommodate the 4 million or so visitors to the 2012 Olympic Games will be ripped up and replaced by a park that will encompass waterways, meadows and lawns. The two and a half mile stretch of parkland will include a concert field for up to 50 000 spectators, allotments and hazel groves and with a focus on health, a network of fitness trails, cricket pitch, novice and extreme mountain bike trails, horse riding tracks, seven miles of waterways for canoeing, climbing walls, walking terrain and ten acres of football pitches.

There is also a focus on carbon footprint reduction and plans for an energy reducing wind turbine, a miniature biomass power station and an education unit named the 'one-planet' pavilion.

The park will take two years to prepare before it is handed over for Olympic Games after-use to its owners the London Development Agency (LDA) and Lee Valley Regional Park Authority. The newly built Games facilities of a velodrome, aquatics centre and Olympic stadium, reduced to 25 000 seat capacity, will remain as key features of the site, while the overlooking athlete village will be converted into 4000 apartments. In order to raise finance, land will be sold from the site to investors.

The plans for the park were launched in 2008, some 4 years ahead of the Games. However, while there were outline plans for an urban legacy from the site at the time of the bid, designers, and therefore costs, were not brought in to the planning cycle until after the bid was won. However, the bid team did always recognize the critical need of handing back a site that needed to be prepared for post-Games use and to the identified owners, the LDA and Lee Valley. Thus these after-users were involved early in the planning of the concept of this legacy.

Meanwhile, the Olympic stadium, and even plans for a reduction in spectator capacity, was planned without any involvement of future after-users. At the time of the launch of the plans for the park, a possible handover to a football club remained only in negotiation.

Source: Booth (2008)

There need to be changes in the way long-term benefits are strategically planned for. It is necessary to consider their after-use at the concept stage of the planning process. In determining if the objectives are feasible, the identification of after-use and the involvement of after-users become critical. Furthermore, the involvement of those who are responsible for the design of facilities that are expected to be successful over 30 years or more is also critical at this stage.

SOCIAL REGENERATION

The regeneration and legacies of events are not always of the built environment. The benefits of city renewal programmes can create a new focus for social activities, while new sports facilities, as a result of an event, can clearly provide longer-term benefit. Hall (1997) also maintains that events can improve the cultural identity of a host city, develop community involvement and integration and instigate local economic benefits. Event tourists also benefit from this (Getz, 1997).

The regeneration of land, the building of new facilities and the planning of events provide employment opportunities prior to the event. The implementation of the event also provides short-term event jobs but, as can be seen in Sheffield, in the Events Unit, major sports events can also lead to the employment of personnel in the long-term. If the facilities are going to be legacies, they require teams that will plan their economic futures either to provide local community services or to attract further events which, in themselves, provide further employment opportunities. The origin of Sheffield's plans to bid for the World Student Games was focused on a solution to the downturn in its economy due to the steep decline of the local iron, steel and coal industries in the late 1980s. Unemployment was as high as 20% in some areas of the city and an event-led strategy offered a way forward (Gratton and Taylor, 2000) and still provides employment today. In Manchester, too, there were clear long-term targets for increased employment as a result of staging the 2002 Commonwealth Games and these were set to come from the prescribed local area around Sports City. There are also a number of key event management roles that have emerged as permanent jobs in city departments where the focus is firmly on ensuring the games legacies are sustained over the long-term. The city has staged and developed numerous new events since 2002 including a half marathon and world champioships.

On the negative side, there are issues concerning how local the social benefit can be. In building new facilities in a regenerated area there may well be objectives concerning the improvement of housing, job opportunities and facilities for those that are local to that area. That being the case, it is important that the economic status of such residents is considered and that the new opportunities are financially within their reach.

POLITICAL DEVELOPMENT

The improved profile of government at national and international level as a result of staging a successful major international sports event is considered of value. The extent to which profile and prestige can be improved though is clearly difficult to assess, but economic development as a result of the improved profile is perhaps more quantifiable and can result in an enhanced political image if successfully achieved. Preuss (2004) refers to this as a new type of politics, the politics of mega-events, where cities for a short time can receive worldwide recognition and welcome international guests.

Individuals as well as larger bodies can benefit at both collective and individual levels (Hall, 1997). The frequenting of key sports events by politicians can gain them much desired exposure to their target publics. For example, President Chirac and Prime Minister Jospin, despite their different political persuasions, showed higher poll results at the time of the 1998 FIFA

World Cup in France (Dauncey and Hare, 1999). Administrators too can achieve certain political credibility as a result of perceived success. Peter Uberroth is an example of an event manager who is now credited with the mantle of having turned Olympic Games finance around with his success in directing the first Olympics to make a considerable profit in Los Angeles in 1984 (Catherwood and Van Kirk, 1992). Meanwhile, in the UK, both the Chairman and Chief Executive of the Manchester Commonwealth Games received the Queen's New Years honours and the Chief Executive of Manchester City Council, Howard Bernstein, received a knighthood.

Political impact is thus perceived as being of benefit at both the micro- and macro-levels. Hall (1997) maintains that, despite the fact that some events generate negative impact, more commonly, individual politicians and governments view them as being of benefit, due to their capacity to promote an attractive image that can lead to increased investment and tourism.

Another recent example in the UK serves well here. The government, in its embarrassment over the loss of the 2005 Athletics World Championships, as detailed earlier in Chapter 3, decided to give British athletics a £40 million injection. Out of that grant, several new indoor stadiums were planned and, ironically, included the site where the 2005 event would have been staged, Picketts Lock in North London. The Culture Secretary, Tessa Jowell, used her 'political weight' to ensure that this grant went through and saw it as due compensation for the way that government let athletics down (Mackay, 2002a). The government saw the granting of funds as a way of retrieving its political face and, indeed, the same might be said of the individuals concerned. This level of political impact though is arguably short-term.

National and cultural identity is also claimed to be affected by events and therefore available for political manipulation. It is claimed that the 1992 Barcelona Olympics were used to enhance the Catalan regional profile, identity and pride and not just the Spanish national profile (Roche, 2000). Three consecutive Summer Olympic Games were boycotted over political standpoints. In 1976, African nations did not go to Montreal in a protest over New Zealand's rugby tour of South Africa and, in 1980, the USA and allies did not go to Moscow in protest over the then Soviet Union's invasion of Afghanistan. In 1984, Warsaw Pact Nations, including the Soviet Union, did not go to Los Angeles with accusations of US violations against the Olympic Charter and, it should be said, among accusations of retaliatory activity against the USA for their previous boycott. More recently, Beijing stated that it wanted to showcase Chinese culture to the rest of the world via its staging of the 2008 Olympics. This was while it was being scrutinized by the rest of the world for percieved human rights issues. There is more detail on Beijing's 'Peoples Olympics' in Beijing Insight 3.1 in Chapter 3.

The lengths individuals will go in order to maintain their political standpoints through sports events have also been remarkable in many ways. The silent statements made by two black athletes, Tommie Smith and John Carlos, on the medal rostrum at the 1968 Mexico City Olympics over American civil rights issues and the Zimbabwean cricketers, Andy Flower and Henry Olonga, over human rights issues in their country at their opening match in the 2003 Cricket World Cup, were undoubtedly political in their nature. Thus, keeping politics out of sport may be seen as a distant Utopia when individuals and governments seek to put their politics into events in these ways, but this point aside, such activity is testament to the powerful political profiles sports events can have.

CULTURAL DEVELOPMENT

Major sports events can offer wider programmes that are seen to be culturally and socially beneficial. The Spirit of Friendship Festival, part of the overall 2002 Commonwealth Games programme for example, was planned by Manchester to offer more than just sport to its local community. They saw the opportunity to provide food, drink and music events that would be entertainment for incoming event tourists, participating teams and businessmen, as well as the local community (Manchester City Council, 2000). The long-term benefit of this will be difficult to measure, but the importance of the effect it has on attracting future tourists to a city that tries hard to be an attraction should not be overlooked. The IOC recognizes the importance here and requires cultural events to be an 'essential element of the celebration of the Olympic Games' and a required provision by any bidding host city (IOC, 2002). Taking the 2002 Winter Olympics hosted by Salt Lake City as an example, 60 performances, 10 major exhibitions and 50 community projects were staged in its Olympic Arts Festival (Salt Lake City, 2002). Hall (1997) argues that the success of major sports events should not just be measured in economic and tangible terms but also in social and cultural impact.

MacAloon (2003) goes further and maintains that culture is not just one form of an Olympic legacy, it is the source of all the other forms. This view proposes that all tangible benefits such as stadiums, transport infrastructure and tourist facilities and intangible benefits, such as sports history making, rituals, national profiles and political developments are accumulated cultural capital. He proposes that the most important things an Olympics can leave behind are systems that can contribute to the increasing of the accumulated cultural capital and states that these local legacies can then be transformed into global legacy. An example of this is the international perception held of Sydney 2000 where national pride, comradery and goodwill between volunteers was experienced, although this is not necessarily one universal perception.

The period leading up to an event can also be effectively used to widen cultural strategies. There were five Cultural Festivals from 2005 to 2008 in the lead up to Beijing's 2008 Olympics where the objective was to engage with the local population and promote the characteristics of Chinese culture.

Smaller-scale events can also offer opportunities for different cultural groups to come together in sporting competition. Programmes consisting of such events are also arguably required in order that the initial short-term cultural impact and impetus created by major events is sustained over the long-term. Manchester, for example, developed 112 'Cultureshock' projects in an attempt to capitalize on the benefits of the 2002 Commonwealth Games. Sixty-eight of those projects had specific links to ethnic groups from Commonwealth countries (Manchester City Council, 2003). However, if there is no follow-up development then the danger is that the impact will remain short-term. The memory of being a volunteer at the Sydney Olympics in 2000, for example, is all that remains and whether this is a useful legacy is difficult to determine. MacAloon (2003) argues that anything that is not repeated, renewed in performance, ceremony or other representations is in danger of being forgotten and so follow-up strategies are a necessity.

One way of enabling events to achieve positive cultural impact is to embody existing local culture into them so that, when the event has passed, the legacy is contributing to what is already there. Garcia (2003) maintains that this can also maximize the marketing of an event because an understanding of the local cultural contexts and values will provide opportunities for event promotions. By including arts and cultural programmes that are representative and distinctive of the local community, a sports event can therefore more successfully appeal to a key customer base.

This does raise an important point concerning the evaluation of events. A legacy is something that is simply left behind and, as MacAloon (2003) maintains, it takes time for a legacy to develop and become culturally significant. Its evaluation then is something that can only be implemented in the long-term.

SPORTS DEVELOPMENT

Another area of benefit that is also difficult to measure is the level of development a sport can achieve as a result of being showcased by a major event. National and international governing bodies are aware of the importance of exposure via events like the Olympics and, of course, the profile television brings to any potential participants in their sports. UK Sport (1999) states that hosting events can lead to the winning of more medals and a greater stage for sports. This benefit is one a sporting organization might be more interested in than the event host. The IOC is an example of a body that is concerned with the broader goals of competitive sport including the provision of facilities that become legacies for sports and actually advises thus (Felli, 2002), although it should be pointed out that IOC President Jacques Rogge, in his official opening of the 2002 IOC Annual Symposium, stated that physical legacies are not an IOC responsibility (Rogge, 2002). The important point though is not who benefits or who most benefits, it is that the planning for the event would be incomplete without such provision.

The showcase an event can provide has been exemplified recently in Athens and Manchester. The Paralympics in Athens in 2004 featured four new sports that are popular in Greece, boccia, goalball, powerlifting and wheelchair rugby (Athens 2004, 2002b) which helped develop the profile of those sports by providing them with important national exposure through the media. The profile of paralympic sport in general was further enhanced by the fact that the Paralympics and Athens Summer Olympics were run for the first time by one organizing committee (Athens 2004, 2002c).

Manchester has estimated that take up of new and existing sports facilities since the 2002 Commonwealth Games is 250 000 visits made up of new and existing users. The new facilities are also expected to provide over 31 500 places on sports development courses (Manchester City Council, 2003). The strategy has been put in place to capitalize on the interest in sports following the 2002 event.

It is not just large-scale events that can perform as shop windows for the development of sports. Any event that offers participation opportunities, particularly for new starters, can potentially be used for grassroots sports development. However, this short-term impact requires considerable thought and planning if it is to be developed into long-term legacy. The ongoing management of further opportunities for watching and participating in sport requires strategies that follow up on the initial initiatives. For example, at a local level the opening up of tennis clubs in the UK to non-members and new players as part of the Lawn Tennis Association's National Tennis Day initiative is only the first step. It is incumbent upon the clubs then to offer further opportunities to those that attend in an effort to develop their interest in playing tennis.

ENVIRONMENTAL DEVELOPMENT

In an age of concern about our environment, major sports events can play a key role in incorporating operational policies that can not only be efficiency conscious for the event itself but also lay down environmental legacies for the host city for the future.

Sydney has played what has turned out to be an important role in the development of this area with a comprehensive 'green' approach for the 2000 Olympics. Athens 2004, for example, planned to leave behind a cleaner, healthier environment that improved environmental awareness and performance and had the intent of becoming a lasting legacy (Athens 2004, 2002a). Its programmes included new planting, building with environmentally friendly materials and improved waste management. Torino had similar objectives for the 2006 Winter Olympics and, as a result, a new type of feasibility study was introduced. A strategic environmental assessment (SEA) verified the compatibility of the environmental and economic works to be implemented before they were carried out and, in effect, put long-term strategies for the protection of the environment into place (Torino 2006, 2002).

Beijing's 'Green Olympics' was a major objective and included afforestation and the promotion of environmental awareness in a city that is beleagured by poor air quality. For example, the newly built road route out to the rowing and canoeing venues, 60 kilometres out of Beijing, is lined with newly planted trees and the water put in place at the venues themselves is important for future air quailty. Its naming of its main Olympic site as the 'Olympic Green' was also a key political and promotional consideration. With five months to go before the Games, the IOC Medical Commission was monitoring the air quality closely and amid worldwide media coverage of athletes and their concerns over the impact of poor air on performance. Plans had in fact been put in place early to measure air on a daily basis at the Games so that the IOC and any relevant sports federation might postpone an event if required (IOC, 2008). With two weeks to go before the Games, only four out of 14 days failed to meet the national air quality standard (Tran, 2008). Incredible effort was put into clearing polution. Many factories were shut down for the Olympic period, construction was halted and it is reported that 2 million vehicles were taken off the roads in an exercise that is claimed by some researchers to be an 'experiment' that had never been seen before and something that is unlikely to be possible again. A number of scientists made their way out to Beijing in order to conduct experiments while Beijing implemented these measures. Experiments focused on how pollution travels across continents and how dirty air impacts on cardiovascular functions.

David Chernushenko has served on the IOC Sport and Environment Committee and maintains that, to create successful legacies out of sports facilities, they need to be designed with conservation and environmental protection in mind and not just because this is now more socially demanded, but because it can also be of benefit economically too (Chernushenko, 2002). He maintains that too few designs for new stadiums consider the importance of reducing resource consumption and eliminating waste. This is possibly because of a perception that it is more costly to make such considerations and then implement appropriate processes in the building of facilities. However, while designing for sustainability can be more costly at the outset, the implementation of energy and resource saving processes can be made to be cost effective in the long-term. The Lillehammer Olympic ski jumps were designed to follow the contours of the hills for example. This not only made them less obtrusive, it also kept construction material costs low.

Negative environmental impacts, certainly in the short-term, include the non-disposal of waste and the destruction of the habitat. In order that such impacts are avoided, event managers need to plan for the post-event handover of sites and facilities that are not disturbed and are returned in their original state. Event shutdown is not complete without comprehensive clear-up systems being in place and ready to be implemented at the right time.

ECONOMIC DEVELOPMENT

The economic impact of major sports events is of critical importance when it comes to justifying the investments made. The impact, if negative, can be a lasting and costly legacy for local taxpayers. Take the 1976 Montreal Olympics which left the city with a debt of £692 million (Gratton and Taylor, 2000) or Sheffield and its significant negative legacy as a result of its 1991 World Student Games, as mentioned in Chapter 3. The mortgaging of the latter's debt will have taken 25 years to pay off at a rate of £25 million per year by 2025 (Wallace, 2001). If positive, however, the impact can bring important revenue to bolster municipal budgets. Uberroth's Los Angeles Olympics achieved a £215 million surplus (Gratton and Taylor, 2000) but, perhaps critically for some host cities, achieving revenue from the operation of a major sports event that exceeds the initial investment is not as important as the long-term economic benefits that will come from tourism and future usage of the facilities.

The staging of major sports events may incur losses for those that make the investment. However, host cities and governments may well be looking for not much more than a break-even position from the actual operation of the event itself as the wider benefits to the community in additional spending are a higher priority. The 2002 Salt Lake City Olympics is reported to have produced a relatively small surplus of US$40 million but there are significant expectations for the future return on the original investment through inward investment, new business and tourism (Mackay, 2002b). Larry Mankin was the President of the Salt Lake City Chamber of Commerce at the time of the Games and recognized the importance of the event delivering in the long-term (Mankin, 2002). The event managed to pay back the State of Utah's original loan and also achieved surplus monies that were put into funds that were to ensure that the facilities would continue to be operated, maintained and developed in the long-term. It was expected that the economic growth experienced during the Games would slow but the impact of further inward commercial investment into the city would impact positively on tourism and convention business in the long-term. This has been further developed by the State of Utah with an event-led strategy and a destination marketing position that is focused on the region as the 'State of Sport'.

The results and, indeed, the forecasts of economic impact are often the focus of attention when it comes to the questions raised over whether to stage major sports events or not. The media will use it to extol or berate the event and those who are responsible for selling an event to stakeholders will be looking for all that is positive both in the short- and long-term economy. The measurement of economic impact, however, can be an abused process (Coates and Humphries, 2003). Multiplier analysis is commonly used in order to assess costs versus benefits both in feasibility studies and post-event impact analysis. However, the fact that there are a number of different multiplier calculations that can be used leaves the industry in need of a standard that can be used for fair comparison from event to event.

This point aside, the general focus for multipliers in this context is a calculation of the additional expenditure into the local economy as a result of staging an event. The calculation includes the discounting of the expenditure that does not remain within the economy, such as the income generated by those that are not resident in that area, for example, suppliers. After these 'leakages' are accounted for, what remains is the monetary benefit that has been achieved. The more sustained this benefit, the more the likelihood of improved employment. It is clear, therefore, that economic impact and forecasts are a key factor in the decision-making of event hosts. The greater the case is for a return on investment, the greater the case is for staging the event. The multiplier process is further explained in Event Management 12.1 in Chapter 12.

Case study 4.3 focuses on Sheffield and provides an insight into the long-term impact gained from the staging of sports events in the facilities built for the 1991 World Student Games. Case study 4.4 considers the 2002 Commonwealth Games in Manchester. It compares the forecasted impact of the event (1999 feasibility study) with the impact data from the first post-event evaluation report in early 2003. The report shows all targets being exceeded but a possible 2009 target short fall for gross value added. Case study 4.5 shows a number of sports events and economic impacts data in the USA, Australia and Germany.

Case Study 4.3

Event Economic Impact: Sheffield

Additional Expenditure Generated by Sports Events 1990–1997

The table shows the event that generated the greatest economic impact each year (not including 1991 World Student Games)

Year	Event	Actual Gross Expenditure Generated
1990	McVities Invitation International Athletics	£248 991
1991	Yorkshire vs West Indies vs Rest of World Floodlit Cricket	£649 697
1992	UK Athletics Championships & Olympic Trials	£353 854
1993	European Swimming Championships	£1 271 454
1994	AAA Championships & Commonwealth Trials	£590 010
1995	All England Womens Hockey Centenary Celebrations	£207 655
1996	FINA World Masters Swimming Championships	£3 333 875
1997	English Schools Track & Field Championships	£346 951

Source: Kronos (1997)

Economic Impact of Sports Events by Financial Year 1991–2001

Year	No of Events	Actual Gross Expenditure	Additional Visitors to Sheffield	Full Time Equivalent Job Years Created
1991/92	55	£2 177 000	57 000	67
1992/93	30	£2 398 000	72 000	74
1993/94	47	£3 477 000	83 000	104
1994/95	49	£2 444 000	67 000	73
1995/96	41	£1 502 000	34 000	42
1996/97	43	£11 444 ,000	127 000	291
1997/98	30	£2 370 000	43 000	62
1998/99	30	£2 070 000	35 000	49
1999/00	34	£2 900 000	25 000	73
2000/01	36	£2 822 000	33 000	66
TOTAL	395	£38 232 000	576 000	901
Average per year	40	£3 823 000	58 000	90
Average per event	N/A	£97 000	1460	2.00

Source: Kronos (2001)

Case Study 4.4

Event Economic Impact: 2002 Commonwealth Games

A Comparison of the Economic Impacts in the City of Manchester Predicted and Gained as a Result of Staging the 2002 Commonwealth Games

Impact	1999 Feasibility Forecast	2003 1st Impact Study
Total direct permanent & 10 year equivalent jobs	4494	6100
Net additional direct permanent and 10 year equivalent jobs to Manchester	988	2400
Regenerated land area	40 ha	60 ha
Regenerated employment floor space (square metres)	51 223	72 000
Gross value added	£110m (1998–2009)	£22m Plus 300 000 additional visitors per annum spending £12m per annum

Source: Manchester City Council (1999, 2003)

Case Study 4.5

Event Economic Impact: An International Perspective US Sports Council Events

Atlanta Sports Council
- 2000 Super Bowl XXXIV   US$292m
- 2000 Major League Baseball All-Star Game US$49.6m

Los Angeles Sports & Entertainment Commission
- 1999 FIFA Women's World Cup   US$30m

Minnesota Amateur Sports Commission
- 2000 ISI World Figure Skating Championships US$3.58m
- 2000 National Junior Wrestling Championships US$497 000

Sources: Atlanta Sports Council (2003), LASEC (2003), MASC (2003)

Nashville Sports Council

2001/2002 Year
- US$24m impact
- 56 hours of network television coverage
- 100 full pages of print media coverage
- 116 391 participants – spectators, volunteers, media and competitors

Source: Nashville Sports Council (2002)

Perth, Western Australia
- 2000 Telstra Rally Australia   AUS$23m
- 2000 Quantas Triathlon World Champs AUS$16m
- 1999 Australian University Games   AUS$10.3

Continued

- 2001 Heineken Classic Golf Tourney AUS$7.1m
- 1999 Pan-Pacific Masters Swimming AUS$2.6m

Source: EventsCorp (2000)

Hockenheim 1997 German Grand Prix
- DM87m local economy impact

- 70% (DM61m) spending by non-locals
- 258 000 spectators spending on average DM336 per day on tickets, parking, lodging, food and drink, tourist retail

Source: FIA (2004)

TOURISM

Event tourism is currently a key area of study and, as can be seen from the previous sub-section, is a key aspect of economic impact. Events are seen as catalysts for driving tourism but not just for the event itself. Major sports events can develop high profiles for host cities, particularly if they are televised and are claimed to be good for attracting future tourists after the event has been staged. However, just how long-term this impact can be is disputed.

It is clear that host cities regard it as an important objective. Many of the objectives and criteria set out by Sheffield's Event Unit in deciding on the staging of an event are linked to how much media attention it can gain and hence improve its tourism profile. Tourists are also attracted to future staged events and can therefore potentially improve the local economy that way.

Research was undertaken in Wales following the 1999 Rugby World Cup. Three hundred and thirty thousand people were estimated as having visited Wales because of the event and only 20% had been to the country before. Seventy percent thought that they might return on holiday and 25% of those who watched the event on television thought they were more likely to go to Wales as a result. The research estimated that Welsh tourism might benefit by £15 million over the 5 years after the event (Cardiff City Council, 2000).

Other cities have also set tourism objectives. The Sydney 2000 Olympics bid documentation, for example, claimed that there would not only be event tourism but also national tourism growth up to 2004 (Brown, 1999) while Sion's failed bid for the 2006 Winter Olympics was seen as important for the host city, the Valais region and for Switzerland generally. The Swiss saw this as an opportunity to reposition the national brand for increased tourism growth.

While some authors agree that tourism is a benefit of events (Getz, 1997) and that every destination should formulate an event tourism plan to enable it to contribute to the national economy (Keller, 1999), others doubt whether the growth levels achieved in the short-term out of event tourism are sustainable over the long-term (Hughes, 1993) and that tourism therefore cannot be viewed as a potential event legacy.

Sustainable event tourism growth has to be strategically planned. This would include pre-event as well as post-event strategies. Chalip (2003) refers to the need to leverage an event in order to achieve tourism legacy. In Sydney's case, this included four pre-event strategies that focused on visiting journalists, event media programmes, sponsors and industry programmes, respectively. This involved the provision of background information and support to enable Sydney to be used and featured as an attractive destination. This suggests that awareness of and interest in a destination that increases as a result of an event, requires further strategic consideration if they are to be converted into longer-term benefits. This can be achieved by further marketing. The difficulty, however, lies in the likelihood that budgets for this will be reduced after the event.

Beijing Insight 4.1
Beijing 2008 Olympics: Qingdao's sailing legacy
In 1999, the city of Qingdao, China, launched its bid to be the 2008 Olympic Sailing venue and, by the time Beijing had submitted its bid for the overall Games, Qingdao had beaten off other Chinese city rivals to provide the sailing component of that bid.

In June 2003, BOCOG approved the Qingdao Sailing Committee and, in the following year, building work began on the new Qingdao International Sailing Centre. The Olympic Sailing Village was not completed until January 2008 but all the other buildings and marina were completed in time for two key test events to take place.

With the 2006 and 2007 International Sailing Regattas staged (as test events), the city's staging of its stopover stage in the Clipper Round the World Yacht Race in February 2008 and now the Olympic sailing event itself behind it, the Qingdao International Sailing Centre is beginning to realize its original objectives of becoming a world renowned sailing centre.

While the Olympic Sailing event was a fundamental event, it was, nevertheless, only one element of a wider strategy for Qingdao to establish itself on an international basis. Sailing and the building of a first class sailing centre were the spine of a strategy to achieve objectives for increased awareness, economy through business investment, shipping, tourism and employment.

By the time the 2008 Olympics were staged and as a part of this wider strategy, Qingdao had already achieved the following as a result of this wider strategy during the previous year:

- US$17 billion aggregate capital investment since 2003
- Increased value of imports and exports to US$100 billion

Continued

Beijing Insight 4.1—cont'd

- The arrival and investment of 166 Fortune 500 firms in the city, including Olympic sponsors GE and Volkswagen

- Increased gross tourism income to 40 billion Yuan from the spending of 30 million tourists

- Increased shipping container throughput to 9.46 million container equivalent units

- Increased airport passenger numbers to 7.87 million

- Construction of the Centre and related infrastructure created 100 000 jobs

- 46 000 new homes built for low-wage workers

- Heated floor space for business surpassed 30 million square metres

The city's gross domestic product was rated at 378.6 billion Yuan (US$54.9 billion) in 2007 and was forecast to reach 490 billion Yuan in 2010 with the port handling 12 million containers.

Key to this strategy was the attention to detail in the planning of the marina and its serving facilities. A total of 3.2 billion Yuan was invested in the 45 hectare site and a keen regard for the objectives for a green, hi-tec and people focused Games was a main driver in the innovation applied to the planning and building.

Sydney and Athens had both attempted previously to achieve a sailing event that was nearer to the shore in order for more spectators to experience it. Both cities had tried to plan a new spectator dam but were forced to abort those plans for security, construction and expense concerns. Qingdao overcame similar issues and built their 534 metre long breakwater dam so that up to 10 000 spectators could watch sailing taking place 100 to 200 metres off-shore.

Prior to the Games, the International Sailing Federation (ISAF) declared the Centre the best in Olympics history but also recognized the city's innovation in its supply of an international sailing legacy.

In addition to the dam, there were a number of remarkable provisions to enable a long-term benefit. These included the following:

- A row of 41 windmills on the breakwater that not only provided an aesthetic touch but also a sailing wind indicator and power source that reduces electricity consumption by 300 000 kilowatts per year

- An advanced pontoon system without stakes that ensures consistent position for mooring

- The widest launching ramp in the world at 150 metres

- Solar powered buildings

- Use of seawater to regulate ambient temperature in the 8138 metre media centre via an underwater heat exchange system which, in turn, reduces greenhouse gases and also saves on electric consumption.

Source: China Daily (2008a, 2008b)

The above photograph shows the newly built legacies of the Aquatics Centre, the 'Water Cube', National Indoor Stadium and Fencing Hall at Olympic Green, Beijing. Also at Olympic Green were the sponsors showcase buildings and the 'Bird's Nest' national stadium. (Below) The Olympic Green site covers a formidable 1153 hectares and alone provides Beijing with an inner city park. The tranquil settings of lake, recreational and sports facilites as seen below demonstrate the scale of this intended municipal legacy. Jacques Rogge, President of the IOC, claimed that 'no white elephant had been built and that the after-Games use of Beijing's venues would be optimal' in his closing press conference for the 2008 Games. He indicated that, in particular, university students, the workers unions and the appointed venue owners would all benefit. He also referred to the environmental legacy of water cleaning and remediation as well as the planting of trees for sustainability (Rogge, 2008). The measure of this will of course be made in the long-term.

SUMMARY

The potential impacts of staging sports events fall into several categories. Major international sports events can be used by municipal authorities as catalysts for the regeneration of key areas of their cities. The redevelopment of disused or contaminated lands and buildings in inner or outer urban areas is an important first stage for many, though not all, host cities. The second stage is the choice of strategy for the achievement of the objectives set for the development of the economy through increased business investment, tourism and employment. Event-led strategies that provide new facilities and venues for long-term use have proved popular choices. The same applies to smaller-scale redevelopment and the relative impacts that they can have.

Such choices can also prove of great value politically to those that are involved in the decision-making process. Social benefits in the form of jobs, cultural and environmental development, increased community value and quality of living are clearly important political decisions as well as objectives of worth in their own right.

Sports events also offer the potential for sports development that again bring enhanced opportunities for both participants and spectators. The profile gained via the media and, in particular, television helps a sports event to put its sport into a shop window, though just as important are local events that encourage newcomers to take up the sport.

For any long-term impact there is a need for strategies to be put in place and at the appropriate stage of the planning process. These strategies must plan the handing over and/or development of short-term benefits so that they can be realized into sustainable legacies.

QUESTIONS

1. Identify the main types of positive- and negative-event impact with the use of your own researched examples. Evaluate the extent and nature of the short- and long-term impacts involved.

2. Research and analyse how one city of your choice has used sports event-led strategies to achieve wider municipal objectives.

3. Identify the event management that is required to ensure that risks are minimal and benefits are optimal.

4. Consider how Restormel Council will make a sustained success of the developments at Fistral Beach.

5. Critically compare and contrast the New York 2012 planned after-use and contracted after-users approach to that of other cities of your choice.

REFERENCES

Allen, J., O'Toole, W., McDonnell, I. and Harris, R. (2002). *Festival and Special Event Management*, 2nd edn. Queensland, Australia, John Wiley & Sons, Chapters 2, 5 and 13.

Athens 2004 (2002). www.athens.olympics.org (accessed 24 April 2002): (a) /Home/Legacy; (b) /Home/Paralympic Games/Sports; (c) /Home/Paralympic Games.

Atlanta Sports Council (2003). *Economic Impact Studies*. www. metroatlantachamber.com/macoc/sportscouncil/economicstudies (accessed 26 February 2003).

Beijing 2008 (2008). www.beijing2008.cn (accessed 11 February, 2008).

Benjamin, A. (2002). Storm warning. *The Guardian*. 7 August. London, Guardian Newspapers.

Booth, R. (2008). *Olympics will leave east London an open space to rival Hyde Park*. The Guardian, 17 March 2008.

Bowdin, G., Allen, J., O'Toole, W., Harris, R and McDonnell, I. (2006). *Events Management*, 2nd edn. Oxford, Butterworth Heinmann.

Brown, G. (1999). Anticipating the impact of the Sydney 2000 Olympic Games. In Andersson, T. (ed.), *The Impact of Mega Events*. Ostersund, Sweden, ETOUR, pp. 133–140.

Cardiff City Council (2000). *The Economic Impact of the Millennium Stadium and the Rugby World Cup*. Report by the Economic Scrutiny Committee, Cardiff City Council. Edinburgh, Segal Quince Wicksteed Ltd and System 3.

Catherwood, D. and Van Kirk, R. (1992). *The Complete Guide to Special Event Management: Business Insights, Financial Strategies* from Ernst & Young, Advisors to the Olympics, the Emmy awards and the PGA tour. New York, John Wiley & Sons, Chapter 1.

Chalip, L. (2003). Tourism and the Olympic Games. In Moragas, M., de., Kennett, C. and Puig, N. (eds), *The Legacy of the Olympic Games 1984–2000*. Lausanne, IOC.

Chappelet, J. (1997). From Chamonix to Salt Lake City: Evolution of the Olympic Village Concept at the Winter Games. In De Moragas, M, Llines, M and Kidd, B. (eds) *Olympic Villages: A hundred years of Urban Planning and Shared Experiences, International Symposium on Olympic Villages*. Lausanne, Documents of the Museum.

Chernushenko, D. (2002). Sustainable sports facilities. A paper delivered at the *IOC-UIA Conference: Architecture and International Sporting Events*, Olympic Museum, Lausanne, IOC. June.

China Daily (2008a). Special supplement: Qingdao sets sail in fresh breeze of exapansion. 5 March.

China Daily (2008b). Qingdao reaps gold from Olympic development. August 13.

Coates, D. and Humphries, B. (2003). *Professional Sports Facilities, Franchises and Urban Development*. University of Maryland, Baltimore County, working paper 03-103. www.umbc.edu/economics/wpapers/wp_03_103.pdf (accessed 7 January 2004).

Dauncey, H. and Hare, G. (1999). *France and the 1998 World Cup: The National Impact of a World Sporting Event*. London, Frank Cass Publishers.

Dawson, L. (2004). Fit for Football. www.stadia.tv/archive/user/archive_article (accessed 28 March, 2005).

Essex, S. and Chalkley, B. (2003). Urban transformation from hosting the Olympic Games. University lecture on the Olympics. Centre d'Estudis Olimpics, Univesitat Autonoma de Barcelona. www.olympicstudies.uab.es/lectures (accessed 19 March. 2005).

EventsCorp (2000). www.eventscorp.com.au/history/index (accessed 5 March 2003).

Felli, G. (2002). Transfer of Knowledge (TOK): a games management tool. A paper delivered at the *IOC-UIA Conference: Architecture and International Sporting Events*, Olympic Museum, Lausanne, IOC. June.

FIA (2004). *The Economic Impact of the European Grands Prix. A Study*. www.fia.com/Etudes/F1_Impact (accessed 25 January 2004).

Garcia, B. (2003). Securing sustainable legacies through cultural programming in sporting events. In Moragas, M., de., Kennett, C. and Puig, N. (eds), *The Legacy of the Olympic Games 1984–2000*. Lausanne, IOC.

Getz, D. (1997). *Event Management and Tourism*. New York, Cognizant, Chapters 3 and 4.

Gonzalez, M. D. (2004). Director of Venue Planning, NYC2012. NYC2012 Presentation. New York University, 4 November, 2004.

Gratton, C. and Taylor, P. (2000). *The Economics of Sport and Recreation*. London, Spon, Chapter 10.

Hall, C. M. (1997). *Hallmark Tourist Events – Impacts, Management and Planning*. London, Bellhaven Press, Chapters 3–7.

Hall, C. M. (2001). Imaging, tourism and sports event fever. In Gratton, C. and Henry, I. (eds), *Sport in the City: The Role of Sport in Economic and Social Regeneration*. London, Routledge, Chapter 11.

Holloway, G. (2001). After the party, Sydney's Olympic blues. www.europ.cnn.com.2001 (accessed 13 March, 2002).

Hughes, L. (1993). Olympic tourism and urban regeneration. In *Festival Management and Event Tourism*, Vol. 1. USA, Cognizant, pp. 157–162.

IOC (2002). www.olympic.org/uk/organisation/missions/cities (accessed 13 March 2002).

IOC (2008). *IOC analyses Beijing air quality data.* IOC Press Release, 17 March 2008.

Isozaki, A. (2001). Designing an Olympic City. A paper delivered at the *IOC Conference: Olympic Games and Architecture – The Future for Host Cities.* Olympic Museum, May, Lausanne, IOC.

Keller, P. (1999). Marketing a candidature to host the Olympic Games: the case of Sion in the Swiss canton of Valais (Wallis), candidate for the Winter Olympics in the year 2006. In Andersson, T. (ed.) *The Impact of Mega Events.* Ostersund, Sweden, ETOUR, pp. 141–156.

Kronos (1997). *The Economic Impact of Sports Events Staged in Sheffield 1990– 1997.* A report produced by Kronos for Destination Sheffield, Sheffield City Council and Sheffield International Venues Ltd. Final report, December.

Kronos (2001). *The Economic Impact of Major Sports Events in Sheffield, April 1991–March 2001.* A report produced by Kronos on behalf of Sheffield City Council Leisure Services Department, August.

LASEC (2003). *Economic Impact of Major Sporting and Entertainment Events.* www.lasec.net/econimpact (accessed 26 February 2003).

London 2012 (2004). London 2012 Candidate File. www.london2012.org/en/ news/publications/candidate+file/London 2012 Ltd. (accessed 23 November, 2004).

MacAloon, J. (2003). Cultural legacy: The Olympic Games as 'World Cultural Property'. In Moragas, M., de., Kennett, C. and Puig, N. (eds) *The Legacy of the Olympic Games 1984–2000.* Lausanne, IOC.

Mackay, D. (2002a). Picketts Lock to get indoor track. *The Guardian*, 30 April, Manchester, The Guardian Media Group.

Mackay, D. (2002b). Tainted games hailed a success. *The Guardian*, 26 February, Manchester, The Guardian Media Group.

Manchester City Council (1999). *2002 Commonwealth Games: Background Information and Overview.* A report produced by KPMG, 16 June.

Manchester City Council (2000). *Spirit of Friendship Festival Executive Summary.* Manchester, Manchester 2002 Ltd.

Manchester City Council (2003). *The Impact of the Manchester 2002 Commonwealth Games.* A report by Cambridge Policy Consultants, Executive summary. www.manchester.gov.uk/corporate/games/impact (accessed 25 February 2003).

Manchester 2002 Ltd. (1999). *Manchester 2002 Commonwealth Games: Corporate Plan.* Manchester, Manchester 2002 Ltd., October.

Mankin, L. (2002). Cited in 'Keeping the winter alive'. In Britcher, C. (ed.) *Host Cities: A Sportbusiness Guide to Bidding for and Staging Major Events.* London, Sportbusiness Group.

Marcopoulou, A. and Christopoulos, S. (2002). Restoration and development of the Faleron Bay, Athens. Paper delivered at *IOC-UIA Conference: Architecture and International Sporting Events.* Olympic Museum, Lausanne, IOC. June.

MASC (2003). *Major Championship Events: Minnesota Hosts the World's Best*. www.masc.state.mn.us/events/championship (accessed 26 February 2003).

Meinel, K. (2001). Sustainability: management issues for the design – the involvement of the future manager of a new competition facility during planning and design phase: an indispensable prerequisite for sustainability. A paper delivered at the *IOC Conference: Olympic Games and Architecture – For Future Host Cities*. Olympic Museum, Lausanne, IOC. May.

NYC2012 (2004). Candidate File – Bid Book. www.nyc2012.com/en/bid_book. html NYC2012 Inc. (accessed 23 November, 2004).

NYC2012 (2005). Urban Transformation. www.nyc2012.com/index_flash.aspx (accessed 15 February, 2005).

Nashville Sports Council (2002). *Nashville Sports Council Announces a Total Economic Impact of $24.2 Million during the 2001—2002 Year*. 22 October. www.nashvillesports.com/nsc/impact_release102202 (accessed 4 March 2003).

Olympic Review (2005). Legacies and costs of the Olympic Games. April, 2005. Lausanne, IOC.

Preuss, H. (2004). *The Economics of Staging the Olympics: A Comparison of the Games 1972–2008*. Cheltenham, Edward Elgar.

Roche, M. (2000). *Mega-events and Modernity: Olympics and Expos in the Growth of Global Culture*. London, Routledge, Chapter 5.

Rogge, J. (2002). Opening address at the *IOC Annual Symposium: Legacy*. Olympic Museum, Lausanne, IOC. November.

Rogge, J. (2008). Press conference and release. Beijing, IOC. 24 August.

Salt Lake City (2002). Olympic Arts Festival. www.saltlake2002.com/sloc/cultural (accessed 24 April 2002).

Spilling, O. (2000). Beyond intermezzo? On the long-term industrial impacts of mega-events – the case of Lillehammer 1994. In Mossberg, L. (ed.) *Evaluation of Events: Scandinavian Experiences*. New York, Cognizant, Chapter 8.

Stadia (2005). German transport and infrastructure to receive funding boost. www.stadia.tv/archive/user/news_article (accessed 28 March, 2005).

Torino 2006 (2002). www.torino2006.it/Venues (accessed 24 April 2002).

Tran, T. (2008). Beijing's blue-sky thinking gives scientists a golden opportunity to study the effects of pollution. *The Guardian*, 8 August. Manchester, The Guardian Group.

UK Sport (1999). *Major Events: A Blueprint for Success*. London, UK Sport.

Wallace, S. (2001). Behind the headlines. *The Telegraph*. 15 June. London, Telegraph.

www.surfnewquay.co.uk (accessed 14 March 2008).

Financial Planning and Control

A 5 a'side football event in Tyne and Wear, UK where the football strips were supplied in a sponsorship-in-kind agreement with a local hire car firm.

LEARNING OBJECTIVES

After studying this chapter, you should be able to:

■ understand the importance of assessing financial feasibility in the planning process

117

■ identify key practices in the planning and control of sports event finance

■ understand the importance of financial risk assessment and identify key risk management practices

INTRODUCTION

This chapter considers the importance of implementing financial planning and control at the feasibility stage by describing the process involved. The role of budgeting and targets are discussed as a key part of this process. The complementary area of income generation, also a key activity at this stage of planning, is covered in the next chapter. Event finances have to be managed on an on-going basis and throughout the process however, and so the central focus here is on how that can be achieved. Key areas such as the acquisition of funding and the control of expenditure are considered, as well as the need for financial risk management emphasized.

EVENT FEASIBILITY

A decision to go ahead with a sports event is a managerial one and can therefore be subjective, but this decision-making process can be made more reliable via planning. The purpose of determining if an event is feasible, prior to a decision to go ahead, is needed to ensure that expenditure or effort is not wasted. Furthermore, it is essential that an event is deemed affordable, desirable, marketable and manageable before it is bid for and/or the decision to proceed is made (Getz, 2007). Therefore, the importance of the feasibility stage in the event planning process cannot be underestimated. The model, proposed in Chapter 3, in the main considers an iterative process but is cautious about early progression from stage to stage. At the feasibility stage, progression should not occur unless the event can be successfully implemented to achieve its objectives. This is achieved by considering if the event concept does indeed meet objectives and, while it is improbable that a dress rehearsal of the event is practical, the determination of the financial status of the project is a pre-requisite. This involves financial planning and, in some cases, may require implementation of those plans prior to any decisions to go ahead with the event. It may require other forms of planning and, in particular, the implementation of key partnerships that make the event feasible. It may also require the assessment of financial risk in determining plans for its on-going management.

FINANCIAL PLANNING

This book does not consider generic financial planning and business accounting in great detail but does focus on the aspects that are pertinent to the strategic planning of sports events. There are, however, a number of texts recommended at the end of the chapter that will serve well for theory and practice of event financial management.

There are a number of stages in the financial planning and control process that need to be considered (Berry and Jarvis, 2006). These are as follows.

Stage 1: Objectives

There are two levels of objectives involved in the management of events. First, there are the organizational objectives that are desired by the event owners for the future direction of the organization. Then there are the objectives for individual events. The first level of objectives will have wider implications for the organization as a whole and will impact on the objectives that are set for any event it owns and/or organizes. Whether there are one or more events, the objectives set for each event need to be aligned with the organization's objectives. This congruence of goals will become a greater issue the larger an organization becomes and as the aspirations of managers may conflict with those of others and the organization itself. The issue here in the events industry is that many events are run by event management organizations on behalf of event owners and the lack of goal congruence between the two may be a critical factor in the running of the event and the company's success.

Secondly, there are business objectives that are set for events, for example the maximization of sales, the maximization of profits, the improved return on investment through dividends to shareholders or the re-investment of profits into the business for growth. These are all quantitative objectives and are therefore quantifiable with targets that can be set and, importantly, easily assessed.

Non-financial objectives may also be set and, for organizations involved in non-profit events, these can be an important aspect. For example, local authorities may be most concerned with objectives that ensure that their sports events deliver an amount and quality of service. Even with non-financial objectives, however, there are implications for the financial planning and control of the event.

Stage 2: Strategic decisions

For the organization as a whole there are strategic decisions to be made regarding the future of the business that will be in accordance with the organizational objectives. For event owning organizations this may well involve the divestment of properties or the investment in other areas of business, either for security purposes or to develop and grow. These decisions are long-term decisions and are made at a senior level. Consequently, they may impact on the management of individual events.

The decision to create a new business that would open up opportunities for the development of International Management Group (IMG) was taken by the late Mark McCormack, when Trans World International (TWI) was formed. This new division was to explore the television opportunities for both IMG and its clients' events and has claimed for some years to be the world's largest independent producer, packager and distributor of televised sports programming (IMG, 2008). Their clients include the All England Lawn Tennis Club and Wimbledon, European Golf Tour, Premier League (England), The Royal and Ancient Golf Club of St Andrews and The Open Championship. For the International Rugby Board and the Rugby World Cups, TWI assists in the delivery of two objectives, growth in worldwide coverage and the achievement of increased broadcast revenue, and the development of the game of rugby on a worldwide basis.

Stage 3: Operating decisions

Operating decisions are mainly concerned with pricing and the level of service to be offered (Berry and Jarvis, 2006). These decisions need to be aligned with the strategic policies that have been set previously in order for them to be effective and are the basis of the short-term financial plan for the event. This short-term plan is referred to as the event budget.

Budgets differ according to the requirements of the organizations involved but will typically represent the duration of the event planning process. Depending on the size of the event, an event budget can cover a very short period of hours or days or be run over a number of years. For example, a cycle road race organized by a local club may be advertised to its members, entry fees collected and catering supplies and a trophy purchased only a week in advance of the event. The club treasurer will operate a very simple budget covering that period and those types of revenue and expenditure. In contrast, the winning bid for the 2000 Olympics in Sydney necessitated an accounting period that lasted from 1993 and an operational budget that involved divestment and handover elements that lasted well into 2002 when Sydney Olympic Park Authority eventually took over the Olympic facilities (Adby, 2002).

Stage 4: Monitoring and correction

In the setting of the budget, personnel are individually made responsible for revenues and costs and therefore should have contributed to the formulation of the budget and its targets. As the planning for the event progresses, the budget can serve as a valuable tool in the measurement of performance for individuals as well as organizations as a whole. A reporting system is required so that individuals and teams who are financially accountable can report on actual performance against the budget so that deviations or variances can be identified. This is commonly referred to as a process of responsibility accounting. Through this monitoring of performance, causes for variance can also be identified and the necessary management decisions can be taken.

BUDGETING

A budget can be beneficial in a number of different ways. First and foremost, in order to prepare a budget there needs to be a degree of forecasting and this at least gets a management team to look ahead. The preparation and research required engages an organization in planning. Budgets also serve as communication tools by identifying what is required of the event and its managers. Regular updates on performance against budget also serve as control mechanisms and as a means to inspire improved managerial performance. The larger the organization, the more a budget can serve as a catalyst to increase inter-team or departmental cooperation in both its preparation and in the application through the achievement of targets.

Budgeting for events consists of identifying where revenue will derive from, determining costs and the setting of performance targets that will realize the objectives set. These targets also aid the on-going control of performance against this budget and therefore act as a means of ensuring alignment with objectives. The key contents of an event budget are summarized as follows.

Revenue targets

Revenue can derive from funding and/or income generation and targets for each will be set as a part of the budgeting process. Funding is associated with investment in the event and the securing of monies with or without any return on investment, whereby income generation is associated with the exploitation of the event and its assets. Each of these areas of revenue is represented in the budget line by line so that the value of funding and generated income sources can be separately identified.

Expenditure targets

The expenditure for an event has to be off set against the revenue raised in order to calculate profit or loss. Each area of expenditure is referred to as a cost centre and can be related to management or programme aspects of the event. For example, typical cost centres would be expenditure on staffing, participants, transportation and marketing. These centres consist of individual line costs such as wages, prize monies, accommodation, limousines, fuel and printing. This makes both the identification of detailed expenditure line by line and reviewing centre by centre an easier process.

Costs can be direct and variable in that they are clearly identified with the event and can be allocated to a specific centre. Variable costs are those that may increase or decrease according to the size of attendance by audience or participants, or numbers of events and performances. Typically, these might be accommodation, subsistence or participants appearance fees and they would increase for every extra participant that takes part in the event. Another variable cost might be the employment of a predetermined number of extra catering staff for every predetermined number of extra corporate hospitality packages sold. It is important that events provide an adequate level of service as the revenue increases and this means identifying the levels at which this will occur within the budget so that the costs can be identified as they become active.

Costs can also be indirect, sometimes referred to as fixed or overheads, where they may not be as clearly allocated and may need to be apportioned to one or more centre. They are costs that are paid regardless of the revenue gained. Typically, they could be capital costs such as equipment or buildings, or venue rental fees and guaranteed prize monies. They may also be costs that extend over a longer period than the event and are therefore not easily allocated, for example, those that are associated with the running of the organization on an annual basis such as office rental and utilities. Such indirect costs require management to decide where they will be allocated and if they can be apportioned to different costs centres.

For many events, the costs are predominantly fixed and this has significant implications for pricing strategies. An over reliance on non-guaranteed revenue that comes in on the day of the event, such as for tickets, merchandise and programmes, can leave the event exposed and financially at risk. Pre-event revenues that are guaranteed and can cover fixed costs are one solution. Another is to set prices so that those sales that are confidently expected cover fixed costs.

For many businesses, the budget will remain fixed but for events there is a need for flexibility. The longer the event planning period, the more this becomes a necessity. A plan that runs over a number of years will be faced with increased costs over those years as economic influences on suppliers take effect. The costs for the 2000 Olympic Games in Sydney exceeded original forecasts and, in order for the same objectives to be realized, the revenue earning operations had to respond accordingly (SOCOG, 2001). Case study 5.1 demonstrates how the budgets were revisited at various points in the long planning period for that event. External forces can dictate not only that events remain flexible in their budgeting, but also that they either adapt to new constraints or they do not run. After the New York terrorist attacks of 11 September 2001, insurance premiums and security provision for events became major financial issues. Prior to the Federation Internationale de Football Association (FIFA) 2002 World Cup, there was concern over the increase in premiums by AXA, the insurance company, that at one point jeopardized the taking place of the event (Shepherd, 2001). The staging of the Winter Olympics in Salt Lake City only months after the New York catastrophe also presented new budgeting issues for the organizers. These examples emphasize the importance of continuous monitoring in the on-going financial control of the event and the need for flexibility in allowing for adjustments.

Case Study 5.1

Financial Management: Sydney Olympics, 2000

The pre-bid budget for Sydney's staging of the 2000 Olympic Games was prepared by Sydney Olympics 2000 Bid Ltd (SOBL) in 1992. It forecast a surplus of AUS$25.9million

Despite winning their bid in 1993, the Sydney Olympic Project Management Group had focused and restricted their activities to programme planning and observation of the 1996 Atlanta Games. The pre-bid budget was therefore still in play until the first post-bid budget, set in 1997.

The Sydney Organizing Committee for Olympic Games (SOCOG) reported in to the New South Wales (NSW) State Treasury and undertook four formal major budget revisions throughout the planning of the Games.

April 1997:
The first post-Bid budget revision following observations at the Atlanta 1996 Games

June 1998:
A total reforecast of the budget

June 1999:
A budget rebalancing due to the identification of shortfalls in sponsorship revenue

February 2000:
Only months prior to the Games a second budget rebalancing due to further shortfalls

The major revisions were as a result of consistent monitoring and review, including activities such as staff level rationalization in 1999 and monthly financial reporting and accounting, bi-monthly forecast updates following input from each of the SOCOG departments.

Allowances were also required for inflation as the planning period covered such a long period. A factoring

Continued

process was installed whereby projected annual inflationary factors were applied to the then current year values.

Contingencies were required in order to cover cost risks and sponsorship revenue shortfalls but, while contingencies were built in to each budget revision, it still took AUS$70million from the NSW Treasury to cover shortfalls in June 2000 and then another AUS$70million to cover expected increased operating costs.

Source: SOCOG (2001)

Getz (1997) identifies that, in the budgeting process, there are a number of key stages. These include the involvement of operational managers, or committee chairs, in the research, preparation and even negotiation of the budget. Essentially, there must be agreement on event objectives and financial planning by all involved if an event is to be successful. For an operational budget to be successful managers have to be in support of the budget and so their input into its preparation is required. Managerial input into the preparation of budgets is a necessity. In practice, however, this is not always the case as individual managers may have conflicting agendas in submitting the revenue targets when they may affect the achievement of their bonuses. The problem of goal incongruence increases the larger the organization (Berry and Jarvis, 2006) and this is especially the case when it comes to the budgeting for major events. Budgets are often a fundamental part of business plans and the presentations made to acquire funding and political support. They can also form a distinctive part in the determination of event feasibility.

Flexibility for revision is therefore clearly required when sources for funding and income generation can change accordingly. Issues also arise at a later point when the budget has been revised and then set for an incoming and newly appointed team of event managers. While accountants may be contracted to supply the preliminary budget in the determination of feasibility, the event managers that are eventually appointed are not a part of that preparation. The 2002 Commonwealth Games appointed a team of commercial managers that struggled to respond to the unrealistic income targets that were set. Over the planning period these targets were changed and, as costs also escalated, funding requirements were also stretched. A government commissioned report in 2001 revealed that the organizers were £110 million short in funding. The result was further injection of funding by the government, Sport England (via its National Lottery distribution) and Manchester City Council. Funding that was not originally planned (Chaudhary, 2001).

FINANCIAL CONTROL

The financial planning of an event is a key component in the objectives set. The budgeting process clearly allows for an alignment with the objectives at the outset, but ultimately, the financial control of an event involves further key elements.

It has been established that a budget can be used as a performance indicator in that its targets can be reviewed to identify any deviation from revenue or expenditure forecasts. Management accounting practices involve the formulation of internal reports at prescribed times so that performance can be reviewed and thus aid decision-making. Useful texts for further reading on this are recommended at the end of this chapter.

Cash flow can also be used as a performance indicator and, for the financial control of an event, it is a key tool. Events have common revenue streams that are realized nearer to the execution of the event that are prepared for at the front end of the planning process, for example ticket income, sponsorship fee instalments and broadcast royalties. As stated earlier, however, expenditure seldom follows the same pattern and payments are often required in advance of the event. Even the costs involved with ticket sales, sponsorship recruitment and broadcasting, as well as venue deposits, equipment rentals and overheads, can all be due for payment prior to the event. A review of the budget at this point can indicate a healthy position in that a break-even or better financial position is forecasted. However, it is imperative to look at the position of cash flow and the capacity to pay bills at required points throughout the accounting period and identify those costs that will require payment prior to when sufficient revenue will be available. The production of regular cash flow reports throughout the planning of an event are therefore essential for the financial control of an event.

Cash flow shortfalls are a common occurrence in the events industry, but they need not be insurmountable problems. The shortfalls can be made up and there are various solutions on both sides of the budget. Cash flow can be made more fluid through the negotiation of payment dates and arrangements. Costs centres can be reduced, possibly by limiting the levels at which variable costs will increase and possibly through the reduction or elimination of fixed costs. On the revenue side, arrangements for both funding and greater income generation can be made to reduce exposure to risk of cash shortfalls.

The reduction of financial risk can also be addressed in the planning of revenue as well as expenditure with the use of strategic partners. For some events, the involvement of key partners is critical if the event is to succeed and such partners can be used to generate revenue as well as reduce expenditure.

It is therefore often a requirement for such partnerships to be not just planned for, but negotiated and even implemented at the feasibility stage. Joint ownership of an event can alleviate the risk by sharing the financial accountability. This accountability might be in the form of equal shares on expenditure and the resulting profit. It might also be made up of partners with responsibility for certain areas of expenditure, funding and revenue generation. At the outset, the London bid for the 2012 Olympics involved a joint partnership between the Greater London Authority (GLA), the British Government and the British Olympic Committee (BOC). With London as the host, the financial onus lay with the GLA, but the Government approved the use of the national lottery for the selling of new and specific tickets that would raise funds when and if the bid was successful. The plans by Camelot, the organization that operates the lottery, included a daily lottery draw and other games that were launched in 2004 (Kelso, 2003). The model used in the financial strategy for London 2012 is presented in Case study 5.2.

Similar risk reduction might also be achieved for an event owner with the appointment of agents to recruit sponsorship, advertising, ticket and hospitality revenue. For larger events, this can involve the agreement of guaranteed payments whereby the agent will pay a fixed amount to the event and try to acquire sufficient sponsorship deals that realize more than that amount in order to make a business profit for themselves. Clearly, the recruitment of agents in these cases needs to be done early in the planning process but, if

Case Study 5.2

Financial Management: The London 2012 model

The London 2012 Olympics financial model consists of two key organizations:

London Organizing Committee of the Olympic Games and Paralympic Games (LOCOG)

LOCOG is a private sector company with the sole task of delivering the 2012 Games. It has to raise its own £2 billion budget for this from the sale of tickets, merchandise and a domestic/national sponsorship programme.

Olympic Delivery Authority (ODA)

The ODA is a public sector organization that has been created to deliver the facilities, new or refurbished, required for the Games. The budget for this task is drawn from the public sector, namely the Government via its Department for Culture, Media and Sport, The Greater London Authority (GLA) and the Olympic Lottery Distributor.

National Lottery:
The UK National Lottery provides £2.2 billion to the ODA.

GLA:
The GLA is providing £925 million and another £250 million via its agency the London Development Agency (LDA) to the ODA. In addition, the LDA is also funding the ODA's clean-up of the Olympic Park at a cost of £220 million.

This model clearly differentiates between the operation of the Games and the strategic provision of facilities that will serve the event but will also serve the longer requirements for physical legacies in London.

Source: London 2012 (2008)

arranged prior to the decision for the event to go ahead, then the event will be that much more feasible. Octagon is one such organization and has been involved in raising commercial revenue for a number of event organizations including Cricket Australia, the European Rugby Cup, International Badminton Federation, The English and Scottish Premier Leagues and USA Track and Field. The company was recently appointed by the Italian Olympic Committee (CONI) to represent their worldwide marketing and sponsorship sales interests of the Italian teams going to the 2009 Mediterranean Games, the 2010 Winter Olympics in Vancouver and the selling of packages associated with the Beijing 2008 Olympic Games. Octagon has worked with the US Youth Soccer Association since 1994 and has helped build their brand in a very competitive field. Between 1998 and 2003, they were able to increase sponsorship revenue 10-fold and bring in 11 partners. Following an asset audit that revealed there were over 3 million registered youth players, they created two key tournaments, the Tide America Cup and the Uniroyal TopSoccer Programme. The key asset was their capacity to reach what the organization refers to as the 'Soccer Mom' and the involvement of a domestic product like Tide shows how the agency was able to attract an appropriate sponsor (Octagon, 2003, 2008).

'Supply-in-kind' arrangements can also alleviate financial risk in the same way but on the expenditure side of the budget. The supply of essential as opposed to non-essential equipment, goods or services means that much less expenditure is incurred therefore reducing financial risk. In these circumstances, a supplier might also be converted into a sponsor and the arrangment made sponsorship-in-kind. The local football event featured in the photograph at the beginning of this chapter shows some of the children that took part wearing their sponsored team shirts. The event was organized by students and was staged in a 5 a'side arena for 20 schools teams. The budget was tight but, to enable each team to be correctly kitted out, they approached a local hire car firm to supply different coloured shirts. In return, the firm was able to get media coverage that showed off their logo on the fronts of the shirts. This was a simple arrangement and typical of local events of this kind but was essential for the event to achieve for it to go according to plan. Similarly, media partners can supply some or all of the events promotional needs. Clearly, the risk is not reduced in such circumstances if the budget is still fully spent on further promotion. The decision here is whether the risk can be covered elsewhere and the event gain through the added promotional value through increased sales or the achievement of other objectives.

With 2 years to go before Vancouver hosts the 2010 winter Olympic Games, the organizing body VANOC was demonstrating strong financial control in its planning and implementation. Its quarterly report released in March 2008 revealed that it was in a positive financial position with a cash balance of CN$56.5 million, a position that was above targets for the period. Its planned spending of CN$17 million more in this period than the previous was also on budget and was due to a move away from planning and into the implementation phase. This quarter also showed the importance of cash flow in monitoring performance with planned 'milestone' sponsorship payments of CN$43 million being paid on time (CN$4.3 million was due in the previous period). Other less objective performance indicators were also used in the form of VANOC's first trial event, the FIS Alpine World Cup hosted at Whistler, enabling VANOC to take heed of athlete and sports federation feedback to make valuable changes for sports performance in response to weather changes (Sports-City, 2008).

FINANCIAL RISK MANAGEMENT

While risk management is required to be an on-going concern throughout the planning process, it is also a major aspect of feasibility assessment and is a required part of the financial planning and control process. The sections above addressed the reduction of cash flow risks via the strategic use of partners and innovative revenue attainment, but there are other areas of risk that affect the financial planning for events. Getz (1997) maintains that event financial risk management is a process that consists of anticipation, prevention and minimization and that would indicate that it is a necessary consideration at an early stage of planning and therefore strategically important.

There are two key factors. On the one hand, there is a requirement for an event to be safe and there are minimum levels of event health and safety that are governed in most countries by law. This will involve the planning of expenditure that will be incurred in the provision of security and medical services, for example, and these will be different at every event. The unique nature of the event will determine the provision required and so the risk management process is a necessary inclusion as early as when the event is first conceptualized. The very numbers and nature of the audience and participants, and their likely behaviour, may well impact on the financial outlay for the event and for sports events there are particular considerations to be made. The provision of safety glass at ice hockey, for example, will require expenditure on special facilities and the monitoring of no go zones at motor racing will additionally incur special stewarding and zoning, both of which have necessary financial implications.

On the other hand, there is the production of entertainment and a spectacle. This may also require expenditure that was not spent at last year's event, or is not spent by a competitor to exceed customer expectation and gain competitive advantage. It is just as important to make these decisions early in the planning process. The unreliability of weather is a common risk for sports events and contingencies for the provision of cover against foul weather can include insurances against financial loss and the provision of extra facilities such as marquees. There are often greater risks in not taking such precautions, of course, and it is therefore a dangerous gamble not to be fully prepared or covered. Additionally, in order to gain competitive advantage, there are financial considerations that may appear to be superfluous at the outset and will require the event manager to assess cost versus benefit. The decision of whether to spend more on extra facilities, equipment and entertainment for example will require an assessment that may well require research. The provision of half-time entertainment for the crowd or better changing facilities for participants may not be directly benefiting revenue but may, in the long run, attract greater target market take-up. Only target market research will effectively support such decision-making as the NFL's Atlanta Falcons demonstrated when it collected data from its season ticket holders and proceeded to remove commercials from its scoreboard services but added new and increased car parking as well as better furnished rest rooms.

Beijing Insight 5.1
2008 Olympics: Olympic Budget
The Beijing 2008 Olympic budget was prepared in December 2000 and submitted in its bid early the following year. The overall aim was to produce a model that had 'little or no risk' and would produce a surplus. The approach was to produce an operational budget for BOCOG for the Games and a non-Games budget to be governed by the City, Regional and State Authorities plus the private sector for the construction of facilities. Financial services were supplied by both Arthur Andersen and Bovis Lend Lease in the budgeting process.

Aspects of the non-Games budget are covered in Beijing Insight 3.1.

BOCOG's Games budget was set as follows:

Revenues	US$ Million	Expenditure	US$ Million
Television rights	709.00	Capital investments	190.00
TOP sponsorship	130.00	Sports facilities	102.00
Local sponsorship	130.00	Olympic village	40.00
Licensing	50.00	Media village	3.00
Official suppliers	20.00	Media	45.00

Continued

Beijing Insight 5.1—cont'd

Revenues	US$ Million	Expenditure	US$ Million
Coin programme	8.00	Operations	1419.00
Philately	12.00	Sports events	275.00
Lotteries	180.00	Olympic village	65.00
Ticket sales	140.00	Media village	10.00
Donations	20.00	Media operations	360.00
Asset disposal	80.00	Ceremonies	100.00
Subsidies/national	50.00	Medical services	30.00
Subsidies/municipal	50.00	Catering	51.00
Other	46.00	Transport	70.00
		Security	50.00
		Paralympic games	82.00
		Promotions	60.00
		Administration	125.00
		Pre-events	40.00
		Other	101.00
TOTAL	1625.00	TOTAL	1609.00
		SURPLUS	16.00

The IOC had input to the budget in its confirmation of the split of revenues from television and The TOP sponsorship programme. The other key sources of income were BOCOG's National sponsorship programme (see Beijing Insight 11.1) and Olympic lottery and ticket sales (see Beijing Insight 9.1 for ticketing strategy).

One of the issues with forecasting budgets for events that take several years to plan is inflation. The budget set in 2000 therefore needed to convert prices it forecast it would receive in future years back to 2000 equivalent prices.

Television Rights
It was estimated that BOCOG would receive US$833 million at 2008 prices. This was confirmed in writing by the IOC in March 2000. The budget converted this to 2000 prices at US$709 million, as indicated in the above revenues column.

TOP Sponsorship
IOC agreed to give BOCOG US$200 million, US$130 million at 2000 prices.

Official Supplies
Various equipment, supplies and services were to be required for the Games and so the budget allowed a figure of US$20 million for supply-in-kind. This was not income.

Lottery
The ministry of Finance operated an Olympic Games lottery from 2001 through to the Games to raise the budgeted US$180 million.

Donations

It was anticipated that BOCOG could raise donations from businesses, social organizations and even invididuals.

Other

Various other sources of income were estimated in one amount of US$46 million and included space leasing and rentals of accommodation in the Olympic Village before and in the short period after the Games.

Post-Budget Revisions

In October 2007, with 10 months to go until the Games, the budget was revised for a second time. The forecast cash flow was expected to have a cash position of US$333.51 million with minus 1 year to go but expenditure was estimated to rise to US$2 billion from the original US$1.6 billion and so in order to realign BOCOG therefore needed to raise a further US$400 million in income.

An official Beijing 2008 Souvenir shop in the busy shopping area on Wangfujing Road in Beijing. Interestingly, a Nike shop (non-Olympic event sponsor) is situated next door and an Adidas shop (Olympic sponsor) is 100 yards down the road. A Li Ning shop sits in between.

Source: Beijing 2008 (2008a, 2008b)

SUMMARY

Financial management and control and the exercise of such throughout the planning process, are clearly recognized as being essential elements for the successful delivery of an event. However, it is perhaps the stage at which the planning for such has to be first implemented that is less widely acknowledged. Certainly, the agreeing of a workable budget is intrinsic to the determination of feasibility. However, the strategic importance of assessing not only the financial feasibility of an event, but also the maximization of finances prior to event execution cannot be underestimated. For many events, the acquirement of funding, the generation of revenue and the recruitment of partners in order to limit risk are an essential requirement prior to the decision to go ahead. It is, however, the use of cost controls and the generation of income that is possible at this stage that can be the deciding factor in the gaining of competitive advantage.

The focus in the following chapter moves on to the complementary area of revenue generation.

QUESTIONS

Select a sports event and:

1. Analyse the strategic importance of financial planning at an early stage.

2. Using the same event identify the key practices exercised in its financial management by identifying any cost controls and then…

3. Identify and analyse the key areas of financial risk, how successful the event was in this risk management and suggest ways in which the event could have been more successful.

RECOMMENDED READING

Finance

Davies, D. (2005). *Managing Financial Information*, 2nd edn. Maidenhead, McGraw-Hill.

Davies, T. (2005). *Financial Accounting: An Intorduction*. Maidenhead, McGraw-Hill.

Dyson, J. (2007). *Accounting for Non-accounting Students*, 7th edn. London, Pitman Publishing.

Glautier, M. and Underdown, B. (2001). *Accounting Theory and Practice*, 7th edn. Harlow, Financial Times.

Lumby, S. and Jones, C. (2003). *Investment Appraisal and Financing Decisions*, 7th edn. London, Chapman Hall.

Westerbeek, H., Smith, A., Turner, P., Emery, P., Green, C. and van Leeuwen, L. (2006). *Managing Sport Facilities and Major Events*. London, Routledge.

REFERENCES

Adby, R. (2002). Email Questionnaire: Director General, Olympic Co-ordination Authority 2000 Olympics. 9 July.

Beijing 2008 (2008a). www.beijing2008.cn (accessed 26 February 2008).

Beijing 2008 (2008b). www.beijingolympic2008.wordpress.com (accessed 26 February 2008).

Berry, A. and Jarvis, R. (2006). *Accounting in a Business Context*, 4th edn. London, International Thomson Business Press.

Chaudhary, V. (2001). Why Manchester may rue the day it won the Commonwealth Games. *The Guardian*, 25 July. Manchester, The Guardian Media Group.

Getz, D. (1997). *Event Management and Tourism*. New York, Cognizant, Chapter 10.

Getz, D. (2007). *Event Studies: Theory, Research and Policy for Planned Events*. Oxford, Butterworth-Heinemann.

London 2012 (2008). www.london2102.com/about/funding (accessed 25 February 2008).

IMG (2008). www.imgworld.com (accessed 25 February 2008).

Kelso, P. (2003). 1p lottery ticket to help fund Olympics. *The Guardian*, 25 May. Manchester, The Guardian Media Group.

Octagon (2003). www.octagon.com/diverts/rights_owner_case_study.php (accessed 12 September 2003).

Octagon (2008). www.octagon.com/about-octagon/in-the-news (accessed 25 February 2008).

Shepherd, R. (2001). World Cup in crisis. *Daily Express*, 13 October. London, Express Newspapers.

SOCOG (2001). www.gamesinfo.com.au/postgames/en/pg000329 (accessed 12 September 2003).

Sports-City (2008). www.sports-city.org (accessed 25 February 2008).

Event Revenue Maximization

An official AS Roma merchandise retail outlet in the centre of Rome.

LEARNING OBJECTIVES

After studying this chapter, you should be able to:

■ understand further the importance of assessing financial feasibility in the planning process

- understand the value and critical nature of strategic exploitation of commercial opportunities

- identify the role and use of an event asset audit for income generation

- consider the key income generating areas of media rights and partnerships, ticket and hospitality sales, space sales, merchandising and licensing

INTRODUCTION

To achieve the greatest competitive advantage, an event needs to exploit fully its revenue potential and much can be achieved at the feasibility stage in the planning process. Indeed, so much does have to be achieved at this point if the event is to be successful. If an event can be financially underwritten as early as this then there is every chance of it achieving its objectives. However, it is not apparent that all events can or, indeed, attempt to attain such a status before progressing.

This chapter continues with the theme of the last by highlighting the need for early strategic financial planning. While the focus of the last chapter was on expenditure and control mechanisms, the focus here is on maximizing revenue.

REVENUE PLANNING

Event external funding

Event operational financial objectives may include the acquisition of income in the form of external funding. The sources that are available for the funding of events differ from country to country. In the USA, UK and Australia, funding for events can be gained via both commercial enterprise and government support. Funding in the UK for larger sports events is provided by the National Lottery, via funds that are allocated for sport and distributed by sports councils, such as Sport England. In all three countries there are provisions for the support of major events by regional government. However, there is one difference between these countries that is worthy of note. In the USA, public money is used more commonly for building stadiums than elsewhere. Typically, there are cities that have built a stadium in order to attract a major league sports team. The competition between cities is intense and so they offer their stadiums at peppercorn rents as inducements (Gratton and Taylor, 2000). The only way for a city then to recoup its outlay is via stadium event sales and marketing programmes that do not include any team rights. Clearly, the demand for major league sports by cities is high.

The new stadiums that have been built in the last decade or so in the USA contain premium price seating areas and corporate boxes, swimming pools, restaurants, hotels and theme park type amusements and represent a much more diverse entertainment centre than did their predecessors. The revenue earning potential has been extended beyond the more traditional ticket, food and beverage and vehicle parking commercial return (Coates and Humphries, 2003).

Research into this area is growing and it currently offers no support to the idea that USA sports stadiums are important catalysts for economic growth. Despite this, proposed stadium construction projects continue to go ahead. In their working paper, Coates and Humphries (2003) identify that, on average, public funding accounted for 65% of the costs of the 26 major league sports stadiums that were built between 1998 and 2003. On average, the amount of public spending was US$208 million per facility. They maintain that these facilities have been promoted to communities on the basis that they will provide economic growth, development and urban renewal and the projections have been calculated using multiplier techniques. They recommend that further more reliable empirical methods be used to help taxpayers make more informed decisions on subsidies for sports facilities.

In the UK, the National Lottery provides funding for sport at various levels and is also used to provide funding for special events. The 2002 Commonwealth Games received lottery funding and a special lottery ticket sales programme is being utilized to provide funds to help support London host the 2012 Olympics as mentioned earlier. One of the issues for sport in general in the UK is that the lottery has suffered decreasing revenue and, consequently, contribution to worthy causes such as sport decrease proportionately. While lottery sales rose between 2003 and 2006, the total of £5013 million is still some way from the high of £5514 million in 1997 (Camelot, 2006). Another issue is that 77% of scratchcard type lottery sales are for 2012 Olympic funding and that too is predicted to affect funds to other sports areas (Culf, 2007).

Income generation

Other operational financial objectives include the development of income through the acquisition of specific revenues. Event operations are considered in Chapter 8 where the focus is on the implementation of plans that have been devised prior to and during the event at an operational level. The focus in this chapter, however, is on what can be planned prior to the event and the degree to which it can be implemented prior to the event in order to secure feasibility.

Rather than simply identify, list and describe the various categories of income generation that exist for sports events, this section seeks to demonstrate that income generation involves a strategic process that requires innovation and sales skills. While the implementation of ticket and corporate hospitality sales, sponsorship, merchandising and licensing programmes is conducted after it has been decided to go ahead with the event, the planning for this exploitation of the events assets is performed at the feasibility stage in the attempt to underwrite it financially. Some revenue may be secured prior to a go-ahead decision and, indeed, some may need to be secured in order for the event to go ahead.

The process consists of determining what the event has that it can sell. This can be a simple exercise and, if considered in great depth, may be very productive. As this exercise can be the deciding factor in the achievement of competitive advantage, the need for innovation is clearly critical. In the North of England in County Durham, there is an established tennis club in the village of Lanchester, founded in 1911 but with few assets and currently only 70 members. In 2003, the club decided to sell corporate hospitality packages locally. Local businesses were attracted by the club's picturesque setting of three grass courts, clubhouse, stream and leafy surroundings and, not unimportantly, the package of champagne, strawberries and a tennis tournament. While corporate hospitality is an established area of income generation and is not new in sport, in this case, the process of determining what would generate income was innovative considering the size of this small village concern. The club identified its assets, an offer was created and a market was targeted. An event was created in order to maximize the commercial potential.

A lot of income generation for events involves the use of sponsorship and, in order to produce a sponsorship programme, an audit of the event's assets is required (see Chapter 11 and, in particular, Event management 11.1 for a greater discussion on this). In addition, the audit can provide many more opportunities. With an innovative approach this task may be able to assist in the maximizing of the event's income.

An event's assets can be categorized into the following areas.

Media rights and partnerships

An event can sell or give the right to use its assets to interested parties. These rights can include the use of logos, a particular status with the event in terms of a title, or sponsorship rights. There are also the much sought after media rights.

The media generally are important stakeholders as events always seek positive public exposure, but media organizations are also important as partners. The selling or giving of media rights to a broadcaster clearly achieves media exposure that is of value to sponsors and for the promotion of the event in the short and longer terms. In addition, and if secured early enough, the rights can therefore become valuable assets in the selling of the sponsorship programme. Thus, it would be advantageous for media rights to be agreed prior to negotiations with sponsors, as the benefits via the media rights will be of value to them.

Television broadcasting

If the event is powerful enough it can sell its rights to home and international broadcasters. This brings in media rights income and promotes the event via either live or delayed scheduling of the event. The securing of such sales in advance of the devising of the sponsorship programme allows for more leverage when it comes to recruiting and developing sponsors.

It can also be beneficial in another way. If the broadcaster values the event sufficiently it will agree to promotional traffic prior to the event. The timely and regular promotional slots that are produced to attract a television audience for the media organization can also act as important promotions for the event.

Pay-per-view is a more recent broadcasting format that has been used in particular with boxing in the USA. UK satellite broadcasters have also been covering football in this way since 2000, albeit take-up by fans has been limited and as a consequence only the higher profile matches are now sold in this way by BSkyB.

Not all events are going to achieve such a status and have attractive television rights but there are other opportunities if the broadcaster is interested at all. It may be of benefit for the event to supply the rights for free or even produce and supply edited tapes itself. It is a cost versus benefit decision. Will the costs in producing broadcast standard material and the supply of it to a broadcaster for free be recouped via the securing of sponsors or other generated income as a result?

There are also ownership issues here. Professional sports teams in particular often have restricted rights to sell as their membership to leagues and other competitions provide limitations. This is the case throughout most of the major sports in the UK but does differ in the USA. Some major league teams in North America can currently sell their television rights to local TV stations and yet national television rights are centrally administered by the leagues. Premiership clubs in the UK may not directly sell their rights in their country under the current contract between the Premier League and its broadcast partners BSkyB and Setanta Sports. However, there have been some developments in this area with the establishment of football club television channels such as those for Manchester United Football Club (MUFC TV) and Chelsea Football Club (Chelsea TV) and their programming of action highlights that may be part of long-term strategies in preparation for when this may be possible. Manchester United has also shown a willingness to use partners to help develop broadcast activity and, in particular, the YES Network and the New York Yankees baseball club franchise.

Radio broadcasting

The same advantages apply to radio broadcasting but are usually less rewarding in terms of actual revenue and audience reach.

However, radio can be a great event friend. Pre-event promotional exposure is often readily available at national as well as local radio stations and, while it is not directly earning revenue, it can be achieved at little cost and can therefore be a saving on promotional expenditure while providing a vehicle for promoting event partners. The latter may therefore provide greater funding as a result. The presence of live radio broadcasts at events can also add to the spectacle and therefore competitive advantage. The use of radio as a means for promotion is considered in greater depth in Chapter 10.

Press coverage

It is possible to secure exclusive rights to press coverage for events. For example, insights into the lives of celebrity sports stars seem to be of particular interest to popular magazines, however, there are dangers. Exclusivity for one written medium means a limitation on coverage for the event. In the UK when the Today national newspaper launched, it sponsored the Football League and it was this sponsorship that helped lead to the demise and liquidation of the tabloid. Neither the newspaper nor the League could have been too happy at the lack of coverage of the sponsor's name by other media when publishing football reports and league tables. However, perhaps it should not have been a surprise that other media would have been unlikely to promote a direct competitor.

There are, however, more innovative ways of making press coverage a more attractive proposition and these are considered in depth, again in Chapter 10.

Internet broadcasting

The technology that is available for webcasting sport offers many opportunities including the development of virtual fans. This began to emerge in the late 1990s and involves rights ownership restrictions wherever there are television contracts. The MUFC example cited earlier is indicative of this.

Some of the early webcasts of sport include the first live National Basketball Association (NBA) game on the Internet between the Dallas Mavericks and the Sacramento Kings in April 2001 (RealNetworks, 2001). The Epsom Derby and eight other races were also webcast live in July of the same year, (BBC, 2003). Webcasting in Asia began earlier and Showei.com, a Chinese sports website, webcast the Union European Football Association (UEFA) Euro 2000 matches and then the Sydney 2000 Olympics live in 2000 (Turbolinux, 2000). The selling of these new forms of broadcast rights has added greatly to the income generation potential for events.

Ticket sales

Many events are dependent upon the revenue derived from ticket sales. When budgeting for such revenue, it is important to predict correctly the times at which tickets will be sold and the revenue collected. The ticket sales life-cycle lasts from the point at which the decision for the event to go ahead is made, through to the end of the event. There is often a need to expend before any of this revenue is realized, not least on promoting the event, and so it is for this reason that so many of the other areas of revenue, if they can be generated early, play such an important role. The problem in selling tickets at any other stage than after a decision to go ahead is that if the event does not go ahead it becomes a costly and time-consuming job to organize refunds.

This is not to say that ticket sales strategies are an unimportant aspect of the assessment of an event's feasibility. The planning of ticket sales income is a fundamental part of the budgeting process but, in order to ensure that revenue is generated as early as possible, it is necessary to be creative.

The encouragement of ticket purchase as far in advance of the event as possible can be the key to this process and this can be achieved in a number of ways. The successful use of event communications to create a sense of urgency in ticket buyers is desired by all events, but customers are not easily taken in by an event that communicates that tickets are 'selling fast' or even 'selling out'. The introduction of early purchase discounts at least offers the customer value and something tangible to encourage early purchase. To succeed in getting large amounts of revenue from ticket sales there needs to be effort in achieving sales volume. Compared with other forms of revenue, such as sponsorship for example, individual tickets carry relatively small prices and so a focus on sales targets where there is potential for block bookings can be both effective and efficient. These might include use of event databanks and sales to previous event attendees, the attendees of other events, members, participants' families, sponsors and the personnel of other partner organizations.

Selling tickets for the next event while staging the current one may be possible and, certainly, offering first refusal via a deadline to purchase is one way of reaching previous event attendees. The freezing of prices up to that deadline can help too.

Ticket pricing policies are an important aspect of financial planning. Ticket income, for admission or participation, can make up the bulk of intended revenue but, the more income streams there are in addition, the more flexible the ticket pricing policies can be. With more flexibility in how much is charged there can be greater focus on the requirements of the target markets and, in the long run, as a result, greater revenue. The policies available to sports events are:

1. *Standard price*: one price for all.

2. *Differential prices*: prices that alter according to the age of the buyer – such as for senior citizen and children's admission. The time they purchase – such as lesser cost for those who purchase by a deadline in advance, lesser cost pro-rata for group numbers. Lesser cost pro-rata for individual multi-visits or season tickets/passes.

3. *Admission plus*: either free or standard priced admission alongside premium charges for specific sub-sections to the event such as for special matches or seat reservation at Wimbledon, or for charges for other requirements such as car parking, and access to catering.

The process by which decisions are made as to which pricing policies to follow is commonly a subjective one for sports events. As Getz (1997) maintains, traditional pricing analysis via the determination of price elasticity and marginal costs is inherently difficult. The problem being that one more person at an event is not necessarily going to affect the costs for that event. The staging of publicly provided events can often mean that there are political motivations behind the choice or pricing policy, take for example free admission. At the opposite extreme, there are commercial events that appear to have both comparatively high admission prices as well as premium charges and a success can be made of both of these extremes if there is sufficient knowledge of the target market and the decision is made in relation to the planning of the budget as a whole. For example, the New York Yankees has a waiting list for season tickets and the San Francisco 49ers have been sold out since 1981 (Berridge, 2003).

Corporate hospitality

The success of different ticket price structures and premiums can be extended via the packaging together of further elements that add to customer value. Adding food and beverage to a ticket price leverages more income from that ticket but corporate hospitality packages are by no means a new concept. The creation of audience hierarchies has been a common practice since ancient times. For example, we only have to look to the Roman Empire and the differences between senatorial seating and the provision for the common citizen (plebians) at gladiatorial events. Indeed, the more recent origins of sponsorship lie in the enhancement of simple corporate hospitality.

The creation of such ticket packages adds further customer value. In addition to the main event, there is the benefit of a meal with good company and possibly entertainment via after dinner speakers. For some events, these packages can raise more revenue and can therefore be potentially more important than ordinary ticket sales. The selling of corporate hospitality in the 120 boxes at the Royal Albert Hall for the annual Nabisco Masters Doubles tennis championships for example, meant that 20% of the audience (1000 people) were paying for food, drink and programmes as well as tickets, and mostly well in advance as a result of renewing their box directly after the previous championships. This not only raised more revenue for the event owners, World Championship Tennis (WCT) Inc, it also ensured revenue well in advance of the event giving an improved cash flow.

The financial planning for such packages clearly needs to be implemented at the feasibility stage. The costs involved in all the package elements, plus the much sought after extra profit level, are required information for the budgeting process. By identifying and securing early corporate hospitality sales, the revenue cash flow can be improved as the costs to be incurred for food and beverage will not be due until much closer to the event. It is therefore only practical sense to determine as early as possible where new and perhaps not so obvious areas for corporate hospitality might exist and, providing that they can be sold, they will provide innovative opportunities for revenue. The audit of an event's assets may reveal new areas for the provision of corporate hospitality facilities, a disused room or building or simply an area where temporary facilities can be erected.

Sponsorship

The art of placing the right sponsorship with the right organization is the key to the development of an event sponsorship programme (see Chapter 11), but this too is another form of the packaging of an event's assets into saleable bundles. The beauty of a sponsorship package is that it contains elements that often have no or little cost. Those events that have built sufficient equity into their brand will command greater sponsorship fees.

There are dangers to be aware of in this process and they need to be highlighted in this chapter. Those elements that are bundled together that do have costs need to be accounted for and so they need to feature as expenditure budget lines. Equally, if the total sponsorship fee is accounted for as an income line in the budget, it is important not to double count it. For instance, if the packages include elements such as tickets, corporate hospitality packages and advertising then it is important to apportion the sponsorship fee revenue into those individual income lines or into the sponsorship line, not both.

Space sales

There is always more space at an event than you think. This section is concerned predominantly with space at the event site, in printed form, and via Internet and mobile telecommunications opportunities.

On-site

The audit can also reveal dead areas that are either disused or non-revenue earning. These can be external or internal concourse areas for example and, if they are situated on regularly used spectator routes, they may be of interest to organizations as exhibition, demonstration or sales space. There are dangers as with most of these considerations, such as over-commodification and the resultant loss of credibility with event stakeholders for the sake of increased revenue. The process therefore involves another assessment of cost versus benefit. The ambience, aesthetics and image of an event are important considerations and even if it is determined that there will be no negative impact, the occupants who pay to go into these spaces need to be appropriate for the event. It may simply be a case of dictating the look of signage so that it complies or matches that of the event or it may be a more sophisticated audit of their merchandise stock and the satisfying of pre-determined quality controls. For even the smallest event, the image and quality of produce created by the burger, drink or ice cream concession is crucial. If an organization is to occupy space at the event it will become a part of the event and its inclusion is therefore an important decision for the event manager.

Available space can also be two-dimensional with opportunities to sell advertising hoarding. There are the commonly sold areas that are within event audience and/or television audience sight lines, such as around the pitches, courts and halls that are used for the main spectacle. In addition, there are other discreet areas that are frequented by event audience traffic such as concourses, seating aisles and even car parks. For the 2002 Commonwealth Games, the prospect of managing event visitors arriving by car was of concern in a city where there were already existing vehicle congestion issues. This is a common event planning issue that requires various agencies to come together to provide solutions. Manchester 2002 Ltd worked with a local public transport provider, First. Two car parks were created in open green-belt areas to the north and south of the city near to motorway networks. First then created bus terminals at both sites. No customer parking was provided at any of the events venues and park and ride tickets were sold. The logistics for the operation were sufficiently complex for First to also work with other transport organizations from around the UK in order to secure provision of personnel and buses at peak times.

Many events realize the potential of their directional signage and sell advertising opportunities to interested organizations. For smaller events, this enables them to approach smaller local companies with opportunities to reach target markets at lesser costs. The 2008 US Open Tennis championships sold space on its hoardings, located in the stands, to IBM, Heineken and Wilson as part of its sponsorship agreements with those organizations and, at the 2002 Flora London Marathon, the mile indicator placards carried the logos of Adidas jointly with the title sponsor.

Space is not just available via on-site physical fixtures. Events also use their people and their clothing to create advertising opportunities. Tennis court officials, ball boys and girls clothing have all been sponsor opportunities for some time but now stewards, if there are enough of them, can become an important way of reaching target audiences. As part of their agreement to sponsor the 2002 Commonwealth Games, Asda, the UK supermarket chain, provided tracksuit uniforms for all of the 12 000 plus volunteer helpers. The tracksuits carried the Asda-owned brand logo for George clothing and were also predominantly purple in colour, the brand colours for Cadbury's, another Games sponsor.

The fee for advertising space of any kind can be set according to prominence and frequency of sightings. For other space sales, occupancy agreements can be a straightforward rental per size of space. For events that are keen to raise such extra revenue and need to try harder to convince potential occupants, there could also be a share-of-profits, but this requires more work in auditing sales for an accurate settlement.

Printed form

Space can also be sold in and on printed event paper materials. Selling space in the event programme is common as is space on event tickets, flyers, posters, corporate headed paper, score sheets, retail and giveaway bags and media information packs.

Internet opportunities

Similarly, there are now opportunities for events to sell advertising space on their websites, the value of which lies largely in their longevity as they can operate year round as opposed to just around event time. However, as this is an event asset, it is also available to partners and sponsors and, as a result, managers must first identify the needs of the latter before entering any potentially conflicting agreements with additional advertisers.

The use of websites, while a relatively new opportunity, has gathered rapid momentum. In many cases, event-related websites have evolved as public relations (PR) tools. The Internet provides a relatively easy way of supplying frequent and updated information to target customers about the event. This can keep adopted fans hooked on an on-going basis. A website can then become a highly productive e-tail vehicle for tickets and merchandise. Unfortunately, some events even use their sites to advertise sponsorship opportunities and even provide application forms by which prescribed sponsorship packages may be purchased online. This latter application rather defeats the objective of building mutual sponsorship arrangements and the attempt to identify a sponsor's needs before proposing their involvement with an event. Nevertheless, the key to getting target customers to hit an event website is utilizing information about the event and, in particular, content pertaining to participants. This is a key driver of site traffic and needs to be sustained for successful ticket and merchandise sales.

Sites can also earn revenue via advertising or sponsorship sales. Creative sites can produce regular promotions, games, auctions and editorial features that can be endorsed by organizations. These may be sold independently of the event's sponsorship programme but run the danger of cluttering both the events and its sponsors' messages. The San Francisco 49ers use creativity to drive revenue from their website, 49ers.com, and predominantly via merchandise, travel, news and competitions as highlighted in Case study 6.1. The site was predominantly a PR function when it was first taken back in-house from CBS Sportsline in 2001 and there is still the objective of controlling while extending the brand as it is recognized that the site is where most fans experience the brand other than via television. The model for most sports teams' sites is one of providing team news of one sort or another to drive fans to the site and then provide sales opportunities. One of the concerns for team sites generally is that, while they impart news and stories about the team, they can be constrained by an editorial process that does not break or cover news on controversial topics. In 2002, when the 49ers released a team coach from his job, there was no coverage at all of that story on 49ers.com. The concern is that such policies may drive fans to visit other sources and that would impact on website traffic and therefore sales.

Case Study 6.1

Website Income Generation: 49ers.com

The San Francisco 49ers.com delivers more than 3 million visitors a day and, as a vehicle for extending the brand, the management evaluate it as being more lucrative than stadium, radio or publishing activities.

Some of the strategies that have been adopted include no use of banners, pop-up or under advertisements and there is a consistent use of the 49ers colours (red, gold with black and white). Other strategies have included limits on the numbers of sponsors for less clutter, a minimum level of investment for entry on to the site, national brand targeting, and no-use of cost-per-click models. Examples of site services are below.

My 49ers ENews

Fans e-mail notification via pre-selected personalized alerts such as breaking stories, injury updates, ticket availability, new arrival merchandise, auctions and special events. Over 100 000 fans were subscribed and, in addition, 12 select sponsors were recruited for revenue.

Business Partnerships

These were rotating advertisements on the homepage.

49ers Store

The site has used partners to deliver merchandise. For example, Footlocker has been used regularly to deliver six-figure annual sales revenue.

49ers Marketplace

This was a private label auction where one-of-a-kind 49ers merchandise was auctioned on-line. For example, the pompoms used by a player in a touch down celebration were auctioned for US$800.00. Players' cars were also auctioned.

49ers Fan Travel

Another partner, Prime Sport Travel, has operated an away match travel service that also produced six-figure revenue annually. In this arrangement, the 49ers received a share of profit.

Games

Regularly changing games such as Pigskin Pick 'Em consisted of free, weekly access to fans for fee-paying sponsors.

The site has also offered photo galleries, 49ers.comTV, Internet radio station, wireless subscription services, foreign language sites, 49ers dating club and ticket exchange services all offering a mixture of information and sales opportunities.

Source: Berridge (2003)

Formula 1 has also shown that creativity in the supply of the information fans want is key. Innovative ways of delivering information is seen as a way to achieve higher web traffic and therefore more sales. Formula 1's site, Formula1.com, offers merchandise, travel and downloads which are fairly typical of most team sites but also offers a service called 'Live Timing'. This is lap practice and race data, as provided to all teams, of cars as they race and supplied direct to subscribing fans via their PC (see Case study 6.2).

Case Study 6.2

Website Income Generation: Formula 1

Formula1.com is a colourful motor racing site that offers news, race and circuit details, results, photo gallery, teams and drivers information and Inside F1 (rules and explanation of the sport). Sponsors' exposure is generally limited to those companies in the sport. The site offers a number of regular services:

Fans can receive *Mobile Messaging* – pictures and/or text messages direct from the race tracks via the Formula One Management Broadcast Centres that are at each F1 race weekend. Subscription packages for the whole season or single races are available.

Other services include downloads of wallpapers, e-mail alerts, RSS feeds and sign-up for offers and giveaways. The on-line travel service offers flight, hotel and hire car packages together with race tickets. The *F1 Store* offers team and F1 merchandise including high-end fashion, accessories such as watches and leather goods, DVD and footwear. The supply of sponsored race-footwear generally and, in particular, by Puma to several teams, including Ferrari, has been a major sponsorship and sales success and the site sells the complete range.

The most creative and fan focused service is *Live Timing* – for a one-off subscription fans can receive practice lap and race data as they are supplied to the race teams live on race weekends. The data include driver names, lap number, lap time, gap times, sector times, weather conditions and speed impact and text commentary. Fans find the technical data and their appearance on screen an attractive near-race experience.

Source: Formula1 (2008)

Another example of innovative website practice was the opportunistic reponse Leeds United FC had to its deduction of 15 points (the equivalent of 5 won games) by the football league in the 2007/2008 season in Division 1. The club regularly provides tickets, merchandise and betting via partner Paddy Power for on-line income generation plus audience drivers such as mobile alerts, season ticket offers, fixture information and player performance voting. However, towards the end of the season when the club and supporters were waiting to hear from an arbitration on whether the 15 points would be reinstated, the website ranked the third most visited football site in the UK, behind Manchester United and Liverpool but ahead of Chelsea, the rest of the Premiership and the whole of the Championship. The evaluation was performed by Hitwise, a company that monitors more than 25 million Internet users with over 1 million websites across 160 industry categories (Leeds United, 2008). In order to take advantage of the situation and to generate income, the club focused on the 15 point theme, something the singing supporters had focused on since the beginning of the season and since the team won its first 7 games. They produced a simple, but best selling, DVD featuring the first 15 games of the season.

Mobile telecommunications opportunities

The advent of wireless communications via mobile telecommunication handsets is an exciting development that has yet to be fully developed. In the UK, there are mobile telecommunication carriers that are providing premiership football match highlights to their customers via their handsets. Fans of teams from many sports can now be served with scores, downloadable logos, ringtones, games, teams statistics and ticket information via mobile handsets. Last-minute ticket availability alerts for teams are also available and are producing income for teams and leagues alike.

Merchandising

The event T-shirt is a memento that is popular with event spectators and, at some sports events, also sells to those that participate in the event. At international racquetball tournaments, the favoured memento to collect is a pin badge, something that Olympic hosts have also recognized as a key part of merchandising programmes. Not all events have this kind of power of course, but the T-shirt example shows that smaller events also have the opportunity to think about where sales might derive.

The development of sophisticated merchandise product lines is achievable for some events and there are also merchandising organizations that will design, produce and sell event merchandise. The more common arrangement will be to pay a commission to the event after an agreed audit of sales. The advantage of contracting external agencies is that there is no event expenditure, only revenue. Handling the programme in-house of course may offer more potential profit but a lot will depend on the retail expertise available.

Beijing Insight 6.1 contains details of how BOCOG went about generating income from its merchandising programme.

Beijing Insight 6.1
Beijing 2008 Olympics: Merchandising and Licensing
The revenue from merchandising and licensing programmes is a significant contributor to an OCOG, but there is also considerable importance placed on the promotional and educational benefits they have for the Olympic Movement. Hence, the importance of quality control and the strategic planning involved in generating merchandise and license income.

Continued

Beijing Insight 6.1—cont'd

An Olympic Games license enables manufacturers the right to use Olympic marks, under strict guidance and agreement, on their products for retail sale. The manufacturers pay royalties to the OCOG for this right. Generally, this includes the use of the rings and the host city logo on clothing, pin badges, toys, ceramics, jewelry and stationery. The development of mascots has also been important for the designs used and, in Beijing's case, they designed a set of five mascots that were used widely on all types of merchandise and by licensees. A banner promoting the mascots can be seen in the photograph.

The Beijing 2008 mascots.

Apart from raising important revenue for BOCOG, the merchandising and licensing programmes for the Beijing 2008 Olympic Games were also used to promote Chinese manufacturing and so the selection criteria and granting of licenses took on particular significance with a key aim being to ensure that 'Made-in-China' meant nothing but high quality.

The general trend indicates that merchandising is a key revenue earner for Olympic host cities. While there was a dip in Sydney 2000 (US$54 million) following the considerable peak in Atlanta 1996 (US$81 million), the revenue rose to over US$80 million again in Athens 2004. Beijing 2008 expected to achieve up to US$90 million from license royalties, merchandise, philately and coin sales (see Beijing Insight 5.1 in Chapter 5).

Beijing's national programme began in late 2003 and internationally after the Athens Games in late 2004. It had over 6000 varieties of product including high-end precious metal models of the venues and even his and hers wedding rings, but predominantly the range was intended for all pockets and so effort was made to keep prices stable as well as affordable locally. The retail network consisted of 3000 outlets selling the goods from over 60 licensed manufacturers.

Pin badges or pins are a favourite item and in Athens provided the single most amount of merchandise revenue after sports clothing. The mascots feature heavily in the designs for Beijing pins as do elaborate designs for each of the sports.

A key point of delivery was the e-retailing strategy. An Internet site was launched on 29 November 2007 with a full range of products. Partners UPS and Visa, both IOC TOP and Olympic sponsors, provided the distribution and payment services respectively and the site was produced and maintained by another partner, SOHU.com, the first Internet provider to be an Olympic sponsor (see Beijing Insight 11.1).

Stamps and coins have traditionally been offered by host cities and, in past years, have provided significant revenue. In 1972, the Munich Olympic Games coin programme provided a major part of the targeted income. While it planned to mint 10 million pieces, it found it had the demand for more and ended up producing 100 million coins which resulted in revenue of US$972 million. Since this peak, revenue has declined, but Beijing launched an ambitious programme with three issues between 2006 and 2008 generally with an athlete/sport theme. The third issue featured a large 10-kilogram gold coin. The mints in Shanghai and Shenyang were used to produce the coins and, following tradition, they were legal tender and not just decorative.

Shopping for coins in one of the franchised stores in Beijing.

Continued

BOCOG generating income during the Beijing 2008 Olympic Games at the Olympic Green retail unit.

Source: Beijing 2008 (2008); Preuss (2004)

Licensing

The more powerful events brands can develop income from licensing pro-grammes. The All England Lawn Tennis Club, the owners and organizers of the Wimbledon tennis championships, have a range of goods available via its website and all around the world as a result of a carefully monitored licensing programme. The NFL also operates a sophisticated licensing operation whereby it is able to command licence fees in the USA as well as other world regions such as Europe and the Far East. Different manufacturers can buy these licences and produce agreed products according to the conditions of the licence. The more powerful the brand, the more manufacturers will be interested and thus the more revenue will be earned. The key again is in the quality of the products produced as they are depicting the image of the events and organizations involved. Quality assurance and control by the rights owner is made all the more complex when the manufacture of the products concerned is conducted by a licence holder, or even a third party, and so strict licence conditions and their policing are required. In the USA, the United

States Olympic Committee (USOC) receives no funding from national government and so it generates further income in addition to its sponsorship and suppliership programmes from licensing. It has a long list of licencees and a set of diverse licensing rights opportunities as Table 6.1 shows.

Table 6.1	USOC Licensing Programme

Together with its sponsorship and suppliership programmes (see Case study 6.3), licensing provides a valuable source of income for the USOC. In 2008, the following companies had the right to license their products and services using USOC's trademarked USA 5-ring logo.

Altius Games: Olympic challenge board games

American Identity: Premium licensee – sponsor premium products

Aminco International: Lapel pins, key tags, magnets and pin collecting trading bags. Money clips, pendants, charms and earrings manufactured in non-precious metals

Asset Marketing: Beijing commemorative coin distributor

b.dazzle: Scramble Squares® 9-piece brain teaser puzzles

The Bob Beamon Collection: Ties and scarves

Colonial Tag & Label Co: Hangtags, sewn-in labels, holograms

Concord Industries: Executive office accessories, golf accessories, leather goods, and 3-D Christmas ornaments

CorpLogoWare: Sponsor premium products

CorpLogoWare Jewelry: Fashion jewelry

Dale of Norway: Norwegian wool sweaters, hats and headbands

Extended Exposure: Scrapbooks, journals, picture frames

Fanticola Adamson Entertainment: Informational DVDs for Italy

Fine Art Ltd: Posters, lithographs and serigraphs

Footlocker: Catalogue sales

Getty Images: Photography

Griffin Publishing: Professional publishing including education material for the USOC.

ICARIA2000: Encyclopedia of documentary archives of the IOC Museum

International Sports Multimedia: Interactive entertainment software

Jon Hair Studio of Fine Art: Olympic-themed sculptures

Jump Rope Tech: High performance jump ropes

Museum Editions: 3-D lithographs

Continued

Table 6.1	USOC Licensing Programme—Cont'd

Nike: Official outfitter: apparel, men's, women's, children's headwear and footwear

The Northwest Company: Throws, pillows, adult and youth blankets

Omega: Watches, clocks

Panda America: One of two Beijing commemorative coins distributor

QVC: Television shopping channel

Roots: Official parade outfitter for the US Olympic team – apparel, men's, women's, children's headwear, leather jackets and leather accessories

Style Science: Lifestyle eyewear

Ultimate Skate: Informational skating DVD

United States Postal Service: US commemorative stamp

WIN Products: Laundry detergent

XP Apparel: Apparel: men's, women's, children's, outerwear, headwear, backpacks, tote bags, sport bags

XP Memorabilia: Olympic memorabilia

XP Retail: Branded brick and mortar retail stores

(USOC, 2008)

Case study 6.3 describes how the IOC has identified and packaged Olympic assets. Clearly, the Olympic offering is a sophisticated programme that has necessitated innovative management in the layering of the partnerships and supplierships available. This is a model that other events have mirrored in an effort to present credible benefits to commercial parties from all types of diversified industries and yet still place them to work effectively together on the same event.

Case Study 6.3

Revenue Maximization: The Olympic Marketing Programme

The Olympic Marketing Programme consists of a number of key elements that are either managed or overseen by the IOC. First, there are three tiers of Olympic sponsors and, secondly, three tiers of supplierships that for the last complete Olympic quadrennium (TOP V, 2001–2004) accounted for 34% of IOC marketing revenue. This has reduced from the previous quadrennium when it was 40%. Broadcasting accounted for 53%, up 3%, ticketing 11%, up 3% and licensing remained the same at 2% (IOC 2008). The IOC retains 8% of its revenue for the upkeep of its administration with the remainder distributed to the OCOGs, NOCs and IFs.

Olympic Sponsorship

The Olympic Partner Programme (TOP VI, 2005–2008)

This programme consisted of exclusive sponsorships that offered worldwide rights year-round and on an on-going renewable basis directly with the IOC: US$866 million was generated from these partners and product category rights:

Coca-Cola: non-alcoholic beverages

Kodak: film/photographics and imaging

McDonald's: retail food services

Panasonic: audio/TV/video equipment

Samsung: wireless communication equipment

Omega: time pieces, timing systems/services, electronic timing, scoring and scoreboard systems and services

Visa: consumer payment

General Electric: select products and services from GE Energy, GE Healthcare, GE Transportation, GE Infrastructure, GE Consumer & Industrial, GE Advanced materials and GE Equipment Services

Manulife: life assurance/annuities

Atos Origin: Information technology

Lenovo: computing equipment

Johnson & Johnson: healthcare products

Olympic Games Sponsorship Programme

This programme consists of exclusive agreements with sponsors for rights to any current Olympiad and are negotiated directly with the host city Organizing Committee for the Olympic Games (OCOG). For the 2008 Olympics, BOCOG implemented two levels of sponsorship ('Beijing 2008 Partners' and 'Beijing 2008 Sponsors'; see Beijing Insight 11.1 in Chapter 11).

National Olympic Committee (NOC) Sponsorship Programme

These programmes are negotiated by each NOC and can be on-going renewable agreements. The US Olympic Committee (USOC) for example has two levels:

Partners	Sponsors
Anheuser-Busch	Allstate
AT&T	Hilton Hotels
Bank of America	Jet Set Sports
General Motors	Kelloggs
The Home Depot	Nike
	24 Hour Fitness
	Tyson Foods
	United Airlines

Olympic Suppliership

Olympic Supplier Programme

Exclusive supplierships offer worldwide rights year-round on an on-going renewable basis directly with the IOC. Current supplierships include:

DaimlerChrysler: rights to supply transport, outside of an Olympic host country, for the IOC. This includes the provision of Mercedes-Benz cars for transportation in Switzerland and for international visits.

Mizuno: rights to supply IOC officials with clothing.

Schenker AG: rights to provide freight forwarding and customs services for the IOC. The firm also supplied these services to BOCOG for the 2008 Olympics.

OCOG Supplierships

Exclusive agreements with suppliers for rights to any current Olympiad are negotiated directly with the host city Organizing Committee for the Olympic Games (OCOG). For the 2008 Olympics, BOCOG implemented two levels of suppliership ('Exclusive Suppliers' and 'Suppliers'; see Beijing Insight 11.1 in Chapter 11).

NOC Supplierships

Agreements are negotiated by each NOC and can be on-going renewable agreements. The USOC, for example, has the following 'Suppliers': Adecco, Amino Vital, Hersheys, Highmark, Kleenex, Maverick Ranch, Oroweat and Schenker too. In addition, it has also implemented a licensing programme (see Table 6.1).

Source: IOC (2008); USOC (2008)

SUMMARY

There are increasing pressures on event managers to be creative in generating revenue. While the traditional methods of selling media rights, agreements with media partners, ticket and hospitality sales, selling space, merchandising and licensing are still appropriate, it is now a necessity for managers to look at these areas for new vehicles that can attract both audience and corporate customers alike. An event audit can reveal new mechanisms and vehicles for commercial properties that, if managed carefully, will not clutter the event but rather enhance it and income figures. As with most businesses today, the dynamic introduction of new technology offers a wealth of new opportunity for the event manager. The increasingly evolving Internet offers events a year-round opportunity to sell and communicate with its customers and wireless technology is now providing instant access to customers round the clock. However, these vehicles can only be as effective as there is care and thought in finding out what the customer wants. The event asset audit can reveal potential products and the event manager can bundle up innovative benefits, but the focus must be on what the customer will buy and that requires market research. Market research as a tool in the marketing planning process is considered in greater detail in Chapter 9.

QUESTIONS

Select a sports event and:

1. From a revenue earning perspective, analyse the strategic importance of financial planning at an early stage.

2. Audit the event and identify the key areas available for revenue generation.

3. Identify the key practices exercised in generating revenue while highlighting specific examples.

4. Suggest new ways in which the event might generate revenue in the future.

5. Now consider Olympic models for revenue maximization and compare and contrast them with the approaches adopted by other events.

6. Critically analyse the costs and benefits of implementing new technology for event revenue maximization.

REFERENCES

Berridge, K. (2003). Marketing and enabling technology: beyond content, turning a team web site into a profit center, paper delivered by Senior Manager of Corporate Partnerships, San Francisco 49ers, at *Sport Media and Technology 2003* November 13–14, New York Marriott Eastside New York. *Street and Smith's Sports Business Journal.*

BBC (2003). www.bbc.co.uk/sport1/hi/in_depth/2001/epsom_derby/ 362059.stm (accessed 12 September 2003).

Camelot Group (2006). National lottery sales hit 5 billion. www.camelot.co.uk/pressreleases/2006 (accessed 21 April 2008).

Coates, D. and Humphries, B. (2003). *Professional Sports Facilities, Franchises and Urban Economic Development.* University of Maryland, Baltimore County, working paper 03-103. www.umbc.edu/economics/wpapers/wp_03_103.pdf (accessed 7 January 2004).

Culf, A. (2007). Lottery sales harming grass roots sport. *The Guardian*, 8 August. www.sport.guardian.co.uk (accessed 21 April 2008).

Formula1 (2008). www.formula1.com (accessed 22 April 2008).

Getz, D. (1997). *Event Management and Tourism.* New York, Cognizant, Chapter 10.

Gratton, P. and Taylor, P. (2000). *Economics of Sport and Recreation.* London, E & FN Spon.

IOC (2008). www.olympic.org/uk (accessed 21 April 2008).

Leeds United (2008). www.leedsunited.com (accessed 29 April 2008).

Preuss, H. (2004). *The Economics of Staging the Olympics: A Comparison of the Games 1972–2008.* Cheltenham, Edward Elgar.

RealNetworks (2001). www.wnba.com/news/ebcast_announcement_030529 (accessed 12 September 2003).

Turbolinux (2000). www.turbolinux.com/news/pr/olympicwebcast.html (accessed 12 September 2003).

USOC (2008). www.usolympicteam.com (accessed 21 April 2008).

CHAPTER 7

The Bidding Process

An artist's impression of the controversial stadium intended as a legacy from a New York 2012 Olympic Games. Linking to sustainable development, section 5.8 in volume 1 of the city's bid book described the stadium as 'the most environmentally advanced building of its kind, setting the highest standards for renewable design and sustainable development'. NYC 2012

LEARNING OBJECTIVES

After studying this chapter, you should be able to:

- identify the planning and management processes required in the bidding for sports events

159

■ identify the key components for successful bids

■ understand how losing bids can be winning strategies

INTRODUCTION

This chapter is concerned with the process undertaken in bidding for the right to host sports events. Before the Los Angeles Olympics in 1984, the terminology used in bidding today was unheard of and the hosting of major sports events, in particular the Olympics, was seen to be a financial millstone (Gratton and Taylor, 2000) until the unprecedented surplus income these games generated. What we have now is a calendar full of events that require host cities to bid and a roster that does not just consist of only high profile events. Now, international events like the World Masters Games, European Wheelchair Basketball Championships and the World Badminton Championships have for sometime been much sought after, as well as a host of national events in many countries (Kronos, 1997). Even individual sporting fixtures can be an attractive target for a host city. The UEFA Champions League final, for example, is a much sought after event and while it takes a season to prepare for it, it is still only one football match. The NFL's Super Bowl is another example. In this chapter, the requirements of the International Olympic Committee (IOC) and the Olympic bidding process will be used as a model to be applied as appropriate to other sports events. The key factors required for successful bidding will be identified as well as an assessment of bids that may be strategically used for legacies and other benefits whether they win or not. A key focus will be on the cities that bid for the 2012 Olympics.

THE BID PROCESS

The preparation and implementation of a bid to host a sports event are an intrinsic part of the event planning process. While the preparation and submission for event candidature requires specialist expertise and project management, it is essential that the process is aligned and integrated into the overall event planning mechanism. For example, it is necessary for the feasibility of the event to be assessed prior to a decision to go ahead and submit a bid. Getz (1997) proposes that a bid is based on at least a pre-feasibility study where preliminary figures for the costs and benefits are assigned. For some events, this can be a relatively low cost and therefore of small financial risk. However, for larger events, the cost of assessing impact can be high but is, nevertheless, a critical undertaking if all potential stakeholders are to be convinced that the benefits of the event outweigh the costs. For major events such as the Olympics, there are planning costs that are entirely at risk, for example in 2002, London commissioned Arup to conduct a study prior to its decision to bid for the 2012 Olympics.

The preparation of any required bid, therefore, does not begin until event feasibility has been assessed and a decision has been made to go ahead with the event. Clearly, any earlier assessments can then be used in the public domain to promote the event and the costs incurred can be included in the budget for the bid.

That then raises a question about bids that fail and how the costs associated with that failure are justified. There are two answers. The first is that the funds raised to finance a failed bid get written off. The loss is accepted as a calculated risk. This further highlights the need for stakeholder support in going to bid because, in Olympic cases, the costs can now be as high as £30 million, as for London and its 2012 bid (Arup, 2002; Culf, 2005). The second is an alternative strategy where the bid can be a means to end and this is discussed at the end of this chapter.

Getz (1997) proposes that a further detailed feasibility study be conducted after the bid has been accepted in order to begin planning the implementation of the event. However, there are dangers here. There is no doubt that this, indeed, is common practice but, for major events that identify new cost factors that are widely apart from the event budget, then any feasibility exercise prior to a decision to go ahead was futile. As mentioned earlier, the Sydney Organizing Committee of the Olympic Games (SOCOG) formally readjusted its event budget on four occasions after it had decided to go ahead and its costs escalated way beyond their original forecasts (SOCOG, 2001) (see Case study 5.1 in Chapter 5). It is not that relignment to actual costs on a continuous basis is not required, the message here is that the feasibility stage is perhaps even more critical than currently the industry accepts.

The Olympic bid process involves two main stages. The IOC awards its games to cities not countries and, in some cases, there are national competitions for interested host cities to win the nomination of that nation's National Olympic Committee (NOC). The NOCs are given 6 months warning by the IOC, approximately 9.5 years ahead of an Olympic Games to decide to nominate a host city (Thoma and Chalip, 1996). Six months is clearly too short a time for interested hosts to consider a bid and so they are in contact with their respective NOC long before. Only an

NOC can nominate a host city to the IOC for the bidding competition. For the 2012 Olympic Games, the United States Olympic Committee (USOC) ran a competition between San Francisco, Houston, Washington and the eventual winners New York. In contrast, the British Olympic Committee (BOC) selected London outright. For some countries with limited resources, the decision of 'which city' requires a simple selection procedure (Thoma and Chalip, 1996), take Cuba and its nomination of Havana for the 2012 Olympics for example. However, the decision by the BOC to select London was more contentious, with rivalry from Manchester and Birmingham in previous years. Manchester had already received national nominations and failed in its bids for the 1996 and 2000 Olympics, as did Birmingham in 1992 and the BOC identified London as the UK's best opportunity to win.

The process for nominated cities becomes more clearly defined and timetabled from this point. For example, the deadlines set for the election of the host city for the Olympic Games of the XXXI Olympiad in 2016 are set out in Table 7.1. The IOC's Bid Process can effectively be divided into four distinct steps. These are discussed below in particular reference to the awarding of the 2012 Games (IOC, 2008b).

Table 7.1   Candidature Acceptance Procedure for the 2016 Olympic Games

Phase 1

13 September, 2007 NOCs to inform the IOC of the name of their applicant city

1 October, 2007 Signature of the candidature acceptance procedure

1 October, 2007 Payment of the fee to the IOC, US$150 000

15 October, 2007 IOC information seminar for 2016 applicant cities, Lausanne

14 January, 2008 Submission of application files/guarantee letters to the IOC

January to June, 2008 Examination of application files by the IOC

June, 2008 IOC executive board meeting to accept candidate cities

Phase 2

August, 2008 Olympic Games observer programme in Beijing

12 February, 2009 Submission of candidate files to the IOC

September, 2009 Report of the 2016 IOC evaluation commission

2 October, 2009 Election of the Host City, IOC Session, Copenhagen

Adapted from IOC (2008a)

THE OLYMPIC GAMES BIDDING PROCESS: 2012 OLYMPIC GAMES

Pre-applicants

This phase is for interested host cities to contact their respective NOC and partake in selection procedures in order to be chosen for nomination to the IOC.

NOCs, if they so wish, may inform the IOC of their nominated applicant city. This was done by 15 July 2003 in writing (9 years out from the event).

Application fees of US$150 000 per city were submitted by August 2003. This fee entitled cities to use a 'mark' that consisted of their city name and the Olympic year '2012'. It also allowed them access to the IOC's Olympic Games Knowledge Management Programme and accreditation for an IOC Applicant City Seminar.

Candidature acceptance procedure

NOC nominated cities were classified as applicant cities and answered a questionnaire in writing, submitted by 15 January 2004. This information was then assessed by the IOC Administration and their recruited experts under the governance of the IOC executive board. No formal presentations took place at this stage, but city visits by experts were allowed. The IOC Executive Board then informed the applicant cities which ones were to be accepted as the candidate cities to go forward to the next stage. It did this by the 18 May 2004 (8 years out from the delivery of the event) with Havana, Istanbul, Leipzig, London, Madrid, Moscow, New York, Paris and Rio de Janeiro going forward.

Generally, applicant cities are assessed on the following:

1. The potential of the cities, including their countries, to host a successful multi-sports event.

2. Their compliance to the Olympic Charter, code of ethics (which includes the right to promote their candidature in their respective NOC territory but not on an international level and the banning of all giving and receiving of gifts by Olympic parties), anti-doping code and other conditions concerning the candidature as set by the IOC.

The questionnaire is concerned with providing the IOC with an overview of the intended event concept using the following seven themes:

1. *Motivation, concept and public opinion*: this section includes the request for maps that show new versus existing infrastructure and an explanation of the motivation behind new build, post-Olympic use and long-term strategies.

The section is also concerned with gauging public support and asks for polls to be undertaken and reported. Detail of any opposition to the bid is specifically required.

2. *Political support*: information on the status of the city's Governmental support is requested and the names of those who would be involved in the future management of the event if won. Letters from the Government, NOC and city authorities are required as testimony to their support of the bid. Details of any forthcoming political elections are also required.

3. *Finance*: details are required on the Games' budget from each applicant city and, in addition, they are to inform the IOC of how the phases of candidature will also be funded. The amount of Government contribution is required information here too.

4. *Venues*: details on existing and planned venues are required including whether they are to be temporary overlay or permanent. Specific plans for an Olympic village, international broadcast and press centres are requested.

5. *Accommodation*: the status regarding hotel provision and media accommodation at the time of the event are required here.

6. *Transport infrastructure*: information on existing and planned transportation is requested and, for new facilities, construction timelines are also needed. This section concerns most forms of transportation including air, road, rail, subway and light rail.

7. *General conditions, logistics and experience*: this section requires information on population expectations at the time of the event, meteorology conditions, environmental conditions and impact, security responsibility, resources and issues. It also requires information on the experience the city has in hosting international sports events and multi-sports events, in particular. Specifically, it asks for the last 10 major events over the previous 10 years.

Each of these themes consists of several questions. Each answer is requested in French and English and is limited to one page, making a maximum of 25 pages in each language. The IOC keenly looks for brevity in this document and emphasizes the importance of fact versus presentation. Answers for certain sections use pro-forma charts, venues for example, and request fine detail on elements such as spectator capacity, construction and upgrade dates, costs of upgrades and sources of finance specifically. Fifty copies of the questionnaire are to be submitted to the IOC.

Candidature

Accepted candidate cities are required to submit a candidature file to the IOC and had between 18 May and 15 November 2004 to complete it. This was then evaluated by a Commission that was comprised of members of International Federations, NOCs, IOC members, representatives of the Athletes Commission and the International Paralympic Committee, as well as IOC experts. The Commission analysed the files received and then, from the end of January 2005, underwent a visit programme, taking in all of the candidate cities. An evaluation report was then compiled and presented to the IOC executive board in May 2005 and a formal announcement was made of the candidate cities that were submitted to the IOC Session (the election). These were London, Madrid, Moscow, New York and Paris.

Candidate cities can, upon submission of their files and acceptance by the IOC, undertake international promotion of their candidature during this stage.

The candidature file provides each city with an opportunity to embellish on the information provided by their earlier questionnaires and the IOC provides a comprehensive guideline for its completion via its *Manual for Candidate Cities*. A fresh manual is produced for every Olympic Games.

The manual supplied to the candidate cities for the 2008 election consisted of a model to follow and included general information on layout, illustration and format, together with clear instruction for the completion of three volumes in order to cover 18 prescribed themes (IOC, 2002). The themes are listed below and, for a comparison, see Beijing Insight 7.1.

- Volume one
    1. National, regional and candidate city characteristics
    2. Legal aspects
    3. Customs and immigration formalities
    4. Environmental protection and meteorology
    5. Finance
    6. Marketing

- Volume two
    7. General sports concept
    8. Sports
    9. Paralympic Games
    10. Olympic village

- Volume three
    11. Medical/health services
    12. Security
    13. Accommodation
    14. Transport
    15. Technology
    16. Communication and media services
    17. Olympism and culture
    18. Guarantees.

The main press centre, MPC, for the 2008 Olympics in Beijing. All Olympic bids are required to state the specific provision a city proposes for media services and its plans for the creation of a press centre. In Beijing, the MPC was supported by the services provided by venue press centres (VPCs) at each venue in order to provide the level of service required by the IOC. The International Broadcasting Centre (IBC) was located opposite the MPC at Olympic Green, the main 2008 site. It can be seen from the overlay that the building used for the MPC, was and will return to being, a hotel.

Beijing Insight 7.1
Beijing 2008 Olympics: Bid Book Highlights
The Beijing bid book for the 2012 Olympics consisted of three volumes and 18 themes as below. Themes 7 and 10 are highlighted in this Insight:

Volume 1
Preface
  Letter of support by President Jiang Zemin
  Letter of support by Premier Zhu Rongji
  Letter of support by Liu Qi, Mayor of Beijing
  Letter of support by Yuan Weimin, President of COC
  Introduction
  Theme 1: National, regional and Beijing characteristics
  Theme 2: Legal aspects
  Theme 3: Customs and immigration formalities
  Theme 4: Environmental protection and meteorology
  Theme 5: Finance
  Theme 6: Marketing

Volume 2
Introduction
  Theme 7: General sports concept
  Theme 8: Sports – archery, athletics, rowing, badminton, baseball, boxing, canoe/kayak, cycling, equestrian, fencing, football, gymnastics, weightlifting, handball, hockey, judo, wrestling, swimming, modern pentathlon, softball, taekwondo, softball, tennis, table tennis, shooting, triathlon, sailing, volleyball
  Theme 9: Paralympic Games
  Theme 10: Olympic village

Volume 3
Introduction
  Theme 11: Medical/health services
  Theme 12: Security
  Theme 13: Accommodation
  Theme 14: Transport
  Theme 15: Technology
  Theme 16: Communications and media services
  Theme 17: Olympism and culture
  Theme 18: Guarantees
  Conclusion

Theme 7: General Sports Concept
This section consisted of details of the venues and facilities. Some of the highlights of the section are detailed below.

Continued

Beijing Insight 7.1—cont'd

List of Venues

Thirty-seven venues were listed including those used in other cities. Information on distance between sites with maps, details of new construction and refurbishment to existing facilities, the current state of construction and financing was supplied.

Guarantee of Use

The post-games proprietors for each venue were identified and it was noted that post-games agreements had been concluded with all (see Figure 4.2 in Chapter 4).

Agreements with International Federations

A list of the 28 IFs that had already given their agreement to the proposed venues and facilities.

Advertising

Confirmation that there would be no advertising at any venue.

Human Resources

Outline of the formation of BOCOG and of future training for personnel

Sports Programme

A schedule of all the sports and their competitions

Test Events

Confirmation that there would be a programme of test events prior to the Games and, in accordance with rule 55 of the Olympic Charter, in the period 18 months to 6 months prior.

Sports Experience

Testimonial for Beijing's experience of managing sports events. This included:

11th Asian Games and National Games (experience of multi-sport events is required)

A list of 55, mainly national, championships covering 24 sports. Of international significance in the listing were the 1999 World Gymnastics Championships, 1993 World Cup Diving, 1994 Shooting World Cup, 1990 World Women's Volleyball Championships plus many Asian Games sports championships.

Theme 10: Olympic Village

This section consisted of details of the village and included:

Design Procedure

Details of the planning phases and the Olympic Green site, including justification of the selection of the site with environmental benefits highlighted. Post-games resale was unspecific except to state that the site was a prime location in Beijing, however, desired legacy arrangements were identified as follows:

Athletes accommodation – to be converted to residential developments

West Dining Hall – to be converted into a neighbourhood recreation centre

East Dining Hall – to be converted into a leisure and shopping centre

Polyclinic – to be converted into a kindergarten

Athletes Weights area – to be converted into a school

These items were offered as plans rather than agreed positions, although the language used was one of 'will be converted for long-term use'.

The athletes' accommodation was designed in 5–6 storey blocks and, to help fulfil technological objectives, all apartments were to be equipped with broadband, cable television, video intercoms, burglar alarms and fingerprint entrance activation.

Construction Schedule

Detailed plans and elevations were provided. Altogether there were 2200 units planned for the athletes consisting of 5870 double rooms and 5860 single rooms; 200 units were for NOCs. Plans were shown for both games and post-games layouts. So far as this accommodation was concerned, it is clear that planning for after-use was evident with architects being briefed to produce layouts that were easily convertible.

Transportation

Details of the transport links to and from the village. Dedicated traffic lanes on express highways, a new bus terminal, car park for accredited vehicles were all identified. Transportation within the village consisted of low noise clean-fuel buses running 24 hours a day. The Olympic Green was so vast that various forms of transport were required to get around.

Low noise clean-fuel buses in operation at Olympic Green during the Beijing 2008 Olympics.

Continued

Beijing Insight 7.1—cont'd

Village Characteristics

A plan and accompanying detail on parking, accreditation centre, shopping and recreation facilities, information centre, dining, worship, training (gym, track, courts, pitch, pool), residences, transportation, freight centre, fire station and polyclinic.

Security

Details of a central security centre with access to video intercoms that extended to the athletes' accommodation.

Paralympic Design

The village would serve both the Olympic and subsequent Paralympic Games and so designs were produced to accommodate special needs including wheelchair access and lifts according to international standards.

Sustainability

Details of how the village would fit with the green objectives including sewage treatment, rainwater collection, brown water treatment.

The Olympic Village, Beijing with VW courtesy cars in waiting. Several team members took the opportunity to place their national flags out of their windows.

Source: Beijing 2008 (2008)

Election

The IOC Session took place in Singapore on 6 July 2005 and the candidate cities each made a presentation of their bid. After all the presentations from each bidding city were received, there were various rounds of voting by IOC members and London was declared the winning city. The four rounds progressed as follows (GamesBids.com, 2008):

	1st	2nd	3rd	4th
London	22	27	39	54
Paris	21	25	33	50
Madrid	20	32	31	
New York	19	16		
Moscow	15			

For each of the candidate cities this represented 6 years of planning in reaching this stage and this all prior to the decision to go ahead with the event. For London, this meant a further 7 years of planning before the implementation of the event in 2012.

In comparison, the election for the 2008 Olympics host city in Moscow on 13 July 2001, was concluded after two rounds of voting. Osaka was eliminated in the first round and Beijing was declared the winner after the second round with more votes than the other cities votes added together. The voting took place as follows (IOC, 2008c):

	1st	2nd
Beijing	44	56
Istanbul	17	9
Osaka	6	
Paris	15	18
Toronto	20	22

The IOC process here is highly sophisticated and, in this comprehensive display of detail and scrutiny, there is the basis for a useful model for bidding requirements for other sports events. Some event rights owning bodies do offer much simpler processes. FINA offers little guideline other than deadlines for receipt of bids, for example for the 13th FINA World Championships in 2009 (swimming, diving, water polo, synchronized swimming and open water events), interested host cities had to put in their bids by 31 October 2004, under 5 years out from the event. For their FINA Junior Diving World Championships the lead-time is under 3 years (FINA, 2003). In contrast, the guideline offered by USA Track and Field (USATF) to bidders for their

National Championships is more informative and highlights the key areas that are to be covered in any bid. It also covers similar criteria to the IOC model as Case study 7.1 illustrates. Both FINA and USATF display their available events over the long term on their websites.

Case Study 7.1

USA Track & Field: Championship Bidding

USA Track & Field (USATF), the US NGB for athletics, provides those cities that want to bid for its events with handbooks. The Request for a Proposal and Bidding Handbook that is provided to those that wish to bid for the US Track & Field Outdoor Championships is a 43-page document with details on what amounts to a three-year process. The handbook is designed to guide interested host cities and advises on how the document can be used to compile a bid.

Timetable for the Award of the Championships:
August: Cities/Communities register interest
October: Submit 10 Bid documents to USATF

A \$25 000 deposit is required. This is one-third of the rights fee that is required from the winning host; \$3000 is retained from all deposits by USATF for administrative purposes.
December: Final presentations by bidders if required
December: Awarding of the Championships 2 years out

The bid document itself is required to cover the following criteria:

1. Local organizing committee
2. Management committee and staffing
3. Bidding host city/community characteristics
4. Facilities
5. Housing and meals
6. Logistics: transportation, security, medical
7. Climate
8. Business arrangements: budgets and sponsorship

Following the award of a championship, a contract is agreed and signed. This includes an operating addendum that includes a list of the parties responsible for equipment, facilities, clerical work. This contract has to be executed at least 120 days prior to the championships or as otherwise determined by the USATF. If it is not the award may be cancelled.

Source: USA Track & Field (2008)

KEY BID COMPONENTS AND CRITERIA

There are a number of key factors that may be critical in the winning of bids. They include the gaining of stakeholder support (in particular the local population), political risk analysis, knowledge of the bidding and evaluation process, the recruitment of key management, communications and a thorough bid book.

Bid book and presentation

The bid book, sometimes referred to as a bid document, is the hardcopy of the proposal prepared and delivered by each bidding city. The IOC requires

20 copies of what it refers to as a candidature file, in English and French, and controls the release of the contents into the public domain. In addition, copies of the file are distributed to a number of other recipients including IOC members, the International Sports Federations affected and the library at the Olympic Study Centre, based at the Olympic Museum in Lausanne. This distribution is important for future candidate cities and their capacity to learn from past bids.

The preparation required needs to be thorough and the list of considerations in the previous section provide only the headers for the level of detail necessary. There is an opportunity to make a presentation and, for the Olympics, this is limited to 1 hour.

These two essential elements of the bid process are the critical tools by which a bid city can seek to differentiate itself from other bids. The 18 themes of information required by the IOC, as listed above, are the key elements by which a city is evaluated and so it is in these areas where the differential is required. For example, Sydney, in its bid for the 2000 Olympics, is famed for its 'Green' approach. The Australian Government claims that it was the first true Green Games and was the force behind the introduction of environmental criteria for Olympic hosts (Department of the Environment and Heritage, 2003). The Sydney bid made much of this approach and is now seen as a key factor in its election, but the bid also focused on the care of athletes in its attempt to set itself aside from the competition (Meisegeier, 1995). The competition included a bid from Beijing that was clouded by human rights issues. Beijing bid again and won the 2008 Olympics under similar clouds, but used Weber Shandwick as its communications agency, as Sydney had done previously. The importance of experience in both previous bidding and bid communications is highlighted here. Weber Shandwick focused the communications efforts for the 2008 bid on de-linking the city with political issues, emphasizing social changes within China and making the case for a country with the world's largest population as 'deserving the games' (Weber Shandwick, 2003). These themes were considered to be key content in Beijing's 2008 candidature file.

For other events, there are other opportunities to gain a differential advantage. The team owners vote for the host city for an NFL Super Bowl and, for the winners for 2008, Phoenix, Arizona, the key factor was their newly planned stadium. The stadium was completed in 2006 with a 75 000 seat capacity and a retractable roof. Prior to the secret ballot, several team owners were freely exalting the attraction of Phoenix's bid. It was recognized as early as during the recruitment for funding that the new facilities would provide the differential needed to win (Harris and Bagnato, 2003; Sports

Tricker, 2003). The other bids from Washington and Tampa (New York had previously pulled out) did not involve new facilities.

Hockey Canada has a reputation in the world of ice hockey for excellent event management. Canada has staged the World Junior Championships seven times, most recently in Vancouver in 2006 and will do so again in Ottowa in 2009. The International Ice Hockey Federation president, Rene Fasel, stated that no country does a better job than Canada in putting on these championships due to their unparalleled fan attendances. A record attendance of 242 173 was set in Halifax in 2003 and, as a result, the 2006 event returned to a Canadian city in what is the quickest return to a country in the event's bidding history (Spencer, 2003). They clearly repeated that feat again for their winning of the 2009 event and, in so doing, Hockey Canada demonstrated its expertise in knowing exactly where its strengths lay and how to maximize them.

Stakeholders

Commitment from all events' stakeholders is a necessary element in order to win a bid. Clearly, funding and organizing partners from both the public and private sectors are key stakeholders, as is the evaluation committee representing the awarding body.

A principal stakeholder group is also the local community. It is essential for the community to be behind a bid and most events recognize this importance by researching their interest and involving them in consultation. A contemporary tool for this process is a website and, early in the planning process, both London and New York developed sites with information on the benefits of hosting the 2012 Olympics.

The name of the game at this stage is to convince stakeholders that there are more benefits than costs in hosting an event. Other media are also key vehicles and the use of public forums, launches and press liaison are all key communications activities. Websites form suitable anchors for the distribution of event strategies, impact reports and feasibility studies, spokespeople comments and progress to date (London 2012, 2003; NYC2012, 2003a).

New York recruited volunteers with the help of its website and then used them in turn to spread the word. Their 'Go Team' was utilized at other sports events, such as the 2003 New York City Triathlon and the USA National Weightlifting Championships. They also distributed promotional materials at stadiums, subways, and festivals and conducted telesales campaigns to recruit further volunteers (NYC2012, 2003b).

The Toronto bid for the 1996 Olympics was marred by public protests and anti-Olympic demonstrations against spending on sports events when poverty and homelessness were a city challenge. Toronto was thought to have the early lead with its bid at the time (Thoma and Chalip, 1996), but did lose out to Atlanta. The costs of getting to that stage and still not understanding the needs and feelings of the public were clearly very high. It is important to programme the campaign so that, when the bid is launched, there is a tide of public welcome. Late in 2002, Britain was expressing some interest in staging the 2012 Olympics. The media followed the story as London Mayor, Ken Livingstone, pushed the claims of the city, supported by the BOC, but against the seemingly cautious national Government. The previously completed impact study by Arup was used as evidence of short- and long-term impacts. Later, a public meeting and a Government fact-finding trip to Lausanne were reported widely in most media. The Government's decision of whether it would support a bid was further delayed by war and an invasion of Iraq. The media and public speculation increased as a result to a point where it appeared unlikely that the Government would provide a sanction. That, in turn, appeared to inspire a feeling of support for a bid. The media were used to enhance that and, on 15 May 2003, the Government announced that it had set aside £2.375 billion to pay for the staging of the 2012 Games in London (London 2012, 2003). The delay, possibly delaying tactics, appeared to have driven public support.

Research plays a key part in this public education exercise. Measures for levels of perception are necessary before a communications plan can be devised. In polls conducted in November and December 2002, New York City and state residents were surveyed about their perception of a potential games in 2012. Around 84% of city residents and 74% of state residents were in favour, and 90 and 89% respectively believed that a games would have a positive impact on the city (NYC2012, 2003b). Research of this kind serves two purposes. First, it provides a benchmark and, secondly, it provides good content for communications activities. Interestingly, in subsequent polls and as disgruntlement grew over the building of a new stadium, the popularity measured lower and to a level that was reported to have affected the city's chances of winning.

Political risk analysis

Thoma and Chalip (1996) stress the importance of assessing the risk of political issues. While strife of any kind is likely to influence the decision to award an event to a bidder, there are other considerations for the bidders themselves. For example, changes in government in stance or personnel may alter bid support. The Millennium Dome in London was initiated by a Tory government and was hampered by problems when, in 1997, a Labour government was elected. The new Prime Minister, Tony Blair, came very close to ending the project despite considerable already high costs. Economic changes, whether taxation or importation related, can also have affect. For example, Manchester City Council's candidature file for the 2000 Olympics was submitted to the IOC with a question over the amount of value added tax (VAT). The file was submitted when it was not clear whether the event would be liable for VAT and so the financial implications at the time were unknown (Department of Environment, 1993). It still remains unclear as to whether VAT will be due for London's 2012 Olympics.

Knowledge

Knowledge of the bidding process and how candidates are evaluated is essential but is, perhaps, only attainable through experience. Patterns exist to substantiate this. Consider those cities that continue to bid after failure, as discussed later in this chapter. There are also those events that have recognized the importance of key personnel and prior knowledge. Vancouver used the expertise of Calgary to support its winning bid for the 2010 Winter Olympics and the 25 Sydney 2000 executives who worked on the 2002 Commonwealth Games were clearly considered to be experts in their field.

Emery (2001) conducted research with 400 major sport events organizers and identified key elements for the improving chances for future successful bidding. They were all concerned with superior knowledge. He identified that a portfolio of events and evidence of successful event management was an advantage for any bidding candidate and, if that was not possible, at least the recruitment of carefully selected personnel was required. In this way, a bid can gain professional credibility. An understanding of the formal decision-making process and those that are to evaluate it was also considered key. One point was that it should not always be assumed that those who evaluate a bid are, in fact, experts and thus bids should reflect that in the way that they are presented. The formal processes and, in particular, the protocols, were identified as essential knowledge and, for those who are new to bidding, this can be a steep learning curve. Individual response from the research demonstrated that not knowing the voting panel members well enough and not being able to compete politically with others on that basis were fundamental barriers to success. Relationship building is clearly important here and knowledge of the needs of the decision-makers is critical.

In addition to knowledge of the processes involved, knowledge of the owning body and its existing corporate partners is also important. More complex organizations like the IOC have various levels of sponsors and suppliers and there are certain rights that they exercise at Olympic events as well as on a year-round basis. For other events, the owners may have existing partners and so it becomes important to recognize how these will relate to the plans for any commercial activities for the event (Graham et al, 2001). Inclusion of competing partners may well weaken the bid, for example.

Knowledge of other past bids and scrutiny of games reports is also necessary (Allen et al, 2002). Where bids went wrong is just as important as where they went right. The transfer of Olympic knowledge via the Olympic Games Knowledge Management (OGKM) service is now well developed for future Olympic bidding cities and currently has useful knowledge on Sydney 2000, Salt Lake 2002, Athens 2004 and Torino 2006.

The bidding process is a competition and, as with all competitions, knowing the nature and extent of the competition is paramount. This is sport after all. One further key factor identified by Emery (2001) was that bidding teams should acquire knowledge not only of rival bid content but also of those individuals who will be presenting it. The capacity to highlight where one bid is better at meeting the required criteria can only be achieved once information on other bids is understood.

Management

In addition to experienced executives, bid teams also need leaders and figure-heads. At all levels of bids, it is personnel that make it winnable. Olympic bids commonly use key figures with national and international influence in their teams. The English FA employed Bobby Charlton and Geoff Hurst, members of the 1966 World Cup winning England football team, in its bid for the 2006 World Cup. Germany utilized Franz Beckenbauer, a member of the West German team that lost the 1966 World Cup Final and won that bid. David Beckham, Tony Blair and Matthew Pinsent were used by the London 2012 bid team with comments of support and attendance at key events including the IOC session in Singapore. These are examples of the use of spokespersons but, what is of more importance, is the appointment of the senior executive that drives the bid through. Emery's research identified that a known key figurehead for inside knowledge of the decision-makers in the bid process was crucial (Emery, 2001). As far as the New York and London bids for the 2012 Olympics were concerned, this turned into a battle between two Americans, Daniel Doctoroff and Barbara Cassani respectively, although significantly Sebastian Coe was brought in to replace the latter.

Communications

The importance of the use of strategic communications in the winning of bids has already been highlighted, but a key aspect of this is the need to create a strong brand. The larger the event the more agencies, partners and organizations are involved and so the importance of having one message becomes even greater. Whatever the scale of the event, a brand will help integrate communications. Of course, neither a brand nor communications alone will win a bid and, if a bid does not meet all the specified requirements, as discussed above in the IOC model, then it will be technically flawed.

Key components of the branding process are the creation of themes and logos and London and its four rivals were all active with designs launched in late 2003. However, it was the ability to overcome key issues as a part of the content of the bid and how that was incorporated into that brand, or at least it was the perception by the IOC members of that ability, that determined London's win. Previously, the issues that Beijing overcame to win the Olympics for 2008 involved the building of a brand that required the repositioning of a city and changes in international perception. The brand of 'New Beijing, Great Olympics', was key (see Beijing Insight 3.1 in Chapter 3). Aside from the controversy that still remains, this re-imaging was at least achieved as far as was required to win the bid; the objective in hand at the time.

LOSING BIDS/WINNING STRATEGIES

Bidding can be an expensive and risky exercise but it can be used as a means to an end in itself.

For both large- and small-scale events, there are lessons to be learned from the bidding exercise. The lessons learned, as discussed above, can become invaluable in winning next time or at least putting in a bid document that is better prepared.

Several cities have continued to bid for Olympic Games and then used that experience to win. Table 7.2 shows that since 2000, three out of the eight past and known future games hosts, Winter and Summer, have had previous bids and finished in second place in those elections. In addition, while the other five cities had not bid in recent history, there were previous bids from neighbouring cities from each of the countries concerned. However, Sweden has made five consecutive bids and not yet hosted an Olympics (Ostersund in 2002, 1998 and 1994, Falun in 1992 and 1988). There is therefore no conclusive relationship between bidding and eventually winning. However, the use of previous experience has probably been of use in improving and developing bids and it is worth noting that, of the cities that bid for the 2012 Olympics as shown in Table 7.3, Paris and Istanbul, each had two recently previous failed bids and no doubt called on their previous experience in an attempt to be more successful in 2005 when the winning city was declared, albeit unsuccessfully

Table 7.2	Recent Successful Olympic Bidding Cities Indicating Recent Previous Bidding History by Each City or Cities from the Same Country Since 1988	

Host		Previous Bidding History
Sochi	2014	Nil Moscow 2012 (5th), St Petersburg 2004 (1st round)
London	2012	Nil Birmingham 1992 (5th), Manchester 1996 (4th), 2000 (3rd)
Vancouver	2010	Nil Toronto 2008 (2nd), 1996 (2nd), Quebec 2002 (4th), Calgary 1988 (host)
Beijing	2008	2000 (2nd)
Turin	2006	Nil Rome 2004 (2nd), Aosta 1998 (5th), Cortina 1992 (5th), 1988 (3rd)
Athens	2004	1996 (2nd)
Salt Lake	2002	1998 (2nd) Anchorage 1994 (3rd), 1992 (6th)
Sydney	2000	Nil Melbourne 1996 (4th), Brisbane 1992 (4th)

Adapted from GamesBids.com (2008)

in the end. Madrid and Rio de Janeiro are also applicants for the 2016 Olympic Games and, at one point in 2008 (early May), Rio was standing favourite (Gamesbids.com, 2008). In January 2009, Tokyo had taken up the running.

If there are objectives that can be achieved via the submission of a bid, whether that bid wins or not, then stakeholder support may be that much more forthcoming. If the local population can see that there are benefits in

Table 7.3	2012 Olympics Bidding Cities Indicating Previous Olympic Hosting and Bidding History – The Final Resulting Positions are Shown in Brackets, London Being the Winning Hosts

	Previous Bidding History
Havana	2008 1st round elimination
Istanbul	4th 2008, 5th 2000
Leipzig	Nil
London (Host)	Hosted 1948 Games
Madrid (3rd)	2nd 1972
Moscow (5th)	Hosted 1980 Games, 2nd 1976
New York (4th)	Nil
Paris (2nd)	3rd 2008, 2nd 1992
Rio de Janeiro	Nil

Adapted from GamesBids.com (2008)

the short term even from a failed bid then they may be more supportive. It is important not to lose sight of the overall goal, however, and so there must also be a strong case for the benefits that will be gained during and post the event in the longer term. Torino did not expect to win its bid to stage the 2006 Winter Olympics and the IOC needed to spend time with the city in order for it to consider more fully constructing facilities that would be of long-term sporting benefit in the city (Felli, 2002). Naturally, Torino's objectives changed once the bid was won.

The extent of the loss for non-successful bidding cities is a contemporary issue. At city authority level, where there is an increased need for account-ability, there is surprisingly little in the way of evaluation of the bidding process from that perspective and, in particular, of the risk of losing. The question therefore does arise, why do so many cities bid to host such complex projects when there is no real prize for even coming second (Emery 2002). London, for example, had a budget of £29.1 million for its 2012 Olympic bid, made up of £10 million contributions from the Government via its Depart-ment of Culture, Media and Sport and the London Development Agency, and just over £9 million from commercial partners and sponsors (Culf, 2005). The immediate answer may well be that winning, and all that can be achieved because of that, is a risk worth taking. This is hardly a strategic approach, however. It also begs the question, can bids be used more productively?

There is a necessity at each stage of the bidding process for further resources and, as a consequence, there is an increase in bureaucracy and numbers and levels of stakeholders that need to be involved. This all adds up to greater levels of uncertainty (Emery, 2002). On the one hand, a winning bid entails that the newly appointed host city become a 'time bound fran-chisee' with all the responsibility that comes with seeing the project through to a successful conclusion. On the other hand, a losing bid ends up with only sunk costs. Research has been undertaken to identify why so many local authorities bid and, more specifically, if they attempted to eradicate such risks and if they did, how (Emery, 2002)? A number of key factors for the winning of bids were identied but what was also revealed was that there was a propensity for bidding local authorities to make key decisions outside of the normal processes they would typically go through. Essex and Chalkley (2003) also suggest that this is an important factor in that there tends to be less formality to decisions concerning the development of a bid and such deci-sions can even be perceived as undemocratic where pre-evaluations and feasibility assessments are not comprehensive and are 'fast-tracked' without public consultation. In other words, there is little attention paid to diligent event planning processes let alone political requirements and, as a conse-quence, risk is increased.

An example of 'fast track' practice may well be found in the decision to award the 2010 Super Bowl to The New York Jets football organization (Roberts, 2005). The NFL made its award in March 2005 with the condition that the Jets become the owners of the new 'West Side Stadium' that was to be built and also used as the main Olympic stadium if New York won its 2012 Olympic bid. For this particular Super Bowl, the NFL waived its rule that dictates that a team must use its stadium for two seasons prior to the event (the stadium was scheduled to be built by 2009). The body also made its 2010 venue decision ahead of its decision for 2009. The decision was made shortly after the IOC 2012 bid evaluation delegation had visited New York and recent media had expressed concern over whether the stadium would be in place in time for 2012. A critical assessment of this process might assume that a number of interested parties had collaborated in order to help get the stadium built and allay fears in the public domain prior to the IOC decision the following July and the award of the 2012 Games.

What about the immediate loss of those cities with unsuccessful bids, what is the financial extent of their loss? Alderslade (2001) estimates that it costs a bidding city at the national round, up to US$10 million and that this cost then escalates to approximately and, on average, US$30 million for each city that then goes on to compete at the international round. However, there is another cost factor to consider. When there is public/private spending on event bids, there are detractors that will claim there are opportunity costs, for example, the same amount not spent on new and needed housing, medical welfare and investment for employment. In addition to the loss of the financial investment, there can also be a loss of public confidence. One of the few arguments a city has in therefore still going ahead with a bid is to demonstrate that there are longer-term benefits in the form of legacies, thus events are used as a justification for local development as well as a stimulus for it (Andranovich et al., 2001). Salt Lake City, for example, justified its bidding for the 2002 winter Olympics by claiming that it was to use the bid in order to achieve its goal of becoming the 'US winter sports capital' and that it would achieve this whether it won the bid or not. In 1989, the city passed a referendum to support a bid on the back of this justification locally and then spent a further 6 years in winning the Games. This period of legacy building then extended over the next 7 years of Games preparation. This would appear to be a rare case, however.

To date, bidding has been mainly done from the risky position of 'if the city wins it will gain, but if it loses it will not', in other words, legacies will be provided only if a Games is hosted. London, in its bid for the 2012 Olympics, conducted a poll in late 2004 in order to determine the extent of public support for its bid. The survey revealed that most people in Britain believed that a London Games would leave behind a legacy; 77% of respondents believed the Games would bring long-term after-use benefit and, of those respondents who were Londoners, 81% saw these as advantages (Marketing Week, 2004). London was using the Olympics as a catalyst for a speedier approach for an already planned regeneration of East London but, if the bid was unsuccessful, no new sports related physical legacies would be built.

So, can bids be made with a less riskier undertaking if there are legacies that can be produced even when the bid is unsuccessful? Adopting a long-term perspective for bidding may be one way of attempting to reduce all the risks involved in making a bid to stage a major international sports event, including the gaining of public confidence. As discussed above, an initial bid may be used as a pre-requisite to develop important relationships (and experience) to give future event bids more chance of winning. In particular, this can come down to the individuals that are involved, for example, the same executives Australia used in successive attempts to win the 2000 Olympic Games (Westerbeek et al 2002). In this sense, bidding can be used by some as a vehicle for long-term objectives which may necessitate a number of bid attempts. This can be described as being a cyclical or a continuous process (Ingerson and Westerbeek 1999). There are other examples. Brisbane bid for the 1992 Olympics and lost, however, the bid is claimed to have focused the city on bidding for other events and, in 2001, they staged the Goodwill Games. Having lost its bid for the 1996 Olympics, Athens duly bid for and won the 1997 World Athletics Championships and, only days after that event, was selected as the host for the 2004 Olympics (Alderslade, 2001).

This long-term planning perspective is clearly being strategically used by some. The research undertaken by Alderslade (2001), for example, cites the thoughts of several executives from US event organizations that had been involved in bidding for major international sports events. The managing director of the 2012 Florida Olympic bid that failed at the national round of bidding is reported to have highlighted the importance of the legacy component at the bidding stage for both winning and losing. He claimed that a bidding community can still benefit from the relationships that have been developed because they can still enable future growth. Executives from three other US cities that lost at the same national round of bidding, Tampa, Cincinnati and Dallas, were reported to agree. It is claimed that Dallas, for example, was still able to gain a legacy from the profile it gained despite its early elimination in launching a Dallas/Fort Worth Regional Sports Commission that was charged with marketing North Texas for the recruitment of future events.

A long-term perspective in evaluating the return on investment on bidding might be an approach that not only sees a reduced risk over the long term but a legacy from the initial failed bid. In other words, the experience and relationships that have been acquired are the legacy that can be exploited in order to produce a more improved bid next time. What the examples above do not identify, however, is whether or not there might also be legacies in the form of physical facilities, win or loss, and whether they might then be featured in future bids. There is an irony concerning Torino and its winning bid for the 2006 Olympics, for example. It submitted its bid in order to use the process as a catalyst for the development of new facilities, whether it won or not and, as indicated above, it did not expect to win. This is not something that would necessarily be in the public domain but it might explain the attention paid to the city by the IOC's Gilbert Felli after they had won and his encouragement of them to provide more legacies for winter sports in the city, as discussed earlier.

There are examples of cities that have gained physical legacies as a result of bidding and losing. Manchester, in particular, as previously explained was intent on following its event led strategy of regeneration of its east side and, despite not succeeding with either of its bids for the 1996 and 2000 Olympics, it still built its aquatics pool, Sport City and the City of Manchester Stadium. However, it did require there to be another event as the catalyst, the 2002 Commonwealth Games. Otherwise, the fast-tracked infrastructure and stadiums may or may not have been built until a later and undeterminable point in time. Toronto, on the other hand, bid for and lost both the 1996 and 2008 Olympics and yet it is claimed that it has gained from these bids not least with new physical structures. Many of the city's bid-generated plans to develop its largely underused waterfront are, in fact, still going ahead. It is estimated that this CD\$12 billion project will extend through to at least 2020 and that it will involve residential and commercial buildings as well as a new freeway, parks and waterfront greenbelts. Toronto clearly used its bids as a catalyst for development that was not dependent on whether the bids were successful (Alderslade 2001). It is important to note though that this does assume that strategies for physical legacies were developed as a part of the planning for the bids.

There are more recent examples of strategic bidding for long-term success whatever the outcome. As discussed in Chapter 4, in contrast with the London 2012 Olympic bid, an analysis of New York's bid for the same games, provides an example of a city that had planned to benefit from its bid, win or lose. New York provided details on how they would be providing social, cultural, economic and sports legacies in its bid with plans for the infrastructure and physical building of facilities for long-term use. As indicated earlier, the IOC does not require that a host city build new facilities and therefore does not require that there be physical legacies of any sort. It does, however, look to protect against the prospect of 'white elephants' and therefore does require that, if there is to be new construction, there are long-term after-use plans in place (Olympic Review, 2005).

A bidding city can therefore be judged on the planning details it provides in a bid book. London was quite ambiguous in its plans for after-use and was clearly only planning to build new sports facilities if it won as stated above but, in contrast, New York had a more impressive plan for its planned facilities. Despite the confusion over whether its preferred new main Olympic stadium would be on the west side of the city (Manhattan), every single one of its planned permanent sports venues at the time of the bid not only had its after-use decided but also had its after-use management and operators nominated and therefore in place (Gonzalez, 2004) (see Figure 4.1 in Chapter 4). There was a firm statement in the bid that all proposed Olympic venues had a detailed post-use plan and that a New York Olympic Legacy Foundation would be set up to help maintain facilities in the long term (NYC2012, 2004, 2005). Perhaps more importantly though, every single one of its planned new sports facilities, apart from a bridge that was a part of the rowing lakes development, was to be built whether the city won the bid or not (Gonzalez, 2004). This was at least the stated position at the time.

Though difficult to evaluate, there is also political impact and benefit that may be gained from bidding for the right event and submitting it knowing it probably will not win. This can also be used to develop business links and demonstrate a commitment to staging sports events that may bear well for future political and trade profile. There have no doubt been other Olympic candidates that have prepared their bids and not thought that they would ever be successful. A bid for 2012 by Havana can at least be part of a wider strategy for the development of tourism in particular and possibly the lobbying for the lifting of US embargos (the city also bid for 2008 and was eliminated prior to the final IOC session).

SUMMARY

The bidding process is becoming increasingly more important as sports events become catalysts for wider strategies. While this is a relatively recent phenomenon, it is, nevertheless, one that has also become quite sophisticated for some events. The comprehensive model provided by the IOC and the bidding for Olympic Games is one that can provide important guidelines for those parties that want to bid for other sports events. There are many event owners that do not require such a comprehensive bid and, yet, with competition becoming more intense, bid teams could do worse than follow such a detailed approach.

Key factors in the winning of bids include the management of and communication with stakeholders, in particular with the local community. There are cases and research to propose that without the support of a local community a bid will not win. For the IOC, it is a required measurement via survey methods and is also a key factor for the recruitment of volunteers, sponsors and media interest, all of which are important if the bid is to be won. An analysis of the political risk, the recruitment of key management, including leadership, and knowledge of the competition and the bidding process are also all considered to be vital factors.

Bidding can be an expensive strategy, even if the objectives are wider set and involve tourism and facility development over the long term. The cost implications need careful consideration at this stage of the event planning process. One strategy is to write-off any costs for a failed bid. Alternatively, and from a strategic standpoint, it is also possible to identify positive outcomes from failed bids. There may be long-term legacies that can be gained. If costs are high and yet it is still possible to achieve benefits, then it is more likely that the bid will receive support from stakeholders. The long-term benefit of stadiums, tourism or social benefits may exceed the costs. Additionally, it seems likely that previous experience of bidding for an event is a key factor in formulating a better bid next time and so a long-term strategy of possibly several bids may also be considered to be cost effective if the event is eventually won.

QUESTIONS

Visit the websites for the 2016 Olympic bidding cities of Chicago, Madrid, Rio de Janeiro and Tokyo (include Baku, Doha and Prague: those bidding cities that did not make the final round if you can) and consider the following:

1. Compare and contrast their efforts in attempting to win local support for their respective bids.

2. What key elements would you consider as important considerations for each city in their preparation of their respective bids?

3. What might each city have gained in the long term from their bid despite failing to win the right to host the 2016 Olympics?

REFERENCES

Alderslade, J. (2001). Focus on sports facilities & conference centers: Olympic loss, economic win. Economic Development Now. International Economic Development Council. 11 November. www.iedonline.org/EDNow/11_15_01/page3 (accessed 28 May, 2003).

Allen, J., O'Toole, W., McDonnell, I. and Harris, R. (2002). *Festival and Special Event Management*, 2nd edn. Queensland, Australia, John Wiley & Sons, Chapter 5.

Andranovich, G., Burbank, M. and Heying, C. (2001). Olympic cities: Lessons learned from mega-event politics. *Journal of Urban Affairs*, 23(2), 13–131.

Arup (2002). *London Olympics 2012 Costs and Benefits: Summary*. In association with Insignia Richard Ellis, 21 May 2002. www.olympics.org/library/boa (accessed 11 November 2002).

Beijing 2008 (2008). www.beijing2008.cn (accessed 11 February 2008).

Culf, A. (2005). The man who is making a £2bn mark on London. *The Guardian*, 27 October. The Guardian Group.

Department of Environment (1993). *The Stadium Legacy, in The British Olympic Bid: Manchester 2000*. Manchester, Department of Environment, Section 12, Vol. 2.

Department of the Environment and Heritage (2003). *Why the Green Games?* 19 September. Australian Government. www.deh.gov.au/events/greengames/whygreen (accessed 15 December 2003).

Emery, P. (2001). Bidding to Host a Major Sports Event: Strategic Investment or Complete Lottery? In C. Gratton, and I. Henry (eds), *Sport in the City: The Role of Sport in Economic and Social Regeneration*. London, Routledge, Chapter 7.

Emery, P. (2002). Bidding to host a major sports event: the local organising perspective. *International Journal of Public Sector Management*, 15(4), 316–335.

Essex, S. and Chalkley, B. (2003). Urban transformation from hosting the Olympic Games. University lecture on the Olympics. Centre d'Estudis Olimpics, Univesitat Autonoma de Barcelona. www.olympicstudies.uab.es/lectures (accessed 19 March. 2005).

Felli, G. (2002). Transfer of Knowledge (TOK): A games management tool. A paper delivered at the *IOC–UIA Conference: Architecture and International Sporting Events*, Olympic Museum, Lausanne. June 2002, IOC.

FINA (2003). www.fina.org/feds_bids (accessed 14 December 2003).

GamesBids.com (2008). www.gamesbids.com/english/past (accessed 1 May 2008).

Getz, D. (1997). *Event Management and Event Tourism*. New York, Cognizant, Chapter 4.

Gonzalez, M.D. (2004). Director of Venue Planning, NYC2012. NYC2012 Presentation. New York University, 4 November, 2004.

Graham, S., Neirotti, L. and Goldblatt, J. (2001). *The Ultimate Guide to Sports Marketing*, 2nd edn. New York, McGraw-Hill, Chapter 12.

Gratton, C. and Taylor, P. (2000). *Economics of Sport and Recreation*. London, Spon Press, Chapter 10.

Harris, C. and Bagnato, A. (2003). *Valley is Super Bowl Favorite*. The Arizona Republic, 30 October. www.azcentral.com (accessed 14 December 2003).

Ingerson, L. and Westerbeek, H. (1999). Determining key success criteria for attracting hallmark sporting events. Pacific Tourism Review, 3, 239–253.

IOC (2002). Manual for Candidate Cities for the Games of the XXIX Olympiad 2008. Part 2.2 Model Candidature File. 13 February. www.olympic.org/uk/utilities/reports/level_2k (accessed 15 December).

IOC (2008a). Candidature Acceptance Procedure: Games of the XXXI Olympiad 2016. www.olympic.org (accessed 1 May 2008).

IOC (2008b). Candidature Acceptance Procedure: Games of the XXX Olympiad 2012. www.olympic.org (accessed 1 May 2008).

IOC (2008c). www.olympic.org/uk/games/beijing/election (accessed 5 February 2008).

Kronos (1997). The Economic Impact of Sports Events Staged in Sheffield 1990–1997. A report produced by Kronos for Destination Sheffield, Sheffield City Council and Sheffield International Venues Ltd. Final report, December 1997.

London 2012 (2003). www.london2012.com/London/Timeline_of_the_Bid (accessed 9 December).

Marketing Week (2004). Jumping the final hurdle. Centaur Communications 2000, 25 November, 2004.

Meisegeier, D. (1995). Sydney Olympics and the Environment. Case No. 184, The TED Case Studies Online Journal. www.american.edu/TED/SYDNEY (accessed 15 December 2003).

NYC2012 (2003a). www.nyc2012.com/team.sec6.sub1 (accessed 9 December).

NYC2012 (2003b). www.nyc2012.com/news.20021028.1 (accessed 12 December).

NYC2012 (2004). Candidate File – Bid Book. www.nyc2012.com/en/bid_book.html NYC2012 Inc. (accessed 23 November, 2004).

NYC2012 (2005). Urban Transformation. www.nyc2012.com/index_flash.aspx (accessed 15 February, 2005).

New York City 2012 Bid Book (2004). *Candidature file for the Games of the XXX Olympiad.* 15 November 2004, New York, NYC2012.

Olympic Review (2005). Games success and the importance of leaving a legacy. April, 2005. Lausanne, IOC.

Roberts, K. (2005). NY stadium set for Super Bowl. 23 March, 2005. www.sportbusiness.com/news (accessed 24 March, 2005).

SOCOG (2001). www.gamesinfo.com.au/postgames/en/pg000329 (accessed 12 September 2003).

Spencer, D. (2003). *Canada Awarded 2006 World Junior Championship*. 18 September. Canoe.com www.slamsports.com (accessed 14 December 2003).

Sports Tricker (2003). *Arizona to Host 2008 Super Bowl*. 30 October. Sports Tricker Enterprises. www.clari.net/qs.se/webnews (accessed 14 December 2003).

Thoma, J. and Chalip, L. (1996). *Sport Governance in the Global Community*. Morgantown, Fitness Information Technology, Chapter 6.

USA Track & Field (2008). www.usatf.org/groups (accessed 1 May 2008).

Weber Shandwick (2003). www.webershandwick.co.uk/imia/content.cfm (accessed 14 December 2003).

Westerbeek, H., Turner, P. and Ingerson, L. (2002). Key success factors in bidding for hallmark sporting events. *International Marketing Review*, 19(3), 303–322.

CHAPTER 8

Event Implementation

Breakdown after the Piazza Di Siena equestrian event in the Borghese Gardens in Rome.

LEARNING OBJECTIVES

After studying this chapter, you should be able to:

- Identify the implementation planning and execution requirements for sports events

- understand the requirement to align implementation planning and the execution of the event to long-term objectives

- understand the importance of preparing for a successful event breakdown, handover, after-use and long-term event evaluation

189

INTRODUCTION

The next two stages in the event planning process occur after the decision to go ahead with the event. Collectively, these two stages involve the implementation of the event. The first involves the pre-planning of all that is required to produce the event where the aim is clearly to deliver an event at the right time and on the day required. The second stage is the execution of the event itself, that being the management of all that has been planned. Both of these stages are discussed in detail in this chapter with the intention of highlighting the processes that are required rather than being a definitive production list.

While it is the period that lasts from the decision to go ahead through to the closing of an event that is the theme of this chapter, the focus will be on how important it is strategically to identify these areas at an earlier stage in the planning process. The processes to be discussed are required whatever the scale of the event. While the level of complexity and quantity may differ from event to event, the same kind of organization, planning, division of responsibility and careful attention to detail is required as much for the local sports event as it is for the major event (Hall, 1997). This chapter is therefore concerned with the processes that are applicable for all scales of event rather than with a detailed checklist approach. The chapter will conclude by identifying all that needs to be implemented during this period for the achievement of long-term requirements, principally by discussing the needs for after-use and of after-users during implementation planning and the implementation of the event itself.

EVENT IMPLEMENTATION

Having made the decision to go ahead with the event, the planning that is required becomes very specific and complex. Initially, there is the planning of all that is required for the production of the event and then there is the execution of the event itself. The focus here is not just to identify how these two stages are managed in real time, but also how and why it is strategically important to have considered the areas at the concept formulation and feasibility stages of the event planning process.

Implementation planning

The duration of this stage of the planning process can vary greatly. An Olympic host city gets to know it has won its bid 7 years ahead while fixture lists for major professional sports leagues can be available up to 3 months before kick-off. Annual events of all sizes are often scheduled more than 12 months ahead and yet there are those that have shorter lead-times, particularly those that are rescheduled or relocated. The nature of the planning of an event, whatever the lead-time and whether there are existing models from previous events to follow or not, can become extremely complex.

The process here is concerned with everything that is required to execute the event successfully. This requires special management skills. The event, whatever its timescale, is transient, with a start and finish. It is a project and it requires project management.

At this stage, an event manager needs to be able to draw on organizational skills, manage personnel, market, sell and negotiate (sometimes barter), relate to different publics, read a balance sheet, be a role model and often get his or her hands dirty. Above all, it is the ability to multi-task effectively and efficiently that is prevalent here. It is a complicated requirement that becomes more sophisticated as the event gets larger and therefore requires systems and methodology to ensure effective management. Project management methodology is wholly appropriate for the task (Emery, 2001; Allen et al, 2002). Emery suggests that sports event management is a subset of project management and is bounded by three key factors: external pressures, organizational politics and personal objectives. The complexity of the task may be explained by further evaluating the relationships that have to be managed. For example, as the numbers of people and resources grow so does the requirement for new relationships. The event management project can be further complicated by the requirement for long planning periods.

The successful management of an event project therefore requires a system that will manage the assessment of what has to be done, by whom and when, and plan it in sufficient time so that the execution of the project is as a result of the planning that has gone before. The process is as follows (Allen et al, 2002):

Step 1: Scope of work

An assessment of the amount of work that is required. This is not such an easy first step as it will be modified at each of the next five steps. The process must therefore be iterative.

Step 2: Work breakdown

The categories and sub-categories involved in an event need to be identified and broken down into manageable units. The following serve as a general list of typical areas and provide a guideline on the time lines involved in their planning. Key issues for long-term planning are discussed where appropriate.

Personnel

Staffing. Managers, crew, stewards and security staff are required for event management teams and, depending upon the scale of the event, there will be different points at which they will be recruited. In bidding for the Olympics, the New York 2012 Olympic Bid Organization and London 2012 bid teams started recruiting in 2003. The latter appointed Barbara Cassani, the former chief executive of budget airline, 'Go' in June 2003 as Chairperson. She is an American by birth but this appointment is an example of an organization appointing the best person for the job at the time. Interestingly, this changed as the bid process and period progressed and, despite doing a lot of the hard work, she was replaced shortly before the bid was submitted.

The appointment of managers is key for all the decisions concerning the implementation of the event and most events start with the appointment of the leadership. Barbara Cassani was appointed prior to any other members of the current team but she was quickly involved in the selection of a Chief Executive, Chief Operations and Marketing Officers.

In creating an event, the creator can remain in control and appoint key personnel as and when required once the decision to go ahead has been made. In the case of New York's bid for the 2012 Olympics, the idea of bidding was first conceived by Daniel Doctoroff, who was the Deputy Mayor of the city. He first had the idea in the late 1990s and it was inspired out of his role in leading New York's economic development and rebuilding efforts (NYC2012, 2003). He also oversaw the city's physical and economic response to the events of 11 September 2001 ('9/11') including coordinating other city agencies and the federal government. His appointment in strategically leading the New York bid secured the enthusiasm of a creator as well as harnessed the efforts of an event bid that incorporated long-term redevelopment plans and legacies (see Chapter 4).

In a top-down process, managers are appointed into position. Which positions are filled is dependent upon the remainder of the breakdown of the work that follows. This process begins post the decision to go ahead with the event but, if there is a bid involved, then the process starts at the point after a decision has been made to bid.

Once a senior management structure is in place, further decisions concerning the implementation planning of the event can take place and there are two key components of this process:

1. Senior management needs to be appointed as soon as possible in order for planning to continue effectively.

2. An event leader has to be put in place first.

One further factor here is that it is essential that there is a clear line of management that has one and only one leader. Leadership is a discipline for discussion elsewhere but, for the effective project management of sports events, one clearly identified leader is necessary. The management of an event needs to be integrated, flexible and dynamic (Hall, 1997) and, while it requires clear management procedures, management decision-making needs to be responsive and effective and, when decisions are required from the strategic apex, they are better from one leader. Emery's (2001) research showed that this was an important factor for the bidding process and most major events have made the appointment of their figurehead their first task.

Volunteers. Hall (1997) indicates that one of the key management problems to be addressed is the dependence of events on the support of both the local community and volunteers. The latter are, in fact, dependent on the former. Management complexity may depend on the size of the community in which the event is hosted which will, in turn, affect the numbers of volunteers that are able to assist the event. It is clear that at major events the need for volunteers is large. The 2002 Commonwealth Games recruited over 12 000 local volunteers from the surrounds of Manchester. Salt Lake City provided up to 30 000 for the 2002 Winter Olympics and Sydney had up to 62 000 (47 000 for the Olympics and 15 000 for the Paralympics), which is claimed as the largest gathering of volunteers at one time, in one place, in Australia's history (Brettell, 2001). The implications are that this is an area that requires considerable planning and also costing. While they are volunteers, there are still costs for recruiting processes, uniforms, food, transport, etc. (Graham et al., 2001). The partnership  with agencies in training is also an educational component that requires planning. The 2002 Commonwealth Games intended there to be educational benefits for those that volunteered and provided senior appointees to receive certificated training. The Pre-Volunteer Programme and Passport 2002 was set up by the North West 2002 Single Regeneration Board in order to engage people in local communities and was intended as being of social importance in the long term (Manchester' City Council, 2003).

A record number of volunteers were used at the 2008 Beijing Olympics, up to 70 000 for the Games and 30 000 for the Paralympics. Volunteers have to be recruited, trained, clothed and managed and accommodation may also have to be provided. Students stayed in the city of Beijing for the summer and via collaborations between BOCOG and various universities, student lodgings were used to house thousands of temporary residents. Volunteers also have to be fed and in the middle of Olympic Green a pleasant sunken area was used exclusively as a catering and site management catering zone as seen here.

Volunteers are kitted out with clothing and refreshment for the day ahead at Olympic Green, 2008 Beijing Olympics.

Beijing Insight 8.1
Beijing 2008 Olympics: Volunteer Management
The management of the recruitment, training and deployment of Beijing's 2008 Olympics volunteers was a long and complex process. The following is a breakdown of what was involved.

Recruitment

The Volunteer Programme sought to recruit the following types of volunteers:

'Towards Olympics' volunteers were deployed early in the planning process and were used in events to help popularize the Olympic Movement, to promote Beijing's new image and the volunteer programme itself.

'Games-Time' volunteers were recruited by BOCOG to help with accreditation, spectator, athlete and official liaison from the end of August 2006 for both the Olympic and Paralympic Games.

'BOCOG Pre-Games' volunteers assisted at the offices and events in the run-up to the Games and were mainly made up of student and professional cohorts from March 2004. Specific roles included translation, technology and project management support.

'City' volunteers recruitment began in early 2007 and sought those that could fulfill roles that could attend stations that gave out information in the streets, hospitals, hotels, and cultural centres. They were also involved in translation services, news collection and editing, secretarial services and at pre-Games events including the Torch Relay.

'Social' volunteers were recruited to serve during the Games to assist in keeping social order and maintain the environment.

There were a number of different types of volunteer role, some requiring extensive training and others requiring specific skills and education. These were:

Translation and interpretation

Protocol and reception – receiving IOC, NOC and international federation officials

Contest organization – venue and equipment preparation

Environment management – inspection and protection implementation

Market development – sponsor liaison and support

Technology – venue and media systems operations

Food and beverage – catering services

Spectator services – turnstile and steward operations

Medical services – medical provision for spectators, athletes and officials

Continued

Beijing Insight 8.1—cont'd

Anti-doping services – testing and reporting

Venue management – staff supervision and deployment

Security services – venue security

News operations – support services for accredited media

Photography services – support services for accredited photographers and broadcasters

Logistics and distribution – venue inventory and supply control

Transportation – courtesy driving services

Venue administration – venue office and administrational support

Accreditation service for athletes, media and officials

Ticketing services – ticket sales and distribution

The basic requirements of volunteers were laid out in manuals and were as follows:

1. Capacity to work voluntarily

2. Born prior to 30 June 1990 and in good health

3. Willingness to abide by China's laws and regulations

4. Capacity to participate prior to the Games

5. Capacity to serve for at least 7 consecutive days during the Games

6. Native or learnt Chinese speaking but with the ability to speak other languages

However, more specifically, they were obliged to undergo training for identified roles and adopt Games-time policies.

Teachers and students in Beijing, including those from outside China, could apply via dedicated institution based recruitment offices. Other volunteers had access to online recruitment sites. Following application, the process included an interview, position assignment, background checks and offers.

Training

There were four different types of training, general familiarization of the Olympic Movement, IOC and Olympic Games and Paralympics, together with Chinese culture and knowledge of Beijing, professional services, venue familiarization of functions and sports and role specific training.

The methods of training included online, face-to-face and experientials and via educational institutions, consultancy services as well as BOCOG appointed managers.

The incentives included an accreditation card for the Games or Paralympics, a uniform, meals during service, transportation and accident insurance.

General guidelines for basic decorum formed the basis of the intial general training. This included rules for politeness, dress, attitude, honesty and guidelines on not becoming over-familiar and respecting cultural differences. Guidelines on how to sit, stand and walk were also given. The exact nature of a handshake was taught and the adoption of 'ladies first' was implemented.

To ensure wider appreciation of cultural differences, taboos in certain cultures were identified. These included the non-use of the left hand to hold food, no finger pointing, not touching heads or personal belongings. The eating orders, limitations in the use of colours and numbers by certain cultures were also included in this training.

Emergency policies and procedure training was also given at this point.

Examples of Specific Training
Quindao sailing rescue team – this team consisted of 37 members and consisted of extensive experiential and on-the-job training of more than 160 hours followed by 300 hours of sea operations that included actual rescues at the pre-Olympic events. The selection process in the first place was rigorous and included tests for agility, swimming, diving and first aid plus interviews.

Language training – a team of volunteers spent a 4-month intensive programme learning Spanish in Cuba in early 2006. The volunteers were selected from four Beijing universities. The volunteer programme aimed in general to cover 20 different foreign languages.

Source: Beijing 2008 (2008)

Officials. Many sports officials that are recruited to work at sports events are also volunteers. During the summer, there are numbers of just such people working at UK athletics track and field meetings as lane and pit judges. Whether they are paid or not, their recruitment can be made easier via association with the appropriate governing bodies and for that there may be long lead and planning times involved.

Stakeholders

Customers. Customers, whether they are purchasers of tickets, hospitality, sponsorship, advertising or merchandising, have the potential to spend with the event again. With care and attention they may remain loyal for the long term. The key is customer relationship marketing

(CRM) where the customer's lifetime asset value to the event is considered over the long term. This is dealt with elsewhere in this book but this process continues throughout the planning and implementation of the event.

The entertainment of customers is part of this process because it is the meeting of these fundamental needs that will help with their adoption. Therefore, the 'show' element of the sports event is critical. Not necessarily dancing and pom-poms, but customer orientated provision that enhances the experience. A tight production that runs seamlessly, can show due respect for the customer and should impress them. Clean restrooms and ambient eating provision is expected but, nevertheless, welcomed. Easy access and transportation systems are appreciated and spectator entertainment and good presentation add to the spectacle. So what is experienced at the event is key for the long-term retention of that customer.

Partners and associate partners. Whether they are investors, media partners, sponsors, providers of key supply to the event or governing bodies, there are the same long-term relationships to be nurtured during these stages of planning and implementation.

Participants. The performers that form the focus for the spectacle are clearly an important element in the provision of customer value. As can be seen above, this is of critical importance over the long term too. Therefore, the choice, if there is one, of who participates is key. If you are identifying potential key teams or individuals who will add value to your event then they need to be nurtured as key customers themselves. This may be in the form of VIP treatment, the care and attention given to their families or the state of their transportation or accommodation. For larger events, this may also require the skills of dealing with agents and/or marketing agencies, charities who 'lend' their supporting celebrities or the media who have the power to bring along key players. What is also critical is that participatory-based events rely on not only these customers re-entering or taking part next time, but also on them being intrinsically a part of everyone else's event experience. Their singular enjoyment will impact on the enjoyment of others and so on. The show in which they participate also needs to give value. As in all of these cases researching the customers' needs provides a way of identifying what kind of show is required.

Yao Ming in action at the 2008 Beijing Olympics, one of the chinese 'celebrity' stars of the 2008 Games. While the accommodation in the Athlete Village is basic, the experience has to be unrivalled and that is why even the highest profile sports stars like the world no. 1 tennis player and 2008 gold medallist, Rafa Nadal, enjoyed staying there.

In the short term, the following categories are important for the successful implementation of the event.

■ **Communication**
  Technology
  Management communication
  Audio visual

- **Venues and equipment**
  Venue agreement and contract
  Procurement and purchasing
  Sponsors supplies
  Franchises
  Show effects
  Access and security
- **Legal and licensing**
  Public entertainment
  Alcohol
  Governing body affiliation and sanction
- **Financial control**
- **Marketing**
  Ticket sales
  Corporate sales
  Communications
  Public relations
  Design
  Sponsorship
  Merchandising
  Space sales
  Advertising sales
  Print and publication
- **Services**
  Transportation
  Accommodation
  Food and beverage
  Merchandising and licensing
  Environmental consultancy
  Sanitation
- **Health and safety**
  Risk assessment
  Certification
  Emergency procedure
  Crisis management process

Step 3: Task analysis

Each of these categories and sub-categories needs to be resourced and so they are assessed for costs, time, staff and supplies. The total costs amount to the total cost of implementing the event. This is an area of planning that must be initiated at the feasibility stage of the event planning process, then continuously monitored and then finalized. The total budget amounts should not change at this stage, although allocations between cost centres can be implemented.

Step 4: Scheduling

Each of the tasks is then put on a time line and deadlines in particular are identified (see Figure 8.1).

Step 5: Critical path

The timelines for each task are then combined into a Gantt chart. This then provides a backbone for production planning and a calendar with deadlines for all tasks.

This chart can become overcrowded and so, in order to identify clashing schedules, tasks need to be prioritized. Network analysis can be applied to determine a critical path; the determination of deadlines by which tasks have to be achieved in order for each to be achieved sequentially. The analysis graphically portrays how many tasks the non-arrival of equipment or the late delivery of merchandise will impact upon. This enables the event manager to

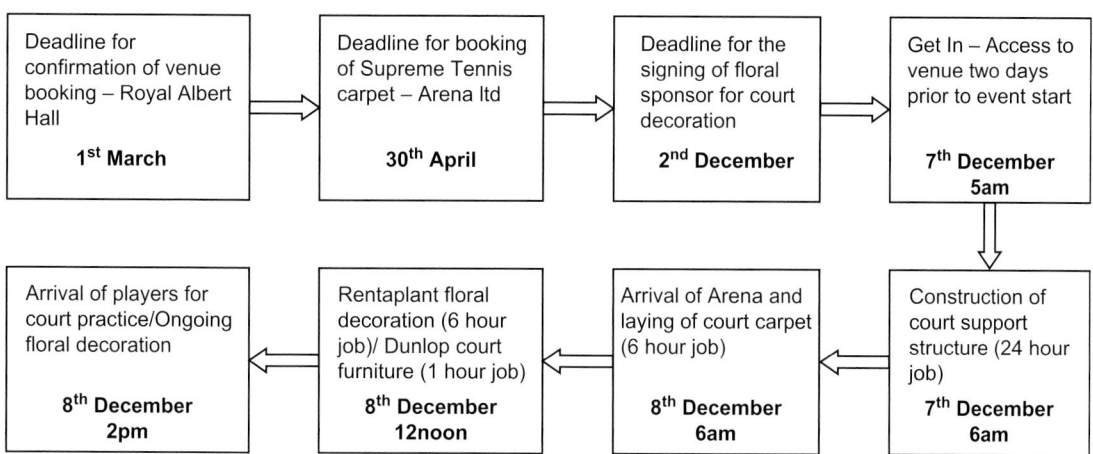

FIGURE 8.1 *A critical path – Nabisco Masters Doubles. A network depicting one set of tasks – the construction of the tennis court for the event at the Royal Albert Hall. The critical path is represented by the arrow and shows that the failure of one task impacts on those that follow.*

identify the consequences of not achieving each task. All aspects involved in the production of the event are integrated into the critical path.

Allen et al (2002) note that the use of Gantt charts and critical paths can become very complex and, as a result, difficult to use for major international sports events. Even the use of software packages has its limitations as the event increases in size.

Step 6: Responsibility allocation

Each task becomes an area of responsibility and, depending on the event, there need to be organizational structures created with appropriate lines of communication so that these areas can be managed in harmony rather than isolation. Each manager may run their own micro critical path but, if they do, it must feed directly into an event master copy. It is essential that the event director controls and maintains the event master copy and that all subsequent and micro paths derive out of it in order to avoid misinformation and dysfunctional operations. Graham et al (2001) cite Frank Supovitz, of the National Hockey League (NHL), and his use of individual production schedules that are incorporated into a master plan document in order to create synergy.

This event project management process is further developed in Event management 8.1. World Championship Tennis Inc, in its management of the Nabisco Masters Doubles, operated with task sheets that were manually derived from a master time-lined plan on a year round basis. No software was available for aiding this process at that time. O'Toole and Mikolaitis (2002) maintain that the fluid nature of events means that milestones, completions of key tasks, are changeable and therefore recalculations of all linked tasks are constantly necessary. This is still unfortunately not achievable with most current project management software. O'Toole and Mikolaitis (2002) recommend the use of Gantt chart and other software for unlinked task approaches.

EVENT MANAGEMENT 8.1

Sports Event Project Management

Successful sports events require an effective project management approach. This applies to all scales of event but, the more complex an event, the more critical this becomes. The scope of the task is determined with the early identification of the work that is involved, who it will be done by and when. The project management process should include:

Work Breakdown Structures (WBS)

Segmentation: a breakdown of the event and the areas of operational work required, first of all by category, such as finance, marketing, HR.

Task analysis: this is followed by a further breakdown of these categories into smaller work units that can be managed as tasks.

Assignment

Any tasks that have predecessors (tasks which have to be completed first) have to be identified and placed in the appropriate sequence.

Each task can then be allocated a timeline or an estimated completion time (ECT). The most commonly used types of ECT for events are latest start and latest finish times because they are absolute deadlines.

The tasks are then allocated for implementation in work packages, either internally or externally to the organization, to appropriate personnel/teams.

For larger events, increased delegation will be required. More discretion can then be applied by individuals for the completion of the schedules in their own task areas.

Schedules

These consist of a calendar covering the whole of the event life-cycle.

All key tasks are entered into the calendar at the appropriate times and dates that they are to be completed by.

This necessitates the consideration of all tasks in relation to each other, the extent to which one is dependent on the other and the sequences involved, so that they can be moved forward or backward for action accordingly.

This can also be put into a graphical display (Gantt chart). By prioritizing the tasks and applying network analysis, the necessity for punctuality can be highlighted. This analysis identifies the critical path for the event by also highlighting all those tasks that absolutely have to be completed on time for the event to be a success.

There are numerous software solutions available that use critical path analysis. However, it is worth noting that the method was first developed and used for decades without the aid of computers and using pencil (to enable the use of an eraser) and paper.

The structure of critical path analysis enables the variance from the original schedule caused by changes to be measured and therefore makes an effective post-event evaluation tool for the identification of the causes and impacts of changes between the original schedule and the actual implementation.

Implementation of the event

The next stage in the event planning process is the implementation of the event itself. This is the execution of an event that has been effectively planned so that it is delivered as intended, at the time and on the day required; the effective management of the project. The above categories covered in the implementation planning now become the areas for execution and so the process of breaking down the work and allocating responsibility also come into play.

LONG-TERM PLANNING

From a strategic perspective, there are two long-term requirements that require consideration both in the implementation planning and the implementation of the event. These concern the after-use of any facilities and equipment and any ongoing projects and strategies that are intended as legacies and long-term benefits of the event.

After-use and after-users

The continued involvement of after-users in these two stages is important if there is to be a smooth event breakdown, handover of facilities, legacies and any long-term evaluation.

The organizations that will own and/or manage any physical facilities post the event need to be involved in the design of those facilities (see Chapter 4). It is the event organization that needs to make the long-term objectives work and so their contribution to architectural design, systems for conservation and choice of sports equipment may be key for that process. There may be contention in agendas, for example, a design for changing facilities, spectator capacity or sports use for the event that does not work for after-use. The determination of the specific objectives and decisions at the feasibility stage are critical if this is to be avoided.

Manchester City Football Club needed to satisfy itself that it was going to be able to use the facilities at the new City of Manchester Stadium before signing the contract for their long-term use after the 2002 Commonwealth Games was over. The consultation that transpired included discussions on the removal of a temporary stand and the year-long preparation of seating; seating capacity being key to the economic proposal that was put to them by Manchester City Council in the first place. This is why there are issues with LOCOG's approach and a decision to reduce the capacity in its London 2012 Olympics stadium to 25 000 spectators for after-use despite there being no direct after-user involvement in that decision (see Chapter 4).

After-users include tourism agencies, local authority leisure departments, commercial sports management organizations, educational institutions, sports clubs and societies, as well as professional sports organizations.

The handover of facilities, either back to original users or to new after-users, needs to be a smooth transition and in a form that presents as few problems as possible. This requires the planning of time and resources in order to return or turn a facility into the amenity that was originally agreed. This might be a stadium or an open field and might involve various time spans in order to be achieved. For example, returning a farmer's field from the orienteering course it temporarily was will involve the removal of overlay, litter and possibly regeneration of some kind. The preparation of the City of Manchester Stadium took a year to get right while it takes only several days for the organizers of the Piazza Di Siena to breakdown and return their site in the Borghese Gardens in Rome to their original state (see the photograph at the beginning of this chapter). There are unwritten rules here. Handover the legacy that was agreed or, if there are no new legacies involved, return the site to its original condition on time. To achieve either, after-users need to be consulted and involved in decision-making prior to the decision to go ahead with an event if risks are not to be taken.

Long-term evaluation

The objectives form the benchmarks for all evaluation and so the question might arise, why is there a need for the handing over of this task at all? Up until now, there has been little long-term evaluation done of sports events. The International Olympic Committee (IOC) only established Transfer of Olympic Knowledge (TOK) 5 years ago and only just as recently claimed that it was considering evaluation systems that would consider the legacies and benefits of events 10 years after they have closed (Felli, 2002). Sydney maintained that it would evaluate the success, or not, of Sydney Olympic Park, in the long term (Adby, 2002). Manchester, too, acknowledged the need to evaualte over the long term in order to measure the success of its 2002 Commonwealth Games legacies (Bernstein, 2002).

As these processes start to develop, there are the following key considerations:

1. At what stages does evaluation need to be implemented and in what form so objectives can be measured?

Case Study 8.1

Nova International: The Great Runs model

Nova International is a significant event management and sports marketing organization, founded some 20 years ago by Brendan Foster and his England athletics team mate and business partner John Caine. Despite its history and wealth of activities in the world of running, the organization is relatively unknown but, in the sports event management industry, it is an innovative leader.

Coming from a background of managing Gateshead Stadium, Gateshead Council Leisure, Nike UK and sports manufacturing with ViewFrom, in 1981 Foster and Caine organized their first event, The Great North Run. Some 27 years later this event is the largest half marathon in the world with 50 000 competitors taking part each year. This is Nova's flagship event and the one that has created the model for the organization and its growth. There are now 29 Nova running events and a Great Run Series that takes in cities all over the UK and Ireland. In addition to the Great

North Run (Newcastle/Gateshead), there is the Great Capital Run (Hyde Park, London), Great Women's Run (Sunderland), Great Ireland Run (Dublin), Great Edinburgh Run, Great Manchester Run, Great South Run (Portsmouth) and the Great Yorkshire Run (Sheffield).

Strategically, Nova has taken its original model for the Great North Run and repeated it in appropriate locations in order to grow the organization and its activities. This has been a successful strategy that has been extended to include junior races and a Tesco Junior Great Run Series that includes many of the Great Run Series locations as bases. In so doing, Nova has also developed a sports marketing service that has seen them recruit significant sponsors such as Nike, Tesco, BUPA, Lucozade, Aqua-Pura, Timex and media partner BBC Sport. The strategy has also enabled Nova to expand internationally with the recent addition of the Toyota Great Ethiopian Run.

Continued

The 2008 Great North Run womens elite race draws to a close. A record 52 000 competitors run.

Nova has continuing ambitions and wants to extend its international strategy into new markets. It has identified that it has been able to grow and replicate its model throughout the UK relatively easily because the original partners and managers have remained intact since origination. The operation of the model has been passed on to newly recruited employees but with the benefit of having this overseeing expertise on hand.

Nova has not implemented the use of any critical path analysis in its event management to date but has now recognized that, to extend this model and create further Great Runs and other events in Europe and beyond, it needs to have operations that are based abroad and, in order to do that successfully, it needs to provide documented management operations that can be followed by newly recruited partners and employees. Operations that can independently manage without any overseeing expertise locally on-hand. In its first step towards this, it has employed an operations analyst in a role that will provide a 'manual' for the Great Run model.

An analysis of Nova's growth shows that it has used its approach for event management operations to expand its portfolio of products and that, to extend still further, it will now seek to document that with more formal information systems.

Source: Nova (2008)

2. Who is responsible for ensuring that the evaluation is implemented?

3. For whom is the evaluation?

4. How will the evaluation be used to contribute to the success of the facility, future benefit, etc?

However, these questions are not for this stage of the planning process. They need to be asked and answered and incorporated into the objectives and, in that way, they can become intrinsic to the event and a part of the alignment process that is ongoing throughout the event.

The important task during implementation is to ensure that those that are to carry out evaluation are supplied with all the necessary information they require when it is available and easy to pass on. When the event ends, this information increasingly becomes obscure as the IOC identified in realizing the need for TOK.

SUMMARY

The implementation planning stage of the event planning process provides the time for the preparation of everything that needs to be implemented for the execution of the event. The short-term focus, for the delivery of an event on time, can become a preoccupation and at the expense of long-term objectives. In particular, the after-use and the after-users need to be considered as well as the process by which evaluation can be conducted in order to assess long-term objectives. A longer-term perspective in the management of key relationships, such as those with stakeholders, in particular, is a more strategic route to long-term success. Depending upon the scale of the event, this process can become complex.

A project management approach is required in order to make a success of this managerial challenge. The use of a process that assesses the scope of the work involved and then breaks it down so that responsibility can be allocated is useful provided that it is implemented correctly and with the right timing. Some of the tasks need to be undertaken earlier, at the feasibility stage, so that budgets can be set. Provided there is flexibility and the managerial system can respond to forces of change, this process should enable the implementation planning and then the implementation of the event to be undertaken.

QUESTIONS

1. Select a sports event and draw up a list of categories and sub-categories that cover the extent of the short-term implementation planning required. What potential issues do you see in the planning for the implementation of this event?

2. Select a different sports event. Research, identify and evaluate the timing necessary for the recruitment of key personnel.

3. What recruitment criteria will you look to achieve?

4. Select a sports event where sports facilities have been built and were intended as long-term legacies. Research, identify and evaluate the use of consultation with after-users during the planning process.

REFERENCES

Adby, R. (2002). *Email Questionnaire: Director General*, Olympic Co-Ordination Authority 2000 Olympics. 9 July.

Allen, J., O'Toole, W., McDonnell, I. and Harris, R. (2002). *Festival and Special Event Management*, 2nd edn. Queensland, Australia, John Wiley & Sons, Chapter 13.

Beijing 2008 (2008). www.beijing2008.cn (accessed 20 March 2008).

Bernstein, H. (2002). Interview: Chief Executive, Manchester City Council at Chief Executive's office, Manchester City Council, Town hall, Manchester. 3pm, 28 June.

Brettell, D. (2001). *The Sydney Olympic and Paralympic Games Volunteer Program*, a Keynote Presentation by the Manager for Venue Staffing and Volunteers for the Sydney Organizing Committee for the Olympic Games. Singapore, July 2001. www.e-volunteerism.com/quarterly/01fall/brettell2a (accessed 9 December 2003).

Emery, P. (2001). Bidding to Host a Major Sports Event: Strategic Investment or Complete Lottery. In: Gratton, C. and Henry, P. (eds), *Sport in the City: The Role of Sport in Economic and Social Regeneration*. London, Routledge, Chapter 7.

Felli, G. (2002). Transfer of Knowledge (TOK): A games management tool. A paper delivered at the *IOC-UIA Conference: Architecture & International Sporting Events*. Olympic Museum, Lausanne. June 2002. IOC.

Graham, S., Neirotti, L. and Goldblatt, J. (2001). *The Ultimate Guide to Sports Marketing*, 2nd edn. New York, McGraw-Hill, Chapter 3.

Hall, C. (1997). *Hallmark Tourist Events:Impacts, Management And Planning*. Chichester, Wiley, Chapter 6.

Manchester City Council (2003). *The Impact of the Manchester 2002 Commonwealth Games*. www.manchester.gov.uk/corporate/games/impact (accessed 25 February 2003).

Nova (2008). www.greatrun.org (accessed 25 March 2008).

NYC2012 (2003). www.nyc2012.com/team.sec6.sub1 (accessed 9 December).

O'Toole, W. and Mikolaitis, P. (2002). *Corporate Events Project Management*. New York, John Wiley & Sons, Chapter 2.

Marketing Planning and Implementation

The facilities and the quality of the product at the magnificent Santiago Bernabeu stadium in Madrid ensure that Real Madrid FC does not struggle to sell its match tickets despite prices being as high as €150 plus commissions.

LEARNING OBJECTIVES

After studying this chapter, you should be able to:

- understand the role of marketing planning and its importance for sports events

- identify the marketing planning process and explain its logical progression

- understand the importance of internal and external analyses and their contribution to the formulation of marketing objectives and strategies

- identify the strategic choices and the role of the marketing mix in achieving a market position

- understand the importance of organization, implementation and control in marketing planning

INTRODUCTION

In today's society, there are a great number of leisure opportunities and substitutes on offer, so much so that it is becoming increasingly difficult to provide a product that is of better value. The common practice of marketing to mass audiences is not an approach that will bear rewards in such operating domains and so the need for marketing planning in the event industry, where customers can be more finely targeted, is becoming more critical. The focus of this chapter is on the marketing planning process and how a sports event can be systematically positioned into a carefully targeted market for better results.

MARKETING PLANNING

The marketing planning process can be implemented in a step-by-step progression that consists of seven stages.

The marketing planning process

1. Organizational goals

2. Internal and external analyses: including an internal marketing audit, situational analysis using tools such as SWOT (strengths,

weaknesses, opportunities and threats) and PEST (political, economical, sociological and technological), customer and competition analyses.

3. Marketing goals: the setting of objectives for the marketing plan.

4. Market selection: segmentation of potential markets and selection of target markets.

5. Marketing strategy: the identification of strategic thrust and the specific marketing mix required for each target market position in order to achieve competitive advantage.

6. Organization and implementation: the scheduling, coordination and execution of the marketing plan.

7. Control: the creation of controls and performance indicators to enable correction throughout the implementation of the marketing plan, post-event measurement and comparison of results against the objectives set with feedback for future performance.

This traditional approach to marketing planning (Boone and Kurtz, 2002; Kotler, 2006; Jobber, 2007) involves a process that begins with a strategic approach and the consideration of organizational goals. As with every business activity, there needs to be an alignment with the mission statement and corporate objectives. The next step is also from a strategic perspective, whereby an analysis of the organization as a whole is required in order to assess internal and external environments. The perspective then becomes more specifically market driven with the tactical planning required for the marketing plan. This consists of devising market and product strategies and the tactics and tools by which these strategies will succeed. The outcome is a marketing plan that then needs to be implemented, controlled and evaluated. Each step of this process is considered in more detail below.

ORGANIZATIONAL AND EVENT GOALS

The plan needs to be aligned with the overall goals for the organization, specifically its mission statement and corporate objectives. If an organization is involved in a range of business activities, then it will set objectives for each of these. Therefore, if it is running an event, it will set specific event objectives that will be aligned with its overall goals. For example, a municipal authority that puts on a sports event has objectives that cover wide issues (community relations, sport and business development and social cohesion) and the event will be used to try to achieve some of those in part. In some cases, an organization is created just to implement the event and so the organizational goals and event goals can become one and the same. For example, Manchester 2002 Ltd for the Commonwealth Games, Beijing Organizing Committee for the 2008 Olympic Games (BOCOG) and New York 2012 Olympic Bid Organization (NYC2012) were all purposely created for an event. BOCOG's goals, for example, can be seen in Beijing Insight 3.1 in Chapter 3, while Manchester's 2002 Commonwealth Games aims were focused on the production of a great event, but also wider urban regeneration legacies as discussed in Chapter 4.

Before the more specific marketing goals can be identified and the event marketing plan created, however, important information is needed in order to progress and this is gained via a series of analyses of the organization's business and its external environment.

INTERNAL AND EXTERNAL ANALYSES

The life blood of all planning is information and therefore the marketing plan requires the collection, storage and analysis of information and from a variety of sources. This can become a complex activity and the more this is the case, the more an organization needs to consider how this information can be managed. First, there are both external and internal sources of information. Secondly, various levels of research can be required in order that a comprehensive understanding of the current organizational situation, competitor activity and customer groups is attained. A marketing information system (MkIS) needs to be developed, however simple the collection and storage of the information is.

An MkIS consists of four elements of data (Jobber, 2007). The first is internal data that are continuously available, such as meetings' minutes, ticket sales data and transactions. The second is internal ad hoc data such as from a one-off analysis of the success of particular sales promotions, such as ticket discount schemes. The third and fourth elements are derived externally, via environmental scanning and market research. The former consists of an analysis of the political, economical, sociological and technological (PEST) forces that may bear influence on the organization. A continuous scanning or monitoring of the environment is required so that a response to change in these key areas can be more effectively implemented. How will new laws for employment, licensing or local bye-laws on the use of pyrotechnics affect the event? How will an unstable market with increasing inflation affect the take-up of tickets? Will sponsorship revenue become scarce? Will the non-take-up of the latest telesales technology leave the event at a disadvantage? Will the hosting of a multi-cultural event positively or negatively affect local issues? What security measures will be appropriate? These are all key questions to consider for the event. Market research is also an essential element so that there is not a total reliance upon inward looking internal analysis on performance (Jobber, 2007). Conducting customer surveys and interviews can reveal insightful data that, if at odds with internal analysis, will serve to enlighten managers.

The beauty of events is that there is a captive audience and on-site surveys become a relatively easy tool to use. The use of the 'mystery shopper' method can also be useful at events where there are opportunities to interact with customers and employees to get more depth in information (Mullin et al., 2000). Research of non-attendees is also an important resource in order to determine why potential audience do not attend and possibly change the product accordingly.

Research will also aid competitor analysis with intelligence on the competition and their marketing activities.

The two key factors in MkIS are that the data need to be collected and stored in such a way that they can be efficiently analysed and then distributed to those that can then use them effectively. Data are a management tool that aid managers in taking decisions. Wood (2004) has developed a model for events organizations that highlights the wide range of sources an organization can tap for information (see Event management 9.1).

It can be seen from the model that information needs to be stored in order for it to be usefully analysed. It revolves around stakeholders and the storage of information pertaining to each so that a greater understanding of them can be achieved. An MkIS provides an effective tool for the collection, storage and dissemination of three key areas that event managers need to gain a full understanding of.

The first key area of information involves the organization looking further into its operating domain for knowledge about its competitors. A competitor analysis will reveal further opportunities and threats in the market. A market-driven approach, such as that of Porter (1980), looks at a number of areas of where competition derives. For an event, his five forces model of market competition would involve an analysis of the extent of the rivalry with other events, the strength of the market to withstand and repel new events, the extent to which substitute entertainment may offer opportunities for purchase switching and the bargaining power held with suppliers and buyers because they can affect the events costs and prices and therefore its ability to compete. Direct competition from other sports events is not

EVENT MANAGEMENT 9.1

Marketing Planning: Marketing Information Systems (MkIS)

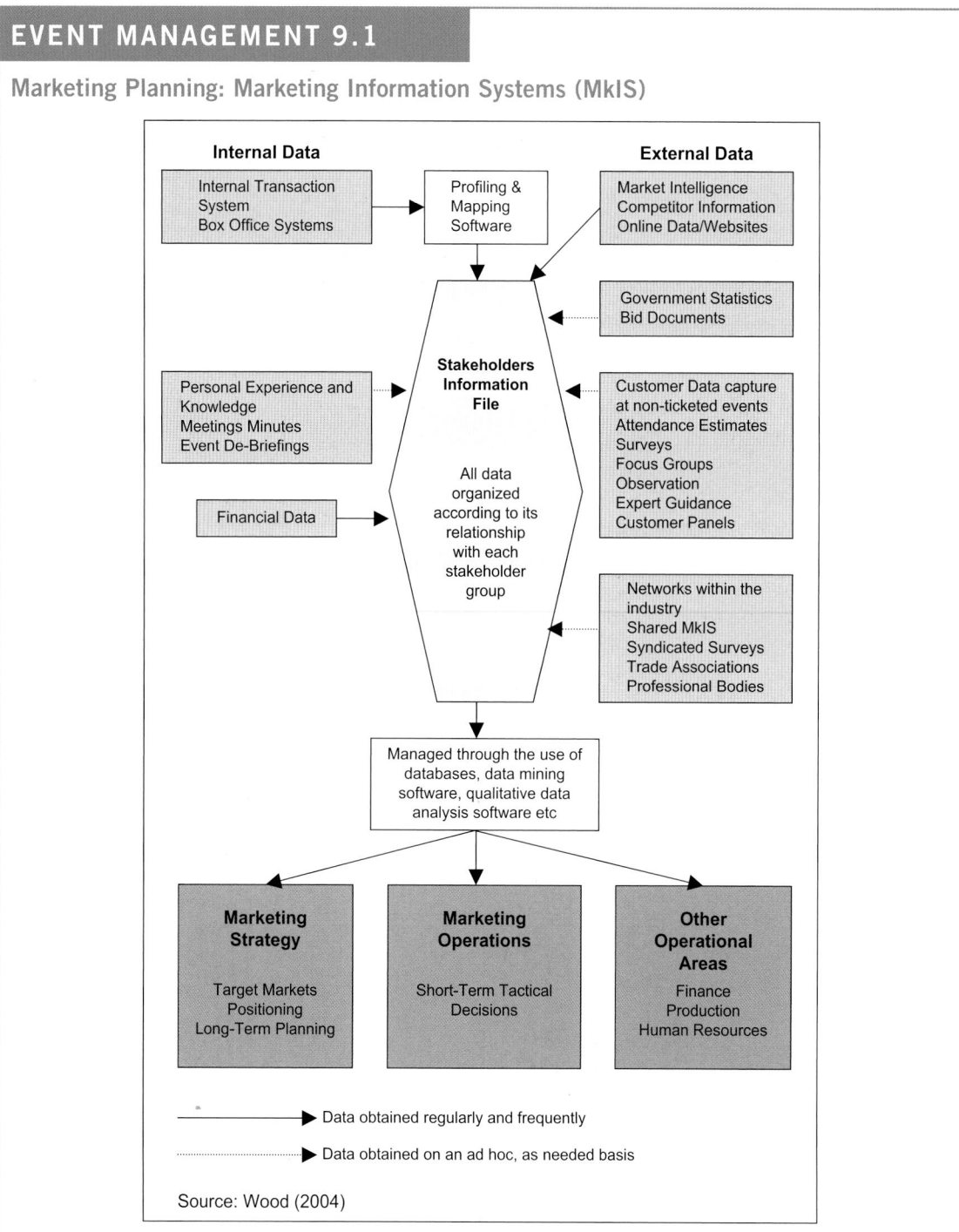

Source: Wood (2004)

often an issue due to the creation of non-competing sporting calendars produced by cooperating sports bodies. For many events, it is the threat that is imposed by substitutes that causes the most concern. When an event is broadcast by the media, an important consideration is clearly to what extent that coverage is having an impact on attendance at the event. Indirect competition from the likes of other forms of entertainment, such as cinema, theatre, family unit leisure, including quality and vacation time, is also an important competitive aspect. For example, the whole fixture list in football in the UK is adjusted when the pre-holiday weekend falls just prior to 25 December. Losing the fan to Christmas shopping is a major concern for clubs.

Research into the competition's current marketing activity is key knowledge. Information on market share and profit is important, but it is the market position and the marketing mix that achieved that share that are perhaps most important. The research needs to focus on the strategies that have been used and, critically, what strategies are to be used by the competition. This may require personal enquiry but can also be available via the regular storing of market reports, media and website activity.

The second key area of information required by the organization concerns an understanding of its existing and potential customers. This provides data that can be used to help the segmentation process and select target markets in the fourth stage.

The third area is a gaining of an understanding of the current situation of an organization: an internal analysis. There are two ways in which this can be achieved. First, via an internal audit of marketing activities that produces information on marketing strategies, resources used and an evaluation of the results produced. The aim is to assess what is required to be changed, this therefore necessitates a review of current activity but may also require a historical perspective in order to gain an understanding of how current activities have evolved.

Secondly, an assessment of the event's SWOT that exist in its operating environment is required. This can serve to summarize all the areas that are assessed. A SWOT analysis can be a dynamic tool for the event manager but, in practice, is not used to its full potential. Piercy (2002) suggests that it is commonly used to look at issues that are too wide, for example considering the organization or the event as a whole, and that organizations also conduct the analysis with an inward look at themselves using their own opinion. As a result, an analysis can produce a set of criteria that are unfocused and lack sufficient depth to be of use. In conducting the analysis, it is important to avoid the ambiguous and unqualified values and statements that are often made when identifying the four SWOT criteria. For example, it is insufficient to list the 'strong image' of the event as a strength and, equally, too vague to describe the event as one with a weakness if it remains in its present venue. For these criteria to be of use in the analysis, each one needs to be broken down until the analysis produces criteria that can underpin management decision-making. For this to be reliable it will involve market research.

Piercy (2002) maintains that, in order for a SWOT analysis to be most productive, there are three key factors. The first is that there needs to be a focus on a particular issue, product or service. For an event, this may mean focusing on one particular marketing strategy, one product line or an aspect of the sales process. In this way, the analysis can highlight the need to gain further knowledge and can thus achieve a greater level of detail than analysing the wider picture. A series of analyses can then be pieced together to form a comprehensive and more global picture. The second concerns the perspective from which the criteria are viewed. What an organization thinks about its own strengths has no bearing if its customers think otherwise and so the analysis also needs to be conducted from the customers' perspective in order for it to be customer focused. The analysis must consider the way in which customers view a particular phenomenon and how and why they consider strengths to be strengths and weaknesses to be weaknesses. A comprehensive analysis, supported by market research, in this case might further breakdown the strength of the event's image and identify that a high percentage of customers are loyal and have had repeat ticket purchase for each of the last four events. A 'strong image' might also be perceived by customers when there is a strong roster of star competitors at the event because that will increase ticket sales. Meanwhile, remaining in the existing venue may be a weakness because customer accessibility is difficult due to a lack of local transport provision and there being insufficient car parking facilities. Similarly, it might be a weakness due to customers experiencing poor catering, seating and restroom facilities. While Piercy (2002) proposes that the external factors of opportunity and threat in the environment should be viewed from the manager's perspective and thus focus on what is attractive or unattractive for the event, it is maintained here that it should also be a consideration that is also conducted with customer perspective. In order to attain competitive advantage, any analysis of the external opportunities and threats will always need to be conducted with customer focus.

Another common failing is not using the analysis as a management tool. The third key factor for SWOT analysis is that it has the capacity to aid managers in deciding on strategy and is a means to an end if used correctly. Piercy (2002) proposes a matching process and the use of conversion strategies as the next stage of the analysis. Having discussed and analysed a full set of SWOT criteria, each criterion can be given an arbitrary score and ranked according to their importance. In this way, strengths may be later matched with opportunities but only if there is a suitable fit (see Figure 9.1). Those opportunities that have no match are those that provide event managers with future challenges. The idea then is to convert the higher scoring weaknesses and threats into strengths and opportunities,

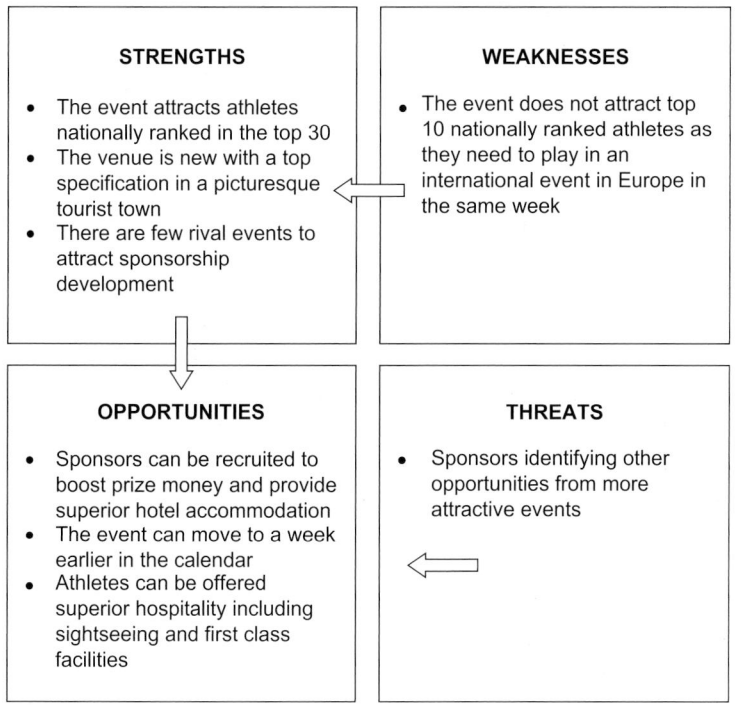

FIGURE 9.1   *An advanced stage of SWOT analysis using a 'matching' approach to produce strategies to achieve objectives. The example used might apply to any regionally significant event that aspires to a national profile. This example is designed to demonstrate how a weakness can be turned into a strength via the opportunities that are available – in this case the top 10 ranked athletes can be attracted to the event by (a) the already existing strength of superior facilities, (b) moving the event to an earlier date, (c) securing sponsors that can provide attractive prize money and superior hotel accommodation and (d) the provision of additional attractions such as sightseeing in a desired tourist location. The threat to this strategy is not being able to secure sponsors if there are more attractive propositions elsewhere.*

respectively. This is not always an easy task and therefore many may remain unmatched, they then act as important limitations and considerations for future business practice.

The Masters Senior tennis event in Madrid, sponsored by Communidad de Madrid, depends on its 'star' players as attractions for ticket purchase. Where would the event be without Boris Becker and John McEnroe for example? To attract these players, not only does the prize money have to be attractive, the quality of the player hospitality that is afforded to the players has to be superior. Jim Courier brought his mother with him to the city for example. This event took place on a weekend in March, 2008 and, to avoid a clash with a Real Madrid FC home match versus Sevilla, it had to ensure it was completed in good time for the football kick-off that night at 9pm. (See the photograph of Santiago Bernabeu at the beginning of this chapter.) Besides Becker, McEnroe and Courier, the six player event also featured Bjorn Borg, Emilio Sanchez Vicario and, importantly, winner and local Spanish hero Sergi Bruguera.

Posters for the Masters Senior, Madrid using the names of its star player attractions as a focus for promotions.

MARKETING GOALS

The next step is to provide a focus for the plan. It is important to consider corporate goals so that the marketing objectives can be aligned with them. Marketing goals can differ from event to event in the way they are evaluated and measured, but will usually involve the maximization of one or more of the following: market share, the building of the event brand equity, target market awareness for the event, target market awareness for event sponsors and partners and their association with the event, event product sales, sponsor and partner product sales and leads and sales for other and repeat events. The key factor here is specifying the extent, level and quality that is to be attained and within what time frame (SMART objectives). By how much does market share and awareness have to grow, for example? Brand equity could be measured via increased repeat sales in the form of customer loyalty and might be considered to be a sign of developing the brand (Jobber, 2007).

Once the goals have been identified the selection of target markets can be implemented.

MARKET SELECTION

Segmentation

While there are various stakeholders that all require attention and directed communications, the business of sports event marketing essentially involves two types of target market. For all events, there are participants and, for many events, there are audiences, spectators and fans too. One of the unique factors of the sports event industry is that both participants and audience are an intrinsic part of the event product. Your fellow runner or the person next to you in the bleachers is contributing to your event experience. With this in mind, the marketer needs to address the most efficient and effective methods of reaching these customers.

Knowledge of customer behaviour allows an organization to identify groups of customers with similar and generic attributes that make it possible for the organization to then be more efficient and effective in reaching them with its communications. This part of the planning process is called segmentation and is a method of dividing large mass markets into smaller identifiable segments where the constituents have similar profiles of needs that may be attractive to the organization.

Knowledge sought can include psychographics as well as geographic and demographic information about customers. The aim of segmentation is to identify customers' needs that can be better met by the organization than by its competitors. There are three criteria for achieving this differential (Jobber 2007).

The basis of segmentation

- *Behavioural segmentation*: what benefits do they seek, how and where do they buy, are they brand switchers, are they heavy or light users and do they view the product favourably?

- *Psychographic segmentation*: what kind of lifestyle do they lead? For instance, are they trendsetters, followers, conservative or sophisticated? What kinds of personalities do they have? Are they extrovert or introvert, aggressive or submissive?

- *Profile segmentation*: age, gender, stage of life cycle, social class, level of education, income level and residential location.

Often, a combination of these forms of segmentation can provide a comprehensive approach to reveal a level of knowledge that will enable event managers to ascertain a number of segments of larger markets that are attractive propositions for its products. For example, the sales of daytime off-peak tickets to appropriate target markets would require demographic information on jobs and personal addresses and psychographic information on interests and availability at those times. The filling of off-peak seats for the Nabisco Masters Doubles at the Royal Albert Hall in London has included the targeting of teachers from schools for blind children based in the home counties of England that were perhaps available for school trips. The offering was made all the more attractive with the help of a partner that provided commentary via personal headphones.

While segments are a division of the mass, niches are an even smaller part of the whole. Segments, in definition, are still quite large and prone to competition, whereas niches can offer single corporate opportunities to provide a small part of a market with a product that will not realize great profits, but can offer market share domination and be more than sufficient for smaller and/or fewer organizations. The identification of a niche follows the same segmentation process. Within the sports event industry there have been examples of organizations creating niches for themselves. In the 1980s, the development of a version of racquetball for the UK was led by two separate manufacturers, Dunlop and Slazenger (they merged at a later date). The game was called racketball (note the name differentiation) and a slower ball was produced so that it could be used for longer rallies on a squash court. There were very few racquetball courts in the UK other than on US Air Force Bases and they had restricted access. There were no sales of racquetball equipment in the UK at the time and, in order to create a market, this niche was therefore organization led. The British Racketball Association was formed and is still organizing events and thriving today (see Case study 2.2 in Chapter 2).

Going through a process of segmentation, however, does not guarantee success. There are four key criteria that must be met (Boone and Kurtz 2002):

1. The market segment needs to offer measurable buying power and size.

2. The market segment needs to be able to offer an appropriate level of profit.

3. The organization needs to be capable of providing the segment with a suitable offering and distributing it at an appropriate price.

4. The organization's marketing must be capable of effectively promoting and serving that segment.

Mullin et al. (2000) encapsulate these four criteria into three measures of identification, accessibility and responsiveness. Dunlop and Slazenger, with their stocks of racquetball rackets (acquired from the USA), were ready to extend into a UK market, but they still had to identify a group of customers that they could access and serve effectively. They identified a mainly female focus on those that could or already did access squash clubs during off-peak hours. The clubs welcomed the idea and worked with the companies to market a game that was easier to learn than squash and utilized courts that were easier and cheaper to book. The clubs developed the offering with the introduction of crèche facilities and the result was that an attractive and sizeable market was successfully accessed by two cooperating manufacturers.

The process for segmentation below has been adapted from Boone and Kurtz's (2002) model.

The segmentation process

1. *Identify the basis of segmentation*: this consists of the choice of the basis for segmentation and the selection of promising segments. Having predefined a segment, a selection can then be made based purely on observation or via market-driven research.

2. *Develop a segment profile*: further understanding of the customers in each segment, so that similarities and differences can be identified between segments. The aim is to arrive at typical customers for each segment.

3. *Forecast the potential*: identify market potential for each segment.

4. *Forecast market share*: forecasting a probable market share by considering the competition's market positions and by designing marketing strategies to reach each segment. The latter will identify necessary resources and weigh up the costs versus benefits.

Target market selection

There are several approaches for target market selection. A mass-market approach entails selecting large numbers where the appeal can still be successful with little wastage of marketing effort and resource. An event that has appeal to people of all ages, either single or part of family units, might successfully select a mass market. However, many events will require differentiated target markets that are more finely selected via the segmentation process. An example here would be an extreme sports event where the appeal is not so widespread. Further differentiation again can be provided via a niche approach. For example, an event that runs during off-peak hours will be required to be more focused still, perhaps in the form of local schools or women's groups.

Following segmentation, an organization can make an informed decision about which segments it wants to target.

THE MARKETING STRATEGY

The stages in the marketing planning process above have so far identified options for a choice of markets. The internal and external analyses offer strategic options and the segmentation process identifies which markets are target options. Having selected target markets and marketing goals, the task now is to determine which strategies will achieve these objectives.

There are four generic approaches for market strategic thrust but two of these are options that are mainly applicable for an organization and its long-term direction. A short-term strategy will consist of penetrating the market in order to increase event sales or, more realistically, improve it each time in order to increase sales via a product development strategy. Over the long term, an organization might adopt a strategy of developing new products for either the same target markets with new sports events or, indeed, move into other sports or entertainment sectors and offer events to those new markets.

The process of segmentation, identification of the events target markets, followed by the selection of market strategies, enables the organization to position the offering in the market so that it meets the target customers' needs by differentiating the offering from that of the competition. The differentiation is achieved via a carefully selected marketing mix. The mix consists of the four Ps: product, price, place and promotion. The determination of the marketing mix for an event involves creating a product that satisfies customers' needs, at an acceptable price, in appropriate places so that it can be promoted in such a way that the whole offering becomes known, attractive and bought by target customers. It is described as a mix because the components of the four Ps cannot be considered in isolation. The event concept may be undesirable at a certain ticket price but more accessible at a certain venue, for example, and so the identification of the options for each component and selecting the right mix is the task here.

Events are services and are therefore subject to the consideration of a separate service sector marketing mix. In addition to the four Ps, three further components should be considered, those of people, physical nature and processes (Jobber, 2007). Events are managed, participated in and attended by people and it is therefore important to consider the personal interactions that take place in the nature of the product. For example, how the audience themselves play a big part in the entertainment at the event or how the stewards and ticket sales staff also play a part in the customer experience. The physical nature of the event and its ambience, in particular, has a large bearing on customer enjoyment and is therefore a consideration in the design of the product and the choice of venue. The processes involved in servicing the customer, such as those of getting tickets and accessing the venue, are critical aspects of the determination of the mix of the four Ps. It can be seen that there is not necessarily any need to add these components to the four Ps when they can be seen as key components of the product.

A successful marketing mix will be developed using the knowledge gained earlier in the planning process and will be designed to meet the goals set for the identified target markets. Creating the differential will achieve a market position from which the event can be competitive. The task is to design a mix that achieves competitive advantage.

Product

The questions asked here are who, what, why and when? Sports event products include the event as a whole and also all the various components that it can consist of. These include goods, services, information and media, places, people and also ideas (Mullin et al, 2000; Pitts and Stotlar, 2002). Prior to the first modern Olympics in Athens in 1896 for example, Baron Pierre de Coubertin pursued and championed an idea that was to become an outstanding sports product. He realized this concept with the formation of the International Olympic Committee (IOC) in Paris in 1894 (BOC, 2003).

The venue and the facilities are an important choice for event organizers. They have to match budget requirements in numbers of seats, suites and commercial opportunities in order to provide and project revenues. From a customer's perspective they have to be accessible, suitably aesthetic and properly equipped. As customer expectation increases, the quality and number of facilities may also need to increase. For example, more bars, car parking and plasma screens that add to customer value, but are of course all at an extra cost to the event. The weather, too, is an important consideration when selecting a venue. While it is not controllable, contingency plans for unsuitable weather are.

The timing of the event is also an inherent part of the product. Consider the ways in which seasons are a considerable part of the offering in UK sport. For instance, a cricket test at Lords, rowing at Henley, or strawberries and cream at Wimbledon. Winter sports depend on their time of year, too.

The product also encapsulates the service that is received via ticket sales processes, purchasing food and merchandise and at the turnstile. The participants also play a key role. One thousand runners or two guest star players are an intrinsic part of the offering. The audience too are providers of entertainment as well as the ones who are entertained. The atmosphere they create is as important as the game on the court, pitch, wicket or ballpark. Empty seats are not just poor for financial reasons.

Price

Pricing strategies are determined in relation to other parts of the marketing mix. A simple meeting of costs and then profit is probably required, for example and a cost-plus strategy might appeal. However, a customer focus is required and so the identification of the customer's idea of what good value is, is needed in order to determine if a profitable event is achievable. Other considerations include the extent of the competitive position and if low prices are necessary or whether differentiation is an option. In order to get customers to adopt and become loyal for example, a discount or free entry strategy may be required. The customer adoption process involves making potential customers aware of the product, giving them information, letting them evaluate the product, then getting them to trial and finally commit to it and then become loyal. Empty seats are a concern and so a seat-filling contingency plan may be a required practice just prior to the event. Attracting groups that have been previously identified as target segments can serve several purposes. One is to sell tickets to them at discounted prices. The second is to use them to fill the seats even without potential revenue so that the atmosphere at the event is not diminished. The third is that these customers get to trial the product and may then adopt it in the future.

Prices have to be determined according to target market requirements. There are those events that can apply a high market price due to having a highly valued product, customers that have the ability to pay, low competition and high demand. This is skimming strategy and many other major events around the world are testament to this, for example the Football Association (FA) Cup Final, the Ryder Cup, the Six Nations Rugby, the Stanley Cup, the Super Bowl and the World Series of Baseball where there is more demand than supply. However, it is not only the end of season finales that attract such demand. Regular season match sell-outs at the majority of National Football League (NFL) games are currently a feature throughout the season and Real Madrid FC also has this power and luxury with a ticket pricing strategy that ranges from €30 to over €150 (including agent's commission) per match. Events that are not in such a powerful position are constrained by different conditions.

Where the only alternative is to offer low prices, there is little differential from those offerings of the competition and therefore competition is high. New events to the market may also apply low prices as part of a penetration strategy and in order to launch the event and get a foothold in the market. In this case, they may also have strategies to make revenue elsewhere through merchandising or catering, for example. An organization with a number of events in its portfolio may strategically launch one event as a loss leader, with low prices, with the objective of making more revenue in the future.

Ticket pricing strategies are determined and balanced in relation to what commercial assets the event has available. For example, there are three levels of corporate hospitality at London's Royal Albert Hall in its Grand Tier, Loggia and Upper Tier levels of corporate boxes and prices can be set accordingly. At the Santiago Bernabeu, the ticket pricing structure for football (there is top-flight basketball too) is determined by the various levels and zones to enable a range of prices that reflect the quality of the view of the pitch. Most venues have similar differentiations. For example, three of the four stands in Madrid have seven different levels of ticket prices (lower, upper, grandstand, 1st, 2nd, 3rd and 4th tiers; see Table 9.1) with the most expensive seat being at the grandstand level in the west and east stands looking across rather than down the pitch. The pricing strategy is further developed with members and more expensive general public prices for each seat. The majority of seats are taken up by season ticket holders and few tickets actually become available for any one game. Season ticket holders are able to reassign their seats quite easily on line and members often have to try and secure tickets on the day of a game.

Season tickets and corporate box tickets are traditional ways of packaging tickets and achieving revenue in advance. These can be ways of also offering

Table 9.1	Real Madrid FC Ticket Prices, Santiago Bernabeu Stadium					
Level	**West Stand**		**East Stand**		**North/South Stands**	
	Members	**Public**	**Members**	**Public**	**Members**	**Public**
Lower level	€80	€95	€80	€95	€40	€50
Upper level	€95	€110	€95	€110	€65	€75
Grandstand	€115	€135	€115	€135	€90	€100
1st tier	€110	€125	€110	€125	€80	€95
2nd tier	€85	€105	€85	€105	€50	€65
3rd tier	€80	€95	€65	€75	€40	€50
4th tier	€45	€60	-	-	€30	€40

Ticket prices in Euros

Real Madrid, 'sold out' at home.

cheaper tickets in advance. Shank (2002) suggests that, in the late 1990s, Personal Seat Licences (PSLs) were a new way of getting similar revenue, whereby a fan could buy a seat(s) for a number of years. With such schemes, sports clubs can achieve large amounts of revenue to contribute to the building of new facilities. In fact, debenture schemes have been around for some time. The All England Lawn Tennis Club (AELTC) first used them at the Wimbledon Lawn Tennis Championships in 1920 to raise revenue in order to develop its grounds (AELTC, 2003). More recently, in a rare example of advertising a high priced product, the AELTC bought space in the Sunday Times (UK) in 2004 to advertise its release of debenture seats in its newly developed Centre Court. There were 2300 debentures available and at £23 150 each for the five-year period 2006 to 2010. Installment payments were possible for those that needed them and the advertisement had a tear-off slip for sending away for further information. Despite this taking place in 2004, there was unusually no reference to a website in the advertisement. The power quite clearly lay with the AELTC rather than the customer.

Place

The question here is where is the product best marketed in order to reach target markets successfully? This would not only include distribution channels that might include the venue, such as ticket offices, but also include the use of websites and ticket agencies and, possibly, via media partners that might distribute tickets directly. The key task for the event manager is to understand where each target market prefers to do its buying. For example, many football fans still prefer to queue for their tickets while the tickets for an Olympics are sold in large amounts to foreign visitors and are only distributed via the appropriate National Olympic Committee and its appointed agents. For the Beijing 2008 Olympics, any tickets bought by residents in Great Britain had to be bought via Sportsworld, the BOC appointed agents.

Beijing Insight 9.1

Beijing 2008 Olympics: Ticketing Strategy

Tickets for the 2008 Olympics were available domestically to China-based residents where they were sold via a number of phases of release. Non-China-based ticket buyers were able to purchase either packages that consisted of tickets, travel and accommodation or tickets only via National Olympic Association appointed ticketing agents.

In the UK, the BOA appointed Sportsworld with whom a UK resident could request individual tickets for any of the events. Each nation requested an allocation of tickets directly from BOCOG to sell on to the general public. The process consisted of a 'booking request', paid for in advance by credit card (surprisingly several types of card could be used and not just Visa, the exclusive credit card services to the IOC and the 2008 Olympics). On the 25th day of each month up to March 2008, tickets were allocated. Tickets were not sent out prior to the Games and had to be collected in person at a designated Sportsworld Ticket Office in Beijing. In order to set ticket prices, BOCOG were guided by criteria, similar to those set in Athens (2004) and Sydney (2000). These were as follows:

- Popularity of the sport – domestically and internationally, domestic only, international only

- Venue capacity – small venues with fewer tickets for possibly higher prices versus larger venues with more tickets for lower prices

- Non-venue events, the marathons and road cycling for example, were non-controllable nor efficient to be ticketed so were free events

- Competition status – pricing via a priority of the importance of the competition, for example medal winning sessions, later rounds, preliminary rounds

- Opening and closing ceremonies were individually priced

- Tickets priced to attract non-sports fans for an 'Olympic' experience

- Tickets priced to ensure the majority were acceptable to a domestic public that receives a comparably lower wage than those from international markets, including some that were free

There were 616 sessions of sport and BOCOG set a pricing structure that consisted of 18 levels of prices. Most sessions consisted of two or three ticket prices, but some sports and venues required only one price, for example rowing, fencing, archery, shooting, gymnastics, sailing, canoe/kayak, boxing, modern pentathlon, BMX and track cycling. The following table provides details of which types of sports and sessions were priced at each of the levels in order to demonstrate how BOCOG implemented the above criteria.

The prices have been converted from Chinese RMB into £ and include agent commission as applicable in most countries and, in the main, indicate where each price was used for medal winning sessions.

Price	Medal and Other Sessions
£363.00	Opening ceremony top price (2nd £230, 3rd £120)
£230.00	Closing ceremony top price (2nd £120, 3rd £63.60)
£80.40	Mens basketball medals
£63.60	Womens volleyball medals, womens basketball medals, athletics medals, mens football medals, womens table tennis medals, table tennis team medals, swimming relay medals
£48.00	Mens volleyball medals, tennis medals, individual swimming medals
£39.60	Mens and womens diving medals, individual table tennis medals, synchronised swimming medals, badminton medals
£32.40	Boxing medals, mens water polo medals, rhythmic gymnastics medals, mens and womens beach volleyball medals
£27.60	Team events final rounds, for example quarter finals football
£24.00	Handball medals, mens artistic gymnastics medals
£15.60	Taekwondo medals, wrestling medals, weightlifting medals, judo medals, equestrian team medals, eventing medals
£12.00	Mens and womens hockey medals, mens baseball medals, equestrian dressage medals
£9.60	Softball medals
£8.40	BMX medals, cycling track medals, fencing medals, archery medals, kayak slalom medals
£6.00	Canoe flat course medals, rowing medals
£4.80	Preliminary matches: football 3rd price
£3.60	Mens triathlon medals, shooting medals
£2.40	Preliminary matches: water polo, boxing 2nd price, swimming open water marathon medals

Continued

Beijing Insight 9.1—cont'd

Rowing.

Womens BB.

Boxing.

Continued

Beijing Insight 9.1—cont'd

Water Polo.

Football.

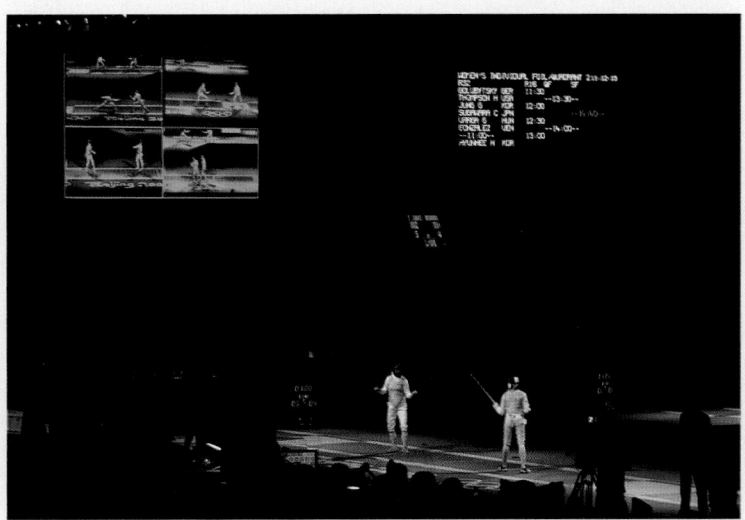

Fencing.

The crowd at a preliminary Womens Football Match. The cheering Beijing workers can be seen in the Foreground.

Continued

Beijing Insight 9.1—cont'd

The Sportsworld ticket collection office in Beijing.

Source: Sportsworld (2008)

Promotions

The promotions component of the marketing mix is also commonly referred to as the communications mix. This consists of the use of tools, such as advertising, personal selling, direct marketing, sales promotion and public relations, to promote and communicate to the event's target audiences. This element of the marketing mix is no more important than the other three elements (product, place and price) but, for event communications to be effective, there is a need for constant innovation and an effective use of a greater range of techniques. The next chapter is therefore devoted to the production of effective communications.

It can be seen that the building of the marketing strategy so far has resulted in an offering that is customer focused. Now it may be necessary to consider what is best strategically for the organization and how it should manage the event over the long term. While this text is ostensibly concerned with the management of events and not the management of organizations, it is worth considering the organizational decisions that affect events. The event organization has four generic options if it has an event product that it manages over a number of times. It can (a) build the market for more sales, market share or profit, (b) hold the market position and maintain current sales, (c) harvest the event by allowing sales to decrease but maximize profits via a decreasing of costs or (d) divest the event by dropping it or selling it off to others. Adoption of any one of these strategies clearly has an effect on the way in which any one event is managed.

Not all event organizations seek the same strategic objectives of course. Many soccer clubs in the championship, divisions one and two of the Football League in England are sufficiently financially challenged to have no desires to have more success on the field of play. They are content to remain in their division. The prospect of promotion to the division above might entail expensive improvements to facilities and would almost certainly lead to greater payments to players and a less stable financial position. This raises the question of events that are focused on playing sport for sport's sake. Even in amateur sports the need for events to break even financially is usually a necessity and so the management of sports events in a business fashion becomes a requirement too. The dilemma that currently exists in European professional football is that the business requirements of football clubs are often in stark contrast to the requirements of fans. This is also an issue in US professional sports. Shareholders demand a return on their investment and, when that requires the sale of a player, it becomes a point of resentment for the fan. The appeasing of disgruntled fans alongside the selling of players is developing into a required art for many clubs.

The development of loyal fans is a particular concern in the sports industry and a common focus for sports marketers in the management of the same event over a number of years or on a regular basis. Kelley et al. (1999) produced a case study for the fan adoption plan that was implemented by the Carolina Hurricanes. In a major relocation of the franchise from its home in Hartford, Connecticut (where they were the Hartford Whalers) to Raleigh in Carolina, the marketing planning required in order to make the transition as effective as possible involved a customer adoption strategy. Raleigh had previously never seen ice hockey in any of its stadiums and so the adoption process not only involved making potential fans aware of the club but also had to educate them in how entertaining the NFL and the game could be. The planning focused on the long-term adoption of a brand new fan base. The Hurricanes used several tactics to grow their relationship with new fans. This included taking their players out into the community and building on the history and tradition of the Whalers at first and on the exciting experience of ice hockey. Milne and McDonald (1999) maintain that, in order to increase fan identification with the team and grow loyalty, there are four key factors. Fans need to be able to access the team and players, community relations need to be developed, team history needs to be a part of communications and there needs to be creation of opportunities for fans to affiliate with the club so that they can feel a part of it. Mark Cuban, in taking over at the Dallas Mavericks, focused on making the fans a part of the club to great effect. The National Basketball Association (NBA) team managed to create loyalty in its fans, despite its losing seasons, by listening to what the fans thought about how they should be entertained (see Case study 10.1 in the next chapter).

Despite there being growth in the use of market research by event organizations, research as a management tool is still much under utilized. The NBA in the USA is active in supporting its member teams and regularly works with the Mavericks and all other teams in supplying research support. Some of their support research is extensive and it enables them to present findings to league teams on what motivates season ticket holders to renew. For example, the location and cost of the tickets are found to be the first two most important factors for customers when deciding on whether to renew. Good customer service also ranks highly as does the attitude and behaviour of a neighbouring fan sat next to you, in other words their effect on your event experience (Cann, 2003). Team performance is only just considered below these in importance with arena cleanliness and in-game entertainment below that. It is important for NBA teams to note that only one of these factors is effectively out of their control (team results) and that they can act on the others in order to improve the product. It is also worth noting that the NBA's research team remains quite small as do others at the US major leagues organizations and so, while the results of research would appear to be important, the use of it is generally not so widespread in the sports event industry.

ORGANIZATION AND IMPLEMENTATION

If an event is fully committed to its marketing strategy, the organizational structure will reflect that. There will be people and roles that are organized in order to get the strategy done. Unfortunately, it is far too common that event managers, particularly in smaller organizations, are required to wear several hats and adopt a number of different roles.

If the marketing planning process is to be followed at all then it needs to be a reflection of the customer's needs and that the offering is produced and positioned so that it satisfies both those and the organization's own needs.

The aim is to provide an offering that is customer driven and for it to be an offering that is better than that offered by the competition. A critical part then is how this is organized and whether the organization structures itself to facilitate the plan it has devised. The problems with the distribution of tickets for the 2000 Olympics in Sydney demonstrate this. Thamnopoulos and Gargalianos (2002) produced a case study on the problems that arose at the Sydney 2000 Olympics Games over ticketing arrangements. The problems revolved around the failure to sell and distribute tickets early enough. Following the research, the recommendations included proposals for organizational structure that would assist in providing better services. These included a structure that could manage operational and customer handling processes effectively when sales activity is at its greatest. While the marketing of tickets for the event was effective in creating the demand, the processing of the sales was not. This was a case of not anticipating the structure required for the handling of the whole of the operation and the treating of one element of the planning in isolation from the other. The research indicated the need for more effective communication between ticket operations and ticket marketing divisions and, in particular, for necessary reports of work in progress to all parties.

There are many events that do not have marketing departments and may only have one titled role even remotely concerned with marketing. This is not necessarily a hardship. The marketing effort needs to be organization wide with all members playing a part. For example, the creation of a marketing mix requires those from financial, sales, distribution and operations areas of the organization to be involved in order to be effective. However, it is critical that there are people, systems and processes in place that reflect the requirements of such integrated marketing strategies.

Another critical factor is the need for a macro- as well as a micro-perspective. The strategic thrust is a key element of the marketing plan and for that to be implemented, the organizational structure needs to be flexible enough to allow managers to get above the day-to-day operational tactics of the event and have time to focus on the longer term. This has ramifications for control as well. In order to keep control, a manager needs to have the time in order to be able to perform that role.

The employment of key figures and professionals into instrumental roles is also a key factor. For example, the Los Angeles hosting of the 1984 Olympics was better off for the abilities of Peter Ueberroth and a US$225 million financial surplus (Toohey and Veal, 2000). The appointment of ex-player and general sports icon Wayne Gretzky as Executive Director of Team Canada was a move by Hockey Canada that the organizers of the 2004 World Cup of Hockey (ice hockey) used to their advantage (*Sports Business*

Daily, 2003). Lord Coe, as chair of LOCOG, has already had a positive impact in heading up the bid for the 2012 Olympics.

CONTROL

This is the stage where alignment with objectives is evaluated and maintained. As the plan is implemented, it may be possible to correct and realign if objectives are not being met. The only way this will be possible, however, is if the objectives are measurable. Improving ticket revenue on last year can only become measurable if there are targets, either with an absolute figure or percentage growth. It can be seen now why the planning process, with its logical development of assessing markets and customer needs prior to the setting of objectives, is an effective approach.

Evaluation needs to be undertaken at the end of the process as well as continually throughout it and so, while it is a final stage in the planning process, it is also iterativley important in all of the previous stages too. The success and failure of future marketing activities determined via post-event evaluation and reporting, documentation and archiving are of paramount importance in the event industry. Many sports events are an annual occurrence and whether the event management team is the same the following year or not, there is a need for accurate detailed feedback the next time the event is being managed.

SUMMARY

Successful marketing planning requires a methodical process that addresses the needs of customers while satisfying corporate objectives. In order to do that, target markets need to be identified and an appropriate event delivered; an event that provides those markets with an offering that makes them choose and stay loyal. To be successful, the event needs to position itself so that it is not only attractive to the customer but it is more attractive than any alternatives. The marketing planning process featured in this chapter is a logical progression through the stages that will achieve that objective.

Recommended by generic and sports marketing theory, the process begins strategically with corporate goals and an assessment of the organizations internal and external environments so that one, the process is aligned to the organizations mission and objectives, and two, that the process begins with an assessment of resources and opportunities in order to provide a relevant base for marketing. The process then becomes more specific with the development of marketing goals and a tactical plan consisting of the marketing mix that will achieve the desired market position. As with most management mechanisms, the plan has to be implemented and so the process leads into the development of suitable organizational structures and systems that can effectively achieve that so that it can be controlled and evaluated against the objectives set.

QUESTIONS

1. Evaluate the importance of the marketing planning undertaken by the Carolina Hurricanes, identifying where possible the progression of the marketing planning process.

2. Select an event and identify the types of internal and external information that is critical for marketing planning.

3. Select two similar events and evaluate how they position themselves in the market by identifying, comparing and contrasting the key features of their marketing mixes.

4. Identify one event manager who, in your opinion, has played a critical marketing role at a specific event. Evaluate that role and the contribution made.

5. Identify one example of innovative sports event marketing and analyse why it was successful.

REFERENCES

AELTC (2003). www.wimbledon.org/en_GB/about/debentures/ debentures_history (accessed 4 November 2003).

BOC (2003). www.olympics.org.uk/olympicmovement/modernhistory.asp (accessed 4 November 2003).

Boone, L. and Kurtz, D. (2002). *Contemporary Marketing*, 11th edn. London, Thomson Learning.

Cann, J. (2003). *NBA Season Ticket Holder Research*. Presentation by Senior manager, NBA Research and Analysis. NBA Store, 5th Avenue, New York. 2 December 2003.

Jobber, D. (2007). *Principals and Practice of Marketing*, 5th edn. London, McGraw-Hill, Chapter 8.

Kelley, S., Hoffman, K. and Carter, S. (1999). Franchise relocation and sport introduction: a sports marketing case study of the Carolina Hurricanes fan adoption plan. *Journal of Services Marketing*, 13(6), 469–480.

Kotler, P. (2006). *Marketing Management*, 12th edn. London, Prentice-Hall.

Milne, G. and McDonald, M. (1999). *Sport Marketing: Managing – the Exchange Process*. London, Jones and Bartlett Publishers, Chapter 2.

Mullin, B., Hardy, S. and Sutton, W. (2000). In: *Sport Marketing*, 2nd edn. Champaign, Il, Human Kinetics, Chapter 6.

Piercy, N. (2002). *Market-led Strategic Change: Transforming the Process of Going to Market*, 3rd edn. Oxford, Butterworth-Heinemann.

Pitts, G. and Stotlar, D. (2002). *Fundamentals of Sport Marketing*, 2nd edn. Morgantown, Fitness Information Technology Inc., Chapter 8.

Porter, M. (1980). *Competitive Strategy: Techniques for Analysing Industries and Competitors*. New York, The Free Press.

Shank, M. (2002). *Sports Marketing: A Strategic Perspective*, 2nd edn. London, Prentice-Hall International (UK).

Sports Business Daily (2003). *Hockey Canada Set to Bring Wayne Gretzky Back into the Fold for World Cup*. 4 November. Morning Buzz. Street and Smith. www.sportsbusinessdaily.com (accessed 4 November 2003).

Sportsworld (2008). Event Guide. www.sportsworld.co.uk/beijing2008 (accessed 24 March 2008).

Thamnopoulos, Y. and Gargalianos, D. (2002). Ticketing of large scales events: the case of Sydney 2000 Olympic Games. *Facilities*, 20(1/2), 22–33.

Toohey, K. and Veal, A. (2000). *The Olympic Games: A Social Science Perspective*. Sydney, CABI, Chapter 10.

Wood, E. (2004). A strategic approach for the use of sponsorship in the events industry: In search of a return on investment. In I. Yeoman, M. Robertson, J. Ali-Knight, U. McMahon-Beattie, S. Drummond (eds), *Festival and Events Management: An International Arts and Cultural Perspective*. Oxford, Butterworth-Heinemann.

Innovative Communications

An unfinished new building is covered for the 2008 Beijing Olympics as all construction work is suspended for the Games period. While the media were critical, Beijing did well to cover up many building sites of this kind but took the opportunity to produce Olympic themed drapes in order to take advantage of the event promotional opportunity.

CONTENTS

241

LEARNING OBJECTIVES

After studying this chapter, you should be able to:

■ understand the role and value of innovative marketing communications in sports events marketing planning

■ understand the process required for achieving successful integrated marketing communications

■ identify the marketing communications tools that are available for sports events

INTRODUCTION

In an increasingly competitive industry where traditional media and methods are no longer as effective as they once were, sports event managers need to be using innovative marketing communication methods. This chapter aims to build up a conceptual framework for the development, planning and implementation of the methods that are now required for successful communication. The focus will be on the importance of effectively integrating a range of tools and techniques to communicate the event.

The chapter is in two sections. The first provides an approach for Integrated Marketing Communications (IMC) planning and its application for the sports event industry. The second provides the event manager with a communications toolbox and considers how personal, interactive and mass media methods are incorporated into an overall strategy for a sports event.

Section 1: Integrated Marketing Communications

In a highly creative industry, it is disappointing to see so many events attempting to communicate with their customers in mass market approaches and not use segmentation techniques to determine more focused target markets. It is also disappointing to see them use such a limited range of tools. The approach has too often been one of managing promotional choices in isolation from the management of the event.

How many events are undertaking research in an analysis of stakeholders and using that research in decisions about the product, its prices and the choice of venue and how it is then promoted? For major events, the importance of communications is generally acknowledged. In the bidding process, for example, it is clear that recent host cities have used extensive communications techniques to win local stakeholder support. Take the Sydney 2000 Olympics and the Manchester 2002 Commonwealth Games and their use of websites and volunteer programmes, for example. The London and New York 2012 Olympic bids followed suit. The London site encourages interaction by inviting messages of support as did Beijing on its site leading up to the 2008 Games. Outside of major events though, the use of innovative communications is scarce. Unfortunately, when it comes to communications decisions, the practice is to reach as many people as possible with only a mass-market mentality. However, due to limited budgets, the selection of mass media advertising for communication purposes is not even an option when the high costs make it an inefficient solution for a return on a promotional investment. A more effective approach should consider the use of focused and highly targeted communications methods.

An IMC approach considers the customer first and then coordinates all communications for a unified organization-wide message. This necessitates agreement and ownership of consistent communications by the organization as a whole. The traditional approach to marketing management has been to create separate functions for sales, mass media activity, public relations (PR) and promotions. An IMC approach, however, integrates all aspects of the communications mix into one effort by devising a customer-focused programme that provides synergy between all activities and messages.

The choice of which media to use, mass, personal or interactive, must effectively meet the communications objectives that are set but must also be an efficient use of resources so that it becomes a costs versus benefits exercise. During the implementation of the strategy, the results need to be monitored so that an alignment with objectives can be maintained.

This approach has developed as a consequence of less confidence in mass media advertising and an increasing reliance on targeted communications. As a result, there is more effort in measuring the success of communications and return on investment. Schultz et al (1996) maintain that the reason for the development of IMC is that marketing communications will be the only way organizations will be able to sustain competitive advantage in increasingly undifferentiated product markets.

The purpose of communication is to create a message that inspires positive action from stakeholders. According to Lavidge and Steiner (1961), this response process moves through a number of effects, a hierarchy of effects. Their model was based on the earlier AIDA (attention, interest, desire and action) theory (Strong, 1925) (see Figure 10.1).

Other models follow a similar process, although not all conclude with purchase. Engel et al. (1994) move through five stages of exposure, attention,

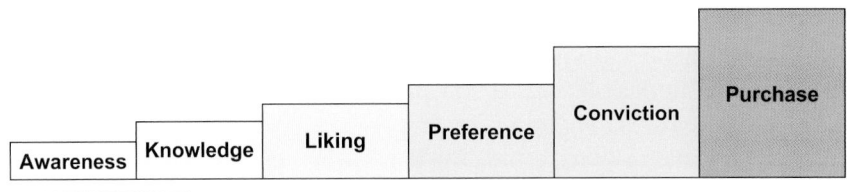

FIGURE 10.1 *Hierarchy of effects (adapted from Lavidge and Steiner, 1961).*

comprehension, acceptance and then retention as the final action allowing for the fact that the communications process is a tool for reaching all stakeholders of an organization not just its customers.

The psychology behind communication is to create as clear a message as possible, one that can avoid the noise and clutter of the market and become memorable. If it is memorable, it may therefore become persuasive and change or enhance opinion (Wells et al, 1995). Vaughn (1980) proposes a useful four-stage view of how communication works. The information feed has to aid learning, appeal with a sense of value and may require relatively long copy such as through the use of e-mail, advertisements, brochures and leaflets. To be effective at stage two, there needs to be a reinforcement of the message that inspires a desire to trial and sample which may be best achieved by image building through the use of large space media, such as billboards and posters. For it to become habit forming in stage three, the aim is to increase use by further reinforcement via small space media such as sound bites and point of sale (POS). Finally, self-satisfaction is achieved when the appeal is socially pleasing and communications reflect that life-style, possible through large space media, print and POS. The task is to identify which target stakeholder should receive which message by what communication method.

There are two choices of focus for this task, to expand or penetrate a market and, for each focus, there are criteria that can guide an event manager in determining the communications plan. This is represented in Figure 10.2.

Once a focus has been identified, the integrated message can be designed. The key is to manage this across the whole of the marketing mix so that, while there are communications to be made about the product, the price and the place, they are not made in isolation. They are considered together and then the appropriate methods are used to impart these communications. This is represented in Figure 10.3. Other models are proposed by Fill (2002) and Pickton and Broderick (2001).

There are barriers to the successful implementation of an IMC approach not least the issue of how it is managed. If external agencies are contracted to supply any part of the process, then their integration becomes an issue when their objectives are different from those of the organization. An advertising

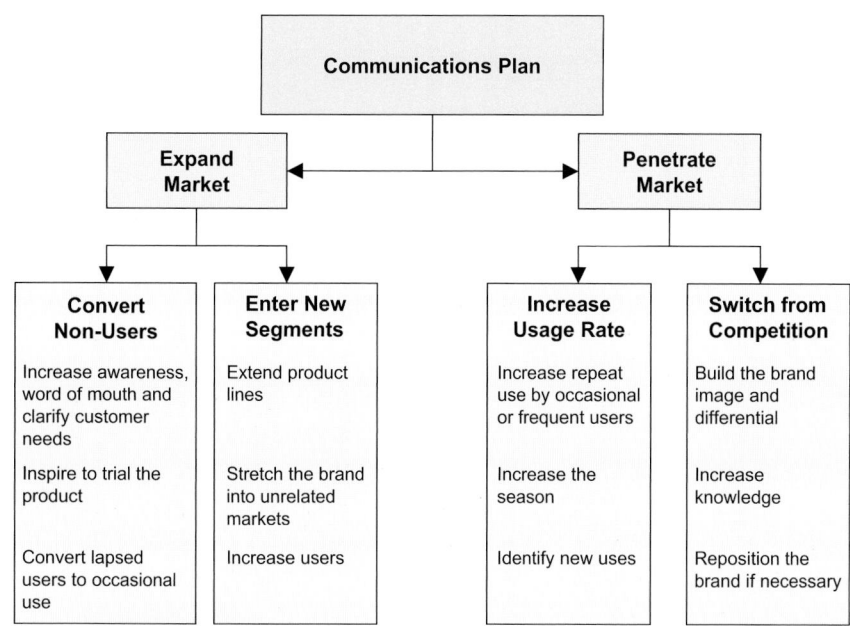

FIGURE 10.2   *Communications plan (adapted from Michell, 1988).*

agency with creative design at the top of its agenda might well be at odds with the client that requires measurable increased awareness or sales not an industry award. The involvement of staff and them buying into the organizations objectives is critical where face-to-face customer relations are concerned, but is not always an easy managerial task. It is also an internal task to manage the transition of those that lean towards the traditional segregation of the communications components, in particular those that manage PR in isolation.

For the current events market there are new and exciting targets. The emergence of the extreme sports market has allowed marketers to reach the teenagers and 20-somethings that are active in skateboarding, surfing, windsurfing, parascending and more. This has attracted mainstream manufacturers such as Nike and Mars as well as those brands that already produce for these markets, opening up new opportunities for event communications. The Ogilvy marketing agency, for example, developed what it refered to as a 360 degrees brand stewardship model. The idea is that it integrates all forms of communications for clients and has had success in reaching these anti-establishment markets for such mainstream clients as Kodak (Ogilvy, 2003).

The approach can be effectively applied in the marketing of teams. Mark Cuban, the owner of the Dallas Mavericks basketball franchise, used an integrated communications programme to turn the organization into a very

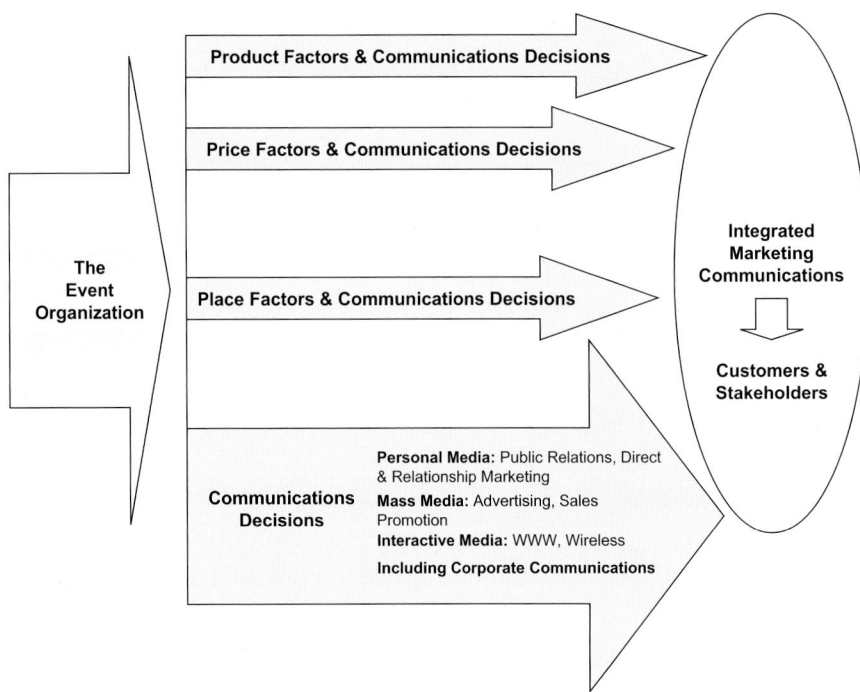

FIGURE 10.3 *The integrated marketing communications process (adapted from Fill, 2002; Pickton and Broderick, 2001).*

successful NBA outfit. From a position of struggling team and poor fan attendance, it took more than just a lot of dollars to achieve the change. The innovatory techniques provide a good example of an integrated approach in Case study 10.1.

Case Study 10.1

Innovative Communications: The Dallas Mavericks

Since taking over the Dallas Mavericks in 2000, Mark Cuban has transformed the fortunes of this NBA franchise. The results, via an innovative approach, include taking half empty home match nights to sell-outs in every game only two seasons later and regularly ever since.

Cuban set out to change the relationship the club had with its fans to enhance their experience. The focus in the beginning was to sell a brand that may or may not win on the court but would provide great entertainment.

He started with the organization culture. He himself got involved at the front end of sales, tripled the number of sales staff and trained them to focus on the entertainment not the on-court results. At one point, there was a target of 100 tele-sales calls per member of staff per day and those staff that could not buy into this culture were asked to leave. Bar codes were put onto tickets so that they could be tracked and when corporate customers did not attend for a number of games they received a phone call to ask if there was any dissatisfaction. The intention was to ensure that every seat was occupied, not just for revenue, but because full stadiums can provide a great atmosphere. This policy continues today via 'Ticket Forwarding' and, in 2008, the US$1.95 cost involved in sending on a ticket to a season ticket holder's nominated 'friend' was paid for by the club.

Cuban himself still sits in the stands with the fans as opposed to in a corporate area. He socializes with them after the games. His personal e-mail address is still accessible via the website and he continues consistently to respond to his e-mail from fans. As technology has advanced, there is now a Cuban Blog. He encourages suggestions for improvement and, importantly, is seen to act on them. In 2001, a fan corresponded that the 24-second shot clock was difficult to see. At that time, such clocks were intended for player information but the Mavericks installed a three-sided clock only weeks after that e-mail. Since then, all NBA teams have equipped themselves with similar equipment.

The rebuilding of the Maverick brand clearly involved the fans. Cuban made the fans, the match night and the experience into the brand itself. When the club sold its naming rights to its stadium in 2007 to American Airlines (American Airlines Center – the AAC) they also created a new fan driven group to inspire the atmosphere at games. Fans can now join the 'Mavericks ManiAACs to be a part of that. The adding of a now extremely successful team on court has only enhanced the brand. When Cuban took over their record was 9 wins and 23 losses but, by 2003, the team had reached its third play-offs in a row and added the Western Conference title. In 2007, the Mavericks reached their first ever NBA Finals.

Cuban also hires key personnel like Matt Fitzgerald from Coca-Cola who embrace this 'have-a-go' approach to marketing. The investment has been there to support errors along the way but ideas are tried out and fans are made a part of that process. Out of 120 sports franchises in an ESPN poll, the Mavericks ranked 5th and 2nd in 2003 and 2004 respectively for overall fan satisfaction.

Maverick by name, maverick by nature!

Source: Caplan (2003); McConnell and Huba (2003); Dallas Mavericks (2008)

Section 2: Communications Toolkit

The basic media forms of personal media, interactive media and mass media will be discussed in this section. PR can be both personal and mass media and is therefore discussed first.

PUBLIC RELATIONS

While the use of PR techniques for successful communications is not without cost, they are, nevertheless, often a less expensive alternative to many of the others that exist in the event manager's armoury. They also carry the highest level of credibility. Consequently, they are arguably some of the most important.

PR has two roles. On the one hand, it supports marketing activity in the form of promotions. On the other hand, it is also the tool that disseminates non-promotional information to other target publics that are important to the organization. PR has a much wider role to play than to support the marketing push, it extends to managing communications with all those organizations, groups and individuals that are considered an important factor in the successful implementation of the event, otherwise known as target publics. These might involve communications concerned with the changing of opinion or provision of information that are targeted at local pressure groups, community leaders, financial institutions and event participants (see Figure 10.4). A target public is an individual or group that has sufficient influence to have bearing upon the success of an organization.

Whatever the nature of the communication, the targets need to be identified. This is achieved via a process of target analysis, the first stage of the process of PR communications. The analysis extends to the identification of all of the event's stakeholders and publics and the form of communication they should receive. At this point, it is critical that these messages are an intrinsic part of the overall communications plan and certainly not in conflict with it. The result is a list of who should receive what communication. An event's publics could consist of any of the following:

- *Customers*: ticket and corporate buyers

- *Participants*: competitors, celebrities, performers and acts

- *Sponsors*: fee paying and supply-in-kind

- *Partners*: for event organization, promotion and funding

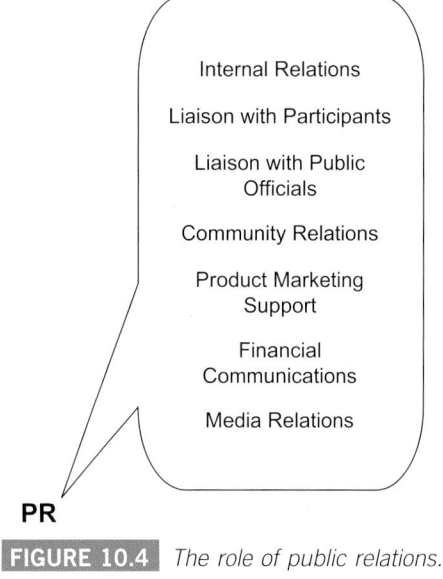

Internal Relations

Liaison with Participants

Liaison with Public Officials

Community Relations

Product Marketing Support

Financial Communications

Media Relations

PR

FIGURE 10.4 *The role of public relations.*

■ *Financial providers*: shareholders, investors and lenders

■ *Suppliers*: event equipment, merchandise and service providers

■ *Staff*: permanent, temporary, sub-contracted and voluntary

■ *Community*: local operating environments and pressure groups.

For economic and efficiency reasons, it may not be possible to reach all of these targets and so this analysis also requires scheduling, costing and then prioritizing. The result is a PR plan that is integrated into the event communications plan. Jefkins and Yadin (1998) follow a six-point process consisting of, appreciating the situation, defining objectives, defining publics, selection of media and techniques, budget planning and evaluation. They emphasize the importance of identifying corporate objectives and aligning PR accordingly. The seven-point process in Figure 10.5 highlights this still further but also acknowledges the need for corporate objectives to be identified at the beginning of the process so that the situational analysis can be aligned too.

The PR planning process

PR encompasses the task of creating media opportunities and so it is important to consider the relationship that exists between events and the media. On the one hand, there is the value of recruiting all-important media partners for the attraction of sponsors, as discussed in Chapter 11, and there is the creation of positive media exposure discussed here in this chapter.

Sports events are reported in or commented on by many media but the event has no control over that content. Whether the comment is negative or positive, the media will air or write what they feel is appropriate for them to meet their objectives and not the objectives of the event. Conversely, an event's overriding aim is to achieve positive coverage for the event without paying for the space or air-time it occupies. Ultimately, it would be desirable for the media to take whatever the event gives it and then disseminate it as it was delivered, but that is seldom the practice. Editors will have the final decision and so the importance of forming positive relationships in media relations is critical. There may be any number of PR objectives to achieve. On the one hand, there are the marketing communication objectives of supporting sales, possibly prior to the event, and also the wider communications that are needed internally with employees, with the community and other target publics before, during or post the event, all of which are not necessarily attractive enough for the media to embrace. Consequently, strong

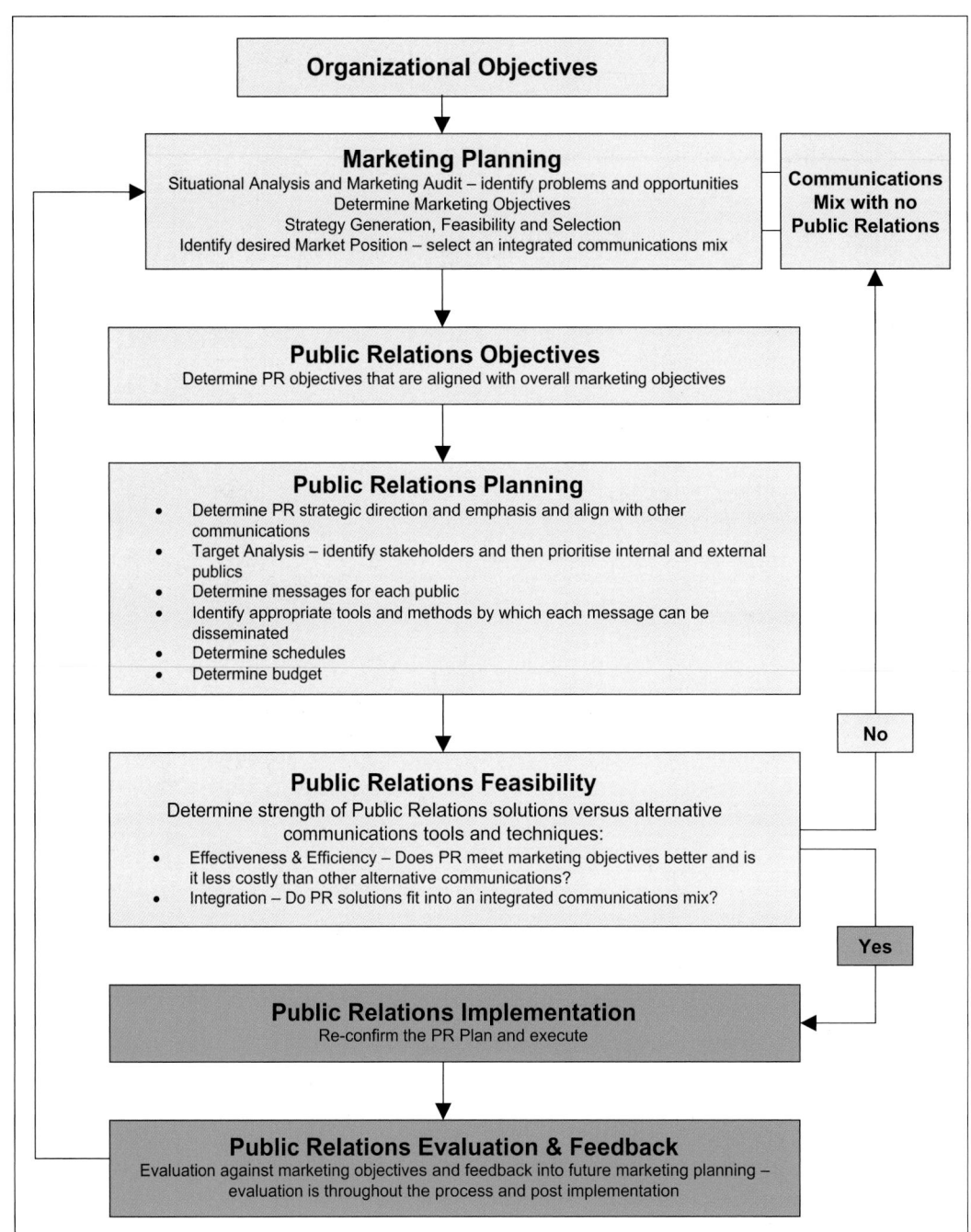

FIGURE 10.5 *Public relations planning process. Process for the planning of public relations in integrated sports event marketing communications (Masterman and Wood, 2006).*

relationships with key media and a range of innovative techniques and tools in order to evoke an attraction are important when trying to create the desired media exposure.

Media relationship building

The cliché of whom you know and not necessarily what you know might easily be applied to the area of media relations whereby having a strong relationship with media can be a key factor. The difficulty of course is getting started, particularly for those events that do not have sufficient power to attract almost any media attention. For new events, the challenge is in creating newsworthy items as well as to build up key relationships.

Maintaining the relationship once it is forged is easier but needs to be an ongoing task. As with most relationships, it often takes giving something you do not want to give on one occasion so that you can have the favour returned on another. The feeding of the media, and the tabloid press in particular, is commonplace in football in the UK. Agents and clubs are prone to supplying reporters with stories that can often start the stories that in effect instigate the transfers of players and other business. The process needs to be handled with care. In 1996, Mars agreed a sponsorship with Team Scotland and its participation in Union European Football Association's (UEFA's) Euro '96. The story was leaked to the press before Mars had given an approval for communications but in an attempt to try to attract further sponsors. Mars took objection to the leak and the action and relations became strained between team and the sponsor.

The recruiting of media partners is a method of forming a strong bond with particular media. Having an agreement with newspapers, local television and radio stations can provide the event with a package of promotional traffic pre-event. The media can also contribute to the event with free entertainment by broadcasting live and distributing products or merchandise. The event can gain more control over the media output in this way by agreeing activities in a contract, but there are dangers. For the smaller event, guaranteed exposure is only to the event's advantage but, for larger events with greater profile, there is the risk of alienating the media with whom there are no agreements.

Event PR techniques

The techniques that are at the event manager's disposal can be broadly categorized as follows:

- *Advertorials*: paid for space but designed to read like editorial. The Athens 2004 Olympics used advertorials to appease concerns over delays in construction of facilities in the lead up to the Games. The content consisted of a focus on the benefits of visiting Greece generally and the Olympics specifically and were targeted at publics in the UK via *The Observer* and in the USA via the *New York Times* within the same month (Masterman and Wood, 2006).

- *Feature articles*: one-off contributions or regular columns that can be 'by-lined' by a representative of the event or by a journalist briefed by event management.

- *Advance articles*: an advance notification of the event using pictures, information and competitions.

- *Spokespeople and expertise*: event managers creating a reputation for always having something to say and a strong opinion so that media will readily call when they want a reaction to a story. The key is to be available at any time and ensure key media know how to contact you quickly.

- *Results servicing*: for major events results there are mechanisms in place that will distribute scores, reports and league standings. For new events and events with a lesser profile, there is more work to be done but results are of general interest to media, particularly local media.

- *Reader offers and competitions*: one of the mechanics that has commonly been used in the events industry is the use of event tickets and hospitality, given to all range of media, printed publications, Internet, television and radio, for use in reader offers and/or competitions. The competition feature will include details of the event and ticket hotlines thus aiding pre-event sales. The exchange of tickets for editorial coverage is mutually agreeable as the media are seen to be providing a service if not extra value to their own target publics.

- *Created news:* when there are no obvious opportunities to use the techniques above, then there is a case for creating newsworthy items. Research and an innovative approach are required in order to create new 'hooks' that will attract media attention and take-up (Masterman and Wood, 2006). Research data can often work. For example, market/public related findings that put the event in a good light will be of interest to the media if they are of interest to readers, listeners and viewers. Poll results on the popularity of an Olympic Games will be important to report and, for the event, important communcations to encourage further support. Other created news of value are links with anything that can extend goodwill. Links and support to charities and the community in general, for example. Special events can also be newsworthy, see below.

Event PR tools

The tools that are available include leaflets, direct mail, newsletters both internally and externally to the organization, special events, sponsorship and the various methods of making personal contact. The hooks or mechanics highlighted above form the focus for the content and these tools are the means by which the target publics are physically contacted. As with most tools, there are advantages and disadvantages depending on their point of use.

- *Leaflets*: the positives are that leaflets are relatively low cost and may be distributed by hand, door to door or by dispenser. The negatives are that there is low retention of the information by readers and high wastage.

- *Direct mail*: these tools offer opportunities to personalize the communication and send it directly to homes and businesses. Events can send them when they want and, by associating with organizations and using their database, the event gains a friendly conduit for the transmitting of the communication. There is, however, a high cost attached to direct mail in that databases can be expensive as can mailing to large numbers. The mail may also be perceived as intrusive and wastage occurs as a result.

- *Newsletters*: this medium can provide an informal and credible communication and can involve and engage the reader. If they are not totally uncritical, however, they may not be perceived that credibly. They need to be carefully targeted for them to have effect.

- *Special events*: events are tools in themselves and media launches are a common form of communication. They require targeted invitees and provide opportunities for social interaction that can be useful in reinforcing the communication. The downside is that they can be expensive and time consuming to organize. Events can also include exhibitions, conferences, seminars and public consultations. Major events use organized public debates as part of their communications activities in the lead-up to bidding. In January 2003, the Greater London Authority organized a debate in conjunction with the Observer Newspaper, part of the Guardian

Newspaper Group, at the Royal Institute of Architecture building in London to discuss the prospect of London bidding for the 2012 Olympics. Anyone was welcome to apply for a ticket and both supporters and non-supporters attended together with a full complement of all media. The Olympic Torch Relay is a special event that is created to promote the Olympic Movement and the games. Sydney created an international relay for its 2000 Games that was so successful that Manchester used the model for its 2002 Commonwealth Games. Manchester even recruited Sydney's key executives to come to Manchester to replicate it. The relay is an event of high cost and is a point of attraction in itself and for Beijing it was a massive international undertaking in 2008 (see Beijing Insight 10.1).

Beijing Insight 10.1
Beijing 2008 Olympics: Torch Relay
The significance of the Olympic flame has developed since ancient times to the present where now there is an international event that sees the lit torch tour on a global route.

It is assumed that the flame itself derives from Hera's temple in Olympia where it was kindled via a skaphia (crucible) and the sun's rays to set a fire. For ancient games, a flaming torch was carried from the temple and handed to a runner to take it across the Olympia site in a ceremony that marked the start of a games. In modern times, the torch was first rekindled, as it were, in 1936 for the Berlin Olympics. Again, the torch was lit using a similar process using a parabolic mirror in Olympia and transported to Berlin where it was used to light a cauldron in the Olympic stadium and begin those games. The process has remained much the same since and is seen as a symbol of the link between the traditions of the ancient games and the modern day epic.

The 'pure' flame is a symbol of the Olympic Movement and is therefore meant to represent peace and harmony. The theme for the Beijing Torch Relay was 'Journey of Harmony' and it was stated that it reflected 'Chinese peoples wish of building a harmonious society of enduring peace and common prosperity'. The slogan for the Torch Relay was 'Light the passion Share the dream' and was intended to tie in to the 'One world One dream' focus for the games themselves.

The Beijing 2008 Torch Relay started on March 24 in Olympia and after seven days in Greece moved on to Beijing for the start of an international tour consisting of 19 destinations across the world. On May 2, the torch reached Hong Kong for the start of a tour of China and 114 different cities before returning to Beijing for the opening ceremony on August 8.

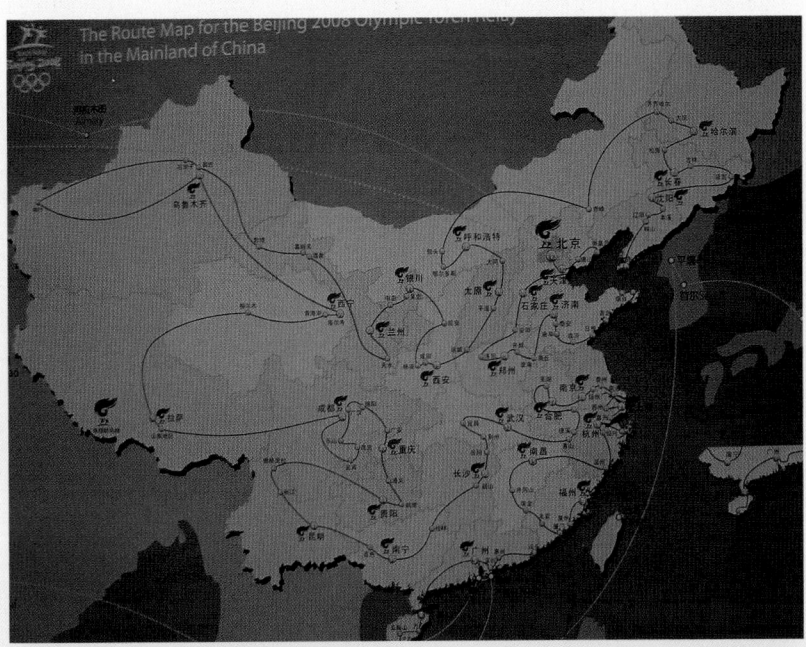

The worldwide and China based routes for the 2008 Olympic Torch Relay.

Continued

Beijing Insight 10.1—cont'd

The Beijing Torch Relay was used to promote the 2008 Games on an international basis but it was also a major event in itself. As a financial exercise, it involved the support of three partners, Coca-Cola, Samsung and Lenovo, all TOP partners who, in effect, were exploiting their own TOP Olympiad and 2008 Games sponsorship rights with further marketing communications. LOCOG also used the visit of the relay to London to promote the 2012 Olympics by taking it through key 2012 sites and using well known British Olympians such as Kelly Holmes, Steve Redgrave and Steve Cram as bearers. To this extent, torch relays are special events that are created to promote a larger event.

The torch relay has arguably become so significant that it has become a target for political message despite the IOC and the Olympic Movement's efforts to strive to keep any kind of party politics out of the Olympics. It is perhaps too tall an order to expect politics to be kept out of sport in this way and the Beijing Torch Relay became a target for a number of protests along its route.

The point to be made here is that this then required considerable effort on BOCOG's part in order to produce communications that could deal with the efforts of others intent on intervening. The interventions in London, Paris and San Francisco were such that the event route through each city had to be altered and positive communications generated to counteract negative media coverage. This was a major public relations effort that also required planned contingencies to be put in place. Throughout this time, BOCOG maintained a focus on the many positive aspects there were on route, including first visits by a relay to Eastern Africa and the city of Dar es Salaam in Tanzania. Keeping a regular updated site of commentary as well as photographs from each visit on-line was also key to this task.

An initial response to the antagonistic interventions from the IOC was that it was to consider the future of international routes for Olympic torch relays and from LOCOG the response was that it had yet to decide what it might do for 2012. LOCOG chairman Lord Sebastian Coe acted as spokesman and was personally on hand throughout the day for media comment including live on the BBC. These are the kinds of statements that are required quickly in order to present as positive a light as possible while negative interventions take impact. Continuous monitoring and action may be required after intervention and, in particular, to counteract media coverage that may ensue. An article entitled 'Fanning the Flames' in *The Guardian* commented on the public relations activity following the visit of the Torch Relay to London and suggested that it was an ideal opportunity for BOCOG to 'refashion the country's image' (Gaber, 2008).

Source: Beijing 2008 (2008); Sports City (2008)

■ *Sponsorship*: event managers might also select sponsorship as a means of communicating their event. The 2002 Commonwealth Games attached its image to a number of sports and cultural events in the 2 years prior to the event. The negatives are that there may be fees attached and further investment is required in order to make the sponsorship work.

- *Personal contact*: such contact can be face-to-face, by telephone or electronically. A very personal communication can be achieved where opportunities to argue the case and overcome objections can be taken. Personal contact also offers opportunities for relationship building but can equally be seen as intrusive with costs that can be as high as they are time consuming.

PR innovation

The above generic PR techniques and tools are commonly used by sports events, so where does the innovation come in? The key stage of the PR planning process above is the situational analysis. It is there that the events assets are evaluated and, as each event is unique, it is there where an advantage may be achieved in the attracting of media attention.

The 2002 Commonwealth Games used product placement in a particularly innovative way on ITV television during the run-up and during the games themselves. Coronation Street was, at the time, and remains one of the UK's highest watched television programmes. The programme is set and filmed in Manchester. An adapted script saw one particular character develop a role as a game's volunteer and wearing an authentic Asda provided and sponsored event volunteer tracksuit. Filming was also conducted at the City of Manchester Stadium.

The categories of assets that are to be considered for the PR plan together form what is uniquely newsworthy for the event, the PR equity in the event. Figure 10.6 identifies the categories of participants, products, programme and partners. They form another set of invaluable 'P's. The equity lies in the interest attracted from the media and how they can become newsworthy entities. The innovation lies with the skills of event managers in maximizing the opportunity.

Evaluation of PR

Traditional evaluation methods of PR for sports events typically include measuring frequency and size. Specific approaches will count up the numbers of opportunities to see increasing or decreasing complaints and enquiries. There are also unfortunate uses of gains/losses in market share that can only be linked to PR campaigns at the most indirectly. Assessing impact value is of use but the allocation of an arbitrary level of importance to each medium is very subjective and a delicate decision.

PR Equity
Participants
The teams and players, either individually or collectively, are unique to any one event at that particular time. Their celebrity, sporting prowess, sporting or other achievements and personality.
Examples:
Taking one or numbers of players and using them as figure head(s) or spokespersons in the marketing communications plan. Specific activities might include interview features in the media, appearances at special events.
Products
The numbers, nature and availability of tickets, corporate hospitality, merchandise, whether free or priced.
Examples:
Use of sold out, sold in record time, record number of sales, exclusive merchandise, limited free merchandise on purchase or attendance/participation.
Programme
Current Perspective: The nature and prospect of the competition and entertainment on offer, player and team matches, its duration, rules used, technology used, calendar position, prices, competition with other offerings (direct and indirect competition), dignitaries and celebrity attending.
Examples:
Sports records under threat, intriguing matches of key participants in prospect. Latest technology and new rules on trial, new dates, timings and ticket prices, head-to-head competition and reasons for competitive advantage.
Historical Perspective: Previous programmes, competition and entertainment provided, records and achievements accomplished, data, facts and figures concerned with competition and event operations.
Examples:
Sports records broken, great archive sporting performances, record numbers of champagne and strawberries served, largest number of stewards to ensure safety etc.
Partners
The sponsors, funding and supporting shareholders and stakeholders.
Examples:
Credible sponsors make news when they are recruited and in their activities. Supporting partners may include local dignitaries, officials or celebrity. Responding to local pressure groups or the competition with comment.

FIGURE 10.6 *PR equity.*

One of the most common evaluation methods consists of quantifying the value of the space/time achieved as if it were advertising. This involves counting up the column inches/centimetres and minutes of PR and calculating how much it would cost to purchase the same as bought space. There are two problems with this method. One is that only rate card cost may be applied as there are no actual negotiations taking place and rate card prices are seldom paid in the industry. Secondly, advertising is a paid for medium and PR is gained via third party acceptance and so it is simply not possible to apply the same value to both. However, the use of Equivalent Advertising Costs (EAC) can be used to evaluate the frequency and quantity of PR over time. By tracking EAC, it is at least possible to see by how much PR activity has increased or not.

In an industry that is increasingly looking for return on investment, the surest methods of evaluation are by market research. The use of survey and interview methods is required in order to get usable evaluation of PR success. The issues are that it is expensive and, as a result, is not a common occurrence.

PERSONAL MEDIA

Personal media marketing methods include the use of PR and direct marketing such as by mail, face-to-face or personal selling, catalogues, kiosks and telemarketing. Other methods that have direct response mechanisms can also be categorized here too and these would include advertising in all media and home shopping television channels, neither of which are currently that common in the sports events industry. Use of interactive methods such as websites and wireless communications are covered below but can also be considered as personal media.

The value of personal media is in the development of customer relationships to a point where they are loyal fans and will consistently return to an event. The Dallas Mavericks provide an example of a sports team attempting to build relationships with its customers where the stages of adoption are to progress non-fans to casual fans and then on to season ticket holders. There are two separate focuses for the management of customer relationships (see Case study 10.1). The first is the corporate business-to-business relationship that is predominantly led by relationships between individuals and face-to-face marketing methods. The other involves the event's target markets where the mass audiences are more difficult to get close to. Personal media marketing methods can be used to try to alleviate these difficulties.

Much is made of the differences between traditional transaction marketing and the new marketing approach of relationship-based marketing.

Piercy (2002) highlights the key differences. He maintains that Customer Relationship Marketing (CRM) concerns the customer and sales to them over the long term and a continuous relationship, not a one-off transactional process. The communication with a customer should be interactive to enable this to happen as opposed to focusing on a single transaction. Technological innovation and the development of new tools for communicating is making this approach much more achievable.

Direct marketing

Methods for marketing directly with the customer include by mail, e-mail, personal selling, catalogues, kiosks and telemarketing. The common thread with most of these methods is that they require the building of databases. This information comes directly from the Marketing Information System (MkIS) as discussed in Chapter 9.

Each method has advantages and disadvantages in marketing events as discussed here.

Direct and e-mail

This involves the sending of highly targeted offers, announcements, reminders, in printed or electronic mode, to a specific address (Kotler, 2006). This is a common event marketing tool that clearly depends for its success on the quality of the database of contact details. Letters, leaflets, flyers, foldouts, audio tapes, videotapes, CDs and computer discs can all be sent out to a named recipient. This targeting capability is clearly an advantage and the capacity to test small numbers also offers efficiency. The ability for events to send out direct mail that is signed by a key figure is another advantage. In the USA, a letter from a major league owner is of value but, in sending out e-mails, the San Francisco 49ers have more success with players' names on a recipients alert screen (Berridge, 2003). Mullin et al (2000) maintain that direct mail can be more than just an offer and propose the use of previous event success data, photos and thank-you quotes as ways of making the vehicle an attractive one.

There are two main disadvantages. Customer response can be as low as 2% and therefore 'cost per thousand' people reached can be high compared with advertising (Jobber, 2007). There can also be a lot of wastage if the database is of poor quality and, clearly, the collection of useful data is also a cost and time consideration. One way to collect address and personal data is to run promotions and offers. The Dallas Stars offered free seats at four games in 2003 with the purpose of collecting data. The result was a database of 50 000 and that was achieved in only 2 weeks. The Stars did run the danger of decreasing the customer value in adopting this approach. It is critical not to devalue the product to existing customers and those that take up such an offer may only be interested in free products. Combinations of discreet and targeted promotions such as sweepstakes or the distribution of very important person (VIP) passes may take longer but may be more productive.

Personal selling

There are two types of selling that are applicable in the sports industry, order taking for in-store operations and order getting by salespeople (Jobber, 2007). In the main, the latter involves the prospecting for new business with key accounts and new organizations such as sponsors, advertisers, etc. Sponsor relations are discussed in greater detail in Chapter 11.

Catalogues

Mail order catalogues are of particular use in event merchandising operations where they can be in printed or be seen in electronic form via a website. They can be expensive to produce and variations in image reproduction can mean the delivery of items that are not exactly as seen previously. The use of website online stores is now a popular way to sell merchandise in the industry and, if they are affordable, they can offer year round visibility for less frequent events. Sports teams continue to use both mail and e-mail order and, in the UK, their use can be seasonal too with Christmas and Season Kick-Off editions a common occurrence. Leeds United Football Club, for example, has used mail order catalogues for dual-purpose merchandise and season ticket sales.

Telemarketing

There can be both one-dimensional telemarketing and the managing of incoming enquiries and the more pro-active two-dimensional approach used to prospect for new customers (Mullin et al., 2000). This direct marketing method is growing and is a major tool in the event communications toolbox. When Mark Cuban first took over the Dallas Mavericks he took on more sales staff and targeted them each with 100 calls per day and the message was one of 'never mind the results, come to our arena for a great sports experience' (Caplan, 2003). They also made calls to those seat holders who do not turn up for games and so for them it was not just about selling, it was also about the building of a relationship. The advantages of telemarketing are that the caller can overcome objections if given the chance. The downside is clearly that a cold call into the home can be seen as an intrusion of privacy and so the key is to ensure that the database is targeted and consists of event friendly people.

Kiosks

Ticket and merchandising booths of various kinds are ways of personally selling event products. They can be located on or away from the event site, prior to or during an event. While they do not require database construction, they can be a means for gathering data. Their implementation on-site during the event is of importance when advance tickets can still be purchased. They are of great importance too for the sales of other tickets for other future events. For major events, high street medium-term locations can be worthy of consideration. In 1999, for example, an Amsterdam shop lease was acquired for the 2000 UEFA Euro Championships that were staged in Holland and Belgium. Kiosk operations can also be achieved with partners for a less expensive solution. In the 2 years preceding the 2002 Commonwealth Games, a ticket operation was implemented out of the City Hall Information Outlet in Manchester. There are also advantages in getting ticket agents to cross-sell from their outlets. However, while having more operable outlets is normally a good thing, the downside is that there is a lack of control over the sales process and in how much emphasis is placed on the sales of one event over another when in the hands of agents.

INTERACTIVE MEDIA

The use of websites is still a relatively new phenomenon and yet there are examples of innovative applications in supply of information and in generating incremental revenue. Those events that are utilizing their sites with interactive communications are exercising advanced customer adoption techniques. In addition, there is the emergence of wireless technology that is still so much in its infancy that many managers are unsure as to how it will manifest itself and be an aid. There are though also many examples of innovation at work.

World Wide Web

The development of event led websites is now widespread and their use as a marketing media is being advanced everyday. Self-managed sites are more controllable but agreements with ticket agencies can also provide supplementary and primary sources. Ticketmaster.com is one of the largest sites on the Internet and serves 20 markets worldwide. In the USA alone it handles sales for over 100 000 events annually (Ticketmaster.com, 2003).

In the main, it is the desire for information that drives customers to such sites and so if merchandise and tickets sales are to be achieved, site sponsors are to be satisfied with site traffic, the content has to be attractive. Sometimes this is best achieved in-house but is not always an operation an event can afford. The National Hockey League (NHL) operates all year round with numbers of hockey events and it can afford to operate its website content in-house. The Manchester United FC site is managed by a contracted company, IMG Media, and is available in three languages.

49ers.com, operated by JA, is a site that has previously run the dangerous game of editing out key team information when it is contentious, as discussed in Chapter 6. However, they continue to build a very commercially driven site that is able to transcend both corporate as well as consumer communications. Promotions such as 'Dynamic Rotator' for example, feature in a corporate online sales brochure that can provide a high yield. The pages cost only US$4000.00 to build for a return of US$100 000.00 per year and also acted as a data collector via registration compliance (Berridge, 2003). My49ers News was an earlier service that offered consumers preferential e-mail notifications of game information, merchandise and special events such as auctions, promotions and competitions, all of which gave the organization ample opportunity to interact with their fans while gaining sponsorship revenue. This has been replaced with their fan community pages titled 'The Faithful', a membership programme with a log-in procedure and access to team information, merchandise, message boards and competitions.

One of the big opportunities for sports teams and their websites is their capacity to offer dynamic action and colour. All websites are unique in that every organization is different but it is critical that all opportunity to create a unique selling point (USP) is achieved. The website needs to create differential therefore and even if the products are similar, one organization needs to look to how it can gain competitive advantage (Bergman, 2002). Sports organizations and events have USP via their logos, action, first hand breaking news and official merchandise and the aesthetics of the site are critical in order to retain visitors. The 49ers, for example, use primary colours (gold, black, red and white) to recreate the look of their official team uniform and have resisted in the past on selling intrusive banner or pop-up spots.

The London 2012 site demonstrated an unusual approach in April 2008 when it innovatively promoted the sport of handball and the recruitment of new players by dangling the 2012 carrot as an incentive for those people who were 16–25 years of age and 180 cm (girls) or 190 cm (boys) in height. Those interested were directed to contact the British Handball Association.

A key factor for the use of websites concerns the development of customer relationships via word of mouth (WOM). WOM is considered an important tool for business-to-business relationships. Good suppliers are commonly recommended within business sectors and this can be the case among individual customers too. This also applies for negative as well as positive recommendation and when in the past it has perhaps taken a lot longer for WOM to have an impact, the emergence of the Internet where bad news can travel faster, has now made this a critical consideration (Strauss et al., 2003).

Wireless communications

The opportunity for communications takes on new meaning with the advent of the wireless age. Mobile or cell phones are commonplace now and technology for playing games, receiving text, organizing diaries as well as managing telecommunications is advanced. What broadband technology has brought is the capacity for telecommunication carriers to send high quality still and moving graphics to mobile wireless devices such as mobile phones. This potential is already being realized on a worldwide basis with sports teams and events sending customers downloadable logos, pictures, ringtones and message alerts. Depending on the deal with the carrier, the sports organization can generate revenue via traffic spend as well as sponsorship. The NHL and the other US major leagues receive a percentage on traffic that they pass on to teams on an incremental basis.

Broadband technology makes it possible to send video clips to mobile devices and so football action is receivable anywhere a signal can be achieved.

On the one hand, wireless technology is giving sports organizations opportunities of new ways of reaching customers, keeping them informed and selling to them. On the other hand, the fact that this is wireless communications means that there are now more opportunities to reach these customers potentially in all places and at all times. This is not achievable with any of the traditional methods available. It is not these two factors that make this technology so much of an exciting opportunity, however. With the right wireless technology, customers can interact with organizations anywhere at any time. For example, with balloting, NHL fans can vote for their favourite players by responding to prompts sent to their mobiles and results can be accumulated for league wide as well as team outcomes. Teams can then post results on their jumbotron screens during games. All kinds of information via alerts get the customer closer to their team and, with instant response to last-minute ticket alerts, they can be at the game that night. Informa Media Group forecast that revenue from game playing on mobiles would rise by US$1 billion a year between 2005 and 2010 to US$9 billion.

MASS MEDIA

In addition to media coverage resulting from PR, mass media marketing methods include the design and placement of advertisements and the use of sales promotions. Event budgets do not always extend to the use of methods that cannot be targeted as well as others but, for some events, mass media are essential. Large scale one-off events with large audiences often require the use of heavy mass media exposure in order to be successful but there are ways in which this can be innovative. For those that can agree media partnerships there are opportunities for advertising packages that can also provide less expensive campaigns.

Advertising

The media available for event advertising include television, radio, printed press and publication, street media in the form of transportation, billboards and street furniture. The latter can include the placing of advertising on bus stops, community information notice boards and, in the UK, advertisers are known to 'sponsor' roundabouts (road network junction points). Also in this area is the use of fly-posting which, in many places, is either illegal or a licensed opportunity at identified locations.

The budgets required for television are often beyond the scope of many events and even major events avoid these high costs. The 2002 Commonwealth Games utilized a number of media but steered clear of paying for television advertising. In particular, it took advantage of several key partnerships not least the building and venue owners and the use of large signage, posters and billboards. One side of one multi-storey building in central Manchester was adorned with a jumbo sized picture of Jonah Lomu, the New Zealand All-Black, throughout 2002 prior to the games.

A sports sector that is still growing is extreme sports print advertising. Oxbow is an example of a manufacturer that has placed advertising in collaboration with their partner events. The Oxbow sponsored Longboard surfing event, in Raglan, New Zealand, has been promoted via Oxbow paid for and derived advertising for example while also gaining editorial features in the same magazine and the assiciated website (The Surfer's Path, 2003; surferspath.com, 2003). The access to this attractive and discerning group that is non-main stream also attracts mainstream advertisers. Alongside extreme industry brands such as Billabong, Ripcurl, Vans, Quicksilver and O'Neil in industry magazines are Snickers in an attempt to reach different segments from the traditional football fans they have targeted. For extreme events, there are possibilities for the attraction of new spenders and perhaps new communications partners for joint media promotions.

The NBA also produced an advertisement in association with partners to promote its 2004 NBA All Star Game in Los Angeles. In collaboration with Foot Locker, Champs Sports, Circuit City, Loews Cineplex Cinemas and Verizon, they ran advertisements that incorporated a public vote promotion (NBA Inside Stuff, 2004). By visiting any of the stores or using a Verizon wireless cell phone, fans could vote for NBA basketball players they thought should play in the All Star Game, the end of season play-off between the best players from each of the two basketball conferences.

The London 2012 Bid team launched its first advertisements in January 2004. The theme was 'Leap for London' and the series of adverts featured famous landmarks as athletes hurdled and leapt over them. The need to use mass media was obviously important to the team even during the bidding process. The target markets were the UK population at large and the effort was to convince the nation that the games would be of great benefit for local communities, the regeneration of the Lower Lee Valley (site of the Olympic Park), UK sport and increased job opportunities, business investment and tourism (London 2012, 2004).

Chicago, a bidding city for the 2016 Olympic Games, took its opportunity to promote its candidature by advertising with a full page in *China Daily*, the English broadsheet newspaper in China, during the first week of the 2008 Games in Beijing. The focus for the advertisement was a picture of Chicago's lake front with a title of 'a spectacular setting for sport'. The accompanying words promoted Chicago as a destination for culture, recreation, entertainment, hospitality and shopping. The 'Visit Chicago' website address was also incorporated into this tourism focused advertisement (*China Daily*, 2008).

One further example of event advertising is unusual in that it is recruiting its participants via a combination of techniques including mass media. The Clipper 05–06 Round the World Yacht Race advertised for crew via a national Sunday newspaper in January 2004, 21 months ahead of the event. The organizers were recruiting crew for its 10 month, 35 000 mile race for amateur sailors in its ten 68 foot yachts. Applicants could come from any background and did not have to be experienced at sea and so a mass media approach was appropriate. The full-page colour advertisement included a phone number and a website address. It also promoted its stand at the London International Boat Show.

The process for advertising decision-making is similar to that in Figure 10.5 for public relations decisions and for any other communications (see Figure 10.7).

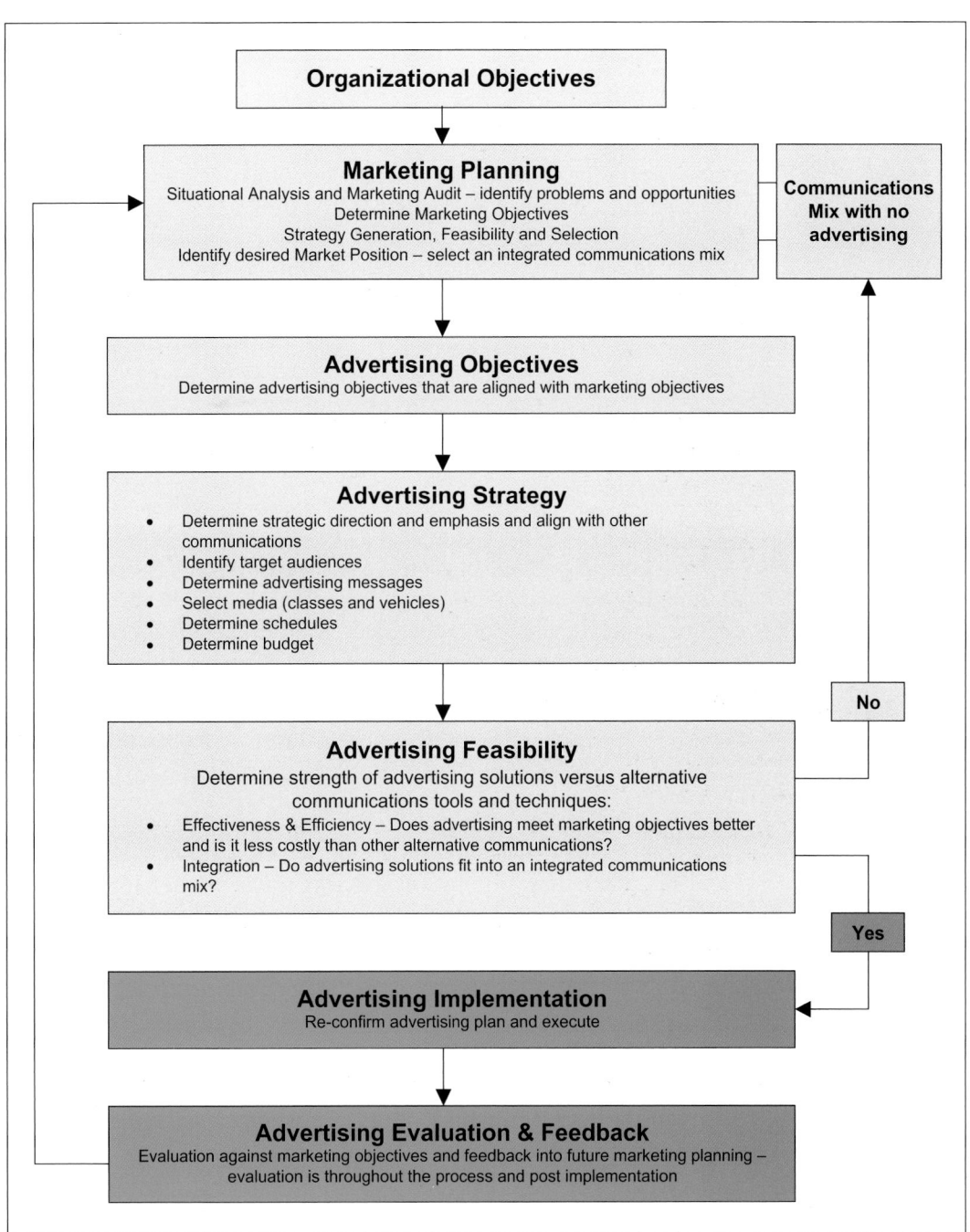

FIGURE 10.7 *Advertising planning process. Process for the planning of advertising in integrated event marketing communications (Masterman and Wood, 2006).*

Sales promotion

Two types of sales promotion apply to the sports events industry, trade and consumer offerings. Attracting ticket and corporate hospitality agents can be achieved by offering discounts for bulk and/or early purchase. Commonplace consumer sales promotions include any discount schemes for tickets with vehicles such as season tickets where the offering has savings over a season/series of events, etc. Other promotions include free giveaways or discounts with early purchase. The following types of promotion, adapted from Jobber (2007), may be used by events.

1. *Price discounts*: ticket agency partners may be offered or they may have sufficient bargaining power to demand discounts on prices.

2. *Money off*: a short-term consumer option is to offer 'money off' but a key factor is not discrediting and cheapening the brand by under-selling.

3. *Premiums*: any merchandise may be offered directly or by mail-in vouchers. A package of goods consisting of tickets, car parking, and programmes may be offered at full price but a value added incentive might be the supply of event 'goody bags' for each member of the party. These may be more cheaply obtained by bringing in event sponsors as suppliers of products for the bags.

4. *Coupons*: coupons as part of PR and direct mail operations may be used so that consumers may access cheaper tickets.

5. *Competitions and prize promotions*: prizes can be offered as inducements to the employees of partner sales agencies for the highest sales. These may also include offering sponsors the same rights. There are two methods. A competition involves skill whereas a prize promotion does not and both offer an attractive solution, as the costs for either may be determined at the outset.

6. *Loyalty cards*: depending on the frequency of events, a loyalty card scheme is a relatively recent retail offering. For event organizing bodies of all kinds the capacity to offer incentives over a portfolio of events is an easy way to reward key customers and build customer relationships.

The problem with most sales promotion tools is that the costs can rise with the success of the vehicle in place. The intention for sales promotion is to achieve any one of five objectives (Jobber, 2007). A fast sales boost, encourage trial, incite repeat purchase, stimulate purchase of larger amounts and gain more effective distribution.

Sponsor Exploitation

It is a bonus for an event's communications effort when one of its sponsors exploits its rights via more spending on positive event linked communications. As explained in Chapter 11, a sponsor that exploits (activates, leverages) its rights by producing more communications that celebrate its association with the event are therefore providing further promotion for the event and are doing so with their own budget. These promotions therefore serve to support and boost the event's own spending. Event managers should therefore seek to encourage their sponsors to exploit and, if they have the opportunity, recruit those sponsors that will venture into this activity. The photographs below are examples of how some of the 2008 Beijing Olympic sponsors exploited their rights. In some cases, exploitation is a very simple and not that innovative tool such as the placing of a logo on a cup or a poster. The innovation is applied in created activities that promote the function the sponsor and its brands play in the event. This is explained in full in Chapter 11.

Adidas using billboards and electric advertising in a busy shopping district in Beijing.

Adidas using billboards and electric advertising in a busy shopping district in Shanghai.

A McDonald's milkshake cup carries the 2008 Olympic logo.

Visa using Jackie Chan to endorse use of the 'Olympic credit card'.

Tsingtao beer and Coca-Cola drink cans bearing the 2008 Olympic logo. Coca-Cola also used the logo on its bottled water.

A Samsung advert at Beijing airport incorporating the 2008 Olympic logo.

UPS went to the lengths of erecting a 'pony express' statue, complete with electronic advertising featuring their status as an official Beijing 2008 sponsor, in one of the busiest shopping areas in Shanghai, a 2008 Olympics host city (football).

Adidas and Samsing collaborated with joint promotions that supported a sports-music phone for training. This test station at Olympic Green during the Games allowed spectators to sample the product. The pre-Games promotion by the two firms helped promote the Games in advance.

China Mobile provided volunteer managed information stations all around Beijing during the Games and helped promote the Games interests in providing a great visitor experience.

Johnson and Johnson focused on their research and development in the exploitation of their sponsorship rights and in this case their lotions have been used to preserve terracotta army statues. This pre-Games message provided a diverse approach for games promotion.

GE provided power to games venues and used this as a promotional focus in its communication activities. A lit model of the Water Cube demonstrates the 308 2000 watt light fittings that were needed to illuminate the facility.

A billboard campaign was used to inform target audiences of the power it takes to light up the Bird's Nest.

Coca-Cola used Chinese culture in one communications programme. A Coca-Cola bottle design competition was rolled out across all provinces in China and received 33 765 entries and 12 million on-line votes to select winning designs. Finalists' designs were modelled and exhibited at Olympic Green. This pre-Games activity promoted the cultural power of the Games.

Kodak is a long-term sponsor at Olympic Games and continues to provide photographic services to both the media and the Games visitors. The showcase building at Olympic Green shown here allowed visitors to download and print their own photographs again demonstrating the focus on a great visitor experience.

Beijing Olympic Games partners were given the opportunity to build their own showcase building at Olympic Green. Here Kodak can be seen alongside Coca-Cola, Adidas and Samsung.

Omega focused on a promotion that saw them create a limited edition of 88 new watches every day of the 17 days of the Olympic Games. The watches were showcased at Olympic Green but were advertised in Chinese newspapers and magazines, including the English China Daily.

Lenovo produced special limited edition Olympic design laptop computers and also focused its integrated advertising campaign on its link with the Olympics – indicating that it was the power behind the world's biggest idea.

SUMMARY

An innovative approach towards event communications is essential for today's sports event manager. Traditional methods of mass or personal media communications are not obsolete but require new and creative ways of being used in order to adopt and retain customers. The key is an integrated effort that consists of communications that work in harmony together and communicate consistent event messages.

The tools that are available include traditional approaches but, alongside these vehicles of print, television and radio for mass media communications, and direct mail, PR and face-to-face selling for personal media communications, sit the bright new applications that are offered by developing technology. The Internet and the opportunities it affords events with websites and the future promise of wireless communications for the development of interactive communications remain exciting prospects for the industry.

QUESTIONS

1. Select an event and critically evaluate its communications activities from an IMC perspective.

2. Using the same event, develop a new plan in an attempt to improve communications to each of the event's identified target markets.

3. What were the key elements of Mark Cuban's marketing mix for the Dallas Mavericks? Evaluate whether and how differential advantage was achieved?

4. Have you experienced innovative event communications that have successfully promoted either the Olympic Games in 2008 or 2012? Analyse why these were successful.

REFERENCES

Beijing (2008). www.beijing2008.cn (accessed 14 April 2008).

Bergman, T. (2002). *The Essential Guide to the Web Strategy for Entrepreneurs.* Upper Saddle River, NJ, Prentice Hall.

Berridge, K. (2003). Marketing and enabling technology: beyond content, turning a team website into a profit center, paper delivered by Senior Manager of Corporate Partnerships, San Francisco 49ers, at *Sport Media and Technology*

2003. November 13–14, New York Marriott Eastside, New York, *Street and Smith's Sports Business Journal*.

Caplan, J. (2003). Business insider: Cuban has the ticket to selling news. *Star Telegram*. www.star-telegram.com (accessed 12 October 2003).

China Daily (2008). Advertisment. A spectacular setting for sport, 8 August.

Dallas Mavericks (2008). www.dallasmavs.com (accessed 6 April 2008).

Engel, J., Warshaw, M. and Kinnear, T. (1994). *Promotional Strategy*. Chicago, Irwin.

Fill, C. (2002). *Integrated Marketing Communications*. Oxford, Butterworth-Heinemann.

Gaber, I. (2008). Fanning the flames. *The Guardian*, 14 April.

Jefkins, F. and Yadin, D. (1998). *Public Relations*, 5th edn. Harlow, FT/Prentice Hall, Chapter 5.

Jobber, D. (2007). *Principals and Practice of Marketing*, 5th edn. London, McGraw-Hill.

Kotler, P. (2006). *Marketing Management*, 12th edn. London, Prentice Hall.

Lavidge, R. and Steiner, G. (1961). A model for the predictive measurements of advertising effectiveness. *Journal of Advertising Marketing*, American Marketing Association, October 59–62.

London (2004). Leap for London. www.london2012.org/en/news/archive/2004/january/2004-01-16-10-27 (accessed 22 January 2004).

Masterman, G. and Wood, E. H. (2006). *Innovative Marketing Communications: Strategies for the Events industry*. Oxford, Elsevier/Butterworth Heinemann.

McConnell, B. and Huba, J. (2003). Case: Dallas Mavericks. www.marketingProfs.com (accessed 24 June 2003).

Michell, P. (1988). Where advertising decisions are really made. *European Journal of Marketing, Bradford*, 22(7), 5.

Mullin, B., Hardy, S. and Sutton, W. (2000). *Sport Marketing*, 2nd edn. Champaign, Human Kinetics.

NBA Inside Stuff (2004). December–January edition. New York, Professional Sports Publications.

Ogilvy (2004). www.ogilvy.com/360 (accessed 7 January 2004).

Pickton, D. and Broderick, A. (2001). Integrated marketing communications. *Corporate Communications: An International Journal*, 6(1), 97–106.

Piercy, N. (2002). *Market-led Strategic Change: Transforming the Process of Going to Market*, 3rd edn. Oxford, Butterworth-Heinemann.

Schultz, D., Tannenbaum, S. and Lauterborn, R. (1996). *The New Marketing Paradigm: Integrated Marketing Communications*. Chicago, IL, NTC Business Books.

Sports City (2008). www.sports-city.org (accessed 14 April 2008).

Strauss, J., El-Ansary, A. and Frost, R. (2003). *E-Marketing*, 3rd edn. Upper saddle River, Prentice Hall.

Strong, E. (1925). *The Psychology of Selling*. New York, McGraw-Hill.

Surferspath.com (2003). www.surferspath.com (accessed 16 November 2003).

The Surfer's Path (2003). Issue 29. November/December. Oxon, Permanent Publishing.

Ticketmaster.com (2008). www.ticketmaster.com/browse (accessed 8 April 2008).

Vaughn, R. (1980). How advertising works: a planning model. *Journal of Advertising Research*, 20(5), 27.

Wells, W., Burnett, J. and Moriarty, S. (1995). *Advertising Principles and Practice*. Englewood Cliffs, Prentice Hall.

Sports Event Sponsorship

CONTENTS

The importance of sponsorship for all scales of event is becoming increasingly important. Here, a City of New York Parks and Recreation organized beach volleyball event has secured a range of sponsors including ADT, Brooklyn Burger and Snapple in order to make the event happen. Image courtesy of City of New York Parks and Recreation.

LEARNING OBJECTIVES

After studying this chapter, you should be able to:

- understand the importance of the role that sponsorship plays in the sports event industry

- identify the objectives that sponsorship can achieve for sponsors

- identify the critical success factors in the production of sponsorship programmes

INTRODUCTION

In 2000, DVAG, a German asset management company, paid Michael Schumacher £5 million for a 10-cm wide space on the front of his cap. A cap that he wore whenever he was in the eyes of the media after winning a Formula 1 championship race which, at the time, was often. Such was his bargaining power that his Ferrari team were able to attract an estimated £60 million of sponsorship that included branding space on the rest of his racing attire (Henry, 1999). This revenue was clearly important to the running of the team and today you do not have to look too far to realize that, to some teams, sponsorship income is critical for survival. In recent times, both the Prost and Arrows teams have departed the Formula 1 motor racing scene with financial problems. Such problems in Formula 1 motor race events are ongoing and a constant source of concern about the re-shaping of a motor-sport events industry that, in 5 years, has grown from £1.7 billion to £2.9 billion in the UK alone. Another £1.7 billion is annually turned over in the marketing, public relations, sponsorship and events management support services for this industry (Motorsport Industry Association, 2008).

Motorsports ably demonstrate how sports sponsorship is now a highly developed communications tool with much of the spending being focused on sports events. The UK market is now back in growth having dipped for the first time in 2003 and 2004, although the increased revenue is still being acquired through higher rights fees as opposed to significantly more deals (Mintel, 2000; Ipsos MORI, 2008). While the sports sponsorship sector is the most sophisticated and developed, other sectors are also in growth. The arts, music, broadcast, cause and community related and education sectors are all developing and with more communication choices like these available, there are key implications for the sports event industry.

Clearly the worldwide recession will take its toll with sponsorship spend likely to decrease. Data from 2008/2009 however will not be produced until

2009/2010. However, with increased spending, the expectations of sponsors increase and, with fewer new deals, there are fewer sponsors to go around. In order to achieve competitive advantage therefore, it is critically important that event managers focus on what those expectations are. There are essentially five key generic areas that sponsors' objectives fit into. These are: to drive sales; increase brand awareness and develop image; increase corporate awareness and develop image; develop internal relations; and to achieve competitive advantage (Masterman, 2007). What sponsors are looking for, therefore, is a return on their investment, clearly showing that sponsorship has moved on from the times when sponsorship decision-making was more philanthropic than it was strategic.

This chapter will first of all set the scene by putting sponsorship into a historical perspective in demonstrating how sports event sponsorship has grown. The direction of this growth is then considered by looking at the types and levels of sponsorship and how sports event sponsorship programmes are structured.

A strategic approach to the process of achieving successful sports event sponsorship is introduced. This consists of four key areas: targeting; building relationships; rights exploitation; and evaluation. Finally, the chapter will discuss two important issues: ambush marketing and the question of ethics, and how they affect the perception of sponsorship.

A HISTORICAL PERSPECTIVE

According to current data sports sponsorship continues to experience growth. On a global scale, the market was worth US$30.7 billion in 2002 and has continued to grow on average 10% per year to US$43.1 billion in 2005 (Sponsorclick, 2003, 2008). The largest contributor to the market is the USA at 38%, but Europe is close behind and is expected to provide an equal contribution by the time 2008 market data are analysed. Its importance can be clearly seen where once the origination of corporate involvement with sport was very much more philanthropic and is now seen to be addressing a number of corporate communication objectives including the driving of sales. The Sanitarium sponsorship of the Weet-Bix Kiwi Kids Triathlon in New Zealand has two main objectives for example, brand building and sales, with increases of 50% (Sponsorshipinfo, 2003). Visa's Olympic programmes are also focused on sales and, in Athens in 2004, along with partner Alpha Bank, it attracted 110 000 subscriptions by the start of the Games that year, easily exceeding its target of 30 000 and leading the way to the achievement of considerable sales performance from its new credit card users (Masterman, 2007).

The importance of sponsorship to events has also grown and, in many cases, is critical to the realization of the event.

There is a worrying issue in the UK, in particular, however. New sports sponsorship deals have been slowing. As stated above, while sports sponsorship continues to be the largest sector in the market, it is fees that are increasing rather than new deals. Recession aside, of concern too is that it is a small number of sports that continue to attract this growth. It was reported in the first edition of this book that 90% of all money spent on sports sponsorship was on the top 10 sports and it is football and motor sports (predominantly Formula 1) that continue today to attract the new sponsors and the increasing fees (Mintel, 2000; Ipsos MORI, 2008). While market predictions were for an increase in wider sports sponsorship spending due to the staging of the London Olympics in 2012, other sectors are on the increase including broadcast, arts and community related sponsorships. Other research has revealed that this shift away from the sports industry is also prevalent in the USA, again showing that the numbers of quality non-sports options are on the increase and the numbers of new deals less (Lachowetz et al., 2003). The implications are that, in order to retain or gain competitive advantage, sports events must improve their sponsorship recruitment processes.

SPORTS EVENT SPONSORSHIP PROGRAMMES

There are two fundamental approaches when it comes to recruiting sponsors. First, there is what can be described as 'off-the-shelf.' This approach is still prevalent within the industry and is the selling of a fixed package that consists of a prescribed bundle of benefits that has been determined prior to any approach to a potential buyer. This clearly entails little involvement of the potential sponsor in the process until negotiations start and gives no credence to the importance of meeting mutual needs. This is a common practice and evidence can be found at any number of event websites. For example, pro-forma agreements that require the sponsor to tick a box to identify the benefits they require can be found on current event websites.

Secondly, there is a tailored or bespoke approach whereby potential sponsors' requirements are considered first and a series of benefits then proposed. The advantages of following something nearer to the second approach are discussed later in this chapter. Prior to that it is important to identify the types and levels of sponsorship that are available via sports events.

Different terminology is used from sector to sector and event to event, to a point where onlookers might be confused as to the nature of the agreement. This need not cause a problem so long as the terminology is understood and agreed by the parties that are involved. There are no rules or standards in terminology.

The term 'sponsorship' continues to have an unfashionable cache about it with a development that sees more use of the word 'partnership' in an attempt to depict a greater relationship and perhaps even increased competitive advantage. This can be seen in the way events construct their sponsorship programmes. There are various levels of status available at an event and these relate to the rights that they receive as a result of their association with the event. These rights consist of a bundle of benefits that can offer the use of certain titles and, more often than not, these titles are an acknowledgement not only of the status that the sponsor has with the event, but they are also indicative of the relationship they have with other sponsors at the event. Here are the levels of status that are available.

- *Title rights*: these rights ensure that the sponsor is named in the title of the event so that all references to the title of the event include the sponsor's corporate, product or brand names as agreed. More often than not this will include rights for inclusion in the event logo graphics. Examples include: Flora London Marathon, Samsung Nations Cup (showjumping), Heineken Open (tennis championships in Auckland, New Zealand) and the TNK Cup (a Russian schools volleyball competition). Bayer, the German multi-national pharmaceutical organization, supports a number of sports teams in its homeland and the name Bayer is fully utilized. Bayer 04 Leverkusen (the soccer club) and TSV Bayer 04 Leverkusen (the basketball club) are two examples. They were also the first to sponsor an Association of Tennis Professionals (ATP) tennis tournament in Russia, the Bayer Kremlin Cup. It is the rights owner's responsibility to manage the use and proper acknowledgement of the event title by other parties, including the media, so that the rights are maximized. This is not always an easy task. In Hong Kong, their famous rugby 7s event has a rare arrangement with two 'co-title' sponsors and an event title of the Cathay Pacific/Credit Suisse Hong Kong Sevens, making it a difficult task in persuading the media they should always refer to the event by its full title.

- *Presentership rights*: this is a status that allows acknowledgement of the sponsor alongside the title of the event (as opposed to being a part of it) and also possible inclusion with the event logo graphics. Corporate, product or brand names can be used. An example is the Bank of Ireland which was the 'premier sponsor' of the 2003 Special Olympics World Summer Games in Ireland (Special Olympics, 2003). A 2003 International Big Air snowboarding event in Bulgaria was sponsored by O'Neill, the sportswear manufacturers, and their involvement entitled them to presenting rights where the event was referred to as the 'Todorca Cup by O'Neill.' Another example is the University of Massachusetts (UMass) whose athletics department was sponsored by Mass Mutual, a financial services company that used the same state abbreviation in its name. The FA Cup also has a presenting sponsor and refers to 'E.on', the power supply company, as an official partner and its other sponsors as supporters.

■ *Naming rights*: these rights are associated with physical structures and, more commonly, in long-term agreements whereby a building such as a stadium can be renamed so that it is referred to using the sponsor in that name. Corporate, product or brand names can be used. Examples are common within the USA and include Edison Field in Anaheim, American Airlines Arena in Miami and the Pepsi Center and Coors Field in Colorado. The McCain Stadium in Scarborough, UK was one of the first stadium naming deals in Europe and one of the more unusual deals more recently is a chocolate brand naming of York City's home ground, Kit-Kat Crescent.

■ *Sector rights*: sponsors with sector or category rights enjoy uncompetitive status with the event in that they are the sole representation from the sector/market in which they operate. These rights offer sector, market or category exclusivity for the sponsor. Title or presenting sponsors may also have these rights. MasterCard for example, as a long-term official sponsor of the FIFA World Cup, enjoys sector exclusivity at those events in the credit card market. Bank of America, Pacific Life and State Farm Insurance have different sector rights, also in the general area of financial services, as corporate partners at the Pac-10 Conference college sports championships in the USA. A prize for the longest acknowledgement might go to Canon and their association with the Professional Golf Association (PGA) as 'Official Camera, Binocular, Facsimile and Copier of the PGA Tour and Senior PGA Tour'. These rights, once seen as a negotiable right, are now generally viewed as being a pre-requisite. Sector exclusive sponsors can sit more comfortably into an event sponsorship programme and work together productively and so most events now understand that they will not be able to attract any level of sponsor without ensuring that they have exclusive sector rights.

■ *Supplier rights*: similarly, supplier rights can and, wherever possible should be, enjoyed by all sponsors. In some way an event should incorporate all its sponsors, their products or brands, as functions of the event. Supplier rights allow acknowledgement to the suppliers of event services, equipment and products they provide. At the 2003 Special Olympics World Summer Games, for example, Aer Lingus provided air transportation as Official Carrier, Toyota supplied fleet cars as Official Vehicle Sponsor and Kodak provided accreditation technology and badges for more than 70 000 staff (Special Olympics, 2003).

These levels of status are important considerations for event sponsorship programmes. They have to be strategically deployed so that the opportunities for the recruitment of the right sponsors can be maximized. For example, key considerations are how many sponsors get what rights.

When developing a number of sponsorships into a programme, the task is to design each one so that it can complement and sit comfortably alongside others. To do this successfully, an event rights owner needs to consider the entire picture and balance the set of rights so that there is sector exclusivity and no unecessary duplication that will lead to over-commodification. Many events have been tempted to attempt to recruit as many sponsors as possible, but this is a risky approach as the cluttering of communications messages can cause sponsor dissatisfaction and, at worst, their non-renewal. One example of this risky approach is at the Valero Alamo Bowl where they recruit 150 local sponsors at a third tier level.

When building event sponsorship programmes there are three basic structural approaches:

- *Solus structures*: Where only one sponsor is involved with the event (see Figure 11.1).

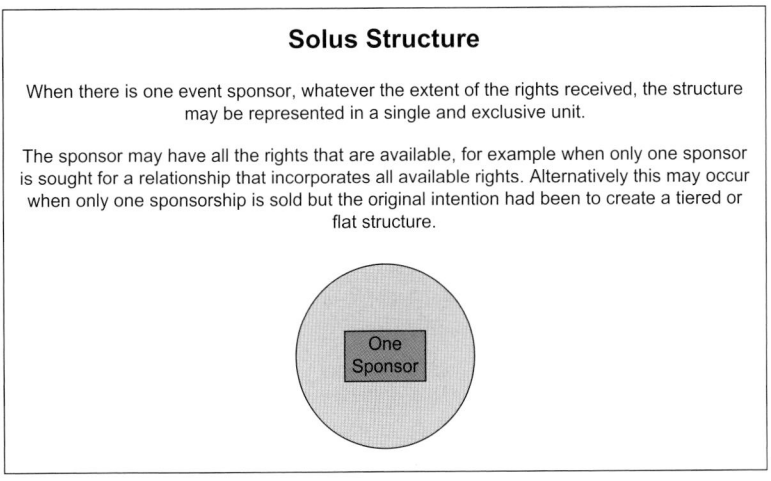

FIGURE 11.1 *Solus sponsorship programme structure (Masterman, 2007).*

■ *Tiered structures*: where there is more than one and a hierarchy of sponsors (see Figure 11.2). In the case of the Nabisco Masters Doubles (see Case study 11.1), there are two fundamental sets of rights, namely those that include television coverage exposure and those that do not and then a further defining set of levels of hierarchy between the title, presenting and other sponsors.

■ *Flat structures*: where all sponsors enjoy the same status though not necessarily the same types of rights or benefits and do not always pay the same (see Figure 11.3). The key is that there is no differentiation in their status and the way that they are acknowledged. This was an approach that was adopted by the likes of the IOC but, because it has since added a secondary level of suppliers to its sponsorship programme, it is in fact now using a two-tiered stucture. Flat structures are more commonly found at local levels where typically a number of sponsors are brought into events that have little media profile and where there is no real need therefore to highlight any hierarchy. Any reference by the event to its sponsors in these cases is done collectively, such as on a printed poster or programme. At the 2008 North Yorkshire Games, for example, there were a number of

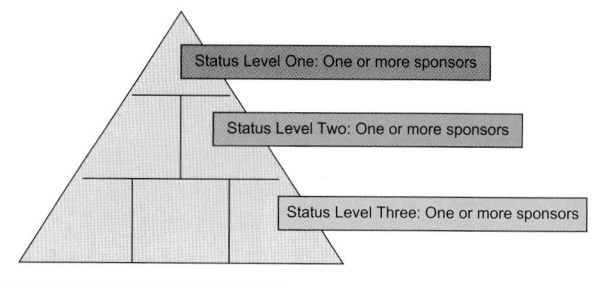

Tiered Structure

When there is more than one sponsor and there is a hierarchy of status, the structure may be represented by a pyramid of levels. Each level has more status than the one below. There can be any number of sponsors at any level and there is a minimum of two but no maximum number of levels. Each sponsor may or may not receive different rights and be on different payment terms, even when they are on the same level, but the status/acknowledgement received at each level remains the same.

Levels may be named in order to highlight the status of sponsors as well as show hierarchy. Crude examples might be gold, silver and bronze level sponsors, but for the Beijing 2008 Olympics there were 'partners', 'sponsors' and 'exclusive suppliers'. Common examples include title, presenting and official levels/sponsors with a fourth level of supplier status. Two-level event sponsorship structures often have official partners and official suppliers.

Status Level One: One or more sponsors

Status Level Two: One or more sponsors

Status Level Three: One or more sponsors

FIGURE 11.2 *Tiered sponsorship programme structure (Masterman, 2007).*

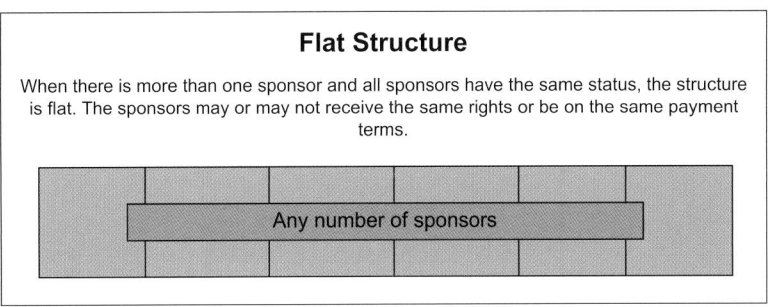

FIGURE 11.3 *Flat sponsorship programme structure (Masterman, 2007).*

sponsors (Hardgear, Asda, Lodestone Patient Care, Skipton Building Society, Yorkshire Itouch, Interserve Plc and Yorkshire County Cricket Club), all receiving the same status and equal billing in the event programme and on posters. One notable example of a higher profile event with a flat structure is the Clipper Round the World Yacht Race. In 2005/2006, the race consisted of 10 boats and each one was sponsored by a city with a particular set of tourism communication objectives; Liverpool 08 (2008 European Capital of Culture), Glasgow (Scotland with Style), Qingdao (Olympic Sailing City 2008), Fremantle (Western Australia.com), Durban (South Africa's Playground), New York, Singapore (Uniquely Singapore), Victoria BC, Cardiff. The city sponsored boats and the photographs below demonstrate how each sponsor had equal status and the same rights.

Clipper 4 Photographs: Ingrid Abery, www.hotcapers.com Clipper Ventures.

It can be seen from the latter two of these basic structures (tiered and flat) that it is possible to have various numbers of sponsors fitting together in one sponsorship programme and all having a productive association with the event. There is a balance to be achieved between what each sponsor receives and what each pays in order for a sponsorship programme to work productively and harmoniously. This can be particularly important when it comes to payment because not all sponsorships have to be paid for in cash.

The use of sponsorship-in-kind is growing. Sometimes referred to as trade-outs or contra-deals, sponsorship-in-kind has no mystery to it and is not any different from any other form of sponsorship. It is just another way of exchanging mutual benefits and, in this case, one that does not involve any rights fee or payment to the event by the sponsor. Instead, they will agree a value of services, resources, goods or products that are clearly useful to the event and receive an agreed level of sponsorship status and benefits in return. While it remains a growing approach for sponsorship, it is by no means a new practice. Sports events have for some time saved on expenditure by acquiring sponsors that can deliver important event requirements such as human resources, equipment, supplies and support services. Case study 11.1 features the contra-deals the Nabisco Masters Doubles negotiated with Mazda, Interplant and American Airlines in the 1980s.

Case Study 11.1

Event Sponsorship Programme: Nabisco Masters Doubles

The WCT Inc owned Nabisco Masters Doubles ran throughout the 1980s in association with the ATP Tour as the men's doubles tennis world championship. Set in the Royal Albert Hall, London, 20% of the audience was seated in corporate hospitality. At its height in 1988, the event was broadcast on television in 20 countries. Star players included Noah, Wilander, Edberg, Forget, McNamara and Fleming. The 1988 sponsorship programme and rights were as follows:

Title Sponsors: Nabisco International

Title sponsorship status and image rights. The objective was for increased corporate awareness as opposed to any brand awareness for Nabisco divisions, such as Huntley & Palmer, Shredded Wheat.

Presenting Sponsors: Nabisco UK

Nabisco UK bought the presenting sponsorship rights in order to prevent them being sold on elsewhere. The use of any titling was not required because of the Nabisco International title sponsorship. The package involved significant additional corporate hospitality including two 12-seat boxes and ticketing.

Courtside Sponsors:

Boss: Official Clothing

Courtside platform boxes for line judge officials with Boss decals. Officials wore Boss blazers and slacks in the day

time sessions and black tie and dinner suits in the evening sessions.

Ebel: Official Timing

Courtside platform boxes for line judge officials with Ebel decals. One courtside clock and scoreboard with Ebel decals.

Schweppes: Official drink

Use of Schweppes drinks on court. Provision of all products throughout the event. Corporate hospitality including two 12-seat corporate hospitality boxes for all tennis sessions.

Dunlop Slazenger: Official ball

Use of Dunlop tennis balls for all tennis. Ball tubes displayed on the umpire chair. Dunlop Slazenger decals on the ball tubes and legs of the umpire chair.

Cundell

No official titling. Cundell, a cardboard packaging company, were converted from corporate box buyers to courtside sponsors (provision of branded towels used by the players). They provided cardboard dining structures for each of the table-less corporate boxes and Harrods (their client) Christmas puddings in Nabisco Masters Doubles cartons for Gold Star corporate boxes.

Continued

There are two important guidelines to adhere to when negotiating sponsorship-in-kind. Often borne out of the development of relationships with existing suppliers and/or the identification of key aspects of the event that incur expense, it is of benefit to the event to get services or products that are required without having to pay for them. The key point here is how much of a requirement they are. Only when they are a budgeted item and an expense that would necessarily occur can a saving be made. The amount saved can also only be up to the amount that was budgeted. For example, the provision of £10 000 worth of IT hardware to an event will only save the event £5000 if the latter figure is all that was entered in the budget. Secondly, the £5000 may be a saving in expenditure but the bottom line may not benefit to the same amount. If the event rights and benefits (tickets, corporate hospitality or advertising etc), that are given in exchange to the sponsor are also targeted as sales and therefore expected revenue, then that will have an impact on the bottom line. For example, £3000 worth of event benefits given over to the sponsor means there is an actual benefit of £2000 on the deal.

It is important though to balance this with the impact the deal will have elsewhere, even though it may not be as objectively measured as in the impact on the budget. The provision of services and products might enable the event to be that much more effective and safe. For example, Qwest provided the 2002 Salt Lake City Olympics with communications equipment including 700 handheld radios and 16 000 public safety radios (Wilcox, 2002). Other provision may enhance the customer experience, participant or spectator, and mean the event surpasses customer expectations and may ultimately lead to increased revenue elsewhere. Gateway paid the 2002 Salt Lake Olympics nothing in dollars but did provide 5700 personal computers and 400 servers. Their CyberSpot at the Olympic Village provided information about athletes and the games to spectators and another such facility in downtown Salt Lake City provided the same for the media. Over 1000 messages of goodwill were e-mailed by spectators to specific athletes.

The negotiation for sponsorship-in-kind begins with the agreement of the value of the exchange to be made. The aim is parity but the practice, of course, is one of trying to get the upper hand in the trade. There can therefore be an exaggeration of the values of provision on both sides. For example, using rate card or retail prices as opposed to actual costs.

Many sponsorship agreements have a mixture of both sponsorship-in-kind and paid fees and it is unlikely that successful title sponsorship will not have some form of provision of products or services to the event. Asda, the UK supermarket chain, paid 10% of the total value of its sponsorship deal with the 2002 Commonwealth Games in cash and the remainder in a provision of uniforms and human resource services.

In determining sponsorship price generally, there is no standard practice. There are various theoretical guidelines offered including Grey and Skildum-Reid (1999) who recommend a price that is at least 100% over costs. There are two considerations here. First, how much the event wants to sell for and secondly, how much the sponsor is willing to pay. The latter consideration is made entirely by the sponsor having first determined the value of the offering. It is therefore essential that the event is also mindful of how much the offering is worth to that particular sponsor, especially if it may be worth more to another. While this can clearly be a difficult task, an awareness of prices in the market will be critical. It is therefore inappropriate to put any standard mark-up on the sale but it is essential to know the exact extent of costs involved in offering it. This should include all overheads apportioned appropriately. Equivalent opportunity cost is a guideline that can be used because sponsors will look to the cost of using other communications tools to achieve the same outcomes. Careful research into how much exposure will be achieved via the sponsorship compared to the equivalent costs for achieving the same through advertising will assist the process.

The event needs to consider the sponsorship programme as a whole and the potential revenue it can bring in as a whole as it may be possible to bring in a sponsor at less than expected but achieve the budgeted sponsorship target revenue. A loss leader approach and the acceptance of a lesser price in the first year might also have the potential for future realization of improved prices.

The Nabisco Master Doubles (see Case study 11.1) devised a sponsorship programme where the sponsorship revenue as a whole amounted to 50% of the overall event revenue. The fee-paying sponsors paid the following percentage of the overall sponsorship target budget:

Nabisco International	52%
Nabisco UK	21%
Boss	7.5%
Ebel	7.5%
Schweppes	4%
Minolta	4%
Dunlop Slazenger	2%
Cundell	2%

Case studies 11.2, the Alamo Bowl and 11.3, the Hong Kong Sevens, provide two more examples of how tiered structures have been implemented. Case study 11.4 presents the sophisticated tiered structure the FA has now implemented from 2006 to 2010. In the previous edition of this book, the FA was used as an example of a two-tiered structure, a structure it used from 2002 to 2006.

Case Study 11.2

Event Sponsorship Programme: The Valero Alamo Bowl

The Valero Alamo Bowl, San Antonio, USA is the play-off game for the Big 10 and Big 12 Football Conferences, but it is more than an important College championship, it is also a month-long festival of related events. Played at the Alamodome, the average crowd since 1995 is 61 131. By researching its target audiences' demographics, the event has been able to target appropriate sponsors and increase its sponsorship revenue by auditing its assets and creating new rights.

- The Bowl has contributed over US$200 million in economic impact.
- Seven of the top 20 most watched ESPN Bowl Games are Alamo Bowls
- The 2006 Alamo Bowl is the most watched Bowl game ever on ESPN (7.8 million)
- The Bowl has received 6112 printed media mentions in 3 years in circulations amounting to over 110 million.

Audience research has identified these demographics:

- Gender: 55% male/45% female (up from 33% in 2004)
- Average household income: US$102 500
- Age: 52% are 25–54 years old
- Education: 32% have a postgraduate qualification, 46% are college graduates
- Marital status: 71% married

The 2008 Sponsorship Programme:

Title Sponsor

Valero

Partners

ESPN: Television partner

American Airlines: Official airline

Chevrolet: Official car

AT&T: Communications partner

San Antonio Conventions & Visitors Bureau

Local Sponsors

There are a further 150 local sponsors involved in the month-long event.

The Cultural programme includes dinners, high school games, sports events, rallies, fan zones with many of the sponsors specifically associated, for example:

The Original Rudy's Bar-B-Q Pigskin Review sponsored by Country Store & Bar-B-Q

AT&T Golf Classic

Wells Fargo Kickoff Luncheon

Valero Alamo Bowl Ball

Source: www.alamobowl.com

Case Study 11.3

Event Sponsorship Programme: Cathay Pacific/Credit Suisse Hong Kong Sevens

Such has been the success of this event since its inception in 1975, that there is now a World Sevens Series (since 2000) run by the International Rugby Board. The Hong Kong Sevens tournament is one of the most popular sports event in Asia and is staged in front of 40 000 people over 3 days in the Hong Kong Stadium, a stadium that was rebuilt in 1994 as a result of the success of the event. Over 20 teams from all over the world take part.

The programme has been developed to now include five tiers of sponsorship.

2008 Sponsorship Programme

Co-Title Sponsors

Cathay Pacific and Credit Suisse

Official Sponsors

Telstra: Telecommunications

Kukrai: Sportswear

Volvo: Motor manufacturer

Coca-Cola: Soft drink

Guinness; Brewer

Broadcast Partner

Pearl

Official Partners

Pacific Basin: Shipping

Invest HK: Business development

Mandarin Oriental: Hotel group

Modern Terminals: Construction

TTI: Home improvement manufacturing

Microsoft: Software technology

Official Suppliers

Group4 Securicor: Security services

HK Tourism Board: Tourism development

Hong Kong Government

Kennedy's: Legal services

March Polo Hotel: Hotel

Sacred Hill: Winery

Lighthouse: Technology

Gilbert: Official match ball

Source: www.hksevens.com.hk

Case Study 11.4

The FA Partner Programme

The English Football Association launched a new sponsorship programme for the period 2006 to 2010, the FA Partner Programme. It consists of three main strands, the England Team, the FA Cup and Football Development.

In a tiered structure, there are ostensibly two primary partners, Nationwide and E.on, with rights to the FA's flagships, the England Team and the FA Cup, respectively. The five secondary partners, Umbro, Carlsberg, National Express, McDonald's and Tesco, each have a mixture of rights associated with these events and/or the FA's core products.

England Team

    Lead Partner: Nationwide

    Supporters: Umbro, Carlsberg, National Express

FA Cup

    Lead partner: E.on

    Supporters: Umbro, Carlsberg, National Express

Football Development

    Men's football partner: Carlsberg

    Small sided partner: Umbro

    Community partner: McDonald's

    Learning partner: McDonald's

    Schools' partner: E.on

    Disability partner: Nationwide

    Girls/women's partner: Tesco

Source: The FA (2008)

STRATEGIC PROCESS

Sponsorship can be an important factor in ensuring that the event is feasible and so consideration of potential sponsors can begin as early as stage two of the event planning process, the creation of the concept. For many events, the lack of sponsors is the one factor that leads to the decision not to go ahead and so the early identification of sponsors and, indeed, early contracted agreement with sponsors can be critical.

There are a number of stages in the development of an event sponsorship programme. Having identified the event's objectives and possibly set optimum revenue targets, it can become clear that sponsorship is an effective tool for the achievement of those objectives. What follows is a situational analysis. This provides an audit of the event assets that can be used effectively in delivering the communications requirements of sponsors. Having identified these assets they can be bundled together to form packages that can then be sold off-the-shelf to interested sponsors. The bundling up of corporate hospitality, programme advertising and use of logo flash opportunities has been much utilized in the past. While this has been the common practice in the industry, it is not a sponsor-focused approach in that it is selling what the event wants to sell and not necessarily what the sponsor wants to buy, sometimes referred to as marketing myopia (Levitt, 1960). This is where it is important to use research to produce more effective sponsorships that can develop over time. The key for event managers is that they recognize that sponsorship is a mutual relationship and that objectives have to be met by all parties.

The process consists of four key areas: targeting, building the relationship, rights exploitation and evaluation.

Targeting

Successful events are managed by those who have researched and identified their target markets. Such research leads to better marketing decisions for the event and is therefore also a key first step in the development of an event sponsorship programme. Potential sponsors are also looking for effective ways of reaching their target markets and an event that can reach the same target market, in sufficient quantity, becomes a potential communication vehicle. The second step is therefore to identify which those organizations are.

Step one

The determination of the event's target markets is arrived at via a process of segmentation. As there is no set way that a market should be segmented (Jobber, 1998), there is an opportunity for innovation. By being creative with the criteria by which the market segments are identified, it is possible to identify further innovative ways in which the event's audience will be of use to sponsors, therefore enhancing the prospects of achieving increased sponsorship revenue (Masterman, 2007). See Case studies 11.1–11.4 and the ways in which those events have been creative in helping their sponsors to reach their target markets.

Research data are required in order to determine the event's target markets. This research needs to determine the nature and characteristics of the various attendees of the event. This could include gaining information about their demographical, socio-economic and geographical profile. More in-depth information would be behavioural or psychographical in nature and would provide information on their lifestyle. For example, information on the types of products or services they buy would be of use. Information at different times in the event life cycle can be of use as well as they may be able to track changes over time. This can be achieved via audience surveys of various types, before, during and after the event. Focus groups and interviews can also be used and can achieve a greater quality of information. Simple observation of audience flow and purchases can also provide useful information. The more comprehensive the information the more clearly defined the target markets will be. Case study 11.2 shows how the Alamo Bowl uses research of its target markets in the recruitment of its sponsors.

The data should be recorded so that it can be used in the identification of the target markets. In addition, the same data are required for the sponsorship sales process and due to their importance to the potential sponsor should feature in any sponsorship proposals.

Step two

The next step is to research the potential organizations that have the same target markets. Sponsorship agencies and consultants can be used to identify whether such sponsors or events can do the job in-house. The process requires time and effort in order to gain an awareness of the market. There is much information that is readily available in the public domain that can be used to target more accurately potential sponsors. This includes company accounts, trading figures, market trends and forecasts, government budgets, trade press, marketing media and, of course, activity at other events and current sponsorship activities. A continuous awareness of the competition is clearly required but the activity of sponsors at other events can also feed the imaginative event manager. In New Zealand, Vodafone entered the market in 1988 with an awareness level of 2%. The company was a target for a number of sports properties clearly with the opportunity for increasing their market status. Vodafone involved themselves with soccer, extreme sports and netball, including the Netball World Cup and, by 2000, increased awareness to 98% (Sponsorshipinfo, 2003).

Building relationships

Having identified appropriate organizations that have the same target markets, the work begins to establish a relationship. An off-the-shelf, or predetermined sponsorship package that has not been designed with any specific sponsor in mind, is unlikely to meet the unique requirements that organization has. Moreover, the key to the achievement of successful relationships is in the provision of a tailored service and the production of a bespoke arrangement that meets the individual objectives and requirements of a potential sponsor. It is important that this approach is not just applied when recruiting new sponsors, as this is also an ongoing requirement for the development of an existing event sponsorship programme. The building of the relationship for the acquisition of a new sponsor needs to continue throughout the relationship in order that it might grow and that future changes in requirements on both sides may be met.

Following on from the general areas of sponsorship objectives introduced earlier in this chapter, direct sales, increasing brand awareness and developing image, increasing corporate awareness and developing image, developing internal relations and the achievement of competitive advantage, the more specific objectives that sponsors seek via sponsorship fall into a number of categories:

- *Development of sales and market share*: the development of new sales opportunities at the event itself, where sales figures can be driven by event audience take-up, and/or via sales promotions in association with the event.

- *Customer loyalty*: the enhancement of relationships with existing customers.

- *Market penetration*: increasing recognition of the brand in existing markets.

- *Market development*: the establishment of brand awareness in new markets.

- *New product*: the launch of new products into appropriate target markets.

- *Product knowledge*: increasing the market's depth of awareness with more specific knowledge perhaps related to specification, capacity and capability.

- *Brand image reinforcement/revitalization*: the use of sponsorship to bolster the personality of brands.

- *Business to business*: the establishment and/or enhancement of key client and customer relationships in organizations markets.

- *Community relations*: the establishment and/or enhancement of the organization's relationship with the local community. This is an important concern, as a business has to be accepted locally in order to be successful, not least because the majority of its employees will live locally.

- *Internal communications*: the enhancement of staff relations.

- *Financial sector confidence*: the use of sponsorship to increase confidence in the city and perhaps with investors through the declaration of corporate intentions and the well-being of the organization in order to depict a healthy perception of the organization.

- *Post-merger identity*: the use of sponsorship to establish and increase awareness of newly formed or merged organizations.

■ *Competitive advantage*: through the above areas, but also through exclusion, whereby an organization blocks the opportunity to its competitors by taking it themselves.

Any one or any combination of these objectives, made specific in order for them to be measurable, could be a sponsor requirement and there is therefore a need for careful consideration of the vehicle that will deliver these successfully. The process that is involved in ensuring this success consists of four clear steps.

Step one

The mutual determination by sponsor and event rights owner of the requirements of the sponsorship.

Step two

The development of measures by which the requirements will be evaluated.

Step three

The development of a series of event rights and benefits for the sponsor that satisfy and meet the requirements of both the sponsor and the event.

Step four

The agreed payment and/or provision of services by the sponsor in return for the event rights and benefits.

As indicated previously, Step three has often included the offering of exclusivity as part of the sponsorship deal whereby a sponsor will enjoy association with the event as the sole representation from its own market sector. In such cases, a sponsor can gain competitive advantage not only through the association but also by denying the opportunity to its market competitors. The Cola wars between Coca-Cola and Pepsi are testament to this. Mullin et al (2000) suggest that offering sector exclusivity is a key benefit and cite that the IOC first designed its sponsorship programme with exclusivity benefits for the 1988 Seoul Olympics. Some 20 years later it is arguable that while sector exclusivity is not entirely 100% used at all events it is, nevertheless, now a virtual necessity. The implications for event managers are that, whereas previously this might have been the cutting edge in recruiting a sponsor, the fact now is that sponsors expect such status as standard.

Exclusivity is not a rigid status, however. Depending upon the negotiating power of the event, it may be possible to segment very finely certain industry market sectors and still achieve exclusivity. The power of Wimbledon and the All England Tennis Championships enables it regularly to have a number of official drink sponsors. For example, in 2005 there were seven including Coca-Cola, the official carbonated soft drink. In 2008, there were five, official wine Blossom Hill, official water Evian, official champagne Lanson, official coffee Nescafe and official still soft drink Robinsons (Wimbledon, 2008).

This four-step process is a continual requirement. Even existing sponsorships that are successful can be developed into being more effective for both parties. An event manager needs to be aware of what it will take for a sponsor to renew their association too. The implications of fewer new sponsorship deals for sports events and the increase of quality options for sponsors is that sponsorship renewal becomes increasingly important (Lachowetz et al., 2003). By using this self-reflecting approach, the changing needs of both sponsors and events can be adequately met and mutual benefits maximized.

For the acquisition of new sponsors, there is an initial wooing which can take a long time, perhaps up to several years, and it is important that the relationship building starts from the first contact. Lachowetz et al. (2003) discuss the concept of 'eduselling,' where an event engages with its sponsors early in the sales process. The research has shown that such relationships can lead to increased loyalty and, as a consequence, their retention as a sponsor. However, it is important that this continues beyond the point at which they first come on board. It needs to continue throughout the relationship and this may require going outside the limits of the contract. While contracts are an essential element of this mutual relationship, there is often good reason to give more than has been agreed and signed off. If there are extra benefits that can be offered to sponsors, they can be used further to enhance the relationship and this is applicable for both the event and the sponsor. If it is an effective arrangement, then both sides will not only want to continue, they will want to develop it further. For the event that means less time spent in seeking replacements and more benefits for the event in both revenue and exploitation.

A key element of relationship marketing is ensuring that it is sustainable and that customers (sponsors) can be retained over the long term (Piercy, 2000). A key customer relationship management (CRM) guideline for events is a development of a mutual trust via effective communication with sponsors (Varey, 2002). Communication is of particular importance considering the complexity and logistical nature of events. However, more than this is required if sponsorships are to be sustainable and this is where the innovation in meeting their objectives makes sponsorship the most creative communication tool. While the continual evaluation of and feedback into a sponsorship will help to sustain it, the exceeding of expectations will go further and also grow. It is therefore important that there is flexibility for change when and where it can enhance the relationship.

While identifying appropriate sponsors that have mutual target market aspirations, an audit of the events assets is also required. The various categories of event sponsorship assets can be seen in Event management 11.1. An event assets audit for many rights holders begins with identification of advertising, corporate hospitality, joint promotions, sales and media opportunities but a more lateral and imaginative approach is required. In addition to these basics, there should also be a consideration of opportunities that are perhaps not yet available. It is also prudent to exhaust all of the possible opportunities even though they may not be feasible in the long run in order that a comprehensive approach to this task is taken. The ultimate decision as to whether a sponsorship is of effective value is taken by the potential sponsor and so it is important that when a sponsorship is proposed to them it has had every possible asset considered in order to ensure that the proposal has every chance of being accepted. This can and should be aided by the event with the considerable use of innovation.

EVENT MANAGEMENT 11.1

Sponsorship Asset Audit

Sponsorship Asset Audits

A sponsorship asset audit consists of an internal evaluation by the rights owner of all possible assets in order to create an 'inventory' of possible sponsorship rights that can be combined to provide sponsors with tailored marketing solutions. The generic audit areas may be categorized as follows:

Physical

The division of rights into physical and geographical assets such as sites, zones, locations, venues, levels, indoor or outdoor.

Territory

The division of rights into local, regional, national catchment and geographical assets. This can include by 'round-of-competition'.

Time

The division of rights into timeframes, including by session, day or, again, by 'round-of-competition'.

Programme

The division of rights into various running order components. This might include pre-event, mid-event and post-event ceremonies, entertainments and other associated and ancillary events.

Communications

Rights holders' direct communications that can also incorporate sponsors messages, such as advertising, public relations and promotional activity via print, broadcast and Internet points of contact.

Status

The placement of one or more sponsors into a sponsorship programme structure that accords that sponsor acknowledgeable status and sector exclusivity, such as via title, presenter, naming or official supplier rights.

Supply

The identification of supplier or services costs that can be reduced or replaced by getting sponsors to pay for or provide those supplies or services, or by getting the suppliers themselves to become sponsors and supply at no or reduced costs, thereby exercising supplier rights to the providers, such as kit, transport, equipment, accommodation and food product. This might include the provision of media activity via the recruitment of media sponsors/partners.

Function

In addition to auditing by supply, rights owners need to identify existing assets or create new ones that are tailored for sponsors whereby any one sponsor can provide a 'function' for or to the rights holder and in so doing showcase their products and/or services, such as runner water stations in a fun run, air transportation or satellite navigation for boats in a yacht race.

Source: Masterman (2007)

The audit will reveal the commonly offered benefits of title and status acknowledgement, use of event insignia and imagery, media and print exposure, ticketing and hospitality. However, the innovation comes in the delivery of benefits that bond the event and sponsor in a way that they are seen to be inseparable. This is called 'sponsorship fit', where the sponsorship relationship between rights owner and sponsor is percieved as having synergy (Masterman, 2007). If the sponsor is intrinsically involved with the delivery of the event, it will make more sense to the target audience. This is more easily achieved with those sponsors that are suppliers of products or services to the event but less so for others and this is where the innovation and creativity are required. The use of fleets of cars as sports event courtesy vehicles is a common idea but nevertheless effective. Rover provided the courtesy fleet for the Manchester 2002 Commonwealth Games where a new model was launched and exposure achieved literally on the road and even away from event sites. At the same event, Boddingtons were able to drive their beer sales with the provision of event site bars. SAP, one of the world's leading software manufacturers sponsored a New Zealand America's Cup boat and received rights to put its logos on the sails. The greater creativity was in its provision of ship to shore wireless technology to the team. Case study 11.2 considers how the Alamo Bowl has audited its assets. In order to maximize revenue, it has innovatively identified sponsors for its many associated events including a preview event, fan zone, various dinners, high school games and golf tourney.

Sometimes the identification of where the bond can be achieved is more sophisticated. Case study 11.1 also gives examples of the ways in which innovation was used to enhance the bond between the Nabisco Masters Doubles and its sponsors. By getting the product in sight and used in the context of the event, the sponsorship can possibly be perceived as a credible facet of the event and provide more leverage from the association in order to achieve their marketing objectives. At this event, the sponsors functioned by providing clothing (Boss), timing display (Ebel), drinks (Schweppes), champagne (Lanson), business machinery (Minolta) and cardboard dining structures (Cundell).

The provision of a function for the sponsor and its brands is the key to ensuring that a sponsorship is bespoke. While any of the assets can be bundled together to form a tailored set of rights, it is the inclusion of rights that are intrinsically 'functional' to the sponsor that will make the sponsorship unique as well as of good fit. As the fit has been driven by the actual function of the sponsor at and in the event, the sponsorship is also more likely to achieve its objectives (Masterman and Wood, 2006; Masterman, 2007). Case study 11.5 demonstrates the effect functionality has had for a number of sponsors at the Boston Marathon.

Case Study 11.5

Event Sponsorship Programme: Boston Marathon

On April 17 2006, the Boston Athletic Association (BAA) staged its 110th Boston Marathon. The first race was in 1897. The race is not surprisingly the oldest annual marathon in the world and, in recent years, the organizers and rights holders have demonstrated equal fortitude in developing a number of key relationships with sponsors. For example, Gatorade has been a sponsor of the race for 14 years.

The 2006 race had 18 sponsors and three media partners in a tiered sponsorship programme structure. It is enlightening to look at John Hancock Financial Services, Adidas and Hewlett Packard in particular and how the BAA has developed relations for stronger and increasingly more successful sponsorships.

John Hancock

John Hancock Financial Services has supported the race since 1986 when it provided the first ever prize money. It continues to provide a prize fund that has grown to over US$600 000 including performance bonuses. In addition, the company provides a wide range of financial services to the communities that form the race course, namely Hopkinton, Ashland, Framlingham, Natick, Wellesley, Newton, Brookline and Boston.

John Hancock is a Boston firm and has been 'principal' sponsor throughout the relationship – the top sponsor in a tiered sponsorship programme structure. In order to grow the relationship though, a number of initiatives have been developed over the 22 years. The sponsor now provides media support with media guides, press material and accreditation coordination and it manages the pressroom. In order to achieve this, it utilizes its own Boston based buildings by transforming them into race centres and 1900 of its employees are recruited as volunteer race helpers. In the last few years, the firm has also provided a giant television screen near the finish line for public viewing.

The sponsor has also been exploiting its sponsorship. A number of key initiatives have been developed with the BAA. The 'John Hancock Running and Fitness Clinic' is a national educational programme that brings the top race winners into schools for demonstrations and training. Notable athlete involvements have come from Kenyans Ibrahim Hussein and Moses Tanui and Portuguese Rosa Mota. More locally, the 'Boston Marathon Kenya Project' has been developed. This is a year-round schools project that celebrates the fact that Kenyan athletes have been the dominant race winners. John Hancock employee volunteers and Kenyan race champions educate pupils on Kenyan culture, language and geography while based at the Boston Zoo's African Tropical Forest exhibit. Another local project was first developed in 1992 – the 'Adopt-a-Marathoner' programme brings the Kenyan elite runners each year together with school pupils in a pre-race rally. These new ideas were all jointly developed to grow the relationship year-on-year and were initiated as exploitation of the rights in order to further achieve John Hancock's objectives for developing corporate awareness and internal relations in particular.

Adidas

Adidas has been a sponsor of the race since 1987 and is now the 'Official Footwear and Apparel Outfitter', a position that ranks it singularly at the next level below John Hancock. After 17 years, it increased its commitment by accepting new rights that saw it provide the runners' bibs and numbers. It had already provided the 7000 volunteers and 1100 media representatives with branded jackets.

In 1992, Adidas sponsored the BAA as well as its Marathon event. After 12 years of involvement, in 1999, Adidas and BAA launched the year-round project, the 'BAA Freedom Run' and also an annual seminar series based at the Boston Marathon Expo. Another new and major exploitation initiative was introduced in 2005 with an Adidas advertising campaign, using its latest shoe 'adistar control', entitled 'It's what happens between runs'. This was a two-week campaign that was exposed extensively across Boston prior to and during the Marathon and it was the largest

campaign of any sponsor to date. Again, these new ideas and exploitation have been introduced at key points throughout the relationship in order to see it grow.

Hewlett Packard

HP has been a sponsor since 1994 and sits on the next level down in the tiered sponsorship programme structure along with 15 other sponsors. In its tenth year, it adapted its technology to provide an exciting new function at the event. It launched the 'HP Athlete Search System', a state-of-the art wireless network to provide data on race participants as they were running. By placing a chip into their shoes or on their wheelchairs, race participants could be tracked during the race. This meant that anyone anywhere in the world could track an athlete via their own personal computer if they logged on to the HP supported race website. Additionally, spectators at the race could stop any of 75 HP employee volunteers and ask them to use their hand-held HP iPAQ Pocket PCs to track an athlete. The technology was therefore providing a number of information-providing functions for race organizers, media and spectators as well as being a piece of entertainment. It also served well in showcasing HP technology and brands.

In order to launch this technology, HP had to work with another sponsor, Verizon Wireless. Here, the collaboration between sponsors provided both firms with cross-promotional opportunities and demonstrates the commitment of both to their relationship with BAA.

Source: Boston Marathom (2004, 2006); HP (2004); Masterman (2007)

Rights exploitation

It is extremely unlikely that the sponsor will achieve its objectives to the fullest capacity by relying solely on the event rights, even with the use of innovation. Reaching the target audiences to a measurable extent requires exploitation of the rights. This consists of communications activity by the sponsor in support of its purchase of the event rights and over and above what those rights alone achieve. Sometimes referred to as leverage, activation or maximization, this involves more time and resources and the complete integration of the sponsorship into the sponsor's overall communications programme. The greater the profile of the event, the more it would seem that this is the case. In 1996, Coca-Cola spent over 10 times the amount it gave for the rights it purchased for the Olympics in Atlanta (Kolah, 1999; Shank, 1999). There have been rules of thumb used in the industry, whereby the ratio of outlay on exploitation has been 3:1 (Graham et al., 2001), but a more accurate rule of thumb has to be that the outlay needs to be whatever it takes to achieve the objectives. This is good news for events. The sponsors that effectively support their rights are the types of sponsors that events want because while the event gains more exposure it gains it at its sponsors' expense. A sponsor that supports its rights effectively is also likely to be happier with the sponsorship and therefore more likely to renew the arrangement. This saves the event the resources it would need to implement in order to find a replacement.

Exploitation is strategically planned and can form the focus or a part of the overall communications strategy of an organization. If the sponsorship sits alongside other communications, the key is that it is integrated. Toshiba, an official partner for the 2006 FIFA World Cup in Germany, for example, ran print media promotions in the UK that depicted computer graphics enacting goal scoring celebrations alongside a competition that entitled purchasers of Toshiba notebook computers to get 66% of the price refunded. A 'fingers crossed' message was used to link the 66% to 1966 and the last time England won the World Cup. Similarly, Hewlett Packard (HP) integrated its UK promotions in 2003 around one theme, '+HP=everything'. Seemingly totally unrelated areas of activity were brought together by this campaign and their sponsorship of the BMW Williams Formula 1 racing team sat alongside associations with Amazon.com, Dreamworks animations, Fedex, birdlife conservation and individual artists (HP Women's Challenge, 2003). The communications consisted of substantial newspaper and television advertising, in addition to Internet spend in order to increase awareness for HP and their ability to help all kinds of organizations on an international basis. The sports sponsorship played its part in the overall campaign but also had dedicated communications activity that HP implemented at their cost in order to make the most of its rights as principal team sponsor.

Flora, in its sponsorship of the 2000 London Marathon, had objectives for increasing its market and value share, awareness through television and employees involvement, all focused on the health of the family. Its UK public relations (PR) communications in support of this sponsorship consisted of schools competitions, charity and pub links, joint branding opportunities, the use of celebrity athletes and chefs, and press trips designed to target women's, children's and life-style media, and its staff internally.

Rover, mentioned earlier, used its sponsorship of the 2002 Commonwealth Games to launch two new cars, the Rover 25 and the 45 Spirit models. The cars were used extensively as a courtesy service for the event and were seen all over the UK with their event insignia. The sponsorship was supported by PR, television advertising and direct mail communications before, during and after the event.

Inmarsat, a satellite communications company, were looking for a sponsorship solution that would showcase the reliability, globality and mobility of its products. Following research undertaken by a sponsorship consultancy, Inmarsat became an exclusive partner of the World Rally Championship (WRC). By using Inmarsat satellite technology, rather than terrestrial transmitters, the WRC was able to facilitate rally teams so that they could send and receive an e-mail and make calls from remote event locations such as deserts. In addition, Inmarsat was able to invite its distributors to entertain end-user customers with corporate hospitality and, from 2003, provided the event's television partners with satellite links that enabled daily highlights and programming that was previously inaccessible (*Marketing Business*, 2004).

Unprompted awareness of the 2008 Olympic sponsors was evaluated just prior to the Games in order to review the impact of expoitation activity both in China and internationally. One of the issues for sponsors during the torch relay was the impact of political protests against China's position in Tibet. In London, Paris and San Francisco, for example, there were demonstrations that attracted international media coverage (see Beijing Insight 10.1 in Chapter 10). However, the evaluation revealed that, on a worldwide basis, awareness of sponsors was not that affected and, in China, awareness was high with Lenovo (38% awareness), Coca-Cola (36%), China Mobile (30%) ranked most highly (Sport Business, 2008). While all sponsors were very active with advertising and other exploitation tactics to achieve these figures in China, a lot of their international exploitation activity was actually temporarily curtailed while the torch relay was happening. According to the evaluators, Sport+Markt, this was delberate as sponsors were unsure as to how they would be perceived. On the one hand, this stand meant that sponsors lost valuable time and opportunity to exercise their sponsorship rights. However, a different conclusion is that the tactic of no activity in these circumstances was positive exploitation in itself. Visa resumed its exploitation activity in the UK one month after the relay had been in London and focused on printed promotions featuring a competition for all card holders to win trips to go to the Beijing games. The advertisements in May 2008 used a link with beach volleyball and the tag line 'blood, sweat and tears aren't the only way to get to the Beijing 2008 Olympic Games'. Samsung, on the other hand, preferred to focus on another of its sponsorships in the UK with both television and printed advertisments in exploitation of its shirt sponsorship with Chelsea FC. For three weeks prior to the clubs appearance in the UEFA Champions League final on May 21, Samsung deployed advertisements that utilized four players in club suits juggling footballs alongside their branded televisions. The tag line was 'imagine design that perfoms' and while the links were not that intricate, this was a positive approach that used integrated communications.

Evaluation

In order for the relationship to grow, there needs to be continuous evaluation of the relationship. This allows for feedback so that changes can be made for the better. This evaluation, like all evaluation, needs to be against objectives and, if they are measurable objectives, then decisions can be made in order to maximize the return on investment.

There are three questions that evaluation can answer:

- *Visibility*: how clear was the sponsorship?

- *Sightings*: who took notice?

- *Objectivity*: did it achieve what it was supposed to achieve?

There are various methods of evaluation. Media value methods are commonly used and quantify the amount of brand visibility at what it would cost to buy the equivalent in advertising space. This method is unfortunately unreliable, first, because there is no evidence that the brand has been seen and, secondly, that rate card prices are used in the calculation when they are seldom actually paid when buying media space. These methods can reveal that sponsorship provides logo or product sightings less expensively than advertising but another issue is that they are not interchangeable in terms of communication effectiveness (Lainson, 1997). Other methods include media audience measurements of circulation, viewing or listenership figures. A different approach is via the customer. By using focus groups, surveys and interview techniques, it is possible to get closer to identifying the extent of the awareness of a sponsor and/or its products.

Increasingly, sales objectives are now being applied to sponsorships whereby sponsors seek to drive product sales via first increasing awareness and developing the image of the product and then using sales results to evaluate performance (Lainson, 1997). A comparison of sales results pre- and post-event and then tracked over time can prove beneficial and provide tangible and measurable evaluation for some decision-making. However, there is no evidence that the sponsorship unequivocally caused the sales results as there are too many contributing factors, such as increased or decreased competitor activity, economic impacts and so forth.

'Direct sales' objectives, on the other hand, can be more objectively evaluated. Sales that have been caused by a sponsorship can be considered as firm evidence of peformance and so an official drink sponsor can measure its performance with sales that have been incurred at the event. Sales do not just have to be at the event, however. A credit card sponsor that produces memberships and sales via its card in association with the purchase of event products, before, during or post an event, is ensuring those sales are because of the sponsorship.

Survey methods are commonly used in sponsorship research and, in late 2007, Ipsos produced the results of its third survey in China, in Beijing and other 2008 Olympic cities, as well as non-Olympic cities. The method used was computer-assisted telephone interviews with a large sample of over 3000. The objective was to measure performance of Beijing 2008 sponsors and compare that with non-sponsors as well as track that comparison on from two previous studies. Twenty-nine partners/sponsors were included in the analysis. Beijing 2008 Partner China Mobile (51.8%) ranked top in awareness among respondents, while TOP VI IOC Partner Coca-Cola (50.7%) came in second, followed by Air China (49%) and Lenovo (46.7%). The survey focused on sponsor identity recognition, sponsor voice, wrong recognition, fit, brand image and enhancement of willingness to purchase. It is refreshing to learn that there was also a focus on sponsor exploitation activity with Coca-Cola's Torch Relay activity ranking top throughout the tracking and Sinopec's 'Green Olympics, Green Oil' losing ground, but China Mobile's 'Fuwa Souvenir Recharge Card' gaining momentum and increasing recognition by the time of the third study and ranking second. Tsingtao Beer's activities did not successfully register (Ipsos, 2008).

Recognition and awareness of image are difficult to evaluate accurately and, for evaluation to be effective, it can also be expensive either to do internally or commission. As a result, evaluation is generally an uncommon practice in the sponsorship sector and therefore an issue for industry. That the evaluation methods available are generally unreliable is leading to more sponsors becoming unsatisfied. It is not necessarily that sponsorship is not

Table 11.1	Event Sponsorship Evaluation Methods
Media related	
Media value and equivalent advertising costs	
Audience levels: printed media circulation, TV viewing, radio listening or Internet hits	
Impact value: quality values applied to media types and coverage	
Frequency of media reports	
Opportunities to see: coverage statistics	
Customer related	
Sales figures and enquiries figures	
Audience spectator numbers	
Merchandise sales figures	
Shifts in awareness assessments: of brands, image	
Quality of awareness studies	
Tracking awareness over time	
Market share improvement and speed of improvement	
Promotional response numbers: distribution of samples, redeemed coupons	

being successful, it is more that sponsors do not know for sure if it is or is not successful in achieving return on investment. The development of a different approach to sponsorship evaluation is therefore required. The only solution at present is to adopt a multi-faceted measurement approach that evaluates the effect of sponsorship using a number of methods, for more reliability, at least until better techniques are developed (see Table 11.1 for a list of evaluation methods). Key for the future is the development of techniques that measure the critical differential that sponsorship has over other forms of communication, it is the value of the sponsorship relationship and the effect that has on target audiences that must become the focus (Masterman, 2007).

AMBUSHING

The increasingly used technique of ambushing is being used to great effect in sport. It is the exploitation of an association with an event by an organization that has not purchased any rights from that event.

The protection of sponsorship rights is therefore a major issue in sport today. Despite considerable effort to police the activity of non-sponsors and their attempts to gain association with an event, there appears to be no end to this type of communication tactic. This form of communication is planned and is designed to gain this association in order to achieve the sorts of benefits official sponsors pay a fee to the event to achieve. Consequently, sponsors are now expecting full protection from ambushing and they expect it from their agreements with their events.

Nike has built itself a reputation in using this type of communication and, in reading sports marketing texts, it is difficult not to find examples of their exploits. Shank (1999) maintains that the organization actually has its own ambush marketing director. One of its largest Nike sponsorships is of the Brazil National Football Team and it exploited this at the time of the 1998 FIFA World Cup in France. Adidas were the official sponsors of the sports manufacturer category of that event and, yet, the awareness figures showed that Nike had a great deal of success. According to a sport and market study, Adidas achieved a sponsor recognition rate of 35% and yet Nike managed a rate of 32% without the purchase of event rights (Hancock, 2003).

The policing of ambush marketing has taken on new proportions. The Sydney Olympic Games Organizing Committee launched an AUS$2 million advertising campaign against the ambushing of the 2000 Olympic Games. In a rather more direct approach, the 2003 Cricket World Cup in South Africa protected its sponsors by not allowing rival brands into its event grounds. In a controversially stringent control of potential ambushing, the event placed lawyers at each ground and warned that any spectator wearing a Coca-Cola T-shirt may be ejected and/or the shirt confiscated (Brown, 2003; Biz-Community, 2003).

New York tried to future proof its possible 2012 Olympics. In its failed bid for the Games, it provided a considerable degree of ambush protection by securing the majority of outdoor media that would be available in the city in 2012. It did this in 2005, 7 years ahead, on index linked prices and managed temporarily to book 95% of the 600 000 advertising signage available.

The Ipsos (2008) research above produced analysis that ranked non-Olympic sponsors very much in among sponsors in terms of recognition and, even though this was 'wrong recognition' it is a worrying trend. Li-Ning, the Chinese sportswear manufacturer, for example, ranked highly in the Ipsos studies despite not being the official sportswear supplier to the 2008 Olympics, a position held by Adidas. Li-Ning actually ranked higher in the third study and significantly so with a recognition of almost 71% against the 66% gained by Adidas. Similar results for Nike have been achieved in other major sports events including UEFA Championships and FIFA World Cups and continues to be a worrying trend for some sponsors (Performance Research, 2000).

One of the biggest ambush coups by any sportswear manufacturer was executed at the Beijing 2008 Olympic Games themselves. Adidas, as a long-term IOC sponsor and supplier, were recruited by BOCOG to its top tier of sponsors, as an official 'partner' (see Beijing Insight 11.1). Meanwhile, BOCOG's magnificent opening ceremony for the Games culminated in one of China's most prolific gymnasts and famous sports stars, Li Ning, being hoisted up and miming a run around the upper rim of the 'Bird's Nest' eventually to light the Olympic flame. While Li Ning is little known outside of China and the world of gynastics, this was viewed on an international basis and there was the opportunity for commentators to enlighten audiences as to who Li Ning is. Li Ning is, in fact, the founder and Chair of the sportswear manufacturer of the same name and, as indicated above, in the run up to the Games the brand was pressing hard in the Chinese sportwear market to a point where it was achieving higher ratings in sponsor recognition polls than Adidas. Its strategy included sponsorship of the Chinese Olympic team but not as an event sponsor for the Games. Li-Ning, the brand, targeted Adidas and its platform of 'Nothing is impossible' by adopting a directly competitive communications theme of 'Anything is possible' in order to achieve this (asia sponsorship news, 2008). The part BOCOG played in this appears unusual and it is interesting to learn that there was little in the way of media interest or in making this a controversy. Perhaps, unsurprisingly, neither the IOC nor Adidas pursued the episode in the public domain.

The more sophisticated sports sponsorship becomes the more sponsors demand protection of the rights they buy. As sports events are prime communication vehicles, they offer opportunities for more than just their sponsors. The implications are that this is an area that will become increasingly important and control will continue to be a key issue. However, sponsors are fair game for ambush activity that is within the law, so the solution should not just be about ambush protection, it should also be about the use of exploitation to promote fully the sponsorship and offensively make the most of an opportunity non-sponsors have been denied. While that is the sponsors' responsibility, rights owners must encourage the practice.

Beijing Insight 11.1
Beijing 2008 Olympics: Sponsorship Programme

Beijing 2008 Partners	Beijing 2008 Sponsors	Beijing 2008 Exclusive Suppliers
Bank of China	UNI President	Schenker
State Grid	ICP/IP	Aggreko
PICC	Yili Group	Synear
Air China	Bhpbilliton	Kinghey
Adidas	Yanjing Beer	Gehua Ticketmaster
Volkswagen	TSINGTAO	Staples
China Mobile	Budweiser	Kerry Oils
CNPC	SOHU.com	Royal
Sinopec	Haier	Technogym
CNC	UPS	Snickers
Johnson & Johnson		Yadu
		Valti
		Beifa
		Mengna
		Greatwall

Continued

Beijing Insight 11.1—cont'd

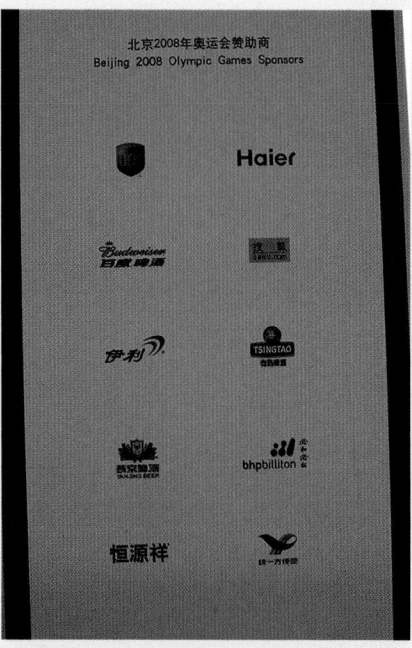

Photographs of Games sponsor boards.

The Beijing Olympic Sponsorship Programme consisted of three tiers, Partners, Sponsors and Exclusive Suppliers. In addition, there was also a minor fourth tier consisting of 17 suppliers: Taishan, Sunglo, Airfly, Crystal CG, Der, Yuapei, Aokang, Liby, Mondo, Newauto, PriceWaterHouseCoopers, Dayun, EF, Capinfo, Unipack, Microsoft, Kokuyo.

Also, in exploitation activities designed to leverage their worldwide TOP VI Olympic Partner status with the Olympic Movement and the IOC were the following: Samsung, Visa, Omega, Panasonic, Manulife, McDonald's, Kodak, lenovo, GE, Johnson & Johnson, ATOS Origin, Coca-Cola.

Photograph of a games Top sponsor board.

TOP VI partners have international rights to promote their sponsorship of the Olympic Movement throughout the lengths of their agreements. Many agreements extend over several Olympiads and are renewed. They also have rights for Olympic Games and these were exercised in Beijing in 2008 (see Case study 6.3 in Chapter 6).

The Beijing 2008 Sponsorship Programme meanwhile is focused entirely at the national level within the host country.

Continued

Beijing Insight 11.1—cont'd

For each of the three main tiers there was a benchmark fee but price variations were allowed in order to accommodate specific industry sector conditions. Adidas, for example, paid US$100 million for their rights. The agreements with each Programme sponsor included their commitment to promote Olympism throughout China, make significant contributions to technology, products and services to support the Games, the Chinese Olympic Committee (COC) and the Chinese Olympic Team.

Exclusive rights were granted in each case, but the extent of rights differed from sponsor to sponsor according to the fee they paid.

Generally the rights included:

- Use of BOCOG and COC marks in marketing communication
- Sector exclusivity and provision of products and services
- Hospitality, ticketing, accommodation and accreditation
- Preferred options for television and billboard advertising
- Preferred options to purchase further sponsorship in the cultural and Torch Relay programmes
- Participation in BOCOG sponsorship workshops
- Participation in the anti-ambush programme.

Outside of these rights, it is down to the sponsors themselves to exploit and make the most of these rights, at further expense, including the provision of technology, products and services that are supplied to the Games as stated above. These are how the sponsors provide a 'function' to the event. For example, the Beijing 2008 Olympic Partners provided functions as follows:

Bank of China: Banking and financial services

CNC: Telecommunications

Sinopec: Petroleum and chemical products

CNPC: Petroleum products

China Mobile: Mobile telecommunications

Volkswagen: Ground transportation (including their Audi brand for VIP transport)

Adidas: Sportswear

Johnson & Johnson: Healthcare products

Air China: Air transportation

PICC: Insurance services

State Grid: Energy products.

Source: Beijing 2008 (2008); IOC (2008); Sports City (2008)

ETHICAL AND MORAL ISSUES

The dominant ethical issue in the sponsorship sector is the one of over-commodification and the selling of an event into the hands of product endorsement. The issue is concerned with how much control is being passed over from rights owner to sponsor. It is equally an issue in the sports industry as it is in arts sectors even though it might appear to have been and gone. On the one hand, it is not only accepted as a financial necessity in order that events can be staged, on the other, there are still examples of rights owners holding back on the 'selling of their soul.' The FA in England still refuses to sell a title sponsorship for its world renowned FA Cup. It is only in recent years that it has allowed a sponsor to be even associated with the competition, first AXA Insurance and more recently E.on but only via presenting rights. While this is not quite as extensive as the rock musicians who resist product overtures for their endorsement over concerns about artist integrity and who controls artistic content, it is, nevertheless, an example of commercially wielded power. The writing, of course, is literally on the wall. In the UK, there are few cases of the use of naming rights and stadiums and, consequently, the likes of the Reebok Stadium, Walkers Stadium and the former Fosters Oval stand-out. In the USA, however, the majority of stadiums used for major baseball, basketball, hockey and football events are sponsored by commercial organizations where the uses of traditional stadium names have been lost.

There are also ethical implications in the sponsorships that involve products that are connected with poor health. Tobacco sponsorship has now ostensibly come to an end but alcohol sponsorship in sport remains. Beer brands still feature on replica football strips as purchased and worn by under-18 football fans. There are also issues with the sponsorship of educational institutions in the USA by sports manufacturers. Of concern are schools that are able to attract the best basketball players as a result of them being able to give them sports gear, and more, via sponsorships and as a result create elite teams. Some believe the solution is to limit or even outlaw sponsorships of this nature. Sponsorship of schools sports by food brands such as Krispy Kreme Donuts has also been controversially received.

The advertising of gambling in sport is another issue and the National Football League in the USA rejected a Las Vegas Convention and Visitors Authority request for advertising space for the 2003 Super Bowl despite there being no gambling content in the proposed advert (Raissman, 2003). Gambling organizations are now very active in the UK in sports events and related sponsorships.

TOP sponsor Omega provided 'countdown' timing displays at various sites around Beijing during the run-up to the 2008 Olympic Games, including here outside the BOCOG office building. These displays exploited the brand's sponsorship rights and demonstrate the importance of its timing function.

The issue of branding in sports is becoming increasingly imaginative and, at the same time, can raise ethical issues. The use of speed-skating suits that are transparent and the wearing of commercial advertising to the body or underwear are of concern to some and there are currently no regulations to restrict it. This has filtered through to boxing too where ESPN, the USA sports broadcaster, wanted temporary commercially related tattoos banned (Christie, 2002). Body billboards have been legal in the state of Nevada as a result of a court hearing and boxers being declared the right to free speech in this way (Raissman, 2002).

Finally, the issue of spending money when times are hard and the message that communicates came into play when the US Postal Service sponsored a Tour de France Cycling Team for US$25 million. While the choices of a communications vehicle in leading rider Lance Armstrong and the synergy of excellence in delivery are perhaps not at issue, the sponsorship is possibly at odds with the organization's US$13 billion debt and downsizing at the time (Pugmire, 2002).

It is clear that there are seldom rules and that ethics are continually evolving especially in markets that are increasingly looking for new ways to achieve competitive advantage. The implications for event managers are that there will often have to be a fine balance between the competitive communication of an event and what will be ethically acceptable.

SUMMARY

A successful sports event sponsorship is one that achieves the independent objectives of both the event and the sponsor, but this is achieved via the building of a mutual relationship. For the event, this relationship is first of all established as a result of targeting the right sponsor. Ultimately, both event and sponsor want to know if the sponsorship has been an effective use of the budget spent and, while evaluation will determine the extent to which this has been the case, it is important that the process starts with clearly defined, hopefully ethical, measurable objectives. After all, it is the objectives that will ultimately be measured. The key issues are that a successful sponsorship is a relationship that has been nurtured to gain an ongoing mutual understanding of requirements and that it is a provision of benefits that will require thorough exploitation in order that those requirements are met. Evaluation will reveal if there has indeed been a return on investment.

QUESTIONS

1. What key market forces are currently affecting the achievement of successful sponsorships?

2. How might the following events structure their sponsorship programmes? Evaluate all the options available:
   - A city school's athletics championship finals
   - A national amateur basketball championship
   - An international junior (under 15s) football tournament

3. By using your own researched examples, evaluate the importance of:
   - Researching and targeting the right sponsors and
   - Auditing event assets

4. Why is rights exploitation a necessary activity for sponsors and desired by event managers?

5. Discuss the role and importance of research and evaluation in the achievement of successful sponsorships.

6. Select an event and provide a critical analysis of the functions its sponsors are providing and the extent to which they are fully integrating and achieving successful sponsorship fit.

REFERENCES

Asia sponsorship news (2008). *Li Ning passes adidas in race for recognition.* www.asiasponsorshipnews.com (accessed 3 September 2008).

Beijing 2008 (2008). www.beijing2008.cn/bocog/sponsors (accessed 19 February 2008).

Biz-Community (2003). *Ambush Marketing Bowled Out of World Cup.* www.biz-community.com/Article/196/48/1477, 24 January (accessed 28 March 2003).

Brown, A. (2003). *World Cup Chief Gets Shirty Over Ads.* www.theage.com.au/text/articles/2003/01/27/1043534003082 28 January (accessed 28 March 2003).

Boston Marathon (2004). www.bostonmarathon.org (accessed 7 April 2004).

Boston Marathon (2006). www.bostonmarathon.org (accessed 3 March 2006).

Christie, J. (2002). New meaning to bottom feeders. *The Globe and Mail.* 23 January. www.sportsethicsinstitute.org/sports_marketing_ethics (accessed 28 March 2003).

Clipper Ventures (2006). www.clipper-ventures.co.uk/2006 (accessed 23 may 2006).

FA, The (2008). www.thefa.com (accessed 18 February 2008).

Graham, S., Neirotti, L. and Goldblatt, J. (2001). *The Ultimate Guide to Sports Marketing*, 2nd edn. New York, McGraw-Hill, Chapter 8.

Grey, A. and Skildum-Reid, K. (1999). *The Sponsorship Seekers Toolkit.* Roseville, McGraw-Hill, Chapter 6.

HP (2004). HP technology keeeps pace for 2004 Boston Marathon. www.hp.com (accessed 6 April 2004).

HP Women's Challenge (2003). HP Women's Challenge sponsors. www.womenschallenge.com/sponsors.asp (accessed 19 March 2003).

Hancock, S. (2003). www.redmandarin.com/viewambush (accessed 28 March 2003).

Henry, A. (1999). Would you pay £5 m for this space? *The Guardian.* 10 November. Guardian Newspapers.

IOC (2008). www.olympic.org (accessed 19 February 2008).

Ipsos MORI (2008). www.ipsos-mori.com (accessed 18 February 2008).

Ipsos (2008). Beijing 2008 Olympic Games sponsorship performance. www.warc.com/ArticleCenter (accessed 19 February 2008).

Jobber, D. (1998). *Principles and Practice of Marketing*, 2nd edn. London, McGraw-Hill, p. 174.

Kolah, A. (1999). *Maximizing the Value of Sports Sponsorship.* London, Financial Times Media.

Lachowetz, T., McDonald, M., Sutton, W. and Hedrick, D. (2003). Corporate sales activities and the retention of sponsors in the NBA. *Sport Marketing Quarterly,* 12(1), 18–26.

Lainson, S. (1997). www.onlinesports.com/sportstrust/sports13 (accessed 10 October 2002).

Levitt, T. (1960). Marketing myopia. *Harvard Business Review*, **38**(July/August), 45–56.

Marketing Business (2004). January, 2004. Chartered Institute of Marketing.

Masterman, G. (2004). A strategic approach for the use of sponsorship in the events industry: in search of a return on investment. In I. Yeoman, M. Robertson, J. Ali-Knight, U. McMahon-Beattie, S. Drummond (eds), *Festival and Events Management: An International Arts and Cultural Perspective*. Oxford, Butterworth-Heinemann.

Masterman, G. (2007). Sponsorship: For a return on investment. Oxford, Butterworth-Heinemann.

Masterman, G. and Wood, E. (2006). Innovative marketing communications: Strategies for the events industry. Oxford, Butterworth-Heinemann.

Mintel (2000). *Sponsorship Report*. Mintel.

Motorsport Industry Association (2008). www.the-mia.com (accessed 18 February 2008).

Mullin, B., Hardy, S. and Sutton, A. (2000). *Sport Marketing*, 2nd edn. Champaign, Human Kinetics.

Performance Research (2000). British football fans can't recall Euro 2000 sponsors. www.performanceresearch.com (accessed 10 September 2003).

Piercy, N. (2000). *Market-Led Strategic Change: Transforming the Process of Going to Market*. Oxford, Butterworth-Heinemann, Chapter 6.

Pugmire, L. (2002). Check's in the mail. *The Los Angeles Times* 17 July. www.sportsethicsinstutute.org/sports_marketing_ethics. (accessed 28 March 2003).

Raissman, B. (2002). TV's fight foe, Inc. *New York Daily News* 14 May. www.sportsethicsinstitute.org/sports_marketing_ethics. (accessed 28 March 2003).

Raissman, B. (2003). All bets off with NFL: Vegas ad out while beer flows. *New York Daily Times*. 17 January. www.sportsethicsinstitute.org/sports_marketing_ethics (accessed 28 March 2003).

Shank, M. (1999). *Sports Marketing: A Strategic Perspective*. London, Prentice Hall International (UK), Chapter 12.

Special Olympics (2003). www.2003specialolympics.com/en/? page=spo_pre_01 (accessed 16 April 2003).

Sponsorclick (2003). www.sponsorclick.com/en/mktag (accessed 24 March 2003).

Sponsorclick (2008). www.sponsorcclick.com (accessed 18 February 2008).

Sponsorshipinfo (2003). www.sponsorshipinfo.co.nz/Site (accessed 24 March 2003).

Sport Business (2008). Olympic sponsors win high interest in China. www.sportbusiness.com/news/166703/olympic-sponsors-win-high-interest-in-china (accessed 30 April 2008).

Sports City (2008). *Olympic Games offer unique path to China markets.* www. sports-city.org/news (accessed 19 February, 2008).

Varey, R. (2002). *Relationship Marketing: Dialogue and Networks in the E-Commerce Era*. Chichester, John Wiley & Sons, Chapter 6.

Wilcox, J. (2002). *Tech Partners Go for Gold*. 7 February. www. news.co.com/ 2100-1001-831393 (accessed 19 March 2003).

Wimbledon (2008). www.wimbledon.com (accessed 18 February 2008).

www.alamobowl.com (accessed 18 February 2008).

www.hksevens.com.hk/sponsors (accessed 18 February 2008).

CHAPTER 12

Research and Evaluation

Planning for Athens 2004 would have been enhanced with better supporting pre-event research and analysis. The main Athens Olympic site now lies predominantly unused. This photograph was taken in 2008.

LEARNING OBJECTIVES

After studying this chapter, you should be able to:

- understand the importance of event evaluation and feedback in the sports event industry

- understand the roles of pre-event, continuous and interactive, and post-event evaluation

- identify evaluation methods and their appropriate use

323

INTRODUCTION

The importance of event evaluation cannot be understated and yet it is a much under used operation. The majority of event planning theory recommends the use of post-event evaluation and yet, in practice, event managers are all too quick to move on and not commit funds or time to this important undertaking.

There is also in practice a perception that there is only one form of evaluation, that which is conducted post-event. This chapter will consider three phases of evaluation, pre-event research and feasibility, continuous and iterative evaluation and the monitoring of an event and its planning in progress and post-event evaluation. It will also identify the various processes, types and methods of evaluation that can be undertaken and the forms of reporting that are necessary. Consideration will also be given to the cost implications involved as they are, more often than not, the reasons for not undertaking the activity.

THE EVALUATION PROCESS

This chapter is intrinsically linked to the event planning process. In Chapter 3, it was established that evaluation of performance is against the objectives that were first set. Therefore, the extent to which evaluation can be an effective tool is totally dependent upon these objectives. If they are specific, have timeframes and performance indicators (PIs) that can be measured, then an evaluation process can be designed that can provide objective and meaningful performance feedback to aid future decision-making.

Evaluation is no afterthought for event management (Hall, 1997). It is a strategic necessity in order to achieve the organizational change required for future success. Event management texts agree that evaluation not only assists an event to become more successful, it also helps professionalize the industry (Getz, 1997; Hall, 1997; Allen et al., 2002).

The methods of evaluation can be both quantitative and qualitative, but the final analysis of all research results will ultimately depend upon one or more manager's interpretation. There is, therefore, clearly room for bias and, in order to achieve as reliable an evaluation as possible, it is essential that several types of research be conducted in order to provide triangulation. This is perhaps more obviously important to the operations for larger events where the same managers may no longer be involved when it comes to consulting past reports. It is just as important, however, for smaller events and continuous management, because time and memory will erode the detail of evaluation needed to feed into the next event.

The usefulness of evaluation and its reporting is further highlighted by the assistance it provides to the industry at large. The Olympic Games Knowledge Service (OGKS), started in 2001, had vast resources from the Sydney 2000 Olympics and provided operational guidance to Manchester 2002, the operating organization for the 2002 Commonwealth Games (see Case study 12.1 for a description of the Transfer of Olympic Knowledge Study (TOK) programme). The Torch Relay that worked so well in promoting the 2000 Olympic Games all over Australia prior to the event was one concept that Manchester directly adopted as a result of the information it gained. For 3 months, the Commonwealth Torch, as launched by Her Majesty the Queen in her Jubilee year, not only served as a promotional tool but also provided community events all over the UK and beyond. The Torch Relay Director, Di Henry, also directed the Sydney Torch Relay.

Case Study 12.1

Event Evaluation: Transfer of Olympic Knowledge (TOK)

The TOK programme was initiated following recommendation by 16 of the IOC 2000 Commission whereby the organization recognized the role it had to play in enhancing the transfer of Games management knowledge from one Organizing Committee of Olympic Games (OCOG) to the next. It began with Sydney 2000, continued with Salt Lake 2002 and Athens 2004 and was implemented for Beijing 2008.

TOK documentation and archives work in tandem with the Olympic Charter, host city contract and IOC guides and specifically provide descriptions of the operations used to manage the Games. The process used in compiling this provision consists of the following:

Observers Programme

Up to 40 observers are installed at the Games (−2/+1 weeks) to analyse the strengths and weaknesses of each functional aspect. The observers are made up of members of National Olympic Committees, International Federations, area expertise and future OCOGs. A series of regular reports are then produced on the previously identified 20–25 key areas of the Games.

Visual TOK

This consists of photographic imagery of 'behind the scenes' operations. Only so many of those concerned with the next Games are able to attend the preceding event and so this visual record is used to help show them key aspects in operation at a later point.

Games Debriefing

This aims to draw main conclusions from the Games and give recommendations for future operations. It also allows the IOC to amend and update its requirements and guides. It consists of 3–4 days of meetings that cover the key areas of the Games. In attendance will be current and future OCOG management together with hired expertise.

The TOK programme is now provided in addition to an Official Games Report that is produced and is a more readily available source of feedback as the latter takes some 2 years to compile.

The IOC also set up a new service in December 2001, the Olympic Games Knowledge Service (OGKS) founded by Craig McLatchey, the former Secretary General for the Sydney Games. Its remit is to use TOK and other sources of information to deliver tailored education to Games and other sports events management teams. OGKS also works outside its Olympic remit and assists other events, for example the 2002 Commonwealth Games.

Source: Felli (2002)

There are costs involved in evaluation and the more sophisticated and extensive are the methods, the more event managers fail to justify this expense. The cost can be in time and effort alone if there are no external agencies involved and, for most event managers, this can be perceived as too valuable to give. Methods that do incur costs can include the production of materials and/or wages/fees and the important factor regarding planning is that these costs need to be included as part of the assessment of event feasibility. There is therefore an amount of planning that is associated with evaluation because, in order to budget for it, the nature of the evaluation, the reporting procedure and the timing involved all have to be considered. It may be that an amount is prescribed for evaluation per se and there are those that recommend a percentage of the event budget be devoted to the task. Those that do make such recommendations would appear to have a vested interest of course, the likes of those organizations that provide impact analysis and sponsorship evaluation services for instance. The key to the costing of evaluation lies, as ever, in the objectives set and who requires it. Is it an internal requirement or are there wider stakeholder needs for such information? The task therefore is to identify those that require evaluation, when they need it, in what form they will accept it and to prioritize what can be produced within budget. This is more comprehensively covered later in this chapter.

PHASE ONE – PRE-EVENT RESEARCH

Having first considered and determined the objectives for the event, the next stage in the planning process is to determine the concept that will deliver these requirements. There is, therefore, a need for research into the opportunities and resources that are available in order that the most appropriate concept is designed. A key part of this process is to identify customer needs. Further research is then required to determine if the event is in fact feasible. This first phase of evaluation is critical because if it is not thorough and conclusive and a decision is made to go ahead with the event, then there will be unknown forces, internally and externally to the organization, which may ultimately prove damaging.

Beijing Insight 12.1
Beijing 2008 Olympics: Pre-Event Research
All organizing Committees for Olympic Games are required to ensure that independently implemented pre-bid polls are conducted. The earliest poll conducted in China in connection with the 2008 Olympic Games in Beijing was implemented in

November 2000. The poll was commissioned by the Beijing 2008 Olympic Games Bid Committee (BOBICO) and Gallup were appointed to undertake a survey of 1626 Beijing residents during the period 8–22 November, 2000.

Sample
All residents were 18 years of age or above and 1322 urban residents were interviewed by telephone and 304 rural residents by personal face-to-face interviews conducted door-to-door.

The telephone interviews were achieved via random digit dialing. To achieve this, 240 bureau (regional code) four digit numbers were selected from all available bureau numbers and in proportion to the populations of the various districts and counties of Beijing. The latter four digits were selected randomly. Non-resident numbers (fax, corporate etc) were screened out and the family member with the nearest birthday to the interview date was selected for interview. Interviewers were divided into supervised groups to cover mornings, afternoons and evenings and no answer and busy line numbers were re-dialled at another time.

Rural residents were selected via a two-stage stratified sampling. First, village committees were selected in proportion to the populations of the various districts and counties of Beijing. Then families were drawn from the committees based on systematic sampling and, again, the family member with the nearest birthday to the interview date was selected for interview. Six interviewers were used under the supervision of a supervisor.

Results
- 94.9% residents were strongly in support of Beijing's bid to host the 2008 Olympic Games
- 62.4% residents were strongly confident that Beijing's bid would be successful

These data were an important guide for BOBICO and provided a 'pre-event' measure of progress to date in the popularity and perception of the strength of the bid. Similar polls for other bidding cities were a guide on how much there was still to do in terms of developing support. The further significance of this 'pre-event' research is that the IOC and its members will base their decision on which city will host a games on how much a city and its residents are in favour of hosting that Olympics.

Source: BOBICO (2008)

The research that is required can be acquired via situational, competitor and stakeholder analyses. An advanced SWOT (strengths, weaknesses, opportunities, threats) analysis, for example, will not only reveal the existing resources and match them with the best opportunities that are available, but also identify any resources required in order to turn weaknesses and threats into opportunities including how to achieve or maintain competitive advantage in response to a competitor analysis. Piercy (2002) maintains that SWOT analysis can be made to work for the realization of strategic insights and is not just another analytical technique that does not produce anything in reality. This is considered in depth in Chapter 9.

A stakeholder analysis will identify those that are important for the event's success and the nature of the relationship that is required. The identification of event stakeholders is important at this stage so that the event can determine those that are necessary for partnerships, provision of resources or, indeed, those that might influence whether or not the event can go ahead. This analysis would therefore include the determination of the nature of any bid, licence or funding application processes and an identification of the event's target markets and publics for the production of an eventual communications plan. The research process and nature of information required for event marketing are discussed in more detail in Chapters 9 and 10. As with any management tool, these tasks are only as successful as the ultimate decision-making performed by event managers.

Chapter 3 identified the need for a cost versus benefit analysis for the event and any long-term objectives provided as a result of staging the event. This is accompanied at this stage by the determination of the event budget. From an evaluation point of view, it is critical that the budget targets that are linked to the achievement of the event objectives have measurable PIs. These PIs are critical for the monitoring of the event throughout its planning in order to maintain an alignment with the objectives.

It is possible to determine a set of criteria by which an event programme can be produced and, in order to determine if the criteria are met, there are areas of research that will be required. Sheffield Event Unit has a clear set of criteria that are inextricably linked to its annually monitored programme of objectives. Its remit is to contract events that are able to meet city objectives that include achieving a higher international profile for example. Therefore, a number of events in any one year is required to receive television coverage to a certain level. This emphasizes the importance of monitoring on an on-going basis as well as post-event evaluation and of programme evaluation as well as individual event evaluation. Because the Unit has to look to a provision of some 30–40 events per year (Coyle, 2002), it can balance its requirements out over the whole programme (see Case study 12.2).

Case Study 12.2

Event Programme Criteria: Sheffield Event Unit

The following criteria are used to assess each event Sheffield promotes and/or hosts.

Major Sports Events Selection Criteria

- Does the event offer an opportunity for the continued development of links with governing bodies of sport emphasizing Sheffield's potential as a venue for their particular major events?

- What are the financial implications and the nature of the deal with the governing body of sport/event promoter? At this stage, involvement and input from sponsors may assist in the decision whether or not to press for a particular event.

- As much intelligence work and information gathering as possible is carried out to assist the decision-making process. Past financial and statistical information is analysed. Potential income sources are assessed against projected expenditure in a cost-benefit analysis.

- Despite the costs of staging major events, there are numerous economic benefits notwithstanding those of civic and community pride, national and international profile (city marketing), together with other forms of secondary income. How does the event fulfil these?

- What will the economic impact be for the city?

- What will the level of media exposure be? In terms of developing Sheffield's regional, national and international profile (city marketing), in particular via the medium of television.

- Is there external funding via Sports Council or grant aid sources available?

- Will the event promote opportunities for sports organizations and governing bodies to relocate to the city? What is the city's potential as a major base for associated activities (training, seminars, conferences, etc).

- How will the event stimulate the local community to collaborate and participate in sport?

- Are there possible links with the development of centres of excellence and the appointment of sports specific development officers?

- Are there opportunities for involving and providing for the sporting disabled?

- What is the status and credibility of the event? How is it perceived in the events market place? Into which category does the event fall, i.e. calendar, participation, entertainment, hybrid/created event?

- Can the city manage the operational implications of the event? In terms of staff, availability of suitably trained volunteers, appropriate resources etc.

- What will the timing and scheduling be? Where possible bid preparations and deadlines need to be identified and assessed to see if they are realistically achievable.

- Is Sheffield Events Unit able to provide a quality service to the customer and satisfy their demands and expectations?

- What will the event bring in terms of 'added value' and also in quantifiable aspects such as TV coverage, estimated viewing figures, over-night stays etc?

Source: Coyle (2002)

PHASE TWO – ITERATIVE EVALUATION

Throughout the pre-event period there needs to be continuous and iterative evaluation, feedback and alignment with objectives in order to execute the desired event. There is, then, the much needed monitoring of the event throughout its duration in order for evaluation to be formative as well as summative (Wood, 2004). This allows for a process that rolls from one event into another.

All aspects of the event need to be evaluated on an on-going basis throughout this period and, due to their nature, there will need to be the use of both quantitative and qualitative techniques. For financial aspects, there is the quantitative use of the ultimate revenue and expenditure targets at the end of the event whereby final accounts will reveal the extent of success. However, the setting of timely deadlines for the achievement of certain levels of revenue, such as for ticket sales for example, will serve as useful PIs that will provide feedback in to the performance of the communications programme, the sales operation and ticket distribution. The use of deadlines as PIs is a straightforward method for the monitoring of a number of qualitative aspects too, for example, the quality of the individual or team participants that have qualified through to a competition can also be useful for communications, sales and distribution decisions.

There is a need for flexibility in the event planning process whatever the duration and continuous monitoring will only be an effective tool if there can be feedback into those aspects that need modification in order that they remain aligned with objectives. If there is no flexibility and this feedback is not actively used, then the event's success is in jeopardy. How else can the long planning periods that are involved with major sports events be monitored and the planning of an event be always contemporary if it is not flexible enough to allow for modifications? The planning period for the Olympics is 7 years, during which the social and legal attitudes and standards may change. Therefore, it is imperative that continuous evaluation be used to ensure an event still meets the objectives it was meant to.

This process also acts as a control for quality. The continuous monitoring against quality guidelines enables the event to control the eventual output through the planning process. This is also important for the delivery of the event itself where the need for a control of the quality of output is most required. Control measures and PIs are therefore required while the event is running.

PHASE THREE – POST-EVENT EVALUATION

The third phase is post-event and while it is difficult not to bask in the aftermath of the event and/or move on to the next project, it is essential that an overall event evaluation be undertaken. This is, of course, important for the organizers so that there can be feedback into future practice, but it is also of value to stakeholders, such as client event rights owners, sponsors, participants, employees and suppliers, partners, investors and local communities and pressure groups. Evaluation has to be against the objectives originally set for the event and, because these can be short- or long-term, a key consideration is also at what point in time the evaluation is conducted. Post-event evaluation may therefore consist of numerous forms of report and produced at various points in time (+6 months, +1 year, +10 years etc.). This only emphasizes the fact that the event is not over until evaluation and feedback has been disseminated and that may be some time into the future.

It will be necessary to prioritize which stakeholders are key recipients of evaluation reports. Getz (1997) recognizes the importance of accountability and the identification of those that require such reports. In many cases, the responsibility to provide these reports lies with the event organizer. For example, financial reporting is required by the state for registered organizations for corporate performance and tax purposes and by investors on their investment's performance.

An evaluation of the success of the event may also be a requirement by sponsors. Whether it is contractually required or not, it might be of benefit to the event to supply research led data on target market awareness, sales figures and media coverage. A successful evaluation can make a convincing presentation of the success of the relationship and, more importantly, make for easier negotiations of renewal or enhancement of the agreement. Sponsors may, of course, produce their own evaluation and their requirements may also be unique. This offers another perspective on the costs of supplying tailored evaluation for each sponsor.

The role of events in sports development is important as they are often the shop window that can encourage a widening of participation and, if this is strategically sought, then outcomes should be measured. Long-term strategies for the development of participation in sport regionally, in local authorities for example, might be measured year-on-year and longitudinally so that annual outcomes can be compared. In the shorter-term, the effect of one year's activity that culminates with an event can be measured to inform next year's planning. North Yorkshire Sport, a county sports partnership and part of the Sport England regional sports network, has strategies for the development of a number of sports across its county. These begin with competitions for teams and individuals that are supported by clubs and schools that then provide winners who go forward to compete at the North Yorkshire Games. The 2008 North Yorkshire Games, despite torrential weather conditions, featured 1500 children across many sports at host venue Ampleforth College. Northumbria University is contracted to evaluate the effect of these strategies and does so via the collection of data from club

Hockey has benefited in North Yorkshire via a strategy for wider participation whereby teams play throughout the year for the prize of qualifying for the North Yorkshire Games. Hockey teams compete here at the 2008 North Yorkshire Games, Ampleforth College.

coaches and school teachers as well as children from the earliest stages of the competitions, year-to-year, in order to determine how many go on to participate further in each sport.

Government at local, regional and national levels may require, or be interested in, economic and tourism impacts. Funding bodies and government agencies, such as those managing the lottery in the UK, may also require evaluation as to where funds have been allocated. National and International Governing Bodies of sport, as event rights owners, may require evaluation against their criteria. They may also require a host or management company to supply an assessment of impact on the development of their sport. All of these requirements shape the eventual reporting format and each can adopt a number of different methods by which to collect the information required in order to make the report. The following methods are available as part of the evaluation process.

Data collection

Much of the information and data required are obtainable via internal processes and operations. They are available right the way through the planning process and the fact that they are gathered over time means that it is also an obstacle to their effective collection and analysis. Management practices need to ensure that not only are data collected but that they are also collated and therefore more easily analysed at the appropriate time. The very nature of the data in question shows why this is a critical factor. Sources include:

- *Sales data*: numbers, price levels and dates/times of sales of tickets, corporate hospitality, sponsorship, advertising, programmes, food and beverage, merchandise, car park and space. Applications for purchase may also include important additional data such as postcodes, gender, age, corporate activity, etc.

- *Audience traffic*: a picture of how the audience flowed in, around and out of the event by collecting attendance figures, times of entry and duration of visit available from turnstiles, car park, transportation or policing sources.

- *Participant data*: a profile of the participants can be gained from their entry forms including dietary requirements, sports activity preferences as well as other demographics data.

- *Budgets and cash flows*: financial reporting that is indicative of performance against prescribed and timely PIs.

- *Meetings records*: chronological collection of agendas, minutes and compendious reports.

- *Communication programme*: updated and corrected mailing lists and copies of all documentation, letters and proposals despatched. Copies of all printed materials such as posters, flyers, leaflets and brochures. Communications plans and schedules including promotions, media release copies, media advertising and public relations (PR) schedules. These may need to be obtained from appointed agencies.

Observation

Observation of the event and then the opinion of the observer are of great value to the evaluation process and all stakeholders can provide such feedback. Alongside the reports from event staff, the police and emergency service groups, sponsors, venue operators, strategic partners and even pressure groups can provide valuable information that can be incorporated into the evaluation process.

Observation by staff, in particular, can be of more use if they are trained beforehand. Allen et al. (2002) advocate the use of benchmarks in order to achieve some level of standardization in the process. By using checklists, for example, a grading can be given on performance of certain aspects of the event so that when it comes to an overall analysis, appropriate comparisons can be made. Getz (1997) goes further and maintains that it is a mistake to rely on casual comment and so there is a necessity for such attempts at standardizing the process.

Observation can also be bought in. In the same way as the retail industry contracts the visits of trained mystery shoppers, the event industry can do the same in order to access perhaps a more objective view (Shone and Parry, 2001).

- *Photographic record*: there are two sides to every event, front of house and backstage (behind the scenes). Both can be captured on film for important visual evaluation that, if achieved in enough detail, can provide a snapshot of the whole planning process and the implementation of the event itself. There are two uses for such footage. Edited visuals are important tools for both future management and for new and developed sales.

The results of the analysis of all collected data and observed information can be used to reflect on target market demographics and operations performance for both internal and stakeholder information. It can also be used constructively in future sales operations.

Olympic games planning also involves observation processes that includes attending a games and feeding into on-going planning of a subsequent games. BOCOG and LOCOG executives for example visited Athens and Beijing, respectively for first hand knowledge for their games (see Case study 12.1).

Debriefs

The use of debriefing meetings takes on many forms. At one extreme, it is the celebration of the event and even a post-event party. These are important aspects and they have a substantial place in the management of an event, but the purpose of debriefing is a separate issue. Having been 'briefed', it is essential that 'debriefing' readdresses the objectives and at a level where all stakeholders have an opportunity to contribute.

The form of debrief will differ from event to event but may involve one meeting, sub-meetings and even a series of meetings. The agenda will address all the aspects of the event but has an important role to play in formalizing the process. For example, there are 20–25 key aspects of evaluation for the Olympics in the TOK programme and Allen et al (2002) suggest something similar with a generic standard 21-point event checklist. Another starting point worth considering is the area of responsibility as given in the briefing of individual roles and as developed in the implementation of the event. Essentially, any checklist is uniquely determined by each and every event.

The question of timing is important too. For some events, the scale and size of evaluation will necessitate a long period before meetings can be convened. In the case of the Sydney 2000 and Athens 2004 Olympics, the final reports were only concluded 2 years post the event. The general guideline is to stage the meetings as early as possible after the event has closed. It is possible to stage a first meeting(s) within a week of the event whatever the scale and this is an important factor if memory is not going to detract from the process.

There is a question of control. It is important that evaluation does not become either self-congratulatory or highly critical, particularly at a personal level. The purpose is constructive evaluation that should feed into the enhancement of performance, not false dawns or recrimination. Therefore, each member of a debriefing session needs time to prepare or contribute to a report for that debrief. Essential considerations for those that lead this process therefore, are the content of the agenda, meetings control and timely notification of meetings dates.

Surveys

A number of event aspects can be surveyed. All stakeholders can be given questionnaires to complete pre-, during and post-event and these can be collected immediately or over time. Audiences are key, of course, and their perception of the event is of paramount importance in an industry that needs to be driven by customer focus. Therefore, feedback on the event from ticket buyers, sponsors, advertisers and participants is required, but it is important to question suppliers, partners, investors, local communities and agencies too.

In addition to questionnaires, there are also the more direct methods of interview, either one-to-one or in groups. Technology has opened up the opportunities where video links and electronic discussion supplement the normal methods.

The quality of the information given from surveys is always of concern and events may well have to seek the guidance, if not the services, of trained professional assistance. Generally speaking, the greater the scale and depth of information required, the greater the costs, but the decision will depend upon who requires what kind of evaluation. Allen et al (2002), nevertheless, maintain that the key considerations when formulating surveys are clear purpose and targeting, simple designs that have unambiguous lines of questioning, a representative sample size, avoidance of bias via the use of randomness in the selection of participants and the need for supporting data for more accurate analysis.

Impact analysis

This form of evaluation is in common use by event hosts in the determination of an event's economic contribution to its locality, region and/or nation. It can provide much needed information of the wider benefit gained over and above the events operational cost or profit. It is therefore also used to calculate a forecasted impact for a potential event by hosts and, as a consequence, becomes a much used reference point for media scrutiny.

Economic impact in this context can be described as the net change in an economy as the consequence of staging a sports event (Crompton, 1995). The change is caused by the use of new or existing sports facilities and services by the event and the resultant visitor spending, municipal spending, employment opportunities and tax revenue as a consequence of staging the event. The impact can consist of three different effects. First, direct effects that are the wages and profits to local residents and businesses as a result of event visitor expenditure. Secondly, indirect effects that represent the rippled effect of this expenditure through to other businesses and workers who supply those who first receive the spending. Thirdly, induced effects where the income received is re-spent locally.

The key data for an economic impact study are derived via surveys of the event visitors. The essence of the study is who spent how much, on what and where. Data are required on who visited the event, why they came and where they came from in an attempt to determine who necessarily came to the event as opposed to who would have been in the locality anyway. Were they spectators, participants, officials or media? Data are then required on spending patterns in relation to the event and could include that spent on tickets, food and beverage, accommodation, merchandise and travel. An average spend per type of visitor can then be determined having next obtained the attendance figures.

UK Sport was set up to support elite sport at the UK level as well as programmes such as anti-doping and major events. It also manages the international relationships and coordinates a UK-wide approach to any international issues. The body is funded by, and responsible to, the UK Governmental Department for Culture, Media and Sport and their Blueprint for Success (UK Sport, 1999) was a strategic framework for the securing of major sports events for the UK. It provided a five-phase approach for the analysis of host city economic impact and included the use of multiplier analysis.

A calculation can be used in order to analyse the extent of impact. Multiplier analysis is widely used to achieve this and is discussed in more detail in Event management 12.1. However, there is contention with the use of multipliers and Coates and Humphries (2003) comment on the use of flawed multiplier techniques and recommend the use of further empirical study and methods in the evaluation of economic impact rather than using calculations that can be manipulated to the user's benefit. The issue with using multipliers is that there can be too much vested interest in disseminating results that suit self needs. The consistent use of such calculations by event organizers to project future economic impact and, consequently, win over stakeholders should therefore be of concern to the industry.

It has been argued in Chapter 4 that there is more to event impact than just economic benefit and it is important that impact analysis considers the

---

EVENT MANAGEMENT 12.1

Multiplier Analysis

In order to calculate the economic impact of an event, multiplier analysis takes the total expenditure, whether direct, indirect or induced, and converts it into a net amount that accounts for any leakages that have occurred. Leakages include the income that does not remain locally, for example, payments to suppliers that are based outside of the area or income that is not re-spent locally.

The aim of multiplier calculations is also to produce estimates of job employment as a result of staging the event. Claims as to the creation of jobs as a result of a one-off event might be somewhat tenuous. Crompton (2001) explains that the use of an employment multiplier assumes that all employees are fully occupied and infer inaccurately that an increase in visitor spending will necessitate local businesses to increase their level of employment just for a one-off event. He maintains that they are more likely to utilize existing levels of employment with short-term transfers. In support of this, a number of Manchester City Council employees were seconded, and 25 former Sydney 2000 Olympics management staff drafted in, to Manchester 2002, the organizing body for the Commonwealth Games. A more common calculation is of equivalent job years. This is where the additional income locally is divided by an appropriate average wage to determine a number that is expressed as being in full-time equivalent job years.

There are numerous multipliers that can be used and, as a result, there is some contention in their use. UK Sport recommends the proportional multiplier be used (UK Sport, 1999). Others are income, value-added and employment multipliers (Archer, 1982; Mathieson and Wall, 1982; Getz, 1997). There are also the discrepancies that can occur due to the inexact nature of calculation. Crompton (2001) maintains that this is not always as a result of a genuine lacking in economic understanding, moreover, it can be deliberate exaggeration that is used to maximize a case for the bidding of an event or the justification for having staged one.

There would appear to be a need for consistency in the methods of measurement used across the industry.

more intangible as well as the tangible, such as cultural and social impacts for example. Conversely, there are also the often neglected negative impacts as a result of staging an event, those of traffic congestion, vandalism, environmental degradation and social disruption that are an important factor in the determination of benefits versus costs. It is also important to consider the long term as well as the short-term impacts as, over the longer period, the benefit may well be of greater value.

Case study 12.3 describes the brief set by Manchester City Council for a cost–benefit analysis of the 2002 Commonwealth Games. The Case shows that the city was mindful for the immediate as well as the long-term view. While it might be implied, there is, however, a distinct lack of specific reference to the requirement of a report of any negative impacts. Cambridge Consultants beat six other tenders for the job (see Case study 4.3, in Chapter 4), for a summary of the results of their immediate impacts report.

Case study 12.4 shows two further examples of methodologies used to report on economic impact and the different objectives of Events Halifax in Nova Scotia and the Hong Kong Sports Development Board.

Case Study 12.3

Impact Analysis Methodologies: 2002 Commonwealth Games

On 28 August, 2001, Manchester City Council dispatched a brief for the commission of a cost–benefit analysis of the 2002 Commonwealth Games. The consultancy brief was to provide a quantitative and qualitative assessment of the impacts associated with the Games and, in particular, the following:

Immediate Impacts – Pre-Games

- The building and preparing of the Games facilities
- Associated environmental and infrastructure improvements
- Associated regeneration activity (including land reclamation, inward investment and employment)
- Training Games volunteers
- Pre-Games operational employment
- Marketing and promotional campaigns
- Enhanced partnership working in order to deliver facilities, infrastructure etc.

Intermediate Impacts – During Games

- Operating the Games
- The opening and closing ceremonies
- Games-related events and cultural activities
- Visitor spend
- Marketing, promotion, media coverage and exposure
- Volunteer activity

Strategic Impacts – Post-Games

The regeneration of East Manchester and wider economic benefits for the City as a whole, including:

- Increased inward and retained investment
- Increased employment opportunities for local people
- Diversification of the economic base
- Increased gross value added

- Enhanced sporting facilities and attendances
- After-use of the stadium by Manchester City Football Club and for other events
- After-use of other Games facilities by local residents, visitors, other sporting events
- Improved environment and visual amenity
- Enhanced national and international image
- Increased visitor numbers and spend
- Cultural renewal

- Social benefits, such as health benefits brought about through the improved participation in sport, a sense of civic renewal, pride and well-being, personal pride and well-being from securing a job or being a Games volunteer
- Spin-off benefits for the wider region: Increased profile, enhanced image, growth in target sectors of the economy, increased education and skill levels, health benefits, stronger regional centre

Source: Manchester City Council (2001)

Case Study 12.4

Impact Analysis Methodologies: Case Studies

Halifax, Nova Scotia

In 1999, Events Halifax, a Canadian Province agency with a mission to bring more events to the city, undertook an impact study of all its events. The strategy was to conduct a multi-event survey of representative events in every category including winter and summer sports. The methodology consisted of random personal intercept interviews of 809 sports event attendees and 12 promoter surveys.

The sports events included Canadian National canoe trials, Nova Scotia Special Olympics, Marblehead ocean race, New Minas soccer tournament, Equestrian championships, Kentville Harvest Valley marathon, Labatt Tankard curling, Alpine ski championships, SEDMHA Easter hockey tournament, Provincial artistic gymnastics championships, Masters national swim competition, and Mastercard memorial cup.

The attendees' surveys acquired data on expenditure patterns for 11 categories of spending: tickets, restaurants, accommodation, concessions, merchandise, entertainment, retail shopping, local transportation, bars, car rentals, equipment, and other.

Survey information collected also included general demographics including sex, age, education, residence, household income, plus travel arrangements, reasons for travel in order to determine the numbers and nature of event visitors.

Average daily expenditure for summer sports events attendees was CAN$72 and for winter events it was CAN$108. The economic impact for 1999/2000 summer events was calculated at CAN$12.7million and for winter events at CAN$30million.

Source: Events Halifax (2001)

Hong Kong

Business and Economic Research Ltd (BERL) undertook an economic impact study of sport in Hong Kong on behalf of Hong Kong Sport Development Board (HKSDB).

Broad industry data sources were used such as the Hong Kong Census and Statistics Department's Household Expenditure Survey, trade statistics and public sector data, and tourist information from the Hong Kong Tourist Association. A selection of face-to-face interviews was also conducted with representatives from companies in specific sports-related industries.

The data analysis indicated that the direct economic impact of sport in Hong Kong is a contribution of $21billion

Continued

to gross domestic product (GDP) per year. The impact, including indirect and induced effects, was estimated at $26billion or 2.1% of GDP. Employment multipliers were also used and estimated that the total contribution of sport to Hong Kong's employment was 81 000 jobs. For comparative purposes, the study reflected on impacts of sport in Scotland (1.8% of GDP), in the USA (2% of GDP), in the UK (1.7% of GDP) and in Canada and New Zealand (just over 1% of GDP).

Source: HKSDB (2002)

Media coverage

In response to the event communications plan and to supplement the collection of communication materials as above, there should be as comprehensive a collection of media coverage records as possible. The sources of information are:

- *Press cuttings*: this can be a bought in service but, the more successful the event, the more expensive this is. This should be compiled in chronological order and, if the coverage has been created via the use of communication tools such as releases or launches, then that too should be recorded. It can therefore be effectively conducted in-house if there is the time available to scour a prioritized list of media.

- *Broadcast coverage*: this can be of the event itself or of the acknowledgements made to the event pre, during and post. Accessibility to material will be easier via the broadcast media themselves. For higher profile events, the task of collection for any media material may involve national or international review and so outsourcing assistance may be more effective and efficient than in-house.

- *New media*: it is important to keep archives of Internet activity. This should track the content and the timing of any changes and the traffic both to own and link site activities. Interactive television traffic for event programming can also provide meaningful information.

The difficulty in financing evaluation is clearly an issue in the industry. There are many other financial pressures that take priority. Time too is a resource that is scarce for most event managers. The prospect then of contemplating long-term evaluation, when short-term assessments are rare in the industry, is daunting. There are also further problems associated with the adoption of long-term evaluation. Organizations, staffing, budgets and even objectives change over time and so usefulness can decrease if focus is not maintained during such longitudinal studies. While these issues are important, they should not detract from an acknowledgement that there is an optimum need for evaluation that can provide the basis for improved future performance.

REPORTING

There are a number of reports that can be produced, written or otherwise. The first consideration is who requires the report and this can often depend on the exact individual personality involved. The report must be written for the reader and this clearly dictates the format that will be adopted.

There is also the consideration of when the report is required. In the case of impact analysis and the evaluation of long-term objectives, there may be a case for an evaluation process that extends long after the event has concluded, as discussed in Chapter 3. Post-event evaluation can therefore be immediate or up to several years after the event. The argument put forward in Chapter 3 maintains that, if there are objectives that involve long-term legacies, then they can only be evaluated over that long term, even if that involves handing over the responsibility for evaluation to after-users.

The next consideration is what kind of analysis of the data should be undertaken and this, again, should be reader focused. The internal requirement for future management decision-making is a comprehensive report that covers all aspects of the event. Not all other stakeholders will be interested in so much detail nor should they be shown the aspects that are confidentially sensitive. Sponsors, for example, may require or be interested in the media coverage obtained, branding activities and target market reach success and the report for each sponsor may also be confidential of course. Investors would be interested in audited accounts and licensing bodies, such as local municipal authorities, in health and safety and economic impact.

The media coverage presentation should be available as a separate and individual record of the results of the communications programme. It can be presented in addition and in support of other stakeholders' evaluation reports. The presentation can then be used in future corporate sales operations in an attempt to increase existing revenue as well as develop new business.

There is no prescribed form to the report but it is a presentation and so all the normal business guidelines apply. It needs to be concise, comprehensive, accurate and reader friendly. There are some elaborately produced forms of event evaluation and, because they are in the public domain and concerned with large-scale events, they have also been expensively produced. Not all events have to go so far. If all an event needs to produce is one written evaluation, for internal use, it need only be at minimal cost.

At least one comprehensive report is required. This will cover all the key aspects of the event and will consider and incorporate the individual reports of as many stakeholders as required. Someone needs to collate it and produce it on time. Other reports, such as those for sponsors, investors and partners can be compiled out of the main report and delivered accordingly. Any debriefing needs to have taken place previously and so the presentation of such reports should not be the first post-event meeting a contributor has had for example. Their input is an integral component.

For more complex events it may be necessary to compile a large report and one that requires several volumes. The report for the 2002 Commonwealth Games for example consisted of five volumes.

SUMMARY

Post-event evaluation may be at the back end of the planning process but, without it, the event is not complete. It provides a measurement of performance that is necessary on the one hand for an assessment of success against objectives and, on the other, an important feedback tool for improved future management.

Evaluation is not just a post-event operation, however. There are three phases that in fact encompass the whole of the planning process. Research and evaluation are necessary in order to develop the event concept and in order to establish feasibility. Then, throughout the event, there is a need for a continual monitoring process thus ensuring that planning is flexible enough to accommodate change, particularly for longer planning periods. Finally, there is post-event evaluation that, together with important feedback, aids decision-making, not just for management but also for all the events' stakeholders.

The shape and form of evaluation reporting is determined by the requirements of stakeholders. The final reports that go to the investors, sponsors, strategic partners and management are different and the needs of the process itself is such that it is incomplete without all their contributions.

QUESTIONS

1. Analyse the importance of pre-event research prior to the decision to go ahead. Support your analysis with your own examples of what types of research can be undertaken?

2. Evaluate the importance of an iterative event planning process and the role of continuous evaluation for the 2002 Commonwealth Games.

3. Discuss the importance and use of post-event evaluation by Sheffield Event Unit.

4. Describe what kind of pre-event research should Athens have implemented in order to have avoided its resultant unused sports facilities and negative legacy?

REFERENCES

Allen, J., O'Toole, W., McDonnell, I. and Harris, R. (2002). *Festival and Special Event Management*, 2nd edn. Queensland, Australia, John Wiley & Sons, Chapter 15.

Archer, B. (1982). The value of multipliers and their policy implications. *Tourism Management*, 3(4), 236–241.

BOBICO (2008). www.beijing2008.cn (accessed 14 April 2008).

Coates, D. and Humphries, B. (2003). *Professional Sports Facilities, Franchises and Urban Economic Development*. University of Maryland, Baltimore County, working paper 03-103. www.umbc.edu/economics/wpapers/wp_03_103.pdf (accessed 7 January 2004).

Coyle, W. (2002). Interview: Manager, Events Unit, Sheffield City Council at Events Unit, Sheffield, Sheffield City Council, 12 noon, 19 July.

Crompton, J. (1995). Economic impact analysis of sports facilities and events: eleven sources of misapplication. *Journal of Sport Management*, 9, 14–35.

Crompton, J. (2001). Public subsidies to professional team sport facilities in the USA. In Gratton, C. and Henry, I. (eds), *Sport in the City: The Role of Sport in Economic and Social Regeneration*. London, Routledge, Chapter 2.

Events Halifax. (2001). *Economic Impact Analysis: Sporting & Cultural Events 1999–2000*. www.sportnovascotia.com/contents/pubs/EconImpactAnal.pdf (accessed 16 April 2003).

Felli, G. (2002). Transfer of Knowledge (TOK): a games management tool. A paper delivered at the *IOC-UIA Conference. Architecture and International Sporting Events*, Olympic Museum, Lausanne, June 2002. IOC.

Getz, D. (1997). *Event Management and Tourism*. New York, Cognizant, Chapter 14.

Hall, C. M. (1997). *Hallmark Tourist Events – Impacts, Management and Planning*. London, Bellhaven Press, Chapter 6.

HKSDB. (2002). *Economic Impact of Sport*: Report to Hong Kong Sport Development Board. August 2002. Produced by Business and Economic Research Ltd (BERL), Wellington, New Zealand. www.hksdb.org.hk/hksdb/html.pdf/research/economicimpactofsportinhk (accessed 16 April 2003).

Manchester City Council. (2001). *Commonwealth Games 2002 – A Cost Benefit Analysis: Brief for Consultants*, 21 November 2001. Manchester City Council.

Mathieson, A. and Wall, G. (1982). *Tourism: Economic, Physical and Social Impacts*. Harlow, Longman Scientific & Technical, Chapter 3.

Piercy, N. (2002). *Market-Led Strategic Change: Transforming the Process of Going to Market*, 3rd edn. Oxford, Butterworth-Heinemann.

Shone, A. and Parry, B. (2001). *Successful Event Management: A Practical Handbook*. London, Continuum, Chapter 12.

U.K. Sport. (1999). *Major Events: A Blueprint for Success*. London, UK Sport.

Wood, E. (2004). Marketing information for impact analysis and evaluation. In Yeoman, I., Robertson, M., Ali-Knight, J., Drummond, S. and McMahon-Beattie, U. (eds), *Festival and Events Management: An International Arts and Cultural Perspective*. Oxford, Butterworth-Heinemann.

Index

345